READINGS
FROM
MENNONITE
WRITINGS

NEW & OLD

READINGS
FROM
MENNONITE
WRITINGS

NEW & OLD

J. CRAIG HAAS

FOREWORD BY JOHN D. ROTH

Good Books

INTERCOURSE, PA 17534

Acknowledgments and Credits

We acknowledge with gratitude the following publishers, authors and editors who granted permission for excerpts from their publications to be included in this collection: Amish Brotherhood Publications, Monroe L. Beachy, Joseph F. Beiler, Brethren in Christ Archives, *Christian History*, Christian Light Publications, CMBC Publications, Conrad Press, DFP Publications, Victor G. Doerksen, Eastern Mennonite Board of Missions and Charities, The Edwin Mellen Press, Evangel Press, Faith and Life Press, *Family Life*, *Festival Quarterly*, Nancy Fisher, Leonard Gross, Marvin Hein, Herald Press, Titus B. Hoover, Isaac R. Horst, Paul Hostetler, Institute of Mennonite Studies, The Johns Hopkins University Press, John E. Kauffman, Kindred Press, Lancaster Mennonite Historical Society, Mennonite Central Committee, *Mennonite Historical Bulletin*, *Mennonite Quarterly Review*, Mennonite World Conference, North Point Press/Farrar, Straus & Giroux, Inc., Dorothy Yoder Nyce, the Old Order Book Society, Victor Peters, *Pennsylvania Mennonite Heritage*, Plough Publishing House, John D. Roth, Lewis B. Sider, Eli Stoltzfus, *Sword and Trumpet*, T. & T. Clark, Ltd., Westminster/John Knox Press, Ida Yoder, Eli Z. Zimmerman.

Scripture set in italics and preceding a reading, unless otherwise indicated, taken from the NEW REVISED STANDARD VERSION BIBLE, copyright © 1989, Division of Christian Education of the National Council of the Churches of Christ in the United States of America. Used by permission of Friendship Press. When initials (NIV) follow citation, scripture taken from the HOLY BIBLE, NEW INTERNATIONAL VERSION. Copyright © 1973, 1978, 1984 International Bible Society. Used by permission of Zondervan Bible Publishers.

The author and publishers have made an extensive search to locate all who hold rights to material, included in this book. Omissions are purely unintentional and the publishers request the pardon of rights holders who may have been excluded. If contacted, the publishers will be happy to correct any omissions in future printings.

Additional details of these acknowledgments appear in the Bibliography.

Cover artwork, "Evening," an etching by Naomi Limont
Design by Dawn J. Ranck

READINGS FROM MENNONITE WRITINGS, NEW AND OLD

Copyright © 1992 by Good Books, Intercourse, PA 17534
International Standard Book Number: 1-56148-064-9
Library of Congress Card Catalog Number: 92-38440

Library of Congress Cataloging-in-Publication Data

Readings from Mennonite writings, new and old / [compiled by] J. Craig Haas.
    p. cm.
Includes bibliographical references and indexes.
ISBN 1-56148-064-9 : $14.95
1. Devotional calendars—Mennonites. I. Haas, J. Craig. 1956- .
BV4810.R34   1992
242—dc20   92-38440
                                                                   CIP

Table of Contents

JULY

AUGUST

Foreword

*S*pirituality has become a fashionable word. From the latest New Age fad of spiritual channeling to a renewed interest in the Christian tradition of spiritual disciplines, it seems as if the language of spirituality has found a firm foothold in modern Western culture. As with all popular terms it is sometimes difficult to know exactly what is meant by the frequent references to spirituality, but there can be little doubt that the hunger for a spiritual reality transcending the rational and material world of daily life is deep and genuine.

Twentieth-century North American Mennonites may have particular reasons to share in this craving for spiritual depth. Not only are we influenced by the spiritual deprivation and impoverishment which is part of modern society, we are also heirs to a religious tradition inherently suspicious of an emphasis on spirituality. For many Mennonites, Christianity has been defined almost exclusively in the language of *sociology* (membership in a particular cultural or linguistic subgroup) and *ethics* (obedience to the *Ordnung* or, more recently, conformity to particular kinds of social activism). A focus on spirituality, with its attendant emphasis on *being* as opposed to *doing*, quickly stirs up in the Mennonite mind caricatures of individualism, cheap grace and charismatic excess.

Mennonite historians have been particularly suspicious of the spiritualist thread in our past. After all, it was a group of spiritualists, concerned with the millennium, who violently overthrew the city of Münster in 1535, thereby besmirching the Anabaptist name for centuries to come. In Mennonite communities of the seventeenth- and eighteenth-centuries, claimed historian Robert Friedmann, a Pietistic spirituality of repentance and inner peace eroded traditional Anabaptist emphases on the visible church and costly discipleship. More recently, historians of American Mennonitism have identified nineteenth-century Protestant revivalism as a baneful source of religious acculturation. Today, charismatic impulses among twentieth-century Mennonites are frequently criticized as a flight from the traditional Anabaptist principles of pacifism and simple living.

Yet the desire to know God more personally and intimately, the desire to enlarge our awareness of God and to experience the living reality of God's presence in daily life, is rarely satisfied by cultural conformity or by the busyness of Christian activism. As a result, many Mennonites have been forced to find spiritual nourishment from other traditions: most of us are much more familiar with the writings of Richard Foster and Scott Peck than with the thought of Hans Denck or Pieter Twisck.

The 366 readings on Anabaptist and Mennonite spirituality brought together in this volume should dispel many of the standard caricatures which have falsely pitted an inner relationship with God against the more tangible expressions of daily discipleship. In this remarkable collection, Craig Haas offers modern

Mennonites an opportunity to recover a tradition of genuine spirituality within the Anabaptist/Mennonite lineage which, at the same time, resonates with the familiar themes of community, pacifism and discipleship.

Drawn from an enormous range of sources—including selections from women and men, lay and learned, contemporary and historical, North American and international—the daily readings offered here address traditional Mennonite concerns in ways which speak to the heart and the soul as well as the mind and the will.

As you follow the daily readings be prepared to move across time and space, and to enter the lives of ordinary Anabaptist and Mennonite writers whose names you have never heard before. Be prepared for a rich and varied smorgasbord of readings drawn from diaries, hymns, poetry, treatises, and letters. But amidst all the diversity of style and genre, be prepared as well to listen to an inner voice of unity giving witness to the One Spirit in whose name Christians of all ages have gathered in confession and worship, and in whose name we are empowered to be disciples in the world around.

John D. Roth
Goshen College
Summer, 1992

A Word of Explanation
from the Author

*T*he book you hold is a compilation of spiritual writings from the works of Mennonite writers. Many of them are short excerpts from longer pieces. Others are articles, poems, anecdotes or journal entries. I have sought a variety of style and expression in the selections.

These readings come from the Mennonite community conceived in the broadest sense. I have looked for a variety of voices to represent the diversity of Mennonite groups, including Amish, Brethren in Christ, River Brethren, Hutterites and Old Order Mennonites. I have selected material from authors from five continents and across five centuries.

The selections are arranged for daily reading—one reading for each day of the year. I have tried to choose selections which were devotional in nature, even though their original intent sometimes may have been historical, controversial or even personal. In any event, the selections are intended to be food for thought, sometimes uplifting, at other times sobering, and occasionally even provocative or disturbing.

I have not simply collected work from famous names, or even those writings which have had the greatest influence or importance historically. You will find the spirituality of ordinary Mennonites alongside that of ministers or teachers. Approximately a third of this book is the expression of first-generation Mennonites: early Anabaptists, satisfied seekers, or the harvest of missionary labors. Some of the selections appear in English for the first time.

Since the selections are presented for daily reflective reading, I have avoided footnotes. For some, I have added a short editorial note or biblical quotation before the reading in order to place it in its proper setting.

In general, the titles for the readings in this book were created for those selections which were excerpted from longer works. Shorter works which appear in their more complete form, or poems, appear with their original titles.

Mennonite writing is notable for the volume of biblical references and citations it contains. In most cases simple references to scripture passages were omitted for smoother reading. Where passages are fully quoted in the text, these quotations were sometimes reduced or omitted in editing if they made a short reading cumbersome.

I provide a short introduction to Mennonite spirituality to the reader seeking fuller understanding of the subject. The aim of the introduction is to show how the various streams of spirituality found in this book developed, and how they divide or mingle. Some readers may choose to jump over the introduction and simply enjoy each reading on its own. Others will find the introduction a point of reference to which they will return from time to time.

There are several indices following the readings, which make the book a useful resource for students and teachers, ministers and worship leaders in their ownpresentations. The general reader will find these indices a helpful map to favorite topics, authors, times or places.

Material for this book was assembled from many different sources. References to sources appear after all selections, and there is a complete bibliography at the end of this volume. The reader is encouraged to turn to these sources for further reading.

I acknowledge the many forms of help required and provided in putting this book together. Some previously unpublished materials were made available to me by John D. Roth of Goshen College, David J. Rempel Smucker of the Lancaster Mennonite Historical Society, and E. Morris Sider and Martin Schrag of Messiah College. Noah G. Good eagerly translated the readings by J. Denner, K. Hildebrand and D. Beiler. The selections from P. Cool's letter were graciously translated from Dutch by Irvin B. Horst.

In my two years of work on this project, Steve Nolt of the People's Place has been helpful beyond measure as a general critic and a guide to American Mennonite sources. Steve was able to correct historical and biographical details as well as provide further information. Stephen Scott, also of the People's Place, aided in the gathering and documenting of material from Old Order groups.

These readings achieved their present shape with the help of Elizabeth Weaver Kreider, book editor with Good Books. Her wisdom in cutting a long passage without gutting its meaning has made *Readings from Mennonite Writings, New and Old* a lively and more manageable collection.

So many people have given moral support to this project and I wish to thank each of them as well as those named above.

The many groups which stem from the Mennonite family tree offer a variety of spiritual delights. In these pages you will experience a family reunion across space and time. This book is an invitation to the reader—whether a member of the family or simply a friend—to come and feast at our table.

J. Craig Haas
Spring 1992

Mennonite Spirituality:
An Introduction

*T*he public mind tends to think of Mennonites as a uniform bunch, different from everybody else, but all pretty much like each other. But Mennonites themselves probably have an easier time distinguishing one party from another than identifying what holds them together *as Mennonites*. It seems to be getting harder to answer the question, "What is a Mennonite?" What distinguishes Mennonites from other religious groups and yet unites them to their own?

An attempt to isolate the "essence" of Mennonite spirituality would involve far too much analysis and discussion for a brief introduction to a collection of Mennonite spiritual writings. Volumes have already been dedicated to probing and unraveling this mystery, and one would need a long winter in the Yukon to ponder it thoroughly.

The matter is further complicated when one realizes—as Mennonites *are realizing*—that the Mennonite movement *never was* a monolithic unity. Diversity has always been a part of the heritage, even in its earliest years, five centuries ago. So it is not only difficult to say who Mennonites are, but also who they were.

I. Anabaptist Beginnings

Members of Mennonite-related communities were not always called Mennonites (and even today this is true). When the movement began in 1525, they were called "Anabaptists," meaning "re-baptizers." The Anabaptists rejected infant baptism, refusing to have their own children baptized. Anyone who joined them was admitted to their congregations by *adult* baptism. That act was understood as a pledge of loyalty to follow the way of Jesus Christ. Baptism therefore had to be entered upon only with mature understanding and by one's own choice. *Genuine* faith and discipleship, following Jesus, could not be *forced* upon anyone.

Here was the rub. Europe had been officially Catholic for a thousand years. The medieval state and church decreed that every child born into "Christendom" be baptized. It was inconceivable to most that an orderly society could be maintained without uniformity of religion. Church and state worked hand in hand.

For over a century before the rise of the Anabaptists, spiritually sincere persons were disturbed by the corruption and political intrigues of the popes and bishops. Immorality among priests and monks was widespread and widely known. The mechanical way in which the sacraments were performed left hungry souls longing for something deeper, yet seemed to offer openly sinful people a false consolation and hope. Further, the church supported the political, social and economic *status quo*—indeed, was a part of it! Yet injustice and inequity penetrated society, and were even institutionalized.

In 1517, when Martin Luther nailed his Ninety-five Theses to the door of the church in Wittenberg, he also drove a wedge into the unity of Christendom. The Protestant Reformation had begun.

This Reformation succeeded because it partially addressed swelling dissatisfaction with the Roman Church. But Luther was also successful because he had the support of local nobles in Germany who were often pious and always looking for independence. They quickly applied Luther's ideas to the churches in their territories. Luther taught that only the grace of God could bring sinful humans into a favorable status with God; that one could not merit such saving grace, but only accept it by faith in Christ whose crucifixion secured it; that the pope had no power to advance or hinder such a work; that even the common people could read the Bible and understand it better than the popes had.

And read the Bible they did! Many found hope in Luther's new message and sided with him. Others, such as the Swiss priest Huldrych Zwingli, read and found ideas that called into question even more practices than Luther did. There were popular uprisings to remove or destroy all pictures and statues from the churches, as idols. The rising movement challenged the way the churches were governed, the way worship and sacraments were conducted, and the power and privileges of priests.

Further, some of the peasants, in the name of Christian freedom, boldly demanded widespread reform in society at large. A full-scale peasant revolt erupted over much of southern and central Germany in 1524 and reached its height in the following year. The peasants demanded from the princes a greater amount of self-government and more access to the resources of the land. They wanted reform in the distribution of property. But the peasants were also in the vanguard of religious ideas, challenging the traditional views of the mass and sometimes questioning the propriety of infant baptism as well. They were highly iconoclastic, demanding the right to choose their own pastors, and questioning whether Luther's views on salvation through faith alone gave adequate support to living a real Christian life. Was Luther offering a new refuge to the careless? To radical readers of the Bible it seemed Luther did not go far enough in many things, yet went too far in others. Among these radicals lay the fertile ground of Anabaptism.

Unrest among the rural folk of Germany had spread into Switzerland too. Rural pastors in the lands controlled by the Swiss city of Zurich, having tasted the new freedoms of the gospel, began to demand rapid reform in church and society. They pushed for the rights of country people to govern their own religious affairs, and to be free from financial obligations to the emerging Protestant church in the city. Meanwhile, a faction within the reform movement in Zurich began to urge more thorough reform based solely upon the Bible, independent of the cautious City Council. After consistent opposition from Zwingli and the Council, this radical group, led by the scholars Conrad Grebel and Felix Mantz and peasant ex-priest Jörg Blaurock, began in January of 1525 to baptize believing adults upon their faith, in disregard of their infant baptisms. Persecution by the state authorities, with approval from the Protestant leadership, was swift. In spite of this, the new Anabaptist movement spread into neighboring parts of Switzerland and southern German lands—drawing many adherents from the restless peasants.

The peasant revolt had by this time become the Peasants' War. It was all too much for Luther and his princely allies. The Lutheran princes were already edgy about opposition from nearby Catholic princes—who also had armies. And the Emperor himself was loyal to the old church. A little word from Luther to suppress the peasants would keep everybody happy—except the peasants, of course. The princes got what they needed. Luther wrote a vitriolic attack on the peasant hordes, characterizing them as crazy fanatics. The princes preferred to attack in person. The peasants were brutally suppressed. Some of the defeated gave up their cause and, feeling betrayed by the Protestants, returned to Catholicism. Others retained their ideals. Chastened against further ferment, some formed their own communities of faith in which these ideals were kept alive. Prepared to go their own way, regardless of society, they too were ready for Anabaptism.

Anabaptism in the Netherlands and northern Germany originated somewhat independently of the southern groups. Already in the 1520s there was a widespread sentiment in the Netherlands that the elements of bread and wine in the mass did not literally change into the body and blood of Christ upon the words of a priest. The elements were instead simply *symbols* of Christ's body and blood; Christ himself was in heaven. This point of view caused many to place less emphasis upon sacramental means of grace and, coupled with popular disillusionment with the Catholic Church, led to the formation of informal study and devotional groups separate from organized religion.

Into this setting came Melchior Hoffman. Hoffman had been an eccentric Lutheran preacher in the Baltic region and Sweden before adopting Anabaptist ideas during a stay in Strasbourg (a city once German, now in France). From there he went to Emden in northern Germany and began baptizing any who accepted it. Hoffman commissioned "apostolic messengers" to spread the news that the kingdom of God was about to appear in visible form, and to baptize believers. After some of Hoffman's envoys were executed for re-baptizing, Hoffman suspended baptisms for a two-year period. Hoffman himself became a wanted man; in his belief that the coming of Christ and the end of the present age were imminent, he turned himself over to the authorities in Strasbourg, where he was subsequently imprisoned.

While Hoffman lay in prison, his following developed into divergent streams. Some of his followers reinstated the practice of believers' baptism. Many of these also followed a violent course (contrary to Hoffman), centering their hopes in the German city of Münster. Here Anabaptists governed the city, and called others to join them in the expectation that Münster would become the New Jerusalem and usher in the return of Christ. Some, however, were expressly opposed to the apocalyptic and revolutionary program of Münster, and developed a more sober, nonviolent Anabaptism not unlike that of the southern groups, but still in the spirit of Hoffman.

Meanwhile, Münster was placed under seige by the troops of the ousted bishop of the city and a Lutheran prince. Conditions inside Münster deteriorated—both physically and spiritually—as the siege dragged on. When finally an inhabitant of Münster betrayed the city to the bishop's troops, vengeance on the Anabaptists was indescribably brutal. Most of the men in Münster were slaughtered, and a general persecution of *all* Anabaptists ensued.

At this time a conscience-stricken priest named Menno Simons saw the sincerity of many disillusioned Anabaptists who had been led astray. He decided that it was time that he openly declared his own Anabaptist convictions. He left the old church to join the peaceful group of Anabaptists, and was soon made a leader. Menno devoted his life to calling the scattered and harassed Anabaptists into a peace-loving fellowship built upon the foundation of Jesus Christ—his teachings, his example, his death and resurrection. Menno was a beloved pastor, and became one of the best known leaders of the Dutch and northern German Anabaptists. Even the government eventually recognized that Menno was no violent fanatic. It was, however, in an edict of persecution that we first find a group of Anabaptists called "Menisten"—the original form of the name "Mennonites."

The Appeal of Anabaptism: A Freedom Movement

In many ways, Anabaptism was a freedom movement. Anabaptists believed that God was absolutely free. This may seem obvious to the point of being silly. Yet for the Anabaptists it meant that God could not be contained by a religious system, confined to a ritual or captured in a sacramental wafer. God acts from himself alone, without consulting any human being. The new emphasis upon God's independence from created things led to a questioning of all that was physical or material in regard to religion. A challenge arose against the use of images in worship. The Anabaptists consistently regarded them as idols which drew the worshiper away from God who is Spirit. No creature lays claim to God, for the Creator is independent of the creation. No product of nature or human hand has spiritual power of itself. Yet God loves his work, created all things for his own pleasure, and human beings in his own image.

The Anabaptists believed that people were free to respond to God's love and able to choose whether to know God and do his will. Human sin—the prevailing tendency of human life and society to go its own way—was a slavery from which Jesus had set people free. Through loyalty to Jesus Christ, the believer was forgiven of sin and empowered by the Spirit to become Christlike. Anabaptists were almost alone in believing that a consistent Christian life—which they termed "discipleship"—was a real possibility in this life.

The free person, they said, is able to take up the challenge of following Christ through difficulty and persecution. The way of the world, with its grasping for power and possessions, is in conflict with the way of Jesus. Christ's way is the way of peace. Disciples put away the sword of war and resistance, and seek to live in harmony with all—even their enemies. If this means becoming sheep for slaughter, so be it; that was, after all, exactly the path Jesus cut. Every disciple must take up his or her own cross.

The Anabaptists also declared the freedom of the "church" from the power of the state. Most recognized the need for governments in a less-than-perfect-world, but differed among themselves on the degree to which a follower of Jesus could participate in the state. No state could stand without force; its laws were upheld by force, its borders maintained by force. Anabaptists held allegiance to another kingdom: Jesus Christ's kingdom of peace. As the resurrected Lord, Christ rules over all, and is to be obeyed even when his way clashes with the ways of the world. The state has authority neither to establish nor to oppose the kingdom of Christ. Jesus reigns by persuasion, not by coercion.

Anabaptism was generally not an attempt to reform the existing church. It was a total break—a rejection of "Christendom"—in favor of a fresh start on the basis of Christ and his apostles as they are presented in the New Testament. This meant that the pope and clergy no longer held a monopoly on the interpretation of the Bible. Anyone who could read could find, with the help of the Spirit, what Jesus or his apostles had really said (or what they did not say), and might in turn teach someone else. In this way, every disciple was a priest—an agent for bringing others into relation to God. Any other priesthood was rendered superfluous.

As common people read the Bible they came to new conclusions about the nature of the church, the proper use of baptism and the Lord's Supper, the relation of the church and state, and the duty of the individual in regard to government, proper conduct in everyday life, and the true knowledge of God. The Anabaptists did not all come to the same conclusions on everything, but they were all committed to the study of the Bible, and cited it over and over. Some read it more literally than others; some believed that it merely pointed to God's word in creation and the human soul.

Differing Spiritual Styles

There were tensions in Anabaptist thought created by the recovery of practical biblical discipleship on the one hand, and the rediscovery of divine freedom on the other. These were resolved differently by different groups of Anabaptists. To delineate all of these various spiritual "styles" in great detail would require more space than is available here. It is hoped that the readings in this book will at least *display* some of them. What follows is a summary of the prevailing spirituality of each *general region* in which Anabaptists were active in the 16th century.

The Swiss Brethren. The Swiss radicals were moved by the belief that the teachings of Christ, found in the Bible, are to be carried out without alteration or delay. Those who led the new Anabaptist movement were students of scripture, and it is clear that they were motivated by the rediscovery of concrete discipleship.   Most Anabaptists in Switzerland read the Bible in a straightforward manner, without a particular scheme of interpretation, and were inclined to implement its teachings in a literal way. Their concern was for right conduct, right order, right baptism, right Lord's Supper and right discipline. True faith issued in obedience, and the more one's obedience conformed to biblical patterns, the surer one's faith could be found biblical.

Everyday things, the basic stuff of ordinary life, became the arena in which real faith operated. True Christians were walking the way of Christ, with the true baptism and the true Lord's Supper. The evidence of their faith could be *seen* by others; and they were gathered into a *visible* community, separated from the "world." In their concrete and practical concern to establish congregations, the Swiss Brethren showed little tension with the spiritualists' vision of God who will not be bound to creatures. To be sure, they had such a belief, but their iconoclastic activities were prompted primarily by their interpretation of scripture.

South German and Austrian Anabaptists. These Anabaptists drew inspiration from late-medieval German mysticism, which viewed all things in God and God in all things. Accordingly, God is not anchored to any creature, but makes himself known through the creation as a whole. Nevertheless, one must let go of all creatures in order to truly know God through himself alone. This happens with great suffering, sometimes physical, but primarily in the depth of the soul. With pain one gives birth to Christ in the heart; Christ must not only die upon the cross, but also *within us* if he is also to be risen in us. One must "let go" to God, or be in a state of *Gelassenheit* (yieldedness, submission, composure), if one is to experience God. This self-sacrifice and suffering is illustrated in nature.

Thomas Müntzer, a mystical pastor and ringleader in the Peasants' War, imbibed this spirituality. He may be the one who taught it to Hans Hut. Hut, as a successful Anabaptist missionary, spread these ideas beyond Germany, into Austria and Moravia. Some of Hut's following developed a congregational life which included a total sharing of property in the manner of Jesus' disciples and the early church. Others developed an individualistic spirituality sometimes characterized by visions or even fanaticism. Hans Denck's views on spirituality were similar to Hut's. Denck was an irenic scholar whose writings display a gentle and tolerant spirit, somewhat in contrast to Hans Hut.

Compared to other Anabaptists, the southern Germans and Austrians were the most impressed with God's independence and freedom. God was not bound to any specific creature, nor to any one way of working. But then what about the water of baptism, or bread and wine in the communion? Should they also be set aside in favor of a "pure" baptism of the Spirit, or the spiritual digestion of Christ in the soul? To emphasize baptism in water too strongly was to risk establishing a new idol. The same could be said of the Lord's Supper or even the visible church community. These were valid insofar as they were symbols of the work of God, but unless they were experienced *in* the believer, they were merely false comfort. The work of God in the depth of the soul was what really saved a person, what truly made one blessed.

These Anabaptists did not disdain the outward and concrete, so long as it led to inward transformation. They too had great respect and love for the Bible—and they quoted from it again and again. But as paper and ink, even scripture was merely a created thing. The Word of God was not exhausted by the printed page; it was the inner light or spark of God shining in the soul.

The southern German and Austrian stream of Anabaptism was the most optimistic in regard to human nature. They saw humanity as made in God's image, and therefore capable of responding to God. Sinfulness did not erase the divine image, nor extinguish the light in the soul. These Anabaptists expected, with God's help, to *succeed* as Christians, to be transformed into the likeness of Christ. They trusted the Christ within to lead them aright, and were therefore least inclined of any Anabaptists to establish specific standards of conduct binding on others.

The paradox in South German-Austrian Anabaptism is that while God is absolutely free and transcendent, God is also completely available and immanent. Because no particular thing is more like God than any other, God is equally present through all things. Nothing is holy—therefore *everything* is holy! God, who is bound to nothing, is always and everywhere present.

The Hutterites. Some of Hans Hut's disciples began to practice community of goods, or the abolition of private property, in Moravia. Other Anabaptists from central Europe were drawn to Moravia because it offered a refuge from persecution. This mix of Anabaptist streams was given its distinctive shape by Jakob Hutter, for whom the Hutterites are named, even though Hutter was not their founder.

The genius of the Hutterites lay in their ability to combine the deep inward spirituality of the South German-Austrian Anabaptists with the concrete congregational life so typical of the Swiss Brethren. There was a strong mystical orientation among the early Hutterite leaders, such as Ulrich Stadler. The *Gelassenheit*, or yieldedness of the mystical tradition was extended to a "letting-go" not only of spiritual claims, but also of material ones. The willingness to part with possessions was the highest attestation that one desired no created thing, but the Creator only. Such sharing of goods made necessary an ordered community living together in a single place, or several communities in proximity. The distribution of material necessities was diligently supervised, and community boundaries (who's in/who's out) were carefully maintained. A sense of mutual care and cooperation was cultivated so that the community could achieve harmony. Without the work of God in the heart, such a situation was deemed impossible.

Dutch Anabaptists. The reform movement which prepared the way for Anabaptism in the Netherlands laid stress upon the purely symbolic meaning of the bread and wine of the Lord's Supper, denying that the communion elements had any value without true faith in the one who partook of them. The Anabaptists extended this reasoning to baptism. No baptism was valid unless there was already faith on the part of the person being baptized; infant baptism could never be genuine baptism. Water alone, like bread and wine apart from faith, was of no account.

After the attempt of the Anabaptists at Münster to organize the kingdom of God in a visible and political manner ended in disaster, Menno Simons began to teach that the kingdom was spiritual rather than material. As long as human beings lived mortal lives in this age, the kingdom of God would be found only in the souls of believers, and seen only in the deeds of a changed life. The kingdom was spiritualized.

Because of the emphasis upon the inner and spiritual nature of baptism and the Lord's Supper, and of the kingdom of God itself, Dutch Anabaptists put clear emphasis on the working of God in the individual soul. The apocalyptic hopes of Münster for the visible transformation of the world were spiritualized into the inner transformation of the heart.

Although the kingdom of God would have to wait for the coming of the Lord, the Holy Spirit was already present in the life of the regenerated believer. Menno Simons and Dirk Philips taught that this new life would express itself in social and ethical dimensions by means of love, peace-making, service, mercy and generosity. They refused to interpret the inward work of the Spirit separately from the spiritual person's outward conduct. The world, so hopelessly corrupt, would be created anew only after the visible return of Christ; but the regenerated believer could begin to live Christ-like in the present, though ever in conflict with the world. For Menno, Dirk and those associated with them, the Spirit was also active in the *common* life of Christians. The community of spiritual believers was *visibly gathered*.

Not all the Anabaptists in the Netherlands and northern Germany supported the idea of such a visibly defined assembly. For some, it was simply too dangerous in light of persecution to organize congregations. There was concern that a visible church would become just another sect, or perhaps like the organized church the Anabaptists had already rejected. A few even abandoned the practice of administering baptism in water or celebrating the Lord's Supper, in the quest for a "purely spiritual" fellowship. It should not seem surprising that these groups, as groups, did not survive long. However, the marks of spiritualism survived among the Dutch, and would be seen again and again in the life of the surviving groups, which did not adopt spiritualism as a program, but were nevertheless influenced by it.

This belief in the importance of a visible community of faith spared the Anabaptists around Menno and Dirk from spiritualism and extinction. But a concrete communion of saints could not survive without problems. As a fellowship based on faith rather than on birth into a particular society, Dutch Anabaptists were faced with having to distinguish between genuine believers and the insincere. At issue was the purity of the fellowship, or its integrity as a gathering of true Christians who have been regenerated by the Spirit. Controversy ensued over which standards marked the true church, the degree of rigor with which standards of conduct were applied, and the circumstances and manner in which warning or excommunication were to be used with members who violated those standards. These tensions would be expected whenever visible congregations formed around high ideals of obedience and service.

Was the effort to sustain the visible congregation or church worth the troubles which accompanied it? Near the end of his life Menno remarked that he loved nothing on earth more than the church. Many who came after him felt the same way. As a result, Menno's friends today are found all around that earth. The development of Mennonite spirituality may best be viewed as the interplay of these spiritual emphases: spiritualism on the one hand, and on the other, congregational concreteness.

Spiritualism emphasizes contrasts or opposites in a metaphysical dualism. It radically distinguishes Creator and creation, spirit and flesh, inner and outer, invisible and visible, Spirit and letter, new and old. In each of these paired opposites the first option is to be sought and the second is to be regarded as an impediment or distraction. Mennonites never fully embraced the most rigorous consequences of such dualism, managing to temper it with concrete congregational life. In the centuries following the era of Menno, many Mennonites were willing to let certain "externals" fall aside as "non-essential" in favor of the "inner reality." But the spiritualist viewpoint alone cannot carry a community of people from generation to generation; spiritualism leads to its own evaporation.

The alternative to spiritualism is the concrete congregational life cultivated by the Swiss Brethren, the Hutterites and the companions of Menno Simons. Here spiritualist themes are not totally excluded, but this congregational viewpoint stresses the *synthesis* of apparent opposites: the creation points to the Creator, the outer expresses the inner, the visible embodies the invisible, the letter voices the Spirit, and the old prepares the new. This is a holistic view in which this material world and everyday life are agents of God in forming ordered community, everywhere at hand. Admittedly, Mennonites have sometimes allowed this synthesis to break down into authoritarian forms, thereby inviting a spiritualist protest. Mennonites have flourished, however, when they have avoided the either/or of spiritualism and authoritarianism, and held heaven and earth together.

II. A Quieter Time

Anabaptism ceased to be a dynamic and revolutionary movement about a century after it began. In part, this was due to the loss of the radical edge among the second and third generations—a phenomenon common to all movements. But the times had changed, too. Governments became increasingly tolerant; Mennonites in the Netherlands were not viciously persecuted by the state at the beginning of the 1600s, although some discrimination against them persisted. To the south, political persecution lasted longer, but was not as common there as it was formerly. New places of refuge were opening up. In addition, Anabaptist leaders were forced to turn their attention and energies inward, to maintaining congregational life in the wake of divisions and controversies.

A new era of Mennonite history was beginning, in which the movement was achieving its "classical" form. This second, or middle period in the development of Mennonite spirituality might be characterized as the *quiet* period. It lasted well into the 19th century. The ferment and drama of Anabaptist radicalism was past, replaced by a more structured and regular community life.

The "sweet Christ" became more meaningful than the "bitter Christ" of martyrdom. Mennonites were content to keep a low profile as a concession in exchange for toleration. They became "the quiet in the land"—hardworking, honest, decent people, but no longer zealous missionaries or angry prophets. It is from this point, therefore, that one would do well to speak of "Mennonites" rather than "Anabaptists," since new ways of self-understanding were replacing the original awareness of being everywhere at odds with the world. How does a people with a martyr-consciousness understand itself when no one is killing them any longer?

The Mennonites of Switzerland and southern Germany developed a carefully regulated discipline *(Ordnung)* to define the community distinct from the "world." If one could no longer "bear the cross" to the place of execution, one could bear it inwardly, by humbling oneself and practicing obedience. This was in some sense an extension of the Anabaptist aim of *Gelassenheit*.

The Dutch ministers were alarmed at how quickly Mennonites became commercially successful and were entering respected areas of public life. In response, T. J. van Braght compiled the immensely influential *Martyrs Mirror*, an account of the sufferings of Anabaptists in earlier times (and accounts of others who suffered or were yet suffering on account of their belief in adult baptism). Van Braght wanted to warn his people of the dangers of spiritual laxity in times of ease. His book traveled around the world with later generations, and is still published and read today. Other Dutch leaders (P.J. Twisck and Pieter Pietersz. among them) wrote strongly moralizing treatises which applied the pressures of conscience in place of the terrors of persecution.

J.P. Schabaelje's *The Wandering Soul* became one of the most widely read of Mennonite classics. His time-traveler engages in discussion about the history of the world with three aged men from different periods: Adam, Noah, and Simon Cleopas (who encountered the resurrected Jesus). Schabaelje's blend of history and imagination is an attempt to instill in the reader a love for God and goodness.

Mennonites were also producing hymns and written prayers during the 17th century. Leenaert Clock was a prolific hymnwriter whose "Loblied" is still used in Amish worship. Clock's collection of prayers long contributed to Mennonite spiritual life.

The Dutch and northern German Mennonites had crumbled into factions even before the deaths of Menno Simons and Dirk Philips. Numerous efforts were made to heal these divisions, and some parties found that they could ally themselves behind confessional statements which pinned down areas of agreement and were sufficiently vague where the parties differed. The "Dordrecht Confession" of 1632 was such an agreement which united three major factions for a time, and ultimately won the endorsement of Mennonites in Alsace and southern Germany as well. Ironically, it later contributed to the schism between the Swiss Mennonites and the Alsatians who followed Jakob Ammann (the Amish).

While some saw common statements of faith as a path toward unity, others rejected any binding written confession. They sought unity on a level deeper than doctrine, upon an authority within the soul. The Collegiant movement in the Netherlands attempted to gather the spiritually sensitive of all religious backgrounds for common informal worship and exchange of ideas. The Collegiants required no dogmatic commitments, but did reject infant baptism, military service and the need for clergy. They stressed the "invisible church" dispersed among and beyond organized religious groups. This simple approach to spirituality attracted its strongest following from the Mennonites, especially those already inclined toward spiritualist ideals. Through the Collegiants the Dutch Mennonites came in contact with more pietistic and rationalistic forms of spirituality, and with creative people such as Rembrandt and Spinoza. In time, the Mennonites practically absorbed the Collegiant movement.

The Mennonite Collegiant Pieter Cornelisz. Plockhoy was a visionary social reformer who established one of the first settlements of Mennonites (and others) in America. His communal utopia in present-day Delaware had the support of the city of Amsterdam. It lasted only a year, however, until it was completely overrun by British troops in 1664.

Amish Reform

Swiss Mennonites lived under continuing pressures from government authorities throughout the 17th century. These pressures caused some Mennonites to jump ship for the state church, often dividing the loyalties of families. At the same time, some members of the state churches were sympathetic to Mennonite ideals and compassionate toward the distressed Mennonites themselves. The help of sympathetic relatives and friends greatly aided Mennonites in their efforts to survive and conduct their lives more easily.

In turn, Swiss Mennonites were cautious not to needlessly provoke the authorities. The Mennonites tended to emphasize the aspects of faith which they had in common with their Protestant neighbors, and to tread softly where there were differences. This meant that the inner, invisible and universal dimensions were stressed, while outer, visible and "sectarian" practices were assigned secondary status. In other words, the Swiss were drifting toward a somewhat more spiritualist position.

Some Swiss Mennonites found relief from government harassment by moving to rural Alsace, a traditionally Germanic region under loose French control. Here the Mennonites again encountered pressures to conform to the officially-sanctioned churches. They did not have the support of family members in Alsace as they did in Switzerland, and their more sparsely scattered members found it tempting to worship with the Protestants. These stresses prompted Jakob Ammann, a young Mennonite elder, to initiate several reforms with support from his community. But what seemed like reform in Alsace was not well received in Switzerland, and Ammann found himself at odds with the established leaders of the Swiss Mennonites.

The controversy between Jakob Ammann and the Swiss elders was about practical matters pertaining to the faithfulness and identity of the community. Ammann's initial reform was to increase the frequency of the Lord's Supper from once annually to twice a year. This arrangement made it possible for his scattered members to participate in the Supper more regularly, even if they were prevented from attending on particular occasions. It also meant that disciplinary concerns were addressed more frequently. Ammann also gave increased attention to such outward matters as the style of clothing and cut of hair. The outer appearance was to be as humble as the inner condition of the heart. These visible practices also meant that members were more easily identified as such, reinforcing the borders between the scattered community and the world.

But the most consequential reform of Jakob Ammann was his insistence that errant members who are excommunicated (expelled from the community) be shunned by the other members. This avoidance involved complete social ostracism, the ordinary relationships of life severed. One was not to eat at the same table as the excommunicated, nor to conduct business with them. Even an excommunicated spouse would have to be shunned. The aim of avoidance was not to destroy the offenders (help was still to be given to those in need or danger), but to shock and shame them into returning and amending their lives.

Ammann had the precedent of Menno Simons and the historic practice of most Dutch Anabaptists to support his position, although the practice was fading in the Netherlands. The Swiss leaders, however, could also claim that it had not been their historic practice to *shun* expelled members, but only to deny them access to the Lord's Supper.

The Ammann controversy was in fact a clash between two differing spiritual "styles" in the Anabaptist tradition. It was Ammann who favored a strong emphasis on the importance and integrity of visible forms, while the Swiss elders inclined toward a more spiritualized view of outward things, preferring to avoid errant Mennonites "spiritually," but not in other ways.

The controversy between Ammann's supporters (the Amish) and the Swiss leaders spread into southern Germany as well, and finally erupted in schism. Most of the German leaders supported the Swiss, but most in Alsace stood behind Ammann. Both sides shared some of the blame for the rupture, which to the present has only partially healed.

The Impact of Pietism

In committing themselves to a more spiritualist orientation, the communities in Switzerland and southern Germany left themselves exposed to a renewal movement from German Protestantism which was just then gaining ground. This movement was Pietism.

Pietists sought to revitalize the Protestant state-run churches from within, by emphasizing a warm emotional piety, introspection, sorrow for sin leading to a heartfelt conversion experience, personal holiness, Bible study and works of charity. In Pietism, the individual heart mattered more than the correctness of outer form. The Pietists had little interest in tampering with Protestant church practices of baptism or communion. These were of little account if the heart was right. Pietists were willing to join across denominational lines with others who shared a similar experience of personal conversion. They reached over to the Mennonites and found an open hand.

Mennonites had several things in common with the Pietists. Both insisted upon the need for individual involvement in spiritual life and a personal commitment to Christ. Each emphasized the importance of repentance as the beginning of the spiritual life, and continuation in moral behavior as a mark of a genuine disciple. And both Mennonites and Pietists were biblicists, believing that the Bible alone, read by ordinary believers, simply and without scholarly or clerical "interpretations," was the rule of faith and guide for practice.

Despite these important areas of consensus—and indeed, within them—there were ways in which the new Pietism differed from the old Anabaptism. For instance, the Pietists' personal commitment often turned into religious individualism for which the visible community of faith was merely a resource to help the individual tend his or her own private garden of the soul. In some cases the community was seen as wholly superfluous, or even as an unwelcome intruder into the private communion of the soul with God.

Most Anabaptists had stood for the integral relation of corporate and personal spirituality, believing that each one comes to God with others, as part of the community which is the people of God. One's relation to God was bound up with one's relations to fellow humans. Peace with God meant peace with one's neighbor. For the Pietist, the "priesthood of all believers" meant that no one needed a priest in order to come to God, each being his or her *own* priest. But for the Anabaptist, the "priesthood of all believers" meant that each one is a priest to every other, leading *one another* into God's presence.

Pietists understood repentance somewhat differently from the Anabaptists. Though each underscored its importance, the Pietists saw it as an inner process of change in the soul, an experience induced by God with much struggle on the part of the penitent. For most Anabaptists, repentance was simply the turning from one way of life to another: not so much an experience as a decision. Some of the southern German and Austrian Anabaptists had anticipated something akin to the Pietist view with their teachings on the "work of God in the depth of the soul."

Pietism and Anabaptism alike stressed morally responsible behavior. But where Anabaptism had focused on bearing the bitter cross in nonresistant love and service in the context of community, Pietism laid weight upon personal morality—the dos-and-don'ts of clean living. But Pietism was not without concern for others. Pietists began many charitable works and beneficial institutions, and showed real concern for the poor. The initiative for their service was usually independent of the organized church.

Both the Anabaptists and the Pietists were readers and heeders of the Bible. Many Anabaptists also wrote confessions of faith to reflect their common understanding of biblical teaching. Pietists were somewhat reluctant to do so, preferring to remain open to new insights which would make old interpretations obsolete. They approached the Bible more subjectively than most Anabaptists, yet the southern German and Austrian Anabaptist belief in the word of God in the heart, to which scripture is merely a witness, was not far from the hearts of many Pietists.

Often these were differences of degree, or changes in emphasis more than content. Yet the subtle re-ordering of ideas in the spiritual kaleidoscope did produce a different image from the one Mennonites had inherited from the martyrs and teachers of their past.

The writings from the middle period of Mennonite spirituality are steeped in Pietism. Jakob Denner, one of the best-known Mennonite Pietists, never bothered to celebrate the Lord's Supper during his more than four decades in a Dompelaar congregation at Hamburg-Altona, Germany. His sermons based on the Gospels are so concerned with knowing Christ in the soul that the historical events of Jesus' life are nearly reduced to parables toward that end. But the warm piety of his sermons had great appeal, not only to Mennonites but to others as well, who would also come to hear him preach.

The Pietist depreciation of all things "outward" rendered the differences between members of rival religious denominations largely irrelevant, especially when they had a common "inner experience" of personal conversion. Pietism had the effect of eroding Mennonite distinctives, and caused some to downplay the unique aspects of Mennonite faith. This may explain why so few persons joined the Mennonite community from outside during this middle period. Why join a marginalized religious group with fewer privileges, if externals don't matter anyway?

Pietism was a factor in the formation of several distinct Mennonite groups. The largest of these groups is the Mennonite Brethren, which formally organized in the Ukraine in 1860. The Mennonite Brethren had criticized the Mennonites of the Russian Empire for a lack of spiritual vitality, coldly formal worship, and routine admission of members apart from a personal conversion experience. Troubled by incidents of emotional excess in its early years, the Mennonite Brethren Church was eventually brought onto a moderate course which merged traditional Mennonite teaching with Pietist spirituality. The Mennonite Brethren differed historically and even today, for example, from the wider Mennonite tradition on the mode of baptism: all their baptisms are performed by immersion rather than by pouring or sprinkling.

Mennonite Brethren still tend to emphasize personal holiness somewhat to the neglect of social ethics, although this is not always the case. Close ties to the Baptists and fundamentalist Protestants probably account for the weakening of the teaching of nonresistance as well. Their strong emphasis on the need for a definite personal conversion experience as the only way to be assured of salvation has made the Mennonite Brethren one of the most missionary-minded groups.

Periodically, Mennonite voices have risen to call the community "back to Menno Simons and the martyrs." Even Pietists such as the Mennonite Brethren often saw themselves as restorers of an earlier zeal. But others saw the way back as a rigorous devotion to the writings of Menno and the *Martyrs Mirror*, a recovery of the "pure teachings of Menno Simons." The Kleine Gemeinde (Little Community) which formed in the Ukraine in 1814 was a protest to the moral laxity which they saw in the general Mennonite community after its migration to the Russian Empire in 1789. The Reformed Mennonite Church which organized separately in Lancaster County, Pennsylvania, in 1812 is a blend of mild Pietism and strict adherence to Menno's teachings, including those on shunning the excommunicated.

Piety Made in America

A few Mennonites appeared in North America in the 17th century, but not until the 18th century did they begin to arrive in larger numbers. The first Amish came in the 1720s. Mennonites reached Canada in 1786.

Since the closing decades of the eighteenth century, American Mennonites have felt the impact of popular evangelistic movements, particularly those which, like Pietism, are strongly subjective.

The Revivalist movement began among American Protestants in the early 1700s and reached its greatest influence during the following century, when it swept the American frontier but also touched Europe. Revivalism is the boisterous daughter of Pietism. Revivalists believe that spiritual renewal can be planned and produced—if humans will do their part, God promises to do his. The best methods bring the best results, when done in the right spirit.

The River Brethren formed sometime around 1780, through the influence of a revival movement among the Pennsylvania Germans in Lancaster County. The central idea of this movement was a crisis conversion experience in which the convert was given the assurance of eternal life. This experience itself, rather than the fruit of one's life, was the evidence of salvation.

Though most Mennonites were less than comfortable with the Revivalists, a few did experience this "heart-felt" conversion. While some united with like-minded members of Protestant denominations, others steered a more traditionally Mennonite course. Such was the case with the earliest River Brethren. These Mennonites, joined by a few Protestants, retained adult believers' baptism, nonresistance and the plain life. In addition, they heavily stressed the sinfulness of every person, conviction of sin by the Holy Spirit, restitution and apology for sins committed, and obedience to the leading of God—all culminating in the crisis experience of conversion. The River Brethren adopted some patterns of congregational life from the German Baptist Brethren (Dunkers): baptism as a three-fold immersion, an adaptation of the Love Feast observed in connection with the Lord's Supper, and regular home visits by the deacons.

Near the middle of the 19th century, the Old Order River Brethren separated from the larger group of River Brethren. After the American Civil War, the larger group was known as "Brethren in Christ." During the following decades the Brethren in Christ adopted the teachings of the holiness movement, which had its roots in Methodism. Characteristic of this movement was the "second work of grace"—an experience of instantaneous sanctification which empowered the recipient to live above the power of sin. Both their origin in Revivalism and their subsequent adoption of the holiness position have inclined the Brethren in Christ toward American evangelicalism.

Mennonites in the early 1800s, like Christian Burkholder and Abraham Godshalk, responded to Revivalism by stressing the nature of regeneration as a careful decision to follow Christ in repentance and faithful obedience, rather than an emotional "experience" produced in part by the use of planned methods. However, by the end of the century, especially through the efforts of John F. Funk and John S. Coffman, Mennonites in general came to accept a mild form of Revivalism. In the twentieth century, Mennonite evangelists, preaching in "revival meetings," continued to bring numerous young people from Mennonite families, as well as non-Mennonite people, into the fold. For many Mennonites, the Revivalist response became the normal way to "come to Christ." It would appear that many of those who responded to the evangelists' messages did indeed become genuine Christians. Numerous Mennonites today would identify such responses as the beginning of their lives in Christ. Revivalism, seasoned with fundamentalism, still influences some Mennonites by way of religious broadcasting.

III. New Fields of Labor

Mennonite spirituality in modern times has become increasingly diverse. The modern period of Mennonite spirituality begins with two related developments: First, the rise of missionary interest both at home and abroad; second, the separation of North American groups into Old Order and general factions. Under the influence of the Protestant missionary movements of the 19th century, some Mennonite groups began to send out foreign missionaries. The Dutch began by sending Pieter Jansz. to the East Indies (now Indonesia) in 1851. Mennonites in the Russian Empire contributed both funds and workers to the Dutch endeavor. American Mennonites got on board (quite literally) in the 1890s. As a result of mission—and Mennonite migrations—there are organized Mennonite-related groups today on all inhabited continents, in over 60 countries, with a total population reaching toward one million. Half of the world's Mennonites live in developing countries; nearly one in every four is African.

The mission field is not just a one-way street. Missionaries and relief and service workers have brought home a richer appreciation for the spirituality of the poor and a deeper awareness of the spiritual dimensions of everyday life. North American Mennonites are becoming more aware that political and social problems are spiritual problems as well, and that spiritual matters cannot be addressed in disregard of material concerns. Consequently, Mennonites in the West are often finding themselves drawn into society by the same conscientious concern which led some of their forebears and others of their contemporaries to draw back.

Old Order Spirituality

Because Mennonites have always been concerned with faithfulness to Jesus Christ in practical and everyday life, change always raises discussion about appropriate behavior, the proper "obedient" way to live under new circumstances. Mennonites have been concerned to not simply conform to "the world." The teachings of Christ stand firm, but the world is ever changing. If Christians change with the times, is the cause of that change found in the world, or in Christ? In what ways may disciples of Jesus accept change?

Differing answers to these questions created tension within most Mennonite-related communities during the 19th century. Not all Mennonites were comfortable with the newer, more subjective forms of spirituality. They were reluctant to accept more formally organized structures in church life, such as Sunday schools, meetinghouses, churchwide mission boards and church sponsorship of higher education. These Mennonites favored both a more personal way of working than the institutional methods being adopted, and a locally-focused congregational life over the rising centralization underway across the church.

Eventually, these more traditional and informal Mennonites formed their own fellowships outside the general groups, in an effort to hold fast to the "old order" of the community. Today they are the Old Order Amish, the Old Order Mennonites and the Old Order River Brethren. (The majority of the Amish who did not follow the Old Order eventually united with the general Mennonite groups in the first half of the 20th century.)

Old Order spirituality is strongly oriented toward the united congregation. Tradition and consensus determine many forms of behavior which are left to personal choice in the more general groups. Emphasis is placed upon simplicity, humility, submission to God's will, and peace and harmony with one's fellow disciples and neighbors—a fuller expression of the Anabaptist goal of *Gelassenheit*. Rather than send missionaries into the world with a highly verbal message, the Old Order groups are a *visible* witness to the world of a better way to live together, in mutual support and care, with a gentle and quiet manner, under the rule and teachings of Jesus.

Old Order groups, which do not endorse revivalism, are frequently accused of "not preaching salvation," or of teaching "salvation by works" because they stress that real faith issues in obedience to Christ, and that obedience rather than a "conversion experience" is the evidence of a true conversion. This charge is really unfair, however. It assumes that conversion can only happen by a method which is nearly the same for everyone. In the Old Order understanding, conversion requires careful deliberation and choice, and strong emotional pleas tend to interfere, disturbing the calm of *Gelassenheit*.

Critics frequently interpret the Old Order concern for the visible and outward forms of obedience as legalism. In reality, this concern reflects the Old Order conviction that *all* of life is meant to be sacred; there is no detail without consequence to God. This conviction can also be seen in the Old Order focus upon home life and the everyday world as the primary arena of spiritual life. Far from a legalistic mentality, the organic wholeness of Old Order spirituality stands in contrast to the thinking of Pietism and Revivalism, where salvation consists primarily of a *legal* declaration of pardon.

New Trends

In the 1920s a communal renewal movement formed in Germany under the leadership of Eberhard Arnold. It attracted a significant following from the Free German Youth Movement, which rose from the ashes of disillusionment following World War I. The Arnold group sought union with the Hutterites of North America, which was formalized in 1930. Today the Hutterian Brethren who trace their beginnings to Arnold's group consist of six *Bruderhofs* in the eastern United States, as well as one each in England and Germany. A new *Bruderhof* is being formed in Nigeria. These eastern Hutterites are often first-generation members, including former professionals and artists, who bring freshness and excitement to their communities, though this has sometimes brought difficulties with the more traditional Hutterites in the western U.S. and Canada. The eastern Hutterian Brethren are notable for their dedication, creativity and optimism.

Around the same time that the Eberhard Arnold's community was adopting Hutterianism, Mennonites in North America were being challenged to rediscover their own heritage. Historians were correcting long-standing misunderstandings about Anabaptism, and offering fresh perspectives of a biblical, pacifist, nonconformist movement as an alternative to the contemporary tug-of-war between fundamentalism and modernism. This renewal of Mennonite identity has been called "the recovery of the Anabaptist Vision." It enabled Mennonites to see their distinctive beliefs and practices as assets—evidence of creativity rather than backwardness. This articulated Anabaptist Vision gave the Mennonites new stature among other churches and attracted new members to the Mennonite community.

The closing decades of the 20th century have seen a flowering of the Charismatic movement among Mennonites in many parts of the world.

Charismatics emphasize the working of the Holy Spirit in creating joy and faith in the individual, lively informal worship, and evangelistic fervor. Especially important are the remarkable gifts of the Spirit for healing, working of miracles, prophecy and speaking in tongues. The movement has had a mixed reception in North America, where its members form a significant minority; but it has had great impact upon Mennonites in Ethiopia as well as in Latin America. The Mennonites of France have felt its influence as well.

Increased involvement in society has exposed North American Mennonites to spiritual influences from established religious denominations. From the Catholic and Orthodox traditions, some Mennonites have found meaning in structured liturgical worship rooted in ancient practice. From these same traditions, other Mennonites have adopted "spiritual disciplines" of fasting, prayer and meditation, as techniques toward "spiritual formation." Adoption of these highly privatized techniques in contact with a personal mentor may be a response to a vacuum created by the waning of congregational discipline in the general Mennonite groups.

Increasing awareness of and involvement in the larger society, along with ecumenical relations, have raised Mennonite awareness of women's concerns, and some have developed spirituality along feminist lines. A few Mennonites have become interested in Creation Spirituality. This movement emphasizes the goodness of the creation and the human body as the work of God, and the importance of holding together the biblical teachings of creation and redemption. It carries a deep concern over care for the earth. A few proponents of Creation Spirituality have adopted a New Age slant, and this has made other Mennonites wary. Yet the recovery of the biblical importance of the creation may recall the point of view of the southern German and Austrian Anabaptists.

How much these trends and movements drawn from other streams will have a lasting influence upon Mennonite spirituality remains to be seen. While many members with a long history in the Mennonite church shop around, many newer Mennonites are finding real inspiration in variously imitating early Anabaptism—sometimes idealized, but more and more seen in its historical reality, wrinkles and all.

IV. A Spiritual Family

Diversity among Mennonites has always existed. Solutions to the quest for the "essence" of Mennonite spirituality are elusive. Part of the difficulty may lie in the way the question is framed. One may be misled by the expectation of finding "the essence." There may be no Mennonite essence at all, yet this need not be a problem!

Modern philosophy of language suggests that it is a mistake to assume that every term in language denotes a single thing in reality, that every expression reaches just as far—and no farther—than the reality to which it points. The late philosopher Wittgenstein has written that words sometimes merely refer to "family resemblances." In his example, the word "game" does not refer to some single common property which all games have in common, but an overlapping of properties between games.

"Mennonite spirituality," therefore, does not need to denote a single phenomenon. It simply refers to a cluster of spiritual patterns which do not have any *one* element common to all, but which resemble one another in the way members of a biological family do: they *look like* each other—some more so, some less so—even if there is no single trait shared by all. The more extended the spiritual family, the more difficult it is to see those resemblances. The similarities remain, however, even when there is some debate as to who looks more like Grandpa or has the mannerisms of Aunt Jane. There are no "pure" Mennonites. Some have married into families which others consider strange, and have children who behave differently, but they are still "us."

This spiritual family will continue as a family for as long as we remember to whom we belong, and from whom we come.

January

Looking Forward

Alma W. Fisher, United States, 1925

We are looking forward into a new year. Many questions arise as we contemplate the twelve months ahead. How will this year differ from the years preceding? What will happen in the world at large? With what great catastrophes may nations be overwhelmed? What scientific discoveries will be made? What new inventions will startle the world? What attempts will be made at the solution of problems of grave import which confront the nations?

*

In the Christian church, what fields of effort will enlist its support? What will be the status of our own church one year hence? How will our individual habits of thinking react toward new ideas as they come? Who of our friends will cease to move among us? Have I lived and shall I live so that I do not fear if I should be among that number?

*

At best I can only project generalities concerning the future. It is well that it is thus. There may be griefs and disappointments before me which I would live in dread of. Or perhaps my cup of joy will be full and even overflowing and I might become too self-sufficient. Events will probably come to pass and conditions arise which I little contemplate or even dream of now. So, paradoxical as it may seem, I shall expect many unexpected things.

Very easily our days can pass by and be spent, for a large part, in a trivial manner. Through ease of communication and modes of travel we are brought together easily whether we live in town or country. Time thus spent with each other can be very profitably employed. On the other hand, it is possible to fritter away our hours in idle, if even harmless gossip, with nothing worthwhile to offer for the time spent.

*

Each year is a sifting and testing of friendships. Our real friends remain true throughout the years and become dearer to us. We share many interests, but differ in our attitudes toward certain questions—yet we are friends. Though we be separated for years we shall remain true. There are others, however, concerning whose friendship I feel less sure. In the coming days I shall probably find some of them moving into the circle of real friendship, and others perhaps unexpectedly receding into the realm of mere acquaintance. I expect also to meet new acquaintances and form new friendships.

I expect my Christian experience to develop more fully. Probably I shall find that I have been emphasizing some less important aspects of life and underestimating some of the more worthwhile things. This re-adjustment of my scale of values I believe to be a normal condition of growth. I should not become pessimistic or cynical when I find that my ideals need revision. I should also become more open-minded, more considerate toward those from whom I differ.

*

Habits of thought and action which I bring with me into the new year will certainly tend to give direction to my life. This being true, it behooves me to so live in this year that the tendencies formed will be forces which will ever carry me into a larger and fuller life.

Fisher (1925): 5, 6

January 2

Love the Earth

Eberhard Arnold, Germany, 1924

We must get rid of an old misunderstanding: the idea that the kingdom Jesus proclaimed is purely otherworldly; that His intention was to make good one day in heaven everything that is and will always remain bad on earth. Then we would have to become people of the otherworld, people who long above all for the hour of our death, people like Trappist monks who lie down daily in their coffins so as to be wholly prepared for dying. To die would then be man's true liberation. Death would then be the redeemer, giving us the final kiss to free us from the shackles of this shameful existence. Then by death we would be lifted out of this accursed bodily life, this pseudo-reality, into a paradise of spirits, a paradise of pure, bodiless joys.

This concept is widespread not only in Buddhism but also in Christianity. It must be emphatically rejected.

*

The great division between God and the devil is not the division between the life here and the life beyond, between matter and spirit, between corporeality and incorporeality. On the contrary, this division runs right through all spirits and all bodies, through all eternities and all times. In every house both spirits are at work in full force. In every body, every human being, both powers are working; both forces operate in every age, in every moment of history, including this one now.

*

Brothers, love the earth. Brothers, be true to the earth, and do not believe those seducers who look longingly at the otherworld so as to cast suspicion on this world. Jesus is the greatest friend of the earth—Jesus who again and again, in the original spirit of Judaism, proclaimed love for this earth, love for the soil, love for the land. Blessed are the peacemakers. They shall have the land.

In Zoroaster's writing we find the startling combination of truth, purity and work on the land, made as the basic demand and promise of divine life. In Jesus and the prophets of Judaism we find that their proclamation of God's coming kingdom testifies to the same miracle of "spirit and land" that comes from God. God, the Spirit of love and justice, of purity and truth, will come; this creative rulership will burst in upon this earth and bring the new earthly regime. This earth shall become the land and garden of a justice and joy, a truth and purity of mutual relationship, such that only then will the true God-ordained joy of life begin on this planet. The earth shall be conquered for a new kingdom, a new order, a new unity, a new joy in true community.

Arnold (1967): 132-135

January 3

The Sting of Death

Millard Lind, United States, 1961

Christians who assume that the primary message of the Bible is "how to get to heaven when you die" must face the embarrassing fact that most of the Bible, the Old Testament, has little to say about life after death. One might respond to this embarrassment with the answer of progressive revelation. This would assume that death was not a problem which was spoken to by ancient religions, but that it was dealt with only at the advent of New Testament times.

However, the opposite is the case. Biblical faith was born in a world where religion was oriented toward life after death. Huge stone tombs for the dead are found in the hill country of Palestine, in Transjordan, in the uplands of Syria, Asia Minor, Armenia, and Kurdistan. These burials date far back and reveal the great emphasis which early man placed upon the afterlife. This compares with the emphasis of the American Indian in our own country upon the "happy hunting ground," with the practice of burying the dead warrior with those objects thought essential to the life in the after world. The example par excellence is that of the pyramids and later tombs of Egypt. These huge monuments, extending back to the early third millennium, were made possible only by devoting the total resources of the state to the service of the dead.

It was not only with life after death that ancient religions were concerned, but also with life here and now. Added to the symbol of the expensive tomb was the symbol of sex. Sex as a symbol of worship seems sensual and vulgar to us.

And much of the practice in ancient religion was sensual and vulgar. Yet to the ancient it was much more than this, for the sex act in worship conveyed life and prosperity to the worshipper. Through "sacred prostitution" the Canaanite believed that he gained fertility for family, for herd and flock, and for field. This belief compares with the faith of those who today practice their religion so that they might "succeed."

*

Biblical faith rejects both of these concerns, the afterlife and prosperity in this life, as the major concerns toward which the energies of faith should be directed. Moses rejected this emphasis because it is not directed toward the amelioration of man's fundamental problem. And since it speaks to the wrong problem, it does not solve those problems to which it speaks.

Moses turned his back upon the emphasis of his contemporaries—life after death. But he had also a unique positive emphasis, an emphasis upon eschatology. Eschatology should not be confused with life after death. For eschatology is not the doctrine that we go to heaven when we die; it is rather the doctrine that the perfect society with a healed relationship between God and man, between man and man, will appear at the end of history.

*

When Jesus came, He proclaimed not life after death but the kingdom of God. He taught us to pray,

> "Thy kingdom come,
> Thy will be done,
> On earth as it is in heaven."

When Jesus used a parable about the afterlife, He used it to teach the importance of the healed relationship. In death the wealthy man opened his eyes in hell because of his broken relationship with Lazarus in life.

Paul also proclaimed—*not* as we would have it, that "The sting of sin is *death*." With him the problem was not that the judgment of death follows upon the broken relationship, and that therefore the broken relationship is to be avoided if we would avoid pain. It was rather that, "The sting of death is *sin*."

Death is unbearable because of the broken relationship, because of guilt.

*

If we cannot understand that the healed relationship is more important than life, perhaps we can learn from a ten-year-old boy, a better theologian than some of us. He had read with his mother an article on the front page of the Goshen newspaper. It told of three girls who had frozen their feet. They had walked barefoot and scantily dressed in 3-below-zero weather, fleeing from a father with whom they had suffered a violent argument. The boy's mother said, "Isn't it terrible to think of children walking barefooted so far on such a cold morning?" The boy replied, "Yes, but it would be worse to have a violent argument with your father!" The boy had pierced to the heart of the message of the Bible!

Erb (1965): 56-60

I Ran Into Myself

Fetty Mae Ndlovu, Zimbabwe, 1970

I walked into a place made entirely of mirrors. I turned expectantly down passageway after passageway seeking an elusive exit. Everywhere I went I ran into myself. The place at every turn seemed to be blocked by a figure. And that figure was always myself. At every turn all I did was to collide with myself. It was a most bewildering experience.

This is what happens to many Christians today. There is one sad trait in common—that is, failing to understand ourselves. Most of the so-called Christians fail to get away from self and, as a result, they collide with it. Self blocks the way of a Christian, and for all the troubles and difficulties that come to him he blames other people, conditions and his friends. He isn't aware of this man "self." In most cases we find self is on the throne while Christ is on the cross.

It is surprising how little a man's outer life needs to govern his inner spirit when he is the integrated master of himself. It is amazing how little outward circumstances contribute to happiness when one is at loose ends in his inner life. The trouble is with ourselves. In the maze of life we have run into a dead end and collided with ourselves. The first solution one has to make is an honest analysis of himself. Many human beings will agree with me that most of our difficulties are within ourselves.

All this is by the way of saying that it took me a long time to learn one great lesson about life. It is this—that most of my failures are caused by one person and that person is *myself*. I've found myself to be the most annoying, distressing and disturbing person with whom I've had to deal. Of course, like every other person, when I've been honest with myself, I've had to confess that I *myself* am the cause of ninety-nine and one half percent of all my failures. This is all because I had partially accepted Christ and self was still on the throne.

Ndlovu (1970): 4

I Sing With Exultation

Felix Mantz, Switzerland, ca. 1526

Felix Mantz participated in the first Anabaptist baptism in January, 1525. Thereafter, he actively spread the renewed faith in Switzerland, during which time he wrote the following song. January 5 marks the anniversary of his martyrdom by drowning in 1527.

I sing with exultation, All my heart delights
In God, who brings salvation, Frees from death's dread might.
I praise Thee, Christ of heaven, Who ever shall endure,
Who takes away my sorrow, Keeps me safe and secure.

Whom God sent as example, Light my feet to guide.
Before my end He bade me In His realm abide.
That I might love and cherish His righteousness divine;
That I with Him forever Bliss eternal might find.

Sing praise to Christ our Savior, Who in grace inclined
To us reveals His nature, Patient, loving, kind.
His love divine outpouring He shows to everyone,
Unfeigned and like His Father's, As no other has done.

Christ bids us, none compelling, To His glorious throne.
He only who is willing Christ as Lord to own,
He is assured of heaven Who will right faith pursue,
With heart made pure do penance, Seal'd with baptism true.

Mennonite Hymnal (1969): No. 40

January 6

Sincere Seekers Find

Jakob Denner, Germany, ca. 1707

*I*t pleased Almighty God when he allowed his Son to be born in flesh, and his holy Son was born for our salvation, to create a new star in the heaven by which the birth of the Savior was to be made known. This was seen by the Magi who were skilled observers of the starry sky and who concluded from this that a new king of the Jews must have been born. From this they knew to go on the way to Jerusalem to see this king and to worship him and to give him gifts.

These wise men were upright children of God. They sought to see Jesus out of pure motives and sincere hearts. They had indeed a rather shallow idea of Christ and about his kingdom, and did not understand at all that the Lord Jesus would not be an earthly, but a spiritual king, or that "his kingdom was not to be an earthly, but a spiritual kingdom" (John 18:36). For this reason they expected to find this king in the large, glamorous city of Jerusalem. In this they were very mistaken. For as has already been said, they did not understand the mystery of this king, that his kingdom would not be of this world. But because their intentions were upright and sincere, the Lord did not let them remain trapped in their error. So from this we can see that if a person seeks the Lord with a sincere and upright heart, and intends only to find the truth, but in this or that thing he might be straying from the truth, God will not allow that person to remain in his error, but will eventually lead him to the truth, on the right way to Jesus Christ, whom he is seeking with the best of intentions. Yes, God protects a simple person—if only he is upright and genuine—and he does not allow that person to walk into destruction, or even to remain in his way of error.

We see an illustration of this in the life of Paul before his conversion. He erred out of a sincere heart in obeying the law of the fathers, persecuted the Christians, the members of the body of Jesus Christ. God saw his sincere zeal even though it was in ignorance. For it was done according to his understanding for the honor of God and the law. Therefore God did not let him remain in this error, but because he was zealous for the truth, God brought him in due time to the knowledge of the truth. For God saw his loyal heart as we can see in Acts 9.

So then let each one see to it that there is nothing false in his heart; but that he tries sincerely to find God. In case he should err in ignorance God will surely lead him to the truth. If a person is seeking nothing but the truth, it can be in any way at all, God will eventually help him to the truth. Any person who is looking with a sincere motive for Christ will eventually find him: God will help him at the appointed time, simply if his intentions are upright and sincere.

Denner (1707): 118, 119 trans. by Noah G. Good

January 7

They Were Not Noticed

Jan Philipsz. Schabaelje, The Netherlands, 1635

An imaginative account—a conversation between a Wandering Soul and Simon Cleopas. The figure of Simon Cleopas is taken from Eusebius, a 4th-century church historian. Simon was purported to have been an acquaintance and follower of Jesus, and to have lived beyond the end of the first century, A.D.

Wandering Soul: The neighbors must have been astonished to see Joseph and Mary return after several years' absence.

Simon Cleopas: Their neighbors did not know what was the cause of their absence; neither did they know that they had fled into Egypt, for Jesus was born among men, as a pearl among a huge pile of stones. The murdering of the children at Bethlehem and the adjacent places was generally known, but none knew the cause of it. Things divine are not so closely examined as earthly things.

*

Simon Cleopas: I do not recollect that there was any rumor made on account of Joseph, Mary or Jesus. Thus little do people regard things that are of more importance than all besides. About trifles there is much ado.

Wandering Soul: Notwithstanding, those who lived with and about them observed more than common things in them.

Simon Cleopas: I acknowledge this, for Mary was in her habits, manners, dress, conversation and in all other things a pattern of virtue. She being my mother's sister, I knew her very well.

*

Simon Cleopas: Her husband also was a man of good manners, honorable, and besides being a laborer he was also very pious. Although he had to maintain himself with his saw and hatchet he would not, like other carpenters, study to enrich himself, but how to please God and to keep his commandments.

*

Simon Cleopas: On account of these virtues, their neighbors and acquaintances were fully convinced of their piety and were astonished at them. Yet they did not take it to heart as they ought to have done.

Wandering Soul: I wish I had known so lovely a company, and particularly the child Jesus, for I desire to hear something concerning him also.

Simon Cleopas: I assure you that should I even spend much time, I would not be able to tell you enough of the virtues of that child. From his very infancy he was so devout and zealous that it was astonishing to see him. His whole mind seemed to be always engaged in heavenly things; and after he could walk, he was obedient to his parents and did their will with such diligence that even they were astonished at him. Everyone who saw him exclaimed, "What a fine child this is! How obliging, mild, lovely and prepossessing. He is not like other children, who play in the streets, full of vanity."

*

Simon Cleopas: All the gifts of nature seemed to have centered in him. Verily, he blossomed like a rose in a field, among other children. O how fortunate are the parents of such a child! But what signified all this—being poor, they were not noticed. What is a carpenter? Were he a priest or another rich citizen, the wisdom of such a son might be of service; but it is to be feared that little will result therefrom. These and the like words were uttered by some when they saw Jesus, yet they knew little of the mysteries of God. This, however, was not at all surprising, for Mary and Joseph themselves, although instructed, did not fully comprehend the true nature of the mysteries of God, which were exhibited in a wonderful and memorable way.

Schabalie (1834): 268-271

Unity Through Love

A. Dyck, Russian Empire, 1826

*E*ven though far removed from one another, the disciples of Christ love one another because each loves the image of Christ and because loving is, in any case, the nature of believers. The mark of a Christian brotherhood is that it is disinterested and selfless, for it does not seek its own gain. It loves, not in order to gain something thereby, but because of Him who loves His own with an everlasting love and has drawn us to Himself out of pure love.

Christ speaks to His disciples: "By this all men will know that you are my disciples, if you have love for one another." The true mark of discipleship is a true and sincere love toward all who love the Lord Jesus unreservedly. For just as no one can be numbered among this group who has not been born again—born of the incorruptible seed, that is, the living, eternal Word of God—similarly no man in his natural state can possess such love, no matter how whitewashed or painted his outward appearance may be. The outward appearance does not impart God's Spirit, nor can it stop or suppress it. This Spirit is free and unconstrained: therefore He blows where He will, and all those souls who have felt His influence in their lives, have waited upon Him, prepared a place for Him to indwell them, and have been called to the true freedom of the children of God are no longer bound to any form!

To such as have been made free the Lord says: "One is your master: Christ; but you are brethren!" They are brothers because one Spirit of sonship in them calls "Abba, dear Father!" and because they share a common inheritance in heaven in which all, through grace, have an equal part. Nor will these souls tolerate any other head over them, any other name, or acquire any other thing under heaven except Jesus Christ alone! To be named after Him—to be members of His body—that is their true glory and their one happiness.

*

Christ is not divided! He alone was crucified for us and only after Him must we be called; otherwise we are carnal, and to be carnally minded is enmity against God! O may the Lord keep us and all his disciples from being thus minded. Brethren, love one another! The Lord is deeply grieved with His kingdom if brethren do not burn with love. . . . Yes, love, let me burn and cling to you! Nothing shall separate me from you, you are the most precious. Oh let me die with you and thereafter inherit the kingdom of glory.

Friesen (1978): 157

A Tame God

Yorifumi Yaguchi, Japan, 1987

You've trapped God
in a cage
You've suspended him
in stained glass
entranced him with organ
and choirs

Cooping him up
in exquisite ritual
you stroke him
with prayers
You've tamed him
like a pet

You exploit
grow rich
live in extravagance
and ease
You let him take away
your sense of guilt

You let him massage
your stiff shoulders
when you please
whistling
to summon him
at will

The once
jealous and ferocious
desert God
now hangs at your neck
an ornamental
amulet

Yaguchi (1989): 56, 57

A Lesson From the Dog

Family Life, United States, 1987

As a mother of young children, I find it is not always easy to be as patient and kind as I should be. We also had a dog that I did not treat as nicely as I should have. He was a good watchdog and helped (and sometimes hindered) us in our work. One thing that especially aggravated me was that he insisted on being on the inside porch. In wet weather, the porch was just about always dirty and hairy. It was simply not fit to let the baby crawl around on the porch. He got hair on his clothes, and if we were not careful, into his mouth.

Then came the day when we found our dog dead. I tried to think what the last words were that I had spoken to him. That forenoon when I was doing the washing, he was lying in the cellar, since the cement was cool and it was a warm day. I coaxed him outside, because I didn't want that dog in the cellar.

How sorry I felt for the many cross words I had said to our faithful dog the last few weeks. For some reason, he had seemed extra provoking to me, but in thinking back now I realized he hadn't been acting any worse than usual. I had to think, "If only I had been nicer to him. . .," but now it was too late to change things.

Then I found out my husband felt the same way. He reminded me how we would feel if it had been one of the children that died instead of the dog. Wouldn't we have reasons to regret our impatience even more then?

I decided it was too late to be kind to our dog, but not too late to be more loving and patient with the children. I am trying to do better. Sometimes when they try out our patience, I remember how it went with our dog, and this helps me to keep myself under control. We still fail many, many times but we are trying to spend more time with our children. We never know how soon they may be called home. And it works the other way, too. If it were a parent that were called to the great beyond, we would want our children to remember us as being kind, loving and patient.

"A Lesson in Patience" (1987): 13

I Prayed For Him With Tears

Thata Book, United States, 1989

In New York, of course, there was much crime and I sometimes wondered how I would react if I were mugged or robbed. I had opportunity to find out.

One Sunday evening we were in service in the chapel just below our apartment. Our chairs were in a circle and I could see the back door from where

I sat. One of the V.S. girls, who was not in the service that evening, came to the door and motioned for me. I went. A stranger was with her, asking for Bibles. I suggested that he come in for the service and I would give him the Bibles afterwards. This he didn't want to do. So I went to get the Bibles requested, which were in our apartment. I unwisely allowed him to accompany me (as I smelled drink on his breath and he looked suspicious).

As soon as we were inside the door of our apartment alone, I felt very uncomfortable, but I went into the guest room where we kept the Living New Testaments in the closet. When I handed him two, he remembered that he wanted two more. Reluctantly I returned for another and this time he followed me. When I turned around he informed me that he wanted money and that I shouldn't make any noise or he would blow out my brains. Upon thinking that it may be the end, my spontaneous response was to call on the name of Jesus. I said, "Jesus, I am ready." I am glad for that assurance at such a time.

He told me to lie down on the bed, but soon ordered me to get up and show him where the money was. Responses at such a time certainly aren't premeditated. At one point, I turned to him and said, "Let me pray for you." His response was to again remind me that he would blow out my brains, even though I don't think he actually had a gun. He got money, which was what he wanted, and got away. I was sorry for him, as I thought that here is another boy who hasn't had a chance in life. I was sorry he got the money, not so much for the money because that was made up to us by friends, but because it only encouraged him in his life of crime. I prayed for him with tears afterwards.

E. Morris Sider (1989): 19

January 12

Permission from Whom?

Pieter Jansz., Indonesia, 1861

The first Mennonite foreign missionary of modern times argues for the independence of mission work from the control of the colonial government.

I, even with the partial accommodation by the government (i.e., the colonial administration), that is still making charges against me without proof or evidence, do not feel free to request permission to perform my service to the government (i.e., Dutch parliament), just as the apostles of the Lord disregarded the prohibitions and threats of the Jewish and Roman authorities. To grant the government the right to require the servants of the gospel of Christ to *ask* for permission to be able to perform their service is to admit that the government also has the right *to refuse* this *permission*. And while I am perfectly willing to obey all commands and laws concerning material and secular affairs, it is my full and firm conviction that we ought not ascribe to it any authority over spiritual affairs, and, above all, in view of the very definite and universal command of our Lord, the Lord of all the earth, that we must obey him rather than man.

*

When Christ brought the glad tidings of grace and salvation for sinners to the earth and sealed it with his own blood, and with that purchased those sinners as his possession to give them eternal salvation, his last command for all who believe in him was: "Go into all the world and preach the gospel to every creature"—make disciples of all peoples, that I may save them by their faith in me.

*

It is truly not our wish or desire that the state as such promote Christianity in any way. But this we ask and beseech with full right in the name of Christ and of the Dutch constitution: Leave the proclamation of the gospel free, even among the Javanese—everywhere. Do not bind them with bonds and limits and legal measures contrary to the law of Christ which would necessarily injure their development. Do not hinder or do not close off the opportunity for the Javanese to be able to hear the Word of God everywhere, and not only the written Word; without good guidance they understand that Word poorly. They do not have support against their priests who explain it incorrectly or declare it falsely; and as to taking the risk of going to a servant of the gospel themselves for enlightenment, that is forbidden by the government; to that place not even a missionary may come!

Therefore eliminate from the law the specification that "every Christian preacher or missionary has to be provided with a government permit to be allowed to render his service in any specific part of the Dutch Indies"—at least, do not require him to beg the secular authorities for permission to fulfill the command of the King of heaven and earth.

Shenk (1980): 87, 94, 95

January 13

Assumptions

Theron Schlabach, United States, 1988

Many branches of the Mennonite community have Old Order groups, such as the Old Order Amish, Old Order Mennonites and Old Order River Brethren. Old Order groups formed in the 19th century in response to modernizing trends in the larger community.

To understand the Old Order outlook, people with modern and progressive outlooks must, at least for the moment, set aside some of their own ingrained assumptions. They must *not* assume:

- That ideas expressed and tested in words are brighter and truer than ideas which take their form in personal and community life.
- That people who accept the ideas of the eighteenth century's so-called Age of Reason are the "enlightened" ones of the world.
- That change is usually good, and usually brings "progress." (The Old Order-minded accepted this change or that—a new tool, perhaps, or rail travel. But they were not progressivists.)
- That the individual is the supreme unit, individual rights the most sacred rights, and human life richest when individuals are most autonomous.
- That the really important human events are those controlled in Washington, New York, Boston, London, Paris and other centers of power—rather than events around hearths or at barn raisings or in meeting at Weaverland or Plain City or Yellow Creek or Kalona.
- That vigor of programs, institutions, activity (including Protestant-style missions) are a test of a Christian group's validity and faithfulness.
- That large organization, organizational unity, and denominational and interdenominational tolerance are better measures of Christian success than is close-knit congregational life.
- That people who imbibe some alcohol or use tobacco have deeply compromised their Christianity.
- Similarly, that people are poor Christians if their sons and daughters wait until adulthood to put off youthful rowdiness and become sober-minded Christians.
- That a structure of rules and explicit expectations (some moral, some mainly just practical for group cohesion) is always legalistic and at odds with the Christian idea of grace.
- That *salvation* refers almost entirely to the individual's original transaction and covenant with God at the time of personal conversion.
- That in church history, words such as *reform* or *renewal* apply only to movements which share the progressivist faith and adopt new methods and new activities; and that leaders who look to the past, or who think faithfulness may come by stricter discipline, are simply reactionary and formalistic.

To set such assumptions aside momentarily does not mean one must romanticize Old Order groups or finally accept the Old Order outlook and critique of modern life. It is only a step outside the prison of mental habits long enough to understand a different view.

Schlabach (1988): 201-203

Plain Is Beautiful!
John L. Ruth, United States, 1978

I have wondered, from time to time, what the effect might have been in my Swiss-Pennsylvania Mennonite consciousness if those sensitive spirits who shared it would have expressed the beauty rather than deplored the narrowness of the plain tradition. In my contacts with my grandparents' generation, or with Amish and Old Order Mennonite friends, I certainly have run across no artists engaging them in any serious dialogue. Borrowing images, yes, but fellowshiping in terms of covenant loyalties, no. It would be too threatening for the liberated artist to open himself again to the incarnation of his past represented in the amazing phenomenon of the plain people, who according to the logic of progress, should not be able to survive.

"Black is beautiful," our black brothers and sisters have learned to say. Who can deny it? But do we ever hear, "Plain is beautiful?" Hardly, outside the pages of the Amish magazine, *Family Life*. We hear, instead, "Plain is narrow, plain is ugly, plain is heartless." Unfortunately, the depth of this discernment is evidenced in tastes that reveal the apparent belief that "Gaudy is beautiful," and present us with "sanctuaries" that appear to have been selected from the same catalog as the churches down the street. Perhaps it is only logical that a Mennonite church furniture firm which has ironically begun to make fonts for infant baptism, and stocks images of Christ and Mary for churches of appropriate denominations, also offered to the ecclesiastical public the option, in 1976, of having its church pews upholstered in red, white and blue.

What would a prophet say in such a situation? Listen to one: "Go through the gates, prepare ye the way of the people." Go before them and lead them in the adventure of returning upon their covenant-sources. Revisit your Bethels. "Cast up the highway"—make it possible for them to travel through this *terra incognita* of their souls. "Gather out the stones"—remove the obstacles to self-knowledge, the sentimentalities, the false images, the confusions in our identity. Show them who, in the story of God's salvation, they are. Use your God-given imagination, un-awed by the important-sounding claims and counter-claims of a miscellaneous secular culture, to "Lift up a standard among the people."

Ruth (1978): 57-59

A Ministry of Reconciliation
Vincent Harding, United States, 1962

*O*ur calling as ministers of peace has led us often to Albany, Georgia—now the focal point of the struggle for justice and freedom in the deep South. It was in the midst of this particular ministry that I was arrested and placed in jail on Monday night, July 23.

*

During the afternoon of that day, a young woman who happened to be a Negro was visiting some friends who had been placed in jail in a town near Albany as a result of their earlier participation in public protests against segregation in Albany. A policeman of the town in which the jail was located kicked the young woman—Mrs. Marian King—from the back, and another then struck her a sharp blow in the face, knocking her to the ground, unconscious for a moment. The policeman who happened to be white, did this simply because Mrs. King would not move quickly enough in response to their orders. However, it was difficult for her to move too quickly, for she was six months pregnant and was carrying her three-year-old daughter in her arms at the time.

When the Negroes of Albany heard of this later in the day, a great wave of anger swept over the community. There were many persons who felt that the only alternative to frightened silence was the returning of violence for violence. Some individuals were evidently ready to do bodily harm to any white person they encountered. Others wanted to go by car to the town where this had happened and retaliate in some way.

In the midst of this potentially explosive situation, it seemed clear to a few of us that some public act of protest and mourning needed to be performed. The Negroes of Albany needed to be shown some way of reacting that would be basically Christian and non-violent in its expression. The young woman who was attacked was a dear friend of my wife and me, and I decided—in conference with others—to go to City Hall that night and pray there.

*

Six other persons joined me.

We talked and prayed together on our way downtown, and though we did not go to seek arrest, we realized that the city was in a tense enough situation to make arrest very possible. We decided to continue still. Shortly before eleven that night, as more than 100 policemen and state troopers looked on, we stood to pray in front of City Hall. The Chief of Police, a personal friend of mine, sought to dissuade us, but we believed it was right for us to pray there at such a time. So he arrested us. I was in jail three nights and two days, basically rejoicing in the privilege of sharing an experience that many Christians had known before me.

As I sat in the confinement of my cell in Albany, and considered my responsibility as a speaker here at World Conference, I was sorely tempted to stay there indefinitely—for the benefit of my Mennonite brothers and sisters. I was tempted to stay there and to write a letter from prison, confessing to you how weary I sometimes get of talking and talking and talking about the church and race. For I do get weary, and I considered seriously staying in my four-man cell and sending to all of you a short, gracious note of invitation, urging you to come down to Albany and share the experience with me. For behind all the other circumstances and peripheral issues, I knew that I was in jail because I believed that segregation is deeply sinful, and I was convinced that many of us here really know this too.

We know it in terms of what it does to human lives. We know that it scars the human spirit and defaces the image of God, and makes the victim feel less than human, and makes a spiritual murderer out of the perpetrator. We know that it makes one group believe that God has cursed them with a darker skin, and makes another group believe that God has especially blessed them with a light one; and both of these are blasphemies against the God who looks only upon the heart.

We know from Scripture that segregation and discrimination and racial prejudice are wrong.

*

We know, too, that the greatest vision of the kingdom of God in the Scriptures is one that speaks of the redeemed as those who come from "every tribe and tongue and people and nation" (Revelation 5:9). We know that a God who intends to have no segregation around His throne surely is not pleased with segregation in our communities and even in our churches.

Dyck ([1962]): 521, 522

January 16

One New Village
Z. Marwa Kisare, Tanzania, 1984

At first I could not accept that God wanted me to become the brother of the missionary, that God wanted me to account the missionary to be of the same village with me. How could I accept that, when I felt the missionary's own ethnic pride so keenly?

The Holy Spirit also showed me that I must honor and respect the Luo people on the Shirati station who were not from my father Kisare's village. How could I accept to do this when I knew all about the gossiping and hypocrisy which stood between us as we struggled for place with the missionaries?

But that evening we all saw Jesus. By that I mean that we saw the crucified Lamb of God whose blood removes the walls that separate people from each other and from God their Father. A great light from heaven shone on us and each saw his own sin and each saw the new village of God. We all saw this revelation together, so it was easy to confess to one another and to forgive one another.

We now saw each other in a different way. Earlier such things as theft, adultery, lying, malicious gossip, and jealousies were not so bad if they were directed against people of another village. But if all were members of the same new village, then we needed to hold the character of each other person as sacred. We needed to ask forgiveness and make things right even with those of a different ethnic background.

*

It was only because of Jesus' blood that Elam Stauffer and I were able to recognize each other. Without that sacrifice he was nothing to me. If he was just an ethnic Mennonite holding to the ways of his Mennonite ancestors, holding to his Swiss-German heritage, then he was no different from what I was when I held to the ways of Kisare's village. My ethnic heritage was as rich and meaningful as his.

An ethnic heritage may be a blessing to us. But there is no salvation there, no new village, no church. Ethnicity alone leaves us separated from God and each other. It is only through Jesus' sacrifice that we can become sons of God and can live within his blessing. It is only through Jesus' sacrifice that we can call each other brother.

Shenk (1984): 81, 82

January 17

Same Old Problem

Johannes Risser, Germany, 1827

When a church has simply presumptuous piety, which is always paired with pharisaical pride, it is likewise in its nature to fear the pure gospel and therefore resist and oppose it, especially when foreign (i.e., non-Mennonite) evangelists unite with it. The evidence for this is clear from the present back to Christ.

It is therefore also clear that the reasons given were only a pretext and that it was really not the men but the gospel that was feared. One is full of mistrust, as if the Holy Scripture had not given us plain standards for proving the spirits. And even though he may not protest against all good proposals, neither does he promote them; and even if one merely passes his mistrust on to his neighbor he is nonetheless causing harm. Another feels his pride is injured because he is supposed to listen to outside counselors and this is sufficient reason for turning his back to them. A third party is so out of sorts that he closes his heart and ears to the truth and actually works against things that are good; he is in serious danger that the truth can become for him an "aroma of death" (2 Corinthians 2:16).

In short, I must confess that in my eyes our church, in its criticism of our outside brethren, has revealed itself as weakest of all.

Risser (1827): 3, 4, trans. Eliz. H. Bender

January 18

From Heart to Action
Pilgram Marpeck, Germany, 1531

Whoever has been inwardly baptized, with belief and the Spirit of Christ in his heart, will not despise the external baptism and the Lord's Supper which are performed according to Christian, apostolic order; nor will he dissuade anyone from participating in them. Rather, he should willingly accept them and practice them, not merely imitating them externally in an apish manner, but in truth and in the spirit with which the true worshippers use external means, such as the mouth, hands and knees. For, as one can see, the heart moves our external members. Whenever the heart laughs, is compassionate, rejoices or gets angry, then the mouth, eyes, head, hands and feet laugh, are compassionate, rejoice, get angry, move and grasp without delay the external things which correspond to anger, joy, mercy or laughter. The opposite is also true. So it is with baptism and the Lord's Supper.

Where they are present in the heart, there they are also practiced externally and practiced according to love. Thus, the heart of the eunuch also moved (Acts 8) all his physical members and his whole body, freely and without any external compulsion, to undergo external baptism. The inner covenant compelled Abraham to accept the external sign of the covenant of the Old Testament. For out of the abundance of the heart, the mouth speaks.

*

Whoever teaches that believers do not need external baptism and the Lord's Supper, or teaches that these ceremonies are not expected of believers or given to them, errs, for Philip demands that faith go before. Christ also placed faith first and, according to the Acts of the Apostles, faith always precedes baptism. Also, the command to break bread is given only to the disciples and the believers, and not the unbelievers. The believers have always practiced it, and only they can practice it in spirit and in truth.

*

The adversary would destroy the internal by discontinuing the external.

Marpeck (1978): 65, 66

January 19

By Simple Water

Pilgram Marpeck, Germany, 1531

*P*eter wished to be wiser than the other disciples; thus, he would not permit the Lord Christ to wash his feet. Peter's assumed humility, which he possessed according to human reason, became sheer pride. Christ wished to break that pride, for He harnessed Peter's salvation to this act of washing his feet and said to Peter's fleshly wisdom: "You do not know what I do now, but hereafter you will understand." Why did Christ not permit the inward and the knowledge of a greater secret, of which the high-minded spirits speak, to come first, to be followed afterward by the outward?

According to this captious wisdom, it is indeed a foolish thing to begin the wisdom and knowledge of God with such mundane things as outward teaching received by faith, and to testify to this teaching by simple water. Immediately, they say: "What good is water, bread or wine to me? It is sufficient if I recognize and inwardly believe." Such reason despises the humanity of Christ to which that reason should be captive.

Marpeck (1978): 79

January 20

What Good Can Water Do?

Menno Simons, The Netherlands, 1539

*C*hrist's sheep hear His voice. True Christians believe and do. If you are a genuine Christian born of God, then why do you draw back from baptism, which is the least God has commanded you? It is a weighty and important command to love your enemy, is it not? To do good to those that hate you, to pray in spirit and in truth for those who persecute you; to crucify your wicked and ungodly flesh with its impure lusts and desires; to tear from mouth, heart and flesh your pretentious pride, your grasping greed, your foul immorality, your bloody hatred, your gluttonous eating and drinking, your accursed idolatry, your jealous slandering, your reckless, hurtful tongue; and to love and fear with all your heart your Lord and God, your Redeemer and Creator, and in all things to govern yourself by His holy will; to serve your neighbor in sincere and unfeigned love with all your powers, with possessions, houses and lands, with your advice, with the fruit of your toil and travail, with your blood if need be; with a sincere heart to suffer misery, disdain and the oppressive cross of Christ for the Lord's Word, and to confess Christ Jesus before lords and princes, in prison and bonds, by words and deeds unto death.

It seems to me that these and the like commands are more painful and difficult for perverse flesh, naturally so prone to follow its own way everywhere, than to be the recipient of a handful of water. And a sincere Christian must be ready to do all this, must he not? If not, he is not born of God, for the regenerated are one mind with Christ Jesus.

*

Herewith I entreat and admonish you, beloved reader, not to be so contrary against the Lord, saying, "What good can water do?" Reflect that Christ Jesus Himself was baptized, although He was without sin, neither was guile found in His mouth; He who was Himself the righteousness, the way, the truth and the life. Tell me, what good could water do Christ who was all in all? The disciples also at Ephesus were rebaptized by Paul because they knew nothing of the Holy Ghost although they had been baptized with the baptism of John. If Christ who was without sin had Himself baptized, and others who had been baptized with the baptism of John, which verily was from heaven, were rebaptized by Paul, why do you despise the Lord's baptism, you who are poor miserable sinners, who were baptized without knowledge and faith?

Menno (1956): 138, 139, 141

January 21

The Beginning of Separation
Kaspar Braitmichel, from earlier sources, Moravia, 1560s

The Anabaptist movement was woven from many strands. The first group to take the step into believers' baptism for persons already "baptized" as infants was the Bible study circle led by Conrad Grebel. January 21, 1525 was the date of those first baptisms, and can rightly be called the birthday of Anabaptism.

*I*t began in Switzerland, where God brought about an awakening. First of all a meeting took place between Ulrich Zwingli, Conrad Grebel (a member of the nobility), and Felix Mantz. All three were men of learning with a thorough knowledge of German, Latin, Greek and Hebrew. They started to discuss matters of faith and realized that infant baptism is unnecessary and, moreover, is not baptism at all.

Two of them, Conrad and Felix, believed that people should be truly baptized in the Christian order appointed by the Lord, because Christ himself says, "Whoever believes and is baptized will be saved." Ulrich Zwingli (who shrank from the cross, disgrace and persecution that Christ suffered) refused to agree—he said it would cause an uproar. But Conrad and Felix said that was no reason to disobey the clear command of God.

At this point a man came from Chur, a priest named Georg From The House Of Jacob, later known as Georg Blaurock.

*

He, too, had first approached Zwingli and discussed questions of faith with him at length, but he had got nowhere. Then he was told that there were other men more on fire than Zwingli. He inquired eagerly about them and met with them, that is, with Conrad Grebel and Felix Mantz, to talk about questions of faith. They came to unity about these questions. In the fear of God they agreed that from God's Word one must first learn true faith, expressed in deeds of love, and on confession of this faith receive true Christian baptism as a covenant of a good conscience with God, serving him from then on with a holy Christian life and remaining steadfast to the end, even in times of tribulation.

One day when they were meeting, fear came over them and struck their hearts. They fell on their knees before the almighty God in heaven and called upon him who knows all hearts. They prayed that God grant it to them to do his divine will and that he might have mercy on them. They were well aware of what they would have to suffer for this.

After the prayer, Georg Blaurock stood up and asked Conrad Grebel in the name of God to baptize him with true Christian baptism on his faith and recognition of the truth. With this request he knelt down, and Conrad baptized him, since at that time there was no appointed servant of the Word. Then the others turned to Georg in their turn, asking him to baptize them, which he did. And so, in great fear of God, together they surrendered themselves to the Lord. They confirmed one another for the service of the Gospel and began to teach the faith and to keep it. This was the beginning of separation from the world and its evil ways.

Hutterian Brethren (1987): 43-45

<hr>

January 22

A Fair Chance
Nancy Sauder, Canada, 1987

*T*hree of my friends and I sat waiting in the back of the Grey Coach bus. Nearly all the other passengers got off at this terminal and we were waiting for a different driver. Two young girls boarded the bus. They eyed us curiously and settled down two seats ahead of us. The one wore a black coat, shirt and jeans. Her hair was tousled loosely in stiff wisps on her head. A rubber alligator about a foot long dangled from the collar of her coat. Her companion looked rather different, too, with her hair dyed to an orange color and eyeshadow to match. A strip of hair above her ears was clipped and the rest cut short.

Unable to hide their curiosity the girls began to ask questions. "Where are you from?" they asked.

"We live on farms near Kitchener."

"Why, your dresses are nearly alike. What are you?"

"We're Mennonites," we answered.

"Mennonites! Mennonites, wow that's weird," exclaimed the girl with the orange-dyed hair. She leaned across the armrest of the bus seat and gaped at us.

"Have you ever heard of Mennonites?"

They shook their heads. "What do you stand for?"

We tried to give a brief and simple explanation of our religion.

One of the girls said, "My mother's a Catholic, but I don't have any religion." Then she asked me, "Do you go to school?"

"No, we only go to grade eight."

"What do you do then?"

"Oh, we work on farms."

"Well, don't ever move to the city. There's too much murder and stuff going on," and she went on to tell how a friend of hers had been murdered.

"Do you ever watch _____ on TV?"

"We don't have TV."

"Oh!" gasped the girls, "You're missing out on a lot. Do you ever have fun? Don't you have any music?"

"Shall we sing a few songs for you?" we asked.

"Yes, do." And they listened intently while we sang a number of our familiar hymns.

"Do you people eat normal food?" burst out one of the strangers.

"Oh, yes," we answered, suppressing our grins. "But we do grow a lot of our own food on the farms."

After a pause, the girl with the orange-colored hair asked, "Have you ever heard of punks? I'm a punk."

"What do you stand for?"

"Rebels," she answered simply. "We have no use for authority, like government or even police." She popped a bubble with her gum. When no one made further comment she said, "Your singing was great, do you know any more?" and they settled back in their seats to listen while we sang some more.

"How old are you?" they asked looking at us from one to the other. We told them and they were surprised.

"My, but you look young," said one of them.

"I know why," added the other. "They don't have on any makeup."

We could not deny it. These girls did look much older than their fourteen and fifteen years. Their faces held a hard look and makeup marred the innocent look of youth.

"Do you ever get drunk, or smoke? What about using drugs?"

"We don't believe in misusing our bodies like that."

"Do you swear or is that bad too?"

"No, we don't swear."

"But what do you do when you get mad?"

"We are taught that according to our works, we will be judged some day. Do you believe in eternity?"

"What's that?"

"A hereafter. Life after death."

"Oh yes, and I want to be happy then. Do you really think the world is going to end in the year 2000?"

"God alone knows that."

"How do you think the world began?"

We put the question back to her: "How do *you* think the world was made?"

"I don't know," she answered. "I wasn't there."

The girl dressed in black got out her purse and began touching up her makeup. Before long they arrived at their destination. They bade us farewell and got off the bus. Very likely we will never see them again.

Now those girls are to be pitied. Do they have a fair chance?

Are we thankful enough for our heritage? We have been given a fair chance. Will we take it or leave it?

Sauder (1987): 30, 31

January 23

Where You Hear of the Cross, There is Christ

Anneken Jansz., The Netherlands, 1539

Anneken Jansz., of Rotterdam, The Netherlands, was a member of the Anabaptist group led by David Joris. Joris' apolcalyptic/visionary spirituality was bitterly opposed by Menno. In spite of such conflict, the following letter of Anneken Jansz. to her son was treasured by early Mennonites.

My son, hear the instruction of your mother; open your ears to hear the words of my mouth. Behold, I go today the way of the prophets, apostles and martyrs, and drink of the cup of which they all have drunk. I go, I say, the way which Christ Jesus, the eternal Word of the Father, full of grace and truth, the Shepherd of the sheep, who is the Life, Himself went.

*

Having passed through, He calls His sheep, and His sheep hear His voice, and follow Him whithersoever He goes—for this is the way to the true fountain. This way was traveled by the royal priests who came from the rising of the sun, as we read in Revelation, and entered into the ages of eternity, and had to drink of this cup.

This way was trodden by the dead under the altar, who cry, saying: "Lord, Almighty God, when wilt Thou avenge the blood that has been shed?" White robes were given unto them, and it was said to them, "Wait yet for a little season, until the number of your brethren that are yet to be killed for the testimony of Jesus be fulfilled" (Revelation 6:9-11). These also drank of the cup, and are gone above to keep the eternal, holy Sabbath of the Lord. This is the way in which walked the twenty-four elders, who stand before the throne of God and cast their crowns and harps before the throne of the Lamb, falling down upon their faces and saying: "Lord, unto Thee alone be praise, glory, power and strength, who shalt avenge the blood of thy servants and ministers, and shalt through Thyself gain the victory. Great be Thy name, Almighty, which was, and is, and is to come" (Revelation 4:8, 10).

In this way walked also those who were marked by the Lord, and received the mark *Thau* upon their foreheads, who were chosen from among all nations of men, who were not defiled with women (understand this) and who follow the Lamb whithersoever He goeth.

Behold, all these had to drink of the cup of bitterness, as will also all those have to do, who are still wanting to complete the number and fulfillment of Zion, the bride of the Lamb, which is the New Jerusalem coming down out of heaven, the city and throne of God, in which the glory of the great King shall be seen, when the feast of tabernacles will be kept and celebrated in the days of eternal rest and joy.

Behold, all these could not attain to this, without first suffering judgment and chastisement in their flesh; for Christ Jesus, the eternal truth, was the first, when it is written: "The Lamb slain from the foundation of the world."

*

If you, therefore, desire to enter into the regions of the holy world, and into the inheritance of the saints, gird your loins and follow after them. Search the Scriptures, and it shall show you their ways.

*

Therefore, my child, do not regard the great number nor walk in their ways.

*

But where you hear of a poor, simple, cast-off little flock, which is despised and rejected by the world, join them. For where you hear of the cross, there is Christ; from there do not depart. Flee the shadow of this world. Become united with God, fear Him alone. Keep His commandments, observe all His words, to do them. Write them upon the table of your heart, bind them on your forehead, speak day and night of His law and you will be a pleasant tree and a sprout in the courts of the Lord, a beloved plant growing up in Zion.

*

O holy Father, sanctify the son of Thy handmaiden in Thy truth, and keep him from the evil, for Thy name's sake, O Lord.

van Braght (1979): 453, 454

The Proper Ordering of the Lord
Swiss Brethren, Switzerland, 1520s

The Anabaptists were careful from the beginning to order everything on the pattern of the New Testament. The selection below is the oldest Ordnung, or congregational order, known in Anabaptism.

Since the almighty eternal and merciful God has made His wonderful light break forth in this world and most dangerous time, we recognize the mystery of the divine will, that the Word is preached to us according to the proper ordering of the Lord, whereby we have been called into His fellowship. Therefore, according to the command of the Lord and the teachings of His apostles, in Christian order, we should observe the new commandment in love one toward another, so that love and unity may be maintained, which all brothers and sisters of the entire congregation should agree to hold as follows:

1. The brothers and sisters should meet at least three or four times a week, to exercise themselves in the teaching of Christ and His apostles and heartily to exhort one another to remain faithful to the Lord as they pledged.

2. When the brothers and sisters are together, they shall take up something to read together. The one to whom God has given the best understanding shall explain it. The others should be still and listen, so that there are not two or three carrying on a private conversation, bothering the others. The Psalter shall be read daily at home.

3. Let none be frivolous in the church of God, neither in words nor in actions. Good conduct shall be maintained by them all also before the heathen.

4. When a brother sees his brother erring, he shall warn him according to the command of Christ, and shall admonish him in a Christian and brotherly way, as everyone is bound and obliged to do out of love.

5. Of all the brothers and sisters of this congregation none shall have anything of his own, but rather, as the Christians in the time of the apostles held all in common, and especially stored up a common fund, from which aid can be given to the poor, according as each will have need, and as in the apostles' time permit no brother to be in need.

6. All gluttony shall be avoided among the brothers who are gathered in the congregation. Serve a soup or minimum of vegetable and meat, for eating and drinking are not the kingdom of heaven.

7. The Lord's Supper shall be held as often as the brothers are together, thereby proclaiming the death of the Lord, and thereby warning each one to commemorate how Christ gave His life for us and shed His blood for us, that we might also be willing to give our body and life for Christ's sake, which means for the sake of all the brothers.

Yoder (1973): 44, 45

Each One

Swiss Brethren, Switzerland, ca. 1540

A listener is bound by Christian love (if something of edification is given or revealed to him) that he should and may speak of it also in the congregation, and again thereupon be silent, according to the text which reads: "How is it then brethren? when ye come together, every one of you hath a psalm, hath a doctrine, hath a tongue, hath a revelation, hath an interpretation. Let all things be done unto edifying," etc. And again, "Let one or another prophet speak (that is prophesying) and the other judge. If anything be revealed to another that sitteth by, let the first hold his peace. For ye may all prophesy one by one, that all may learn and all may be comforted. And the spirits of the prophets are subject to the prophets. For God is not the author of confusion, but of peace, as in all churches of the saints."

*

And he enjoins them thereupon to permit all this to be done—that is, to apply or to use—to the edification of the congregation which comes together, so that it may be a bright light in spite if the presumptous attacks of the adversaries. And it is Paul's intention that if one sitting by or listening receives a revelation or is moved to exercise his spiritual gift or to prophesy, then the first shall hold his peace; and Paul says that all may prophesy, one after the other, and wants that at all times the spirit of the one who prophesies or teaches or preaches first shall be subject to, and silent before, the one from among those seated or listening who has something to prophesy, and shall not show himself discordant or unpeaceful.

*

When someone comes to church and constantly hears one person speaking, and all the listeners are silent, neither speaking or prophesying, who can or will regard or confess the same to be a spiritual congregation, or confess according to 1 Corinthians 14 that God is dwelling and operating in them through his Holy Spirit with his gifts, impelling them one after the other in the above mentioned order of speaking and prophesying?

Peachey (1971): 10, 11

Suffering's Challenge

Dagne Assefa, United States, 1983

An Ethiopian Mennonite describes renewal in his congregation in Addis Ababa. The Ethiopian church is called Meserete Kristos Church (MKC) meaning "Christ Foundation Church."

*T*he spiritual renewal of Bole MKC began with worship. There was a new life and openness in the worship services that had not been characteristic of the congregation. The Sunday morning worship was not only too formal and structured, but also lacked inspiration and flexibility. Then the congregation, because of charismatic influences, turned away from its prescribed pattern of worship to a more spontaneous and diverse style of worship. For a while, the change created a tension between the "old" and the "new" members. Out of this tension and other experiences, the congregation was able to appreciate not only one but different forms of worship.

There was more praying and singing outside the formal church setting. Believers gathered together in households to pray and share testimonies of God's work in their lives. They prayed for courage and love when they were mistreated and persecuted by the enemies of their faith. Through all the harassments they received, both from the government and the society, they showed a persistent faith in what God can do in their lives.

Along with this conscious and active seeking of God's will in prayer also came a new hunger for the word of God. The congregation began to study the Word and listen to each other's interpretations. They examined the Scripture to find out what it meant to live under a regime that attacked their faith. They asked themselves how one could be honest to the teachings of the Scripture and at the same time live in peace with the Socialist Government.

The Bole MKC, because of its willingness to suffer for Christ, became a power that the Government had to reckon with. The more the Government infringed upon the freedom of the Church to worship and to spread the Gospel the more the work of God was done. When the Government restricted the Church from going out into the world in any manner, the world came to the Church to see what God was doing in her midst. The Church could not go out to carry out her "Great Commission" but nothing could stop her from being a witness to what God was doing in the world. It was this challenge that the Government could not deal with. They finally resorted to using force to close down all the Mennonite congregations and put their leaders behind bars without any charges.

Assefa (1984): 14

Sunday Worship in London

Eleanor Graber Kreider, England, 1990

During our ninety-minute meeting, our worship comprises three parts. In the first part we sing, read the Scriptures and pray in ways that people of all ages can participate. Sometimes we present Bible stories in dramatic readings. We like using flannelgraph and other visual aids. Almost every week we sing birthday blessings to someone with a song, "[Name], Jesus loves you!" Simple thank-you prayers and a song complete the first section of praise and worship. At this point the children go to a side room for their special activities.

The second part is the prayers. For many of us, this is the heart of the worship. As members of a local Christian church we are members of the body of Christ, participating in its mission. That mission includes listening to the world, mourning over its pain and interceding for its leaders. We pray about local housing issues, about European environmental questions, about unemployment or housing needs of individual members, about friends who do not yet know Jesus. Jesus taught us to pray for our enemies and for our neighbors, to bless each other, to ask for healing. Jesus promised us overflowing life. In our prayers we get a foretaste of the promise. In our prayers we find Jesus in the middle of our circle. We know that answered prayers may yield surprises and perhaps give new shape to our corporate life. To pray together is our work, and it is our joy.

The concluding part of the worship varies. Once a month it is a communion service. The communion service flows on from the prayers by the peace greeting (holy kiss) and singing. We stand to hear the words from Scripture. Then two members give thanks over the bread and the cup. First we break and serve to each other the unleavened bread. Then we all drink from the common cup. On other Sundays of the month, a sermon comprises the final part of the service. We have elders, but they are not always the preachers. A number of members are gifted Bible expositors. We have relatively few outside speakers. The elders oversee the choice of topics and biblical texts, and also attempt to elicit the prophetic, the free and Spirit-given word that emerges through the life of the church.

We baptize in a small lake in Hampstead Heath, North London. Its public character makes an outdoor baptism an opportunity for witness to passers-by. We usually have members at the edges to explain what is happening to joggers and people out walking their dogs. Many will stand and watch.

Worship in our church is characterized by its familial atmosphere, with numerous common meals, and by its emphasis on corporate prayer. In worship the community discerns God's word through expository and prophetic gifts of the Spirit. In worship we express our joy and thankfulness, our weakness and need. In worship, as in no other way, we the church become the living body of Christ.

Lichdi (1990): 72, 73

Sunday Worship in Mbuji Mayi

Milolo Kabalu, Zaire, 1990

*V*ery early in the morning, at about 8 o'clock, the deacons take care of arranging the sanctuary. They put out flowers, dust the benches and hose down the sanctuary. The children then go to Sunday School, which lasts about thirty minutes. They are given special instruction based on Bible verses, and they learn songs. The Youth for Christ group has its meeting after the service.

The starting time for the service varies from one parish to another. When the bell rings, the faithful enter in order and in silence.

*

When the worship leaders have entered, the moderator reads a Bible verse and the congregation rises to sing a hymn. At the end of the song, praise is given to the Lord by the moderator and the faithful pray silently. The chorister then announces two collective songs and everyone sings with joy under his direction. If the song has a four-beat measure, it will be accompanied by the clapping of hands. After a meditation on the goodness of the Lord, the moderator invites one of the members to thank the Lord for having watched over all the members during the week. The moderator reports to the members the amount of the offering and the number of Bibles and songbooks from the preceeding week. He arranges for the place where the prayer groups will meet that week. He also introduces the visitors. The faithful welcome the visitors with a special song, and a member is chosen to say a prayer for them.

Now comes the participation of the choirs, who sing their melodies in the order given by the moderator. In a parish where there are four choirs, they sing alternately.

*

Not all choirs have the same instruments. There are others who sing only with unaccompanied voices. The songs of the women and the youth are often accompanied by dances. If not the entire body, at least the head will surely be moving. The dance always has meaning and is appropriate to the song. It always manifests praise and joy. In other choirs, only gestures are used.

Taking the offering is done in the following manner. First are the promises that the faithful have made secretly to the Lord concerning personal problems. When the problem is resolved, the person gives a testimony before the congregation. Each one gives what she or he has promised. It can be money, produce or an animal. This part of the service has its special song. The day's balance is tallied and everyone rises, singing and dancing. The children bring their offerings first, then the youth, the women and the men. In this part only money is given. The tithe is given voluntarily by the people involved. This can be in the form of money, produce or animals.

The most important part of the service is the sermon. At this time all the children are watched carefully to see that they do not disrupt the sermon. The preacher for the day announces to his audience the author, page, chapter and verses of the reading. He reads in a loud and clear voice. Afterward, he invokes the Holy Spirit to enlighten and hold the attention of the audience and to help the preacher during the sermon.

The length of the sermon varies from one preacher to another. If the sermon is long, it will be interspersed with verses of song that speak about the same subject in order to give the preacher a break and prevent the faithful from sleeping. The sermon does not often last longer than an hour. The singing is often improvised and can come from any member. Sometimes the preacher asks the audience short questions in order to hold their attention, and the answer is always given collectively. After ample explanation of all the points of the message, he makes a summary and gives the moral.

When the sermon is finished, a member who is chosen gives thanks to the Lord for the message; often the preacher fulfills this task. The choirs sing for the last time. Their songs correspond to the theme of the sermon. At the end, the pastor prays as a closing. The congregation sings the prayer "Our Father" and receives the blessing. Leaving the sanctuary is also done in order, and all the faithful greet each other at the door. The way we worship in Zaire is very satisfying.

Lichdi (1990): 81, 82

January 29

Our Whole Lives in Worship
Sara Wenger Shenk, United States, 1987

*I*n most Protestant worship, both at home and at church, we rely heavily on the unvarnished biblical word. We lean toward a rationalistic approach to religion, imagining that if we can *say* it right we'll finally get it right. We have forgotten that because human beings are a *unity* of mind, body and spirit, we need colors, candles, embraces, dances and drama to fill out our picture of truth.

Why have we forgotten? Why have we forgotten that Christian worship (as distinct from attending lectures and concerts) invites everyone to get in on the act, not as spectators, but as responsive actors? Movement is an integral part of Christian worship. Moving is essential to thinking. Ritual provides a way to harmonize our movements with their meaning.

Why have we forgotten that it is through our senses, all of them, that our hearts are enlarged so that God may enter in? The supernatural reaches us along natural paths, symbolized in the breaking of bread, the rising helium balloon on Easter morning, the hands-on parental blessing. Our senses are the vehicles through which the Spirit of God enters into our constricted thought to make space for grace.

*

Why have we forgotten? The wordy austerity of much contemporary worship life stems in part from the time of the Protestant Reformation. During the 16th century, Protestant reformers ruthlessly condemned external symbols of religiosity such as the Roman Catholic liturgy, vestments, pictures, candles, incense, crosses, organs and processions.

*

The reformers saw correctly, I think, that external ceremonious religion is inadequate and, in extreme cases, magical. A heavy dependence on ceremony can easily slide into crass materialism. The fire of reform did burn up a lot of fluff. Yet that same fire left us with little, other than words, for grasping the intimate relatedness of our humanity and God's transcendence.

We are beings who, while concretely anchoring ourselves in our world, seek to transcend ourselves and our world. When we are discouraged or lonely we turn to music, or to painting, to prayer or to the Eucharist, and "as compensation beyond all price," Madeleine L'Engle writes, "we are given glimpses of the world on the other side of time and space."

Through our senses we are able to reach out toward the supra-sensible. This is a deep mystery! Concrete symbols and ritual play connect us somehow with the eternal, the incomprehensible. And too, they are especially appropriate for children because many of them don't require a certain level of knowledge before one can participate. They make tangible for children what is intangible. They convey a simple, elementary meaning that can grow with us as we grow in our ability to comprehend.

*

It was Christ who drew from the ordinary things of life to point to the reality of God in our midst: a farmer planting a seed, a woman's use of yeast in baking, the relationship of a father and two sons. By God's grace the common stuff of life becomes sacred, leading us toward God.

Shenk (1987): 9, 10

His Abounding Grace

Menno Simons, Germany, 1554

After proclaiming biblical faith since the spring of 1535, Menno renounced the priesthood and departed the medieval church for the Anabaptist cause in January 1536, quite possibly on this date.

*I*t happened in the year 1524, the twenty-eighth of my life, that I assumed the duties of a priest in my paternal village called Pingjum. Two others of about my age also officiated in the same functions. The one was my pastor, fairly well educated. The other was below me. Both had read the Scriptures a little, but I had never touched them, for I feared if I should read them, I would be misled. Behold, such an ignorant preacher I was for nearly two years.

In the year following it occurred to me, as often as I handled the bread and wine in the Mass, that they were not the flesh and blood of the Lord. I thought that the devil was suggesting this so that he might separate me from my faith. I confessed it often, sighed and prayed; yet I could not come clear of the idea.

The two young men mentioned earlier and I spent our time emptily in playing [cards] together, drinking and in diversions as, alas, is the fashion and usage of such useless people. And when we touched upon the Scriptures I could not speak a word with them without being scoffed at, for I did not know what I was driving at, so concealed was the Word of God from my eyes.

Finally, I got the idea to examine the New Testament diligently. I had not gone very far when I discovered that we were deceived and my conscience, troubled on account of the aforementioned bread, was quickly relieved, even without any instructions. I was in so far helped by Luther, however: that human instructions cannot bind unto eternal death.

Through illumination and grace of the Lord I increased in knowledge of the Scriptures daily, and was presently considered by some (not correctly however) to be an evangelical preacher. Everyone sought and desired me; the world loved me and I loved the world. It was said that I preached the Word of God and was a good fellow.

Afterwards it happened, before I had ever heard of the existence of the brethren, that a God-fearing, pious hero named Sicke Snijder was beheaded at Leeuwarden for being rebaptized. It sounded very strange to me to hear of a second baptism. I examined the Scriptures diligently and pondered them earnestly, but could find no report of infant baptism.

After I had noticed this I discussed it with my pastor and after much talk he had to admit that there was no basis for infant baptism in Scripture. Still I dared not trust my own understanding but consulted several ancient authors. They taught me that children are by baptism cleansed from their original sin. I compared this idea with the Scriptures and found that it did violence to the blood of Christ.

*

Shortly thereafter I was transferred to the village in which I was born, called Witmarsum, led thither by covetousness and the desire to obtain a great name. There I spoke much concerning the Word of the Lord, without spirituality or love, as all hypocrites do, and by this means I made disciples of my own kind, vain boasters and frivolous babblers, who, alas, like myself did not take these matters too seriously.

Although I had now acquired considerable knowledge of the Scriptures, yet I wasted much knowledge through the lusts of my youth in an impure, sensual, unprofitable life and sought nothing but gain, ease, favor of men, splendor, name and fame, as all generally do who sail that ship.

*

Meanwhile it happened, when I had resided there about a year, that several launched adult baptism. When the innovators came, or where they were from, or who they really were, is to this hour unknown to me, neither have I ever seen them.

Next in order the sect of Münster made its appearance, by whom many pious hearts in our quarter were deceived. My soul was much troubled, for I perceived that though they were zealous they erred in doctrine. I did what I could to oppose them by preaching and exhortations, as much as in me was. I conferred twice with one of their leaders, once in private and once in public, but my admonitions did not help, because I myself still did that which I knew was not right.

*

Afterwards the poor straying sheep who wandered as sheep without a proper shepherd, after many cruel edicts, garrotings and slaughters, assembled at a place near my place of residence called Oude Klooster. And, alas! through the ungodly doctrines of Münster, and in opposition to the Spirit, Word and example of Christ, they drew the sword to defend themselves, the sword which the Lord commanded Peter to put up in its sheath.

After this had transpired, the blood of these people, although misled, fell so hot on my heart that I could not stand it, nor find rest in my soul. I reflected upon my unclean, carnal life, also the hypocritical doctrine and idolatry which I still practiced daily in appearance of godliness, but without relish. I saw that these zealous children, although in error, willingly gave their lives and their estates for their doctrine and faith. And I was one of those who had disclosed to some of them the abominations of the papal system. But I myself was continuing in my comfortable life and acknowledged abominations simply in order that I might enjoy physical comfort and escape the cross of Christ.

*

My heart trembled within me. I prayed to God with sighs and tears that He would give to me, a sorrowing sinner, the gift of His grace, create within me a clean heart, and graciously through the merits of the crimson blood of Christ forgive my unclean walk and frivolous easy life and bestow upon me wisdom, Spirit, courage and a manly spirit so that I might preach His exalted and adorable name and holy Word in purity, and make known His truth to His glory.

I began in the name of the Lord to preach publicly from the pulpit the word of true repentance, to point the people to the narrow path, and in the power of the Scripture openly to reprove all sin and wickedness, all idolatry and false worship, and to present the true worship; also the true baptism and the Lord's Supper, according to the doctrine of Christ, to the extent that I had at that time received from God the grace.

I also faithfully warned everyone against the abominations of Münster, condemning king, polygamy, kingdom, sword, etc. After about nine months or so, the gracious Lord granted me His fatherly Spirit, help and hand. Then I, without constraint, of a sudden, renounced all my worldly reputation, fame, my unchristian abominations, my masses, infant baptism and my easy life, and I willingly submitted to distress and poverty under the heavy cross of Christ. In my weakness I feared God; I sought out the pious and though they were few in number I found some who were zealous and maintained the truth.

*

And so you see, my reader, in this way the merciful Lord through the liberal goodness of His abounding grace took notice of me, a poor sinner, stirred in my heart at the outset, produced in me a new mind, humbled me in His fear, taught me to know myself in part, turned me from the way of death and graciously called me into the narrow pathway of life and the communion of His saints. To Him be praise forevermore. Amen.

Menno (1956): 668-671

January 31

"Das Ist Menno Simonis"
Walter Klaassen, Canada, 1988

Menno Simons died on his sickbed in northern Germany on this date in 1561, twenty-five years after joining the Anabaptists. He was buried in his own garden.

I first met Menno Simons when I was a child, perhaps eleven or twelve years old. His likeness hung on the living room wall of a friend's house. The room was as plain as the picture. Under the water-stained portrait was a large wooden chest, in which the family valuables had been brought from the Trakt settlement near Saratov on the Volga to the dry, sunburnt prairie of Saskatchewan, Canada.

I remember it clearly. I asked my friend, "Wer ist das?" We still spoke German then. He said, "Das ist Menno Simonis." He said it with a kind of awe and with the certainty that everyone knew who Menno Simonis was. Although

I do not remember what I said or what happened later, from then on Menno Simons was part of my thought world, a gentle man in a skullcap, a long beard, writing with a quill pen. When I met him shortly afterward in the book *Abriss der Geschichte der Mennoniten*, Vol. II, by Cornelius H. Wedel, I gained the impression of a man who never smiled, on whom the sun never shone, a man courageous but not heroic, a man who totally lacked the charismata that might have made him more attractive to a boy of twelve.

I have never been able to shake off those impressions of my youth. Indeed, the reading of the biographies of Menno, as also of his own writings, has simply confirmed them.

*

It is in retrospect that we see Menno Simons as the molder of a tradition. He never saw himself in that role, nor did his contemporaries. He was concerned above all to be faithful to "the heavenly vision" ("dit hemels visioen," Acts 26:19), and his own circle saw in him a faithful witness. There are hints that he regretted decisions he made, which then, nevertheless, lived on in their consequences. Still, what the man was personally, what he wrote and what he did lived on beyond him and became part of an ongoing tradition.

Klaassen (1988): 368, 370

February

"I Have Regained My Identity"
Anne Allen, United States, 1981

An African-American woman reconciles black identity and Mennonite identity.

One hot summer day, the Mennonites from a nearby Mennonite church in southern Lancaster County were canvassing the village and invited my sister and brothers and me to Bible school. Being only a fifth-grader, this meant a new adventure for me.

A year or so later, my family moved near the church where I was still attending on a regular basis. I had accepted Christ as my Savior and had gone through instruction class, and was now a member of the Mennonite Church. I was not aware then of what impact this would have on my life.

My Sunday school teacher took a great deal of interest in me and influenced me enormously. She was very conservative and "plain." Being plain in this congregation twenty-one years ago meant hair parted in the middle, prayer veiling with a band of 1 3/4 inches, veiling, ribbons, cape dress without a collar, long sleeves, black stockings, brown cotton stockings for the younger girls and black shoes. I became a carbon copy of her in attire and thinking. I remember being very proud as a twelve-year-old in my "plain" garb.

My mother was not very pleased with my appearance and even more shocked that my regular clothes had very quickly become obsolete, as far as I was concerned.

*

She could not possibly persuade me to wear anything but my "plain" garb to junior high school or to go with the family to activities and occasional parties that played worldly music, such as jazz or rock 'n' roll, or where anyone was engaging in any form of dance.

This created tension between my family and me. Then, I did not understand fully what being different from the world meant. To me being so-called "plain" was my savior.

My little world of "conservatism" came crashing down on me during my junior high school years. I became the laughingstock of the school. No one else, especially among the few blacks in the school, looked like me. Mennonites were not known very well at that time in the area where the school was located. The

---

next year I enrolled at Lancaster Mennonite High School and I fit right into the mode of attire there and that problem was solved.

*

I lost my black identity. I wished to be like the Mennonites in all aspects. Yet I knew deep within that I could never become a white ethnic Mennonite no matter how hard I tried.

*

But I struggled through racist attitudes and slurs at Lancaster Mennonite High School and managed to graduate as the only black, in the upper half of my class of 115.

As a Christian young person of eighteen I suddenly realized that I had never really thought out or questioned anything that I had been taught. My secret idea I kept in the back of my mind was that I would leave this church when I graduated and go out entirely on my own. This never happened because I realized later that the church had become my whole life. But I had to settle some of this teaching and Mennonite tradition in my own mind.

*

In 1959 I received a call from a Mennonite man asking if I would like to work in Philadelphia. So, being a country girl, I suddenly found myself at the age of eighteen journeying to the large city of Philadelphia into another Mennonite setting which was almost identical to the conservative environment I had just left, although this has changed through the years. The main exception in this Mennonite setting was its situation right in the middle of a large black ghetto-type residential area.

Thus far, all my associations had been with white Mennonites except my immediate family. I left home at age fourteen to go to Lancaster Mennonite High School, a boarding school, and never spent very much time living at home after that. So living in a totally black community and working in a totally black office was quite an adjustment for me.

Many things began to happen inside of me as I really began thinking for myself. I began to really question some of the Mennonite rules and traditions that I had been taught so well over the years.

*

As I began slowly to find my identity as a black person in a black environment, I had to break away from some of these traditions and rules. As a result, I fought an ongoing battle within myself for several years.

Over the past twenty-one years I have had my membership at Diamond Street Mennonite Church. I have had some good experiences there, but I have taken advantage of various opportunities to become aware of as much as possible about the total Mennonite Church. I have made efforts to get to know my black brothers and sisters in the Mennonite Church, and the Black Caucus has been the main channel for this. I have also made special effort to get to know Christians from other denominations. They have a lot to offer too. I am still learning, but through my experiences I have regained my identity and the self-awareness that I need. I have settled to a great extent in my mind what I believe God is saying that we as the church and as Christians should be doing.

I have a deep appreciation for the Mennonite Church and what it stands for. It is because of the Christian principles that were taught to me in the early years of my life that I am what I am today.

Hertzler (1983): 179, 180

February 2

Leaving to Join
Hubert L. Brown, United States, 1976

*L*ike most blacks, I came to Christ through the influence of white people. At first, I did not realize that whites in America have generally related to blacks primarily from a position of assumed superiority. I discovered that whites enter the circumference of a relationship feeling that everything of value is on their side, and that blacks have nothing to offer. I did sense that whites were always extremely concerned about my soul and where my soul would be lodged after death. I came to faith believing in the goodness of whites, having received the benevolent acts of the white community (which I later came to recognize was paternalism in many instances).

And so in the Mennonite Church, as well as in white society, I've had to struggle and deal with what it means to be a black. The rise of black consciousness enabled me to see that I could no longer identify with the white man nor think of myself as being a part of his world. The rise of black consciousness made me understand that blacks are a separate people, with a separate history and separate culture. I can affirm this today and am proud of black history and culture.

The black Christian in a predominantly white institution has to make a decision early in his or her life as to whether or not all that represents the white Christian experience will be internalized. This was the question that I faced. Indeed, a great deal of what I experienced in the white church was internalized and believed by me. However, in my search for my own personal black identity, I began to question my role as a black Christian in the Mennonite Church and what that meant. I became quite discouraged about the church as I saw it, particularly how the church operated in the area of social concerns in trying to resolve the whole issue of racism. I discovered that white racism among Mennonites was not the result of a distorted theology, but of a theological illiteracy. The tragedy as I sensed it was that the church was neither what it professed to be nor what it was told it should be.

To me the church is to participate in the suffering of the oppressed in a godless world; the church is to be wide-awake with Jesus, identifying with the oppressed. As I looked about me I saw the brokenness of humanity. I, too, experienced brokenness—a loneliness, a sense of not being affirmed, of not having my history, my past and my experiences respected and acknowledged. I was depressed by what I considered the irrelevance of the church. I began to see the church as nothing but a resolution-passing community that failed miserably in being a visible manifestation of God in the world. I saw the church as not being God's redemptive agent, but rather being an agent of American culture. The church was failing to create an atmosphere of radical obedience to Christ, failing to be all that God had intended for it to be. It seemed to me that the church was nothing but a fellowship that was more concerned about new buildings than about children who die of starvation, or of men who are killed because they happened to dream about a just society.

I wondered for a time whether I could continue to relate to the church. I had to make a decision. I remember attending a conference where Dale Brown, author of The Christian Revolutionary, said, "Sometimes one must leave the church in order to join the church." That statement had profound meaning for me.

Brown (1976): 22-24

February 3

Worthy Participation
Balthasar Hubmaier, Moravia, 1526

See how bright and clear Paul writes, "Whoever now eats of this bread and drinks from the cup of the Lord unworthily is guilty of the body and blood of the Lord." See here, who wants to see, how Christ above called the drink a fruit of the vine before and after the words of consecration. Thus Paul also calls the bread bread and the cup a drink, and whoever eats of this bread and drinks of this drink unworthily is guilty of the bread and wine.

*

But let the person examine himself, however, etc., as to whether he has real internal and intensive hunger and thirst for this bread and drink, as Christ also had when he said, "With fervor have I desired to eat the supper with you." And all this in faith, so that he wholly believes that his sins are remitted through the death of Christ. Likewise, in love, in which he obligates himself now, and with this breaking of the bread and drinking of the cup publicly before the church commits himself and promises that for the sake of his neighbor he is willing to let his flesh and blood be broken and sacrificed, with which he has now become one bread and one drink. It is also in thanksgiving to God our heavenly Father and his only begotten Son our Lord Jesus Christ whom he has given even unto death for our salvation.

Thus the three thousand people in the Acts of the Apostles first recognized themselves as sinners, believed in the forgiveness of sins through Christ, let themselves be baptized, remained constant in the apostolic teaching, in communion and the breaking of bread, and in prayer. That is true self-examination according to the teaching of Paul.

Hubmaier (1989): 333, 334

February 4

By Grace

Menno Simons, Germany, 1552

*T*hink not, beloved reader, that we boast of being perfect and without sin. Not at all. As for me I confess that often my prayer is mixed with sin and my righteousness with unrighteousness. For by the grace of God I feel—if I but observe the anointing which is in me—when I compare my weak nature to Christ and His commandment, what kind of flesh I have inherited from Adam. If God should judge us according to our deserts and not according to His great goodness and mercy, then I confess with the holy David that no man could stand before His judgment (Psalm 143:2). Therefore it should be far from us that we should comfort ourselves with anything but the grace of God through Christ Jesus.

*

Notice, my dear reader, that we do not believe nor teach that we are to be saved by our merits and works as the envious assert without truth. We are to be saved solely by grace through Christ Jesus, as has been said before.

By grace the human race was created by Christ Jesus when as yet it was not.

By grace it was again accepted through Christ when it was lost.

By grace Christ was sent to us of the Father.

By grace He has sought the lost sheep, taught repentance and remission of sins, and died for us when we were yet ungodly and enemies.

By grace it is given us to believe.

By grace the Holy Ghost was given us in the name of Jesus.

In short, by grace eternal life is given us through Christ Jesus.

This, dear reader, is our faith and confession in the matter in hand. We cannot obtain salvation, grace, reconciliation nor peace of the Father otherwise than through Christ Jesus. As He Himself says, "No man cometh unto the Father but by me." Peter also says, "There is none other name under heaven given among men, whereby we must be saved, than the name of Jesus," and that all those who accept this grace in Christ, preached by the Gospel and accepted by a firm faith, and cordially adhered to by power of the Holy Spirit through faith, become new men, born of God.

Such men are changed in their hearts, renewed and of a different mind; yes, transferred from Adam unto Christ. They walk in newness of life as obedient children in the grace which is manifested unto them. For they are renewed, have become poor in spirit, gentle, merciful, compassionate, peaceful, patient, hungry and thirsty after righteousness. They strive after eternal life and with good works. For they are believing, born of God, are in Christ and Christ in them. They are partakers of His Spirit and nature, and live according to the Word of the Lord by the power of Christ which is in them. This is according to Scripture to be really believing, to be Christian, to be in Christ and Christ in us.

Menno (1956): 506, 507

February 5

A Path to Walk

Hans Denck, Germany, 1526

*H*e whom the entire world confesses in words and denies by its deeds says, "I am not come to abolish the Law but to fulfill it" (Matthew 5:17). The carnal wisdom of this world, always passing for the light of divine knowledge, tears these words out of context and says that since Christ has fulfilled the Law we therefore need not keep it. For if we too had to fulfill it, we would thereby imply that Christ has not fully done so. Thus these words are expounded, for thus they serve our perverted nature to which everything that comes from God is pus and poison, as is evident from everyone's life.

If this were the true meaning, it would be irrelevant how one lives after one's conversion. The whole world is full of people whose fruits and lives were somewhat better before they gloried in their faith than afterwards. And these are supposedly the people by whose good works the heathen are to be moved to praise God the Father in heaven. Indeed, as are the works of these people, so the heathen exalt God. For they say to us with derision: "What sort of God do you have?" As if to say, that he is either not merciful (as you insist) to let you err thus, or else that he is not just to be able to watch you do such evil, or else he is not all-powerful and unable to help or punish you.

Lord, you mighty God, for your name's sake do what you desire not to be left undone, that the perverse refrain from doing what they should not. Amen.

You say: "Is it not true though that Christ has fulfilled the Law?" Answer: Not a single law that has ever been conceived or written is complete until it is perfected in the body of Christ. Whoever desires to be a member of this body and does not realize the Law in exactly the same measure as it is found in the head must take care lest he deceive himself. For whenever the members do not concern themselves with what the head does, something is not quite in order. A member that does not share weal and woe, joy or sorrow with the head is surely a useless and dead member. It is deprived of all the benefits of the body as if it were no longer attached.

You say: "Has not the head made satisfaction and fulfilled all that can be accomplished on behalf of the members?" Indeed, he has made satisfaction for the entire world and has levelled the path which no one could otherwise find so that we might walk therein and reach life. Whoever does not walk it does not reach life and the path proves to be useless. He fulfilled the law, not to place us above it, but to give us an example to follow him.

Denck (1989): 221, 222

February 6
The Middle Path
Michael Sattler(?), Germany, 1520s

*W*hen one speaks of works, one must preach not, after the manner of the work-righteous, the works of law but the works of faith. That is, a turning away from works, creatures and your own self, through faith in Christ the crucified one, not as what man can do from himself, but what he really can do in the power of faith; which hereby are not man's works but God's, since the willing and the ability to turn to God are not of man but the gift of God through Jesus Christ our Lord.

Verily, blessed be he who remains on the middle path, who turns aside neither to the work-righteous (who promised blessedness or the forgiveness of sins through works done without faith), preaching *works* in such a way that they think no more of faith, so that all their works are like wild plums, ceremonies without faith. Nor to the side of the scribes, who although they have forsaken works, then turn aside to the right and teach in the name of "gospel" a faith without works and take the poor obedient Christ (who had no place to lay His head, who speaks without complaint or self-defense) as their satisfaction, but will not hear what He says, "Come, follow me."

Yoder (1973): 115, 116

February 7
No One Who Sins is Free
Klaus Felbinger, Germany, 1560

*W*e are being accused of justifying ourselves. They say, "None is just but God alone; we will wait with the avowed sinner in the Temple till God justifies us." Well and good! If only they came to the true Temple where there is remission of sins! This Temple is the true Christian Church, the community of saints. But as they refuse to enter it, how can God justify them in it?

We, however, came to this Temple and confessed ourselves to be sinners before God and His Holy Spirit. The earnest prayer of the devout justified us and freed us from our sins, for which we praise God. With His help we want to hold on to His justification, just like the avowed sinner in the Temple, and sin no more so that nothing worse may befall us.

You do not even understand that passage, for you are like the Pharisee who wanted to please God without repenting. You let yourselves go and sin against God's mercy. You do not even want to leave behind your disgraceful ways, your sins and wickedness, so that God can put new life into your hearts. If, as you claim, Christ freed you from sin, why do you still *act* in such a godless way? You are just as free as a prisoner who, while his hands and feet are in the stocks, claims he is free; he would rightly be laughed at by everyone. No one who sins is free.

Hutterian Brethren (1978): 124, 125

February 8

Freed By the Word
Hans Denck, Germany, 1527

*A*nyone who says that he lacks grace from God to become righteous is a liar—like all of humankind. In fact, He testifies against God who pours out his mercy upon all of humankind, as he does his wrath even more plentifully. Otherwise, the godless would be without blame, as they like to claim. The truth, of course, does not sustain them.

A perverse person who seeks himself (and never wants to love himself) will not find himself in all eternity. He seeks to achieve and overcome something before he has suffered. He wants to believe before he knows what faith is. He wants to be saved, but knows nothing of damnation. He wants life, but does not know death. It is here that the two contradicting views arise, with some saying that they have free will without having a particle even of that which pleases God. Some say that they have none, because they can partly see that they cannot do anything right, though they freely suffer the work done by the word.

In themselves both claims are true, as was stated above. But they are both lies, too, since people simply make them either to boast of their freedom or else to talk themselves out of responsibility and excuse themselves with its opposite, by saying, "May God give what He can justify."

The first claim regarding free will is plain boasting and foolish security. It allows no room for the fear of God, but presumes the right to do as it pleases. The other claim is false humility and false wisdom. It pretends to honor God and to be nothing itself. Yet, it is unwilling to deny itself and increasingly seeks itself. This is utter folly and arrogance in the sight of God who probes the depth of the human heart and searches out subtle and open sins.

Anyone who is unable to weigh these contradictory statements cannot learn anything thoroughly in the school of the Spirit. For anyone who does not know himself and what he can and cannot do, the same is unable to gain true knowledge of God. In short, the more a person seeks himself and his own, the more fully he is assured by God's Spirit in his heart and conscience that he does wrong. Whoever would lose himself has done his best. We are unable, of course, to do any good of our own making, but the word which has come unto its own (i.e. all creatures) sets us free to be children of God, provided we believe it.

Denck (1989): 257, 258

February 9

"How Can Redemption Be Lacking?"
Robert Friedmann, United States, 1973

The concern as to "how to escape eternal damnation," or in Luther's terms, "how to find a gracious God," was certainly not a major concern of the Anabaptists. They did not start with the crushing awareness of being lost sinners but began rather with the glorious experience of regeneration or spiritual rebirth. This signifies basically a positive experience of God's grace which subsequently leads to a rather different chain of insights.

Granted, it was rather uncommon, this experience which so overwhelmed seekers that they spontaneously joined the flock of Anabaptist disciples wherever they found them. These early Anabaptists were not particularly bothered by guilt feelings; they desired to walk in the footsteps of the Master, "in love and cross," as Sebastian Franck described them. Therefore, the question of "salvation" naturally dropped into the background and was dealt with only casually.

A personal experience may serve to dramatize this situation and make the genius of Anabaptism come more alive. Several years ago, after a conference in South Dakota, a number of ministers decided to visit a nearby Hutterite Bruderhof, the oldest one in the United States, and I was invited to join this group. We were cordially received and shown around, and then the elders were ready to discuss their way of life. One of the first questions the ministers asked was this: "What do you people teach regarding salvation?" Thereupon the very intelligent brother, who had very likely not anticipated this question, paused a moment and then said quietly but with great assurance: "If we live in obedience to God's commandments, we are certain of being in God's gracious hands; we do not worry further about our salvation. Rather, we try to walk the narrow path in the fear of the Lord. We fight sin and practice brotherly love. How then can redemption be lacking?" This reply was as simple as it was authentic. Now it was the ministers, trained in conventional theology, who were surprised and even a bit shocked. They had not anticipated such an answer.

Friedmann (1973): 78, 79

February 10

I Tried Being Mennonite
Nancy Fisher, United States, 1971

*A*t one point in my life I tried to be a Mennonite but somehow I just didn't fit. I've internalized Amishness so thoroughly that trying to be Mennonite was like trying to put a square peg in a round hole. I think that part of Mennonitism which made me most uncomfortable was the pressure I felt in Mennonite circles to verbalize that one was "saved," and to tangibly "witness" (hand out tracts, etc.) to others in an effort to lead them to "salvation."

I remember my college days (Eastern Mennonite College), when one earned extracurricular credits to heaven by spending Sundays "witnessing to the lost," the prisoners, the mountain folks and others. I usually stayed in the dorm involved in relaxing, writing letters, or in serious rap sessions with my dorm neighbors. However, periodically I would feel guilty for being somewhat irreligious. To friends I would give the flimsy excuse that I didn't feel comfortable "witnessing" to people in my oversized Amish bonnet. (College regulations at that time strongly encouraged bonnet-wearing for witnessing and other such activities.)

No longer does such irreligiosity provoke guilt. When I decided that, to a greater theological degree, I was Amish and really valued the Amish attitude toward the specific theological question of salvation, then I could let the Mennonites do their thing without feeling conflict and guilt. The Amish attitude as radiated by my parents during my upbringing seems to be that salvation is more a process than a simple act of "being saved." That seemed to make more sense to me when I seriously evaluated the two attitudes. Salvation, I feel, is a heavy thing, a serious thing, a continuing soul-searching thing. Christ-likeness seems to be more focused on relationships. The Amish emphasis on brotherhood rather than on salvation means, to me, to be more in keeping with this whole theme of Christ-likeness.

Fisher (1971)

Both Bitter and Sweet

Thomas Müntzer, Germany, 1524

*T*here is no other basis of faith than the whole Christ; half will not do; for one does not sneak into a house by the window. Anyone who rejects the bitter Christ will gorge himself to death on honey. Christ is a cornerstone. Just as he had to be shaped, so we have to be knocked into shape by the master-mason if we are to grow into a true living building. Not a cent must go missing at any time of our lives; every Christian must stand up to scrutiny from top to toe, and must strain his utmost, according to his talent or gift, to measure up to Christ. Only he who dies with Christ can rise with him. How can anyone be living the true life if he has not once taken off his old garment? Therefore, those who console before they sadden are thieves and murderers; they want to spring into action before Christ comes; they have no idea what it is to which they say "Yes" or No."

*

On such a foundation true Christianity, destined for eternal life, is built. One only attains it after learning to watch out for, and get rid of, the yeast of those wicked scholars who dare to convert the pure word of God into their yeast with their worm-eaten, hobbling claptrap. For the result of all their teaching is that men strut around with their untried faith, vainly confident, and imagining they will be man enough to cope with any crisis, armed with their bland assurances. In reality, they have not learnt at all how a man can achieve this.

Müntzer (1988): 220-222

The Whole Christ

Eberhard Arnold, Germany, early 1900s

*N*othing but the whole Christ, for the whole of life, will change and renew everything. Half of Jesus for half of life is a delusion, a lie. The spirit of life will not tolerate a selection of guiding principles or elements of faith such as a self-willed spirit tries to pick out for itself from God's truth. Truth is indivisible. Christ cannot be dissected. Whoever does not try in all matters to take the same stand that Jesus established in wholeness and integrity has rejected Him. No justification, no matter how clever, for his half-hearted behavior, will shield him from the judgment, "Whoever is not with me is against me."

There are some who, while they want to hear and read and learn this, that or the other about Him, at the same time have a way of obliterating everything that seems to them impossible by weakening it with explanations. They, together with their whole life, though it appear ever so Christian, will collapse. Jesus says that all who hear His words in the Sermon on the Mount but do not do them are like those who build on a shifting foundation. What they build is lost from the outset. It succumbs to the first attack of hostile forces.

Christ, who is whole, wants us whole. He loves decisiveness. He loves His enemies more than His half-hearted friends. He hates His falsifiers more than His opposites. What He abhors is the lukewarm, the colorless grey, the twilight, the foggy, pious talking that mixes everything up and commits one to nothing. He sweeps all that away whenever He draws near.

He comes to us as He is. He penetrates us with His whole Word. He reveals himself to our hearts in His wholeness, His completeness. In His coming we feel all the power of His love and all the strength of His life. Everything else is deception and lying. Jesus Christ never comes close to anyone in a few hasty, transitory impressions. Either He brings the whole kingdom of God for ever or He gives nothing. Only those who are willing to receive Him, complete and for ever, can experience Him. To them it is given to know the secret of God's kingdom. To all others He veils himself in enigmatic metaphors. Anyone who stops short of a full surrender hears parables without understanding the thing they point to. With seeing eyes, he sees nothing. With hearing ears, he understands nothing. Whoever does not want to have everything will lose the little that he thinks he has.

Arnold (1967): 168-170

February 13

Our Father's Love
Daniel Musser, United States, 1868

*L*ove is the divine nature, and is manifested in all of God's dealings with us. Divine love is entirely different from that love which influences us as long as we are carnal. The Savior, speaking of the difference between the influence which governs the carnal mind, and that which controls the spiritual mind, says: "The Gentiles love and do good to those that love and do good to them," but He said to His disciples, if they do no more than this they prove nothing. But they shall show the nature and disposition which God shows in His dealings with the children of men: "That they may be the children of their Father which is in heaven: for he maketh his sun to rise on the evil and on the good, and sendeth rain on the just and on the unjust" (Matthew 5:45).

The world, we know by every testimony of the word of God, lay in wickedness and was in enmity against God; yet God, out of love to the sinful world, sent His Son to redeem it from this sinful condition.

Christ or His apostles never expressed approval of any act of man, unless it was dictated by the love of God. Nothing is acceptable to God but that which is prompted by divine love. Divine love ever moves man to consider what the will of the Father in heaven is, and to seek His honor. The Savior said He came "not to do mine own will, but the will of him that sent me," and all the duties and commands of the gospel are of the nature of divine love.

God himself is love, and all His dealings with the children of men are done out of love. Out of love He gave the promise to our first parents; out of love He sent His son to redeem us; out of love He follows us with His grace and beseeches us to be reconciled to Him. Out of love He gives those who believe on Him power to become sons of God and bestows upon them the divine nature; and out of love He supports them and enables them to walk in His ways of love. His love toward us is incomprehensible and far beyond expression.

It is the will of the heavenly Father that all men should be brought into this element of love, because they can not enter into the kingdom of heaven without being brought into it. This is the conversion they must experience if they would enter heaven: the soul must be converted or changed from under the influence of self-love to the influence of divine love, or from the influence of the flesh to the influence of the Spirit.

Musser ([1868]): 18, 19, 21, 22

February 14

Only Love
Johann J. Toews, Soviet Union, 1932

J.J. Toews was sentenced to five years of exile in 1929 and sent to the frozen Russian north. In 1931 he was put to hard labor in the forests. Toews died in exile about nine months after writing this letter to his family, and was buried in the forest by a fellow Mennonite minister and a Muslim cleric.

Oh how much you mean to me! May it please God, my eternal Benefactor, to cause you to rejoice, to give you good health, joy and happiness, but also to prepare you for all things. I am so deeply concerned that you, according to the measure of eternal grace, will have a good, a very good life here on earth. Regardless of how important our overall goals are, I know that your main interest is not focused upon the security of the intellect nor the criterion of reason. The thing that is most important is and will remain a conscience sharpened by the Holy Spirit.

Naturally, I don't love anyone more or more intimately than my dear family, especially my dear wife and faithful life's partner who has had such difficult experiences in the recent past. How would I feel if people were to carry that person from my house to the cemetery—who knows all my struggles, my deepest experiences, the most important moments of my life—in a word if one were to take my wife from my side, then words sufficiently profound and heartrending would fail me in portraying it with truth and love!

Several dear people are so exceedingly close to my heart and as comforting to my spirit as I could only wish. My dear wife is so far from me, so very far and yet, what benevolence of grace, so near to my heart. Much nearer than formerly, deeper and more securely rooted and inwardly more united.

My chief struggles here in exile lie on a completely different plane than that of the marriage relationship. Sodom was a temptation for Lot but not for Abraham. That is why God tempted Lot with a region rich in water and with Sodom's riches and glitter. For Abraham this was all of no consequence. His loftier spirit demands more rarefied dangerous temptations. But God only tempts for the good.

*

I have recited no verse as often in exile, with or without tears, as the profound words of the song:

> When I feel nothing of Your might
> You still bring me to my goal
> Even through the night.

I no longer knew anything, felt no help or strengthening. Again and again there was only one thing: God's word—His promise! How often I fell asleep completely exposed with only naked faith. Next day I awoke only to practice this anew. Not I, only the Lord, the Lord securely held me.

*

If we really believe in God we believe in a real God who has taken everything but everything into account. Oh how often this was my bath of faith. When I submerged myself in it, I always became well.

Thus all the leadings of our Father in Christ are only and definitely only love. My exile is love, only love. God's love removed my loved ones out of pure love for me. He fears nothing when He tests our love for He knows: pure love will only gain through such testing. He cannot use and does not want other love. Therefore He comforted and quieted and steadfastly prepared for everything—for God.

Toews (1990): 238, 239

February 15

Insatiable Love

Hans Denck, Germany, 1527

Love is a spiritual power by which one is united or through which one desires to be united with another person. Where there is perfect love, the lover does not deny himself to the beloved. Rather he forgets himself, as if he were no longer anything and does not count anything a loss which he may suffer for the sake of the beloved. Yes, the lover will not be content with anything he undertakes until he has had opportunity to show his love towards the beloved in its highest expression throughout all dangers. And if it were possible to benefit the beloved (as it often is) the lover would willingly and gladly die for the beloved.

Yes, a lover is so wanton (if one might say so) that he would die at the lover's behest, even though he knows full well that no good would come of that, in any case. And the more the beloved fails to acknowledge the lover's love, the more he suffers hurt. Yet he cannot cease loving, but must show his love in the highest measure, even though no one may ever appreciate it. Thus, where there is genuine love, which is no respecter of persons, she reaches out and desires to unite with everyone, insofar as this can happen without divisions and undue inconstancy; for love cannot ever be fully satisfied even by all lovers taken together. Yet, even if all lovers should flee her altogether so that she were unable to rejoice in them, she is nonetheless so vast in riches within herself, that she has always had sufficient, still does today, and shall have in all eternity.

*

Of such a love a little spark may be detected in many a person; more in one, less in another. Unfortunately, it has been extinguished in almost everyone in our generation. However, one thing is certain (since love is spiritual and all persons are carnal); this little spark; however small it may be in a person, does not come from humankind but from the source of Perfect Love. This love is God who cannot create himself although he has made all things; who cannot destroy himself, although he shall destroy all things. He is eternally immovable. He must love himself, since he is good, so that he conceives from within himself and gives birth to himself eternally; who disregards himself utterly on account of those who are in need of him to the extent that he desires to be nothing at all (if that were possible) on their account.

Such love could not be comprehended by flesh and blood if God were not to demonstrate it uniquely in some people who are called godly and children of God, because they take after God, their spiritual Father. The more fully such love is demonstrated, the more known, the more love is practiced. Therefore it has pleased the eternal love that the one in whom it was most fully revealed ought to be called a redeemer of his people. Not that it is possible for a human being to redeem anyone, but rather because God is so perfectly united in love with this person that every divine deed would be his deed and every act of suffering of this person could be reckoned God's suffering. This person is Jesus of Nazareth who has been promised in Scripture by the true God, a promise now fulfilled in the fulness of time, as has been publicly demonstrated in Israel by the power of the Holy Spirit with every deed and activity which is love's just due and prerogative.

Denck (1989): 269-271

Peace Grows Out of Love

Christian Burkholder, United States, 1792

*T*he kingdom of Satan is an unpeaceable kingdom, it being ever engaged in quarrels and wars. The kingdom of Christ, on the contrary, is a peaceable kingdom: it consists of nothing but love, peace and unity. Now if the love to our fellow-creatures is of the right kind, it is of a divine nature, just as is the love of God towards us.

*

Now think, beloved reader, what a pitiable state that is, in which love between brethren is wanting. A blind man who is deprived of all natural light is a poor creature. But if a man is so blinded by sin that he does not see sin any more, he is much poorer and more miserable yet than the man who is deprived of his natural sight. For while he says he does see while he does not see, his "sin remaineth"; and this for the reason that he does not see it any more.

Reader, perhaps you have lived for some time in a state of uncharitableness with your neighbor, and it would not cost you your life (as it did your Savior) to make peace with him. It would only cost a little of your pride and self-righteousness, and can you not give up these? Or do you still want to please yourself?

And should it cost you something of your temporal property to plant and maintain peace, God is rich enough to restore to you all that you may thus lose or sacrifice. And should he not do this temporally, he will richly reward you spiritually, to the welfare of your immortal soul, for his love is of a divine nature and origin. So also a person who, by faith, has become a partaker of the divine nature will "add to his faith virtue, and to virtue, brotherly kindness and charity. But he that lacketh these things is blind, and cannot see afar off" (2 Peter 1:5).

A person who is naturally blind would give all his fortune if he could thereby obtain his sight. But about spiritual sight—the peace and love of God—many a one concerns himself but little, although his whole soul's salvation consists in joy and rest, peace and love. And is it not a great piece of blindness, if we deprive ourselves of the peace of our souls by discord and dissension? But perhaps you say the fault is not in you but in your neighbor. But your neighbor speaks the same language. And thus each one endeavors to shift the fault from himself, in order that he may throw it upon someone else. But consider for once closely the words: "Love thy neighbor as thyself," and then confess whether you can, according to the meaning of the Lord, throw the fault on any other person than yourself, if you live in discord and dissension with anyone. It is not said that you should demand love of your neighbor, but that you should love him.

Christ says: "Have salt in yourselves, and have peace one with another" (Mark 9:50). Now peace grows out of love, and where peace and love are wanting, there the main work of godliness is wanting: whether it be between man and wife, between brother and brother, or between a minister and his congregation. And where there is no love nor peace, there is neither happiness nor prosperity. Discord and uncharitableness are bitter roots out of which much evil fruit grows.

Conversation (1856): 204-208

A Letter of Consolation

Menno Simons, Germany, 1557

According to one writer, the recipient of this letter was Menno Simons' sister-in-law. She had spent a winter in sickness, which was made worse by disturbing thoughts of her own weakness in pursuing holiness. The pastoral heart of Menno speaks to both concerns and points her to Jesus, her comfort and strength.

My elect and beloved sister in Christ Jesus: much mercy, grace and peace be unto you, most beloved sister whom I have ever sincerely loved in Christ.

From your dear husband's letter I understand that during all the winter you have been a sick and afflicted child, which I very much regret to hear. But we pray daily: "Holy Father, Thy will be done." By this we transfer our will into that of the Father to deal with us as is pleasing in His blessed sight. Therefore bear your assigned affliction with a resigned heart. For all this is His fatherly will for your own good and that you may turn with your inmost being from all transitory things and direct yourself to the eternal and living God. Be comforted in Jesus Christ, for after the winter comes the summer, and after death comes life.

*

May the Almighty, merciful God and Lord before whom you have bent your knees to His honor, and whom according to your weakness you have sought, grant you a strong and patient heart, a bearable pain, a joyous recovery, a gracious restoration or a godly departure through Christ Jesus whom we daily expect with you, my beloved sister and child in Christ Jesus.

Secondly, I understand that your conscience is troubled because you have not and do not now walk in such perfection as the Scriptures hold before us. I write the following to my faithful sister as a brotherly consolation from the true Word and eternal truth of the Lord. "The Scripture," says Paul, "has concluded all under sin." "There is no man on earth," says Solomon, "who does righteously and sinneth not." At another place: "A just man falleth seven times and riseth up again." Moses says: "The Lord, the merciful God, merciful and gracious, longsuffering and abundant in goodness and truth, keeping mercy for thousands, forgiving iniquity and transgression and sin, before whom there is none without sin." O dear sister, notice, he says, none are without sin before God. And David says: "Lord, enter not into judgment with thy servant; for in thy sight shall no living man be justified." And we read, "If they sin against thee (for there is no man that sinneth not)." We are all as an unclean thing, and all our righteousness is as filthy rags. Christ also said, "There is none good but one, that is God."

*

We must all acknowledge, whoever we are, that we are sinners in thought, word and deed. Yes, if we did not have before us the righteousness of Christ Jesus, no prophet nor apostle could be saved.

Therefore be of good cheer and comforted in the Lord. You can expect no greater righteousness in yourself than all the chosen of God had in them from the beginning. In and by yourself you are a poor sinner, and by the eternal righteousness banished, accursed and condemned to eternal death. But in and through Christ you are justified and pleasing unto God, and adopted by Him in eternal grace as a daughter and child.

*

I pray and desire that you will betake yourself wholly both as to what is inward and what is outward unto Christ Jesus and His merits, believing and confessing that His precious blood alone is your cleansing, His righteousness your piety, His death your life and His resurrection your justification. For He is the forgiveness of all your sins, His bloody wounds are your reconciliation and His victorious strength is the staff and consolation of your weakness, as we have formerly according to our small gift often shown you from the Scriptures.

Yes, dearest child and sister, seeing that you find and feel such a spirit in yourself desirous of following that which is good and abhorring that which is evil, even though the remnant of sin is not entirely dead in you, as was also the case in all the saints who lamented from the beginning, as was said, therefore you may rest assured that you are a child of God and that you will inherit the kingdom of grace in eternal joy with all the saints. Hereby we know that we dwell in him and he in us, because he has given us of his Spirit.

I sincerely pray that you may by faith rightly understand this basis of comfort, strengthening and consolation of your distressed conscience and soul, and remain firm unto the end. I commend you, most beloved child and sister, to the faithful, merciful and gracious God in Christ Jesus, now and forever. Let Him do with you and with all of us according to His blessed will, whether in the flesh to remain a little longer with your beloved husband and children; or out of the flesh to the honor of His name and to the salvation of your soul. You go before and we follow, or we go before and you follow. Separation must sometime come.

In the city of God, in the new Jerusalem, there we will await each other before the throne of God and of the Lamb, sing Hallelujah and praise His name in perfect joy. Your husband and children I commend to Him who has given them to you, and He will take care of them. The saving power of the most holy blood of Christ be with my most beloved child and sister, now and forever. Amen. Your brother who sincerely loves you in Christ.

Menno (1956): 1052-1054

February 18

I Began to See

Z. Marwa Kisare, Tanzania, 1984

*D*uring my three years at the Bukiroba Bible School, I read my Bible through many times. Slowly I began to see that in Christ my wife Susana and I were equal before God. During the first years of our marriage I insisted on having the last word in our home. We fought, Susana and I. I struggled to make her an obedient wife. Then I saw from my study of the New Testament that a husband and wife are to work together. All our quarreling ceased.

I began to go to the lake to bring Susana water. In my father's village no man carried anything on his head. Heading was for women. A man carried things on his shoulder not his head. But you cannot carry a *debe* of water on your shoulder.

When we were carrying water from the lake at Bukiroba to fill missionaries' rainwater tanks, we carried the *debe* on our heads. That was all right because it was western work we were doing for a white man. But putting the *debe* on my head and carrying water from the lake for my wife to use in my home, this simply was not done by Luo men.

People laughed at me when they saw me carrying water for Susana. They said that I was ruining my wife. "She will become uppity," they warned. "She will become like a white woman telling you what to do."

But I continued to relate to my wife in this new way that I had seen in the New Testament. How I related to my wife was the practical outcome of my realizing that in Jesus Christ we are of equal value before God. In this way Christianity was making a difference in my life.

Shenk (1984): 75

February 19

The Ferment Was There

Christina van Straten-Bargeman, The Netherlands, 1990

*T*wo thousand years ago Jesus Christ equally invited men and women to a new covenant with God and to do the will of God. God became human in Jesus Christ in order to show and teach us how to live together and to liberate us from the power of evil, which is the distortion of the reality God wants for us. Martha, the sister of Mary and Lazarus, confesses it: "I now believe that you are the Messiah, the Son of God who was to come into the world" (John 11:27). This confession, coming from a woman, seldom gets the same attention as that of Simon Peter: "You are the Messiah, the Son of the living God" (Matthew 16:16). Yet Martha is explicitly invited by Jesus to express her faith, just as in another story he invites her to leave the role traditionally allotted to women—that of serving men—and instead come and sit at his feet like her sister Mary and be a disciple. Some of Jesus' other female disciples are mentioned by name in Luke 8:1-3. Not only did they and many other women share the journeys of Jesus and the Twelve, they also financed them.

Women also preached the gospel (the Samaritan woman in John 4:29, 30) and not without results. The disciples were surprised to find Jesus speaking with a woman—a sign that by treating women as equal to men Jesus acted against predominant tradition. After the resurrection Jesus first met with women, who again became the first to preach the gospel of the risen Lord. But, coming from women this was thought a nonsensical story by the apostles; they were able to believe it only after Peter confirmed it. Jesus took the women seriously. The apostles did not. But Luke recorded it in his gospel, the same Luke who recorded that burst of joy coming from Mary about the liberating and renewing power of the word of God, which lifts the humble.

*

Time and again there have been courageous women and men who questioned every explanation handed down by tradition.

*

Anabaptist women clearly showed their independence when they had to give witness to their persecutors. As we read in *Het Offer des Heeren (Sacrifice Unto the Lord)* and the *Martyrs Mirror*, they were quite able to hold their own in the discussions with their interrogators. A good example is Elisabeth Dirks, killed in Leeuwarden in 1549. She had been apprehended because she was a teacher (preacher) in the Anabaptist congregation of Leeuwarden. The interrogators asked her to tell by oath whether she had a husband. Elisabeth answered, "We ought not to swear, but our words shall be yes, yes and no, no; I have no husband." The lords asked, "We want to know what people you have been teaching." Elisabeth replied, "Oh no, my lords, leave me in peace about this and ask me about my belief; it would please me to tell you about that."

It was a dangerous and exciting time, but soon different times came. Influenced by what went on in society and in other churches, Mennonites forgot about the equality of men and women in their congregations. They became "the Quiet in the Land." Women receded into the dark background again but the ferment was there. In the second half of the eighteenth century, women in the Mennonite congregations of southern Germany had voting rights. In the Netherlands women became visible again in the congregations during the nineteenth century, and in 1911 Anna Zernike was ordained as a teacher (preacher, minister) after having studied theology at the Mennonite Seminary in Amsterdam. Though in the beginning people found it strange, soon having female preachers became as normal as having male preachers among Mennonites. (Other Dutch churches followed much later or not at all.)

Now all functions in the congregations and at the conference level are open to both the brothers and the sisters; not their sex but their abilities and their willingness to serve are important.

Lichdi (1990): 153-155

February 20

The Lord's Hand Was in It

Lewis B. Sider, United States, 1989

On one of my visits to Hlatshweyo school, I noticed a little girl sitting in the front row who had great difficulty seeing the blackboard. Somehow, I developed a feeling that she needed special help and also I had the conviction that she had real ability. Makanalia Siziba was in Standard III, about the equivalent of 5th grade. This was the Standard that they needed to pass in order to go to the girls' boarding school at Mtshabezi Mission.

I don't remember just how I was prompted to take her to the mission or just what the circumstances were that caused her parents to give permission, but I am positively sure that the Lord's hand was in it. In any case, permission was given, and she agreed that she would go with me. So when I went back to the mission at the end of that trip to the schools, I took her along in the car, with her small bundle of blankets and clothing. It must have seemed like a big and terrifying thing for her, but she went with me willingly.

When we arrived at the mission, she was given a place to sleep at the Girls Homecraft School, and my wife gave her some work to do while it was being decided what should be done about her. The poor girl could scarcely see well enough to do simple sewing tasks.

*

Dr. Thuma saw that she was fitted with glasses. When she looked through the glasses, she could see the trees and the mountains for the first time.

She was given a chance to work a year for school fees at Mtshabezi, and then she entered Standard IV. She remained at the mission at holiday time and worked every chance she had. She seldom went home during holidays and never again went home to live.

*

She was able to complete the Junior Certificate Course, equivalent of two years of high school and qualified for a Primary Teachers Higher Certificate. She has been a teacher for many years.

She is married to Eniya Dhlamini, who holds a position with the Zimbabwe Department of Education. At present she is a teacher of Special Education for the Handicapped in Bulawayo. They have four children, three daughters and one son.

She has helped to start both the Lobengula and the Bulawayo Central churches in Bulawayo. She has been a wonderful wife, mother, teacher and example of Christian character and leadership.

During our last term in Rhodesia we saw her a number of times, and on one occasion she and her husband and family had a meal in our home. She said to me with great feeling, "I wouldn't be here if you hadn't brought me in from Hlatshweyo."

It is with a feeling of satisfaction and humility that we contemplate that the Lord used us to help a poor country girl with very poor eyesight to become a pillar in the church.

Lewis B. Sider (1989): 56, 57

February 21

Rational Behavior
Thieleman Jansz. van Braght, The Netherlands, 1660

*M*eenen is a beautiful little town in Flanders, three leagues from Rijssel, on the road to Bruges, built on the edge of the Leye. In this town there lived a God-fearing man, Piersom des Muliers, with his wife Claudine le Vettre, who through the preaching of Leenaert Bouwens, and by reading and studying the Word of God, were turned from papal idolatry.

Learning of this, Titelmannus, Dean of Ronse, and inquisitor of the faith, came thither with bailiffs, thinking to apprehend the aforesaid Piersom in his house. But a pious man of the council of Meenen had warned Piersom to flee from the inquisitor, which he did, betaking himself into a certain piece of woods not far from his house. But his wife being engaged with her four little children (one of whom is still living) tarried a little too long, and had just left the house with a child on the arm when the bailiffs entered, who tumultuously asked the children and the neighbors where the husband was; and when they could not learn it they prepared to leave.

Perceiving this, one of the neighbors, kindled with an evil and perverse zeal, said: "Men, there goes the wife with a child on her arm." They therefore forthwith caught her and delivered her into the hands of the aforesaid inquisitor.

*

She was taken from Meenen to Ypres, where many lay in prison for the faith that is because they could not understand that there was another Mediator and Savior than Jesus Christ alone, who was offered up for our sins on the tree of the cross; and could not believe that God had any pleasure in images of wood and stone or silver and gold, but believed rather that such worship was prohibited in the Word of God. And because they also did not believe that dead men can hear our prayers and help us; but much rather that we are to call upon no one but God alone, who alone is the discerner of our hearts and thoughts and knows what we shall pray for even before we have poured out our prayer.

*

At one time a large number broke out of prison and escaped, so that Claudine also could have made her escape, but she would not leave her child; so also a pious brother, who remained with her in prison unto the end, dying with her for the truth, at said place. But Claudine did not apostasize, notwithstanding manifold assaults, continuing one year, but remained steadfast in the faith, refuting, from the word of God, all that the priests and monks were able to bring forward against her, as appeared from diverse letters which she wrote to her husband from prison.

Finally, when they could not prevail upon her, they endeavored to move her by her maternal love for her infant, which hitherto had been nourished at its mother's breast in prison. The child therefore was taken from her and put out to a wet nurse, which was the greatest affliction she suffered during her imprisonment, and on account of which she wept many a tear, constantly praying God for power and strength against such temptation and assault of the flesh, in order that she might not fall, even as many of her fellow believers fell in her presence. God almighty heard her prayer, for the Duke of Alva, having in the meantime entered the country, and commanded to clear all prisons from heretics, she also was crowned with the crown of the godly, without Ypres, A.D. 1568, and with her a brother, who was also burnt for the truth at said place.

Her husband Piersom often said of his aforesaid wife that it was astonishing how well she was versed in the scriptures. For whenever he could not find a passage, he would ask his wife Claudine, who would at once clearly indicate to him what he sought.

It is understood that the child which was taken from her in prison was from that time on seen no more, without the father and the friends ever knowing what became of it.

*

Claudine was beautiful of person, and a good singer, so that she moved the bystanders by her singing. Especially on the last day of her life, people stood before the prison, to hear her sing with a joyful heart, when death was announced to her. One who related it to me had heard her sing with a clear, strong voice the 27th psalm of David: "Le Seigneur est la clarte qui m'addresse."

And the people firmly believed that if they had not gagged her when they brought her to the place of execution she would have departed life singing and praising God.

*

Piersom, at the time of the imprisonment of his afore-mentioned wife betook himself to a miller who lived in or near his mill which stood close under the walls of Ypres, in order to be able there daily to get tidings from his beloved wife, which, gleaned from street rumors were brought to him by the miller's wife, as often as she returned from town, though without knowing that it was his wife or that he was an Anabaptist.

She judged Claudine not to be in her right mind because she had allowed herself to be rebaptized and let so many sufferings be inflicted upon her on this account, and would rather die than do what the priests said. This every time pierced Piersom's heart like a dagger and often compelled him to step aside to give vent to the deep feelings of his heart.

The day when Claudine was to be offered up, the miller's wife, desirous of seeing her being executed, asked Piersom whether he did not wish to go along and behold the scene, which he declined, requesting her kindly to pay strict attention to everything in order to give him an account of it afterwards. When she returned home she related to Piersom how valiantly and undauntedly Claudine went to death, what she said, and how she conducted herself; everything, however, with the idea, that Claudine had not acted rationally. Thereupon Piersom, having warmed up, took heart and disclosed himself to the miller and his wife, saying that he was of the same belief, and that the one put to death was his beloved and very rational wife, and upon what foundations of truth they founded their doctrine and life. This so deeply affected the miller and his wife that they also resolved to amend their life. They were baptized upon their faith, and shortly after sealed the truth with their blood.

van Braght ([1886] 1979): 737, 738

February 22

Two-Way Honesty

R.M.N. (in *Family Life*), United States, 1969

I was on a bus which was traveling from Lancaster to Blue Ball. As we were passing through the Groffdale-Leola area, three plain ladies, Amish and Mennonites, boarded the bus. This in itself is not unusual. After arriving at New Holland, all the passengers got off except myself.

The bus driver was a real friendly chap and soon we had an interesting conversation going. He asked if I had noticed anything unusual when the three ladies boarded the bus. I hadn't been aware of anything so he told me the following story:

"Frequently, when we bus drivers gather at the office, we discuss the method which many of the plain people use when they pay their fares. As they board the bus, their first question is, 'How much to New Holland?' (or to wherever they happen to be going). Even though they always ask, we notice the majority of the people already have the correct amount of change in their hands. This was amusing to us, so we decided to have a little game of our own. As these folks would board the bus, asking the usual question, we would purposefully either increase or decrease the fare by ten cents to see what would happen.

"The result was that nine out of ten would tell us when we requested too much, proceeding to tell us the correct amount and then pay it. However, when we decreased the fare, not one person would tell us about this. They calmly paid what was requested and kept the change."

The bus driver continued, "Of those three ladies who boarded the bus, all had the correct change in their hands, yet not one of them made any kind of remark as to why the fare was decreased."

I stop here and wonder, just what is honesty? I frequently ride this bus, and I wonder if I have ever been tested in this way. Is it leaving a good witness to only correct a mistake when it is to our favor to do so? Perhaps each person should seriously consider this the next time he notices a price change, regardless of whether the price quoted is up or down.

N. (1969): 14

February 23

I Could Not Think That You Had Said That
John F. Funk and Jonas Martin, United States, ca. 1890

Excerpts from a series of letters which passed between bishops John F. Funk and Jonas Martin.

Funk: I see in the several papers there is a report about you and I want to know whether it is true. The saying is that you should have said you would rather see your children go into the grave than see them go to a Sunday school. Now I am a friend to Sunday schools. I think you know that; but I am also a friend to you, and I would not like to have you laying under such a stigma if it were not true. Will you kindly write me and tell me if this is true? If it is not true, I will write to the papers and tell them so.

*

Martin: I have received your letter this evening and can say with a clear conscience that there is not a word of truth about it, what I should have said about Sunday school; but I can say that I am no advocate of Sunday school. I have always said that I would do nothing for it nor against it.

*

Funk: Your kind letter was duly received, and am glad to hear from you that what has been said is not true. That was what made me write. I could not think that you had said that. Of course, if you are not in favor of Sunday schools, you have a right to say so, and if you do not want to do anything for them, you have the right to do so. We cannot compel a man, nor ask a man to do different from what he believes, and we cannot make a man believe different when convictions lead him to believe so or so. I hope I have not hurt your feelings in asking you the questions I did. I believe this is the Scriptural way to do, and I hope God will bless you in your work and help you in the many cares and trials you have in your church. I sincerely sympathize with you in these troubles. I hope all the dear brethren on both sides will be patient and let brotherly love continue in all things, and may the peace of God which passes all understanding keep their hearts and ours.

Horst (1985): 232, 233

February 24

A Word Broken
Ervin Miller, United States, 1989

When I was a school boy, Dad had a nice pair of geldings, full brothers. A non-Amish friend and neighbor wanted to buy them and kept raising his offer. Finally Dad said he could have them. After he left, my brother and I objected. We did not like to see them go. Dad said he would not go back on his word. If we wanted to tell him off, we could but he would not.

So I offered I would go. Away I went and when I got there he came walking out of the house.

I told him we had decided that he couldn't have the team after all. He said, "Okay," and turned around and went back in. My heart seemed to fall to my toes. I walked home with slow steps. Our friendship was broken for a long time.

I will never forget what Dad taught me: "Our yes should be yes, and our no should be no." It might be well if more people got the lesson the hard way like I did. Lord, help me to live up to it.

Miller (1989): 10

February 25

First Love
Christian Lesher, United States, 1850

The person first becomes a spiritual virgin through the original conversion and at that time he or she is washed clean in the blood of Jesus Christ, cleansed of all spots of his former life. And at this time he receives strength and light from God and a new inner pure and virginal life, which the ten virgins, the wise and the foolish, all had acquired. For at the beginning they all were wise enough that they went out to meet the bridegroom and they all took their lamps. And up to this point everything was all right with them, but just at this point their foolishness began, in that they did not earnestly strive to have oil for their vessels, to get it and to have it with them. And this is what needs to be understood, namely, they were satisfied with their one-time conversion, just as if that would be effective for them at this point, but did not go forward in the course of holiness right up to the full indwelling and uniting with God.

*

And so then the vessel of oil is nothing else than the indwelling godly nature, which the faithful, wise souls in their time come to have within them. And actually, it is that first love which at the beginning at conversion was poured out in their heart through the Holy Spirit, an outpouring of the divine nature, out of the vessel of oil. But it is not the vessel of oil itself remaining and dwelling with and in us, but the fact that from it the lamps are filled and caused to burn.

But then just as the supply of oil in the lamps is soon all used up and the lamp becomes pale or goes out unless more oil is poured into it from time to time, so it is in our spiritual life, the strength of the first love diminishes and finally disappears so that one does not know what became of it. Also that sweet feeling, and the sweet incense of faith, and the living hope together with that heroic energy with which one was first drawn all become weaker.

*

And just here is the place where often the half or even more than the half of truly called persons become foolish virgins, who do not break through or persevere till they have the oil vessel, that is to say, the indwelling godly nature. But they continue saying that one cannot get any further, and they concede that their being virgins has ended their preparation and they lie down to sleep, only to wake up to hear the voice calling and they become alert to their mistake.

Lesher (1850): 62, 63

February 26

Clinging Firmly

Abraham Friesen, Russian Empire, 1820

*A*t one time I had a dream that I had prepared myself to ascend up unto a high mountain. After I had proceeded for a short distance the mountain became very steep so that it seemed impossible for me to climb any higher. But when I turned about and wanted to go back I quickly had to cling to the earth for otherwise it seemed as if I would plummet down into the precipice. When I looked upwards it was as steep as a sheer wall. I can hardly express how anxious and fearful this made me. Nevertheless I clung firmly so as not to fall down, and after a tremendous battle I was finally able to descend from the mountain. Then the joy was exceedingly great. Usually I do not care much for dreams but this one did not leave my thoughts.

It always seems to me that one must work for salvation with a similar earnestness and clinging firmly. Yet I will not conclude this from my dream; rather the apostle Paul says, "Work, so that ye will be saved, with fear and trembling." And Peter says, "Govern your life in fear during the time of your sojourn here." For this reason I am also concerned for myself and my fellow brethren. If only we could change ourself about and live according to the will of God and not according to the desires of man. I have much to be concerned for myself.

But beloved friends. If we stand in true communion with each other, then we are many in the body and must protect each other.

Plett (1985): 250

February 27

The Spirit of Resurrection
Eberhard Arnold, Germany, 1922

*T*he knowledge of the Sermon on the Mount can be opened up only to those who know something of reverence for the Creator: who sense that also all powers of body and soul in the life of natural, organic growth are an outright gift from God and utterly dependent on Him. God's creation can never be regarded as the effort of men as a more or less profitable field for their activity. The new creation in Christ's Spirit has nothing to do with the efforts of will by contemporary individuals or by mankind as a whole as it is today. Jesus, therefore, cannot say, "You should be light, you should be salt, you should make yourselves into a city!" Instead, He recognizes that the creation and the new creation is a being and a becoming which evolves and has its being from the Creator.

You are the salt of the earth, you are the light of the world. Salt is salt, or it is less than dung; it is dirt that is fit only to be thrown away. Light burns and shines and warms. If it does not do this, it is not light. Light, like salt, does its task by consuming itself. Here we are concerned with a giving up of one's own life, which then becomes happy in its task, its giving up. The task of love, the self-effacing, blissful devotion to the task—this is the essence of Jesus and His kingdom.

*

It is just as impossible to *make* a communal life of this kind as it would be to produce a tree in a factory. The building up of the church community, coming into being out of the spirit of community, is an action by God just as free and independent of human activity as the creation of a tree and its fruit. As the tree is, so is the fruit. Creation's law of growth and life is here placed in opposition to human doings, just as in the Letter to the Romans the law of the Spirit of life is opposed to the law of sin and death. Living creation takes the place of dead weight.

What man can never accomplish, God does. His creative Spirit is the secret of the law of life, for God is a God of all that is living, not a God of death. The resurrection of Jesus is the ultimate revelation of this law of life. The Sermon on the Mount can be grasped only where reverence for the Creator and the creation is overwhelmed by the Spirit of the resurrection; where Jesus is proven in power to be the Son of God, through this very Spirit of holy consecration whose action goes out from the resurrection. Outside of this the Sermon on the Mount remains an impossibility, a utopia, unwholesome fantasy, nonsense, self-deception or madness.

Arnold (1967): 34-36

February 28

Freedom and Obedience
Samuel Gerber, Switzerland, 1967

*S*ince ancient times much mischief has been raised with the two words "freedom" and "obedience." Adam and Eve already felt it was an unendurable restriction of their freedom that they were obliged to refrain from eating the fruit of the two trees in the midst of the garden, and the deceitful logic of the serpent sounded so reasonable that disobedience immediately became a precept of human dignity.

Through the mischief done with these two words, things have reached the point where the subjects freedom and obedience themselves have fallen into discredit. And yet both pertain to the most precious, the holiest blessings, to the supporting pillars of our existence.

*

In recent times the childish motto "Freedom means one is permitted to do anything" has increased to the demonic-pathological with some thinkers, as when J. P Sartre lets a character in one of his dramas commit murder and then state that he can only now be truly free when he is permitted to do anything, even commit murder.

When whole nations, even those with centuries or even millennia of culture, permit themselves to be imposed upon with the idea that a citizen must obey, even when a crime is required of him and even when irrational self-destruction is called for, then one wishes to call out: "The distortion of the concept of freedom was childish; the distortion of the concept of obedience was diabolical."

Freedom does not consist in anyone's preventing me from playing the saxophone. (No one prevents us at this moment from playing the saxophone!) Freedom consists in my being *able* to play the saxophone. Freedom is *being able to.* The converse of freedom is not merely constraint and subjection, but impotence, bungling, dilettantism; freedom is fullness of power. Therefore, freedom signifies the presence of God. God is He who is truly able, without limitation, to do what He desires. Kierkegaard says: "God indicates that everything is possible." That is why we pray: "Thine is the kingdom and the power and the glory."

*

Freedom also means to find one's place in the godly order. The musician who plays his own part in the orchestra can, of course, suppose it to be inventive or original to play his own melody. But he horribly ruins the harmony of the whole, and he cannot count on applause. The driver of an automobile may come upon the idea to ignore all traffic rules, let go of the steering wheel, and set levers and switches of the car into motion just as he pleases. This departure from regulations is something for which he pays a high price. It does not bring him freedom, but rather hospital or jail.

Our generation is getting to feel, as never before, that excessive individualism presents us with anarchy where we had thought to proclaim freedom. It is to be feared that the pendulum will soon swing in the opposite direction. We will burden ourselves with persons who will carry through their barbarous rules and regulations with Draconian harshness.

Would it not be better for us to think of truly valid standards for freedom and obedience? Should we so-called Christians not know better, ponder, and in a credible way communicate to others that freedom and obedience were demonstrated to us in a unique way by Jesus, grasped and testified to by the apostles with amazing clarity, and—what counts most—since Pentecost have been made accessible to all mankind?

Dyck ([1967]): 36, 37

February 29

Hindrances

Abraham Godshalk, United States, 1838

*H*ow many thousands are there who think themselves orthodox in faith, and were therefore children of God, and have not so much as the will to do that which is truly good? They may indeed be faithful in their attendance on religious meetings to hear preaching, and anxious to pray in order to be heard and seen of men like the Pharisees of old, but mercy, and true and living faith are omitted by them, as they were by the Pharisees. Yea, many are not yet willing to deal according to justice with their fellow men, to say nothing about love and mercy. I therefore say that it is indeed a great thing to have the will to do that which is truly good and right in all things.

Whence come so many of the last described class? The main cause of their existence is man's natural proneness to evil. Again, the belief that Jesus is the Christ is now prevalent in the land, and we are brought up to it from infancy. Now this is a kind of dead thing, learned from our parents and other sources, which may not always be called living faith, as many afterwards experience; for true and living faith embraces Christ whole, namely, in doctrine, example and merits. It embraces the threatenings, as well as the promise in God's word, and thereby the will is created to cease from the evil and learn to do the good.

Another cause for their existence may be that men are not always taught godly truth, or rather not the whole truth. For there is so much said against the moralist, and as it appears to me classing him with the self-righteous Pharisee, that I honestly fear many are thereby hindered from being moral, and made so fearful of self-righteousness, as not to become righteous at all.

Godshalk (1838): 39, 40

March

Envy

John H. Holdeman, United States, 1891

*E*nvy has done much harm both in the world and the church. When envy defiles the minds of the ministers and members of the church of God, then there will be no end of fault-finding and harsh judgments, and peace cannot be made as long as envy is not subdued, for it is of an irreconcilable nature.

*

Paul says: "Let us not be desirous of vainglory, provoking one another, envying one another" (Galatians 5:26).

Is it not a dreadful thing to envy the talents, gifts, prosperity and good report of others? Should we not much more rejoice of all the good gifts God hath given to others, though they excel our gifts? It is an evidence of an unkind spirit where we find a man so blasted through envy that he cannot rejoice over the prosperity of another. Envy is always coupled with hatred: though there may be hatred where there is no envy, there is never any envy found without hatred. When the object envied is evil spoken of, it eases the uneasiness of envy to some extent, and the envious person will help the accusers against the envied person.

*

Envy no doubt has its degrees, and we should always destroy it before it overpowers us, and so blinds our eyes that we misrepresent and condemn the person we envy and thus destroy our own souls. As soon as we are the least mortified at the praise of others, we should pray unceasingly until we can rejoice in the praise, honor and prosperity of others. We should be willing to be passed by in the choice of the church for special work without being mortified. If we are passed by and others are counseled before we are, we should submit without uneasiness of mind, and if we do not, then envy is working in us and should be subdued. The man who has envy in his heart no doubt considers his own worth too highly and undervalues the excellence of the man he envies, and desires the position of another considering himself capable of filling the envied person's place. And thus an envious person often becomes thievish, and would rob the man he envies of his position, honor and prosperity—and this envy will do in diverse ways.

*

This spirit of envy will do like the Hyena that digs dead bodies out of the grave: it will carry old sins, many years ago repented of, and hold them up against the envied persons to as many as can be reached, and oftentimes under the garb of holiness and righteousness, as though it was a duty to do so. Wherever you find a spirit that goes back from the present time fifteen and twenty-five years and after many a communion was held, you will find at least an irreconcilable spirit, if not always the spirit of envy. Envy is therefore thievish, murderous and implacable—that is irreconcilable. Beware of envy.

Holdeman (1891): 192-195

March 2

Foolish Wisdom
Klaus Felbinger, Germany, 1560

*H*ow incredulous are the wise of this world when they are shown the narrow path! The teachings of Christ's Cross can be nothing but folly in the eyes of the lost. They claim that we are much too ambitious; that Christ has paid our debt and has done enough for us; that all a man needs to do is to believe firmly and admit that he is a sinner, for God is merciful. Not a word about true repentance and new birth, without which there is no blessedness. True repentance means sinning no more, beginning a new and holy life with God, and breaking with the world.

The wise of this world flaunt their knowledge and say, "We find it in the Old and New Testament. In our opinion you are aiming much too high. If only those were to be saved who act as you do, the whole world would have to be damned." But we believe God's Word without any question. His Word is established and cannot lie. His Word does not conform to the world; rather, we men have to conform to the Word of God. The wise of this world think that because they have studied the Books and are well versed in them they lack nothing. That applies especially to the monks, clerics and scribes. The foolish men! The wisdom of God cannot be gleaned from books or learned at the university; far from it. "For the fear of the Lord is the beginning of wisdom; and a good understanding have all those who practice it."

So we see that the mystery of the heavenly Kingdom is revealed only to those who faithfully follow Christ; the others have eyes and do not see, they have ears and do not hear. David says that the secrets of God belong to those who fear Him, and He makes known to them His covenant. Those who remain true to Christ's teaching will understand the truth, and the truth will make them free. Knowledge makes people puffed up, but love heals and builds up. The worldly-wise are repelled by the teaching of Christ's Cross. Common sense warns us not to come under the yoke, for our flesh rebels against God.

That is why Paul says, "Consider your call, brethren; not many of you were wise according to worldly standards, not many were powerful, not many were of noble birth; but God chose what is foolish in the world to shame the wise. . .so that no human being might boast in the presence of God," but all honor might be God's. Christ praises His Father for having hidden the truth from the mighty of this world and revealed it to babes.

Hutterian Brethren (1978): 104-106

March 3

Powerful Preaching
Paul Hostetler, United States, 1980

I thought about the 1939 General Conference on the campus of Messiah College. Our family was quartered in a tent. A nearby tent housed another preacher and his wife. Early one morning he was talking to her. Tent walls are thin, and every word was clearly audible to Dad.

The preacher told his wife with some pride that someone had told him he remembered a sermon he had preached forty years before. After a pause to let that profound statement sink in, he declared, "That is *powerful* preaching!" Dad chuckled until he realized that even that slight sound might carry to the next tent.

In the years that followed, the story became a family joke. When anyone remarked that he remembered what Dad had said in a sermon, we would look at Dad in mock seriousness and say, "*That* is *powerful* preaching!" It helped keep him humble.

Hostetler (1980): 123

March 4

The "Doesn't Matter" Spirit
Christian Reesor, Canada, late 1800s

T here are so many things which Satan uses to mislead man, and if possible even the elect. It is sad to see the pride and willfulness taking place in the world, and creeping into the church, which as you know causes much grief to the ministers.

*

With many, the flesh does not wish to bow down. Oh, how the world carries on: what state and pomp is exposed to the eyes—so much capriciousness that one would think it cannot be, yet all will carry the name of Christians, and pretend to have an humble heart.

Oh, how he calls and offers his grace, but so few pay attention, for nearly all wish to carry on in pride and pomp, and still be good followers of Jesus. Each wishes to be the greatest. The Savior says, "How can ye believe, which receive honor one of another, and seek not the honor that cometh from God only?" Oh dear brother, let us hold fast to the nonresistant foundation which we accepted as examples to the flock.

It seems as if the "doesn't matter" spirit was getting the upper hand, which reminds me of the poet who says, "So many stand separated, who still confess to be part of Christ's little flock." Is this becoming for brethren, as members of one body? Do not the Scriptures plainly testify against this? Oh, that each one who confesses the nonresistant faith would seek to humble himself, so that there is a difference between the world and the church.

*

Oh dear brother, how necessary it is to strive against the misleading "doesn't matter" and revival spirit which seems to rise up in all the nonresistant churches and seeks admission, to lead conformity to the world and pride into the church. I must often think how cunning Satan was in the garden of Eden when he cast a net over man's eyes and brought them to ruin; and how Israel became careless, and when Jerusalem was besieged they could no longer gain victory because they departed from the godly commands.

Oh, so let us be on the watch and together give a certain and distinct sound of the trumpet, that there be no confusion among the people, and we neglect not the grace of God, lest any bitter root springing up trouble us, but that rather we direct them down to the lowly, to humility and self-denial, and whatever is most pleasing to God.

Horst (1985): 150-152

March 5

Against New Rules
Gerritt Roosen, Germany, 1697

I am sincerely grieved that you have been so disturbed by those who think highly of themselves, and make laws of things which are not upheld in the Gospel. Had it been specified in the apostolic letters how or wherewith a believer should be clothed, or whether he should go in this or that country and this were disobeyed, then these had something of which to speak. But it is more contrary to the Gospel to affix one's conscience to a pattern of the hats, clothes, stockings, shoes or the hair of the head; or make a distinction in which country one lives. And then, for one to undertake the enforcement of such regulations by punishing with the ban all who will not accept them, and to expel from the church as a leaven those who do not wish to avoid those thus punished, though neither the Lord Jesus in His Gospel or His holy apostles have bound us to external things, nor have deemed it expedient to provide such regulations and laws.

I agree with what the Apostle Paul says in Colossians 2:16, that the kingdom of heaven, or the kingdom of God, is not obtained "in meat or in drink," nor in this or that, in the form or pattern of clothing; to which external things our dear Savior does not oblige us.

*

In all of Paul's letters we do not find one word in which he has given believers regulations concerning the forms of clothing they should have, but in all things he instructed them to "condescend to men of low estate" according to all decency and modesty. I hold that it is becoming to adapt the manner of dress to the current customs of one's environments; but it is reasonable that we abstain from luxuries, pride and carnal worldly lusts, not immediately adopting the latest style of fashionable clothing; which is certainly something to be reproved, but when it has come into common usage then it is honorable to follow in such common apparel and to walk in humility.

But thanks be to God, I do not want showy array or worldly lusts, and have always continued wearing nearly the same pattern of clothes. But if I had dressed in modern fashion, should I then, for this reason, be excommunicated? This would be an injustice, and contrary to the Scriptures. The Lord has indeed made regulations in the church of God, for punishment of the contentious and those conducting themselves contrary to the ordinances of God, as set forth in the Gospel. Herein it must be determined whether the things we wish to bind are also bound there, or are commanded to be bound.

The Holy Scriptures must be our ruling standard; to this we must yield, not running before it, but following; and that not ultimately, but with care, fear and regret. For it is a dangerous venture to step into the judgment of God and bind that which is not bound in heaven.

Mast (1950): 66-68

March 6

No Fruits Of Pride
John M. Brenneman, United States, 1866

Many, with all their pomp and decorations, still console themselves by saying, "It does not matter so much about the externals, if only the heart is right." It is very true indeed that a good heart is the essential qualification in the true Christian character; but a good heart, beyond doubt, is also humble and consequently cannot exhibit any pride; for "a good man, out of the good treasure of the heart, bringeth forth good things."

I know there are persons who say that the religion of the Mennonites consists entirely in their manner of dress and that, in their estimation, the style of dress decides the whole matter. But if this were true, then the state of the Mennonites would indeed be sad to contemplate; for if they had no other Christianity than their manner of dress, they would not have any at all. God forbid that a true Mennonite should believe that Christianity consists merely in simplicity of dress.

A genuine and true Mennonite assuredly believes that true Christianity is to be found only in the humble and regenerated heart, and that out of such a heart can proceed or be manifested no fruits of pride: but that it will much rather feel an aversion to, and abhor, all needless ornament and extravagance in dress. It is sadly true, however, that in our day there are some also who call themselves Mennonites but indulge in the extravagances of dress and fashion, considering themselves good Christians withal and maintaining that it can make no difference what kind of dress one wears. But I think the name Mennonite is very unsuitable for such persons, as long as their manner of life is so directly contrary to the teachings of Menno. I am well aware that merely the name Mennonite will not profit us in the least, if we are not true Christians.

Brenneman (1866): 10, 11

March 7

Walking Hand in Hand
Christian Horst, United States, ca. 1880

*O*h beloved brethren, if we all could only receive enough strength to be truly steadfast on this narrow way, to walk hand in hand in one faith, and be led by the good and Holy Spirit—then the lusts of this world could not lead us poor mortals so easily off to the left, as one sees with regret how everything must be adorned in state and pomp. Now I think if we are children of the good spirit we will adorn ourselves in humility. Now, according to my opinion there are those who are misled to the right, by priding themselves in their good works, which we cannot attribute to ourselves, for it is but a gift of grace.

Now here is something to do for each and everyone that wishes to sow the seed on the narrow path and reap life everlasting on the other side of the wilderness. I hope and pray that we might all join hand in hand all brothers and sisters and all God-fearing people and pray for one another and help each other along on this journey, and not try to push and pull each other off the path of righteousness that leads through the narrow gate into everlasting blessedness, which is too much the case that says this is the way and another that is the way to Heaven.

Some say it is not in the coat nor in the hat, if the heart is right all is right. My opinion is if the heart is right, the coat and hat will soon get right. Still no one is bound to my meaning, but that doctrine has been preached up by some of our ministers.

Horst (1985): 135, 136

Laws and Love
Hans Denck, Germany, 1526

*W*hy then did God give these commandments to his people?

*

By this he intended to show that all human order and decency is in harmony with him, provided it is not set against genuine love. And anyone who works against love cannot excuse himself either with divine or human law. For all laws must give way to love since they exist for the sake of love, and not vice versa. Since they cannot give love, they should not obstruct it either.

Love, on the other hand, gives all laws; hence, it can receive them again, each one as occasion demands. As much as to this day love is lacking, so much it is essential in every undertaking to remind oneself. Therefore, a person who has once been cleansed of the filth of this world would never eat a piece of bread without thereby contemplating how much God loves him and how much he in turn should love God. To wit: that God in his own fashion breaks himself for his benefit like bread and that he in turn ought to break himself like bread to the glory of God; that God renounces his divinity and that he in turn ought to renounce his humanity so that the sacrifice be perfect and that love might become one, as it was in Jesus Christ, the first-born son of God and as it is yet to be in all the elect.

To the extent then to which a person is one with God, he is above the laws of time and place and not subject to their laws. But he cannot enjoy such freedom unless he gladly subjects himself to all the laws. For anyone who does not for God's sake become the servant of all creatures, cannot inherit the kingdom of God together with his Son.

Denck (1989): 240, 241

The Clothes of An Outsider
Magdalene Redekop, Canada, 1988

I remember a visit to a neighboring farm where my friend Mary Penner lived. The Penners (I have changed the name to protect their privacy) were made outsiders by their poverty and this was signaled by the fact that there were no trees in their yard and there was no paint on their house. I have no memory of Mary's father (perhaps he had died), but her mother must have been a remarkable woman. Mary Penner's mother made flowers with tissue paper. Mary Penner's mother could turn a box of pink Kleenex into fragile carnations.

With red crepe paper Mary Penner's mother could produce astonishingly lifelike roses which she sold to be worn as decorations at weddings.

On this particular visit there was hiding and shrieking and chasing and falling which all ended in humiliation for me. I fell, rolled and got up to discover that I had rolled in what we called a cow pie (no money here for fences). My clothes, my arms, everything was smeared with cow manure. I can remember the gentle kindness and tact of Mary Penner's mother; I remember the overpowering smell of fresh cinnamon rolls and the fact that I could not eat them for thinking of cow pies. Since I cannot remember being tormented at school with the incident, my friend Mary—blessings on her, wherever she is—must have kept a loyal silence.

My memory, however, is not unmixed with shame and it is not because of that cow manure. I am still ashamed of myself when I remember that I hated to go home wearing my friend's clothes. I felt revulsion for the high-pitched, soapy smell of poverty that clung to them. My gratitude for her kindness was mixed with a painful sense of my own treachery. If I loved my neighbor as myself, I should surely not mind being her during the time that it took to walk up her long driveway and down the long driveway to my own home. But I did; oh yes, I did! Trying to be myself and yet trying on the clothes of an outsider: for me that is an apt image of what it means to try to be a Mennonite.

Loewen (1988): 230, 231

March 10

My Heart Rejoices at the Recollection
Jan Philipsz. Schabaelje, The Netherlands, 1635

Another imaginary conversation, in which Simon Cleopas relates his experiences with Jesus to the Wandering Soul (see page 33).

Simon Cleopas: At one time we had gone into a ship and suddenly the heavens were spread with dark clouds, and a tempestuous storm arose on the sea. It was so boisterous that there seemed to be no hopes for our lives. The waves dashed against the ship, the sails could not be managed, the ropes broke, the mainmast was bent frightfully, and all of us much troubled.

At last we, in this distress, awakened Jesus who lay quietly and slept. He rose and stood before us like a father of a family when he reproves his blustering servants. The winds seemed to fear him, the clouds disappeared, the sea immediately became calm, the sails hung down by the sides of the masts, the stars appeared in the serene heavens: Orion, the Wagon, the Seven Stars and the Twins were seen directly over head.

*

Wandering Soul: Were it not for your age and experience, as a witness of these things, I would be ready to doubt what you say to be true.

Simon Cleopas: I know that it is almost impossible to believe the great and unheard-of miracles, but I omit many things which would not less astonish you. For he also raised the dead, in a word, cured old chronic diseases, under which many had suffered for twelve, eighteen, thirty and more years: that was all the same to him, for even those who, with a believing heart touched the hem of his garment, were healed without entreating him to do so, so great a virtue proceeded out of him.

The afflicted followed him everywhere—into houses, ships, fields, wilderness—yea, wherever he went they were about him, so that often no time was afforded him to eat, sleep or to be alone for private meditation. The cry that Jesus of Nazareth would come, that he had been seen at that place yesterday and would be there on the morrow was often heard long before he came to a place, upon which the lame and the blind began to move. Each one wished to be there first. And when they could not come to him, the roofs of the houses in which he was were broken open, and the sick let down before him—so anxious were many to be healed of their diseases. And whenever healed, they were also ready to praise God. Oh, how often have I seen the lame run, the blind look up towards heaven, those who were afflicted with gout walk and the sick stand in astonishment on account of the great deeds.

Schabalie ([1834]): 284-286

March 11

I Could Almost Weep For Joy
Jan Philipsz. Schabaelje, The Netherlands, 1635

Wandering Soul: By your talk, I perceive, that you have not been among the people at all times, but often travelled with Jesus alone.

Simon Cleopas: Oh, in that you speak the truth. I could almost weep for joy when I remember the agreeable journeys we had with him. Sometimes we went upon a mountain, then into an open green field, through olive groves, along the banks of fine clear streams, often through thick forests, and the high cedar trees sheltered us from the winds and rain. The palm and lemon trees protected us from the burning rays of the sun. The cypress trees refreshed us by their fragrant smell. Often we found nothing but thorns and thistles. In one field we saw one plowing and another sowing seed. In another, a shepherd watching his flock.

But Jesus knew how to profit by all things we saw; yea, I do not believe that Solomon ever knew the nature of all things as Jesus. For he could speak of all things before the people—of trees, herbs, grain, vineyards, mustard, even of fishes, birds, of nets, pearls, stones, mountains. In short, he was familiar with everything. It seemed as if all were shadows and types of the kingdom of God.

He did not look to outward things nor did he care for them, but alone that the kingdom of God (which continued for ever) might be enlarged: this he always impressed upon our minds and wished to have it made known to all.

He therefore also selected twelve of his followers as apostles, according to the number of the twelve tribes of Israel, again to establish that people. He sent two and two together; they went through the country in the above-mentioned manner, through cities and towns, and wanted nothing. They had ample time to serve God, and to keep all the cares for this life at a distance. He was not at all concerned about the cares of this world, which are the most injurious poison by which the heart of man can be infected. They had to keep themselves clear from having anything in store, in order not to be detained on the way.

Schabalie ([1834]): 286, 287

March 12

Parables

Eberhard Arnold, Germany, 1934

*T*he leading classes of the people, and an increasingly large part of the common people too, rejected Jesus more and more the longer He worked, especially after He had sent out His twelve, two by two, and His seventy, two by two, giving them mighty authority. After they had come back without having won the people of Israel for the kingdom of God, Jesus made a tremendous decision. He withdrew to His parables.

These parables were meant to veil the truth to the obtrusive, in order not to deliver what was holy to the beasts of prey. At the same time the parables were to show the truth all the more deeply to those who really wanted to hear. Those who wanted to hear something with false hearts only to be able to contradict it afterwards were to run up against an impenetrable wall in these parables. In fact, up to the present day no human theology, no false prophecy has ever been able to understand these parables.

To open hearts, however, the church was to be opened up. Here the ultimate meaning of the message of God's kingdom was shown. In the first place it was revealed in the parable of unity, that of the wedding and the supper—the deepest unity possible among men and the most inclusive and yet most intimate fellowship of the table possible among men. Complete uniting and the fellowship of many at one table—this is the mystery of the kingdom of God. But this wedding feast, this supper is seen in connection with the King and the King's Son, so that it may be recognized that this fellowship of God's kingdom among men is not a value in itself. It receives its value only because it is the King who holds the wedding and who invites people to this supper.

The kingdom of God is compared with the royal wedding and with the royal supper. Later parables show us that this unity consists not only in the joy of uniting, but also in the creative activity of this uniting. Therefore Jesus likens the kingdom of God to the work in the vineyard, and in another place to the worker who does yes while saying no. Real unity and community are present only where there is common work, for love is deed. And if we ask what this deed is, then the parables of Jesus show us that this deed is utmost surrender; it is work directed toward the future, work entirely dependent on the blessing of heaven. The sower is likened to the kingdom of God, and so is the farmer who waits for the right weather, and so is the field in which the crop is intermingled with weeds deceptively similar to it.

Total readiness for God's kingdom means work in united love and at the same time a believing and loving expectation of God, that He will bring all things to their completion.

Arnold (1967): 282-284

March 13

Greater Motives
P. Cool, The Netherlands, 1854

Johanna, a young Dutch woman preparing for baptism, was troubled by some difficult sayings of Jesus. The following selection is taken from a pastor's reply to her concerns.

The very morning you wrote to me you had three encounters with Jesus when you read Luke 9:57-62. In these verses he appeared to you in a less favorable light; in sensitive human relations he seemed unfeeling and unnecessarily severe.

Let us first see then if we are able to clear up the objections which have arisen for you in regard to Jesus' conduct, especially in regard to the course of action he took towards the man who offered to follow him wherever he went.

*

"He who comes to me," Jesus said once, "I shall in no wise cast out." And his willingness to help and save everyone who believes and comes to him—to receive them as sheep of his flock—how often Jesus revealed this by striking examples. With what magnanimity of spirit he always stood above the rich and great of this world, and paid no less attention to the man born blind begging by the wayside than to a man of consequence and high standing such as Nicodemus. How magnanimously also he stood above the misconceptions of the people, appearing among them occasionally, but also to Samaritans held in contempt and despised by his own countrymen. And he was so far above the spirit of the loveless and proud Pharisees that he dined with the publicans—those regarded as riffraff of the country, regarded as after all incorrigible and lost, so that he had to hear the complaint that he had a preference for sinful men and women. See, this was the Lord's way of procedure.

*

Jesus, who knew the heart of man, read in the heart of the scribe clearly a lack of the principles and motives belonging to the anticipated step. This man wanted to follow in all the steps of Jesus. But for what reason? For no other reason—Jesus' answer seems more than a surmise—for no other reason than to be included among his followers in the earthly expectation to attain honor and prominence with the people in general—and the scribes and Pharisees not the least—in the kingdom of the Messiah.

*

Surely as a result of this Jesus did not accept the scribe's offer. He desired that men come to him impelled by other motives. We must come to Jesus as sick persons, as dangerously sick to the physician in order to find health, or as a traveler to the guide, realizing that without him we cannot find the way. We must seriously understand that we need him as Savior and Mediator, that without him the great questions of life cannot be answered, that without him we cannot obtain peace with God and ourselves, not find true soul-rest, not attain victory in the battle against sin, sin inside and outside ourselves. In a word, greater desires must impel us to a close relationship with Christ.

Gorter (1856): 13-17, trans. by Irvin B. Horst

March 14

The Prince of Peace for All
Henk B. Kossen, The Netherlands, 1978

When Jesus entered Jerusalem riding a donkey He wished to indicate thereby that He, as the Prince of Peace sent by God, saw a very special way of establishing the messianic kingdom. This was specifically not the traditional method of force opposing force, of fighting and warfare which ultimately led to new injustices and new tyranny. It was instead the way of service and the sacrificing of Himself.

We must understand clearly how the way Jesus chose differed drastically from the way of the Zealots and why the latter group succeeded in getting the support of most of the people. For the Zealots, the fight against the Romans and Caesar was the fight for Israel's God. Thus they would prepare the way of the Lord and thus make ready His kingdom on earth, so that Israel, freed of all her enemies, should rule over the nations of the earth. Although Jesus unquestionably took His stand on the side of the poor and oppressed with all the inherent consequences, He decidedly rejected the method of the Zealots. For He knew that Israel was called not to rule over the nations but to serve them, to become a blessing to them so that they also could praise the Lord for His faithfulness and loving kindness.

This conflict between the way of Jesus and the way of the Zealots came to a head in their conception of the temple of Jerusalem, *the* center of Jewish authority. This temple was clearly not only the spiritual center of the Jewish world community. Here all the yearly temple taxes from Palestine and the diaspora were collected. And with gifts of all kinds besides, an impressive temple treasury accumulated, from which the high priest nobility could live in a way violently contrasting to the painful poverty of the people. To the Zealots the temple had a totally different significance. This lay in the actual fact that it was the only place in the whole Jewish country which no heathen, thus no Roman, could enter. The Romans had agreed to this to prevent the Jews from acts of desperation. And you know how strictly the Zealots enforced this regulation. They would not even allow Roman coins in the temple because of the image of Caesar on these coins. This explains the presence of money changers in front of the temple. There all heathen coin could be changed for Jewish money, and so heathen defilement of the temple was avoided.

Now we can fully understand Jesus' confrontation of authority at the heart of the Jewish order. He had read in Isaiah that God's house would be a house of prayer for all nations. This conception cut straight across the Zealots' idea of the temple. They saw in the temple a sort of last guarantee of God's presence in their midst, the presence of Him who would exalt Israel and humble the nations. They clung fanatically to the temple in the endeavor for religious self-preservation. They were determined to defend it at any cost against every heathen defilement as evidenced in the Jewish war of 66-70.

This was of course no new concept. Jeremiah had detected it in his time and had passionately opposed it. He could even confront his people with the charge that such a use of the temple made of it a robbers' den (Jeremiah 7:11). For robbers and thieves hide in a den what they have unlawfully appropriated as their own. "Now then," Jeremiah would say, "you have appropriated the living God unlawfully. You try to confine Him to your temples as if He were not the God of Israel and the nations, as if He had not chosen Israel for the express purpose that she be a blessing to all nations."

Now then, Jesus rode into Jerusalem on a donkey, Himself the sacrifice to bring peace to all peoples of the earth. That is why He turned against the money-changing practice of the Zealots and cleansed the temple of it, appealing to the words of Isaiah and Jeremiah: "Is it not written, 'My house shall be called the house of prayer?' But ye have made it a den of thieves" (Mark 11:17). His action was not only taking a stand against the Zealots and their way. It was also a direct confrontation with the highest Jewish authority of the day, namely, the high priest and the whole priestly hierarchy. His quoting the words of Isaiah and Jeremiah must be heard as a direct judgement on their luxurious way of living in the midst of a poverty-stricken people and a devastating criticism of their power politics as well. By their course of action they thwarted the purpose of God for Israel, namely, that she, living in true freedom and deliverance, would be a light to the nations (according to Isaiah 49:6).

Thus Jesus brought His attack on the powers ultimately to the Jewish power center of the temple, so that the words of Luke 1:52 might be fulfilled: "He hath put down the mighty from their seats, and exalted them of low degree." Because He would not withhold His love from His enemies, He chose His own peculiar way to this end. Thus He took His stand with the least of His brothers and was obedient unto death, even the death of the cross. The church has confessed through the centuries that He expressly went this way for the redemption of Israel and the nations. For that reason God gave Him a name above every name, that is to say, the decisive place in the history of man. Only He is the Prince of Peace, to whom is given all power for establishing peace. Real peace can come to this world only in His name and in following Him.

Kraybill ([1978]): 72-74

March 15

Meeting Places
Jacob J. Enz, United States, 1957

You will recall that the Pharisees came to Jesus and asked Him about His authority in connection with His cleansing the temple, and He made this statement: "Destroy this temple, and in three days I will raise it up" (John 2:19). But they missed the point. He was talking about His body; they were thinking about an earthly building.

*

So Jesus in the purity of His own flesh and in the constant outgoing of His own love, the expression of the love of the Father, turned His very body into the eternal temple. This temple makes possible the meeting of the enemy—the sinner, the man who is going in the opposite direction from God, yet who got his very existence and his body from God—and the God who is constantly in search of him.

This brings us to the concern of our irresponsibility and idolatry. When we see no more in the temple or our churches than mere buildings, and if we have not that similar concern to carry about in our very body churches, meeting places between man and God, then our churches and our bodies become an idol. We use them to exalt self and perpetuate barriers. They become ends in themselves.

Rather, our bodies, like the body of Christ, are to be a battleground where the trying conflicts of our time are staged. These conflicts are to be fought not at arm's length taking up the weapons of nature, but within our hearts, as we separate ourselves from the world in order that we may gather into our arms that same sinful world in reconciliation. That is what our bodies are to be. They are to be living replicas of the tabernacle and the temple. We should come to think more and more when we say "church," not of brick and mortar, but of flesh and blood. For while flesh and blood express the depths of collapse of God's creation on one hand, in Christ they express also the signal victory of God's creation.

You and I, then, are to regard our lives as the meeting places, as the battlegrounds for these conflicts so that they do not spread out into the realm of the shedding of blood with human instruments of destruction. This helps us to understand what Paul meant when he said that we struggle not against flesh and blood, but against principalities, against powers, against the hosts of wickedness in heavenly places. Therefore, he suggests the suitable instrument to cope with the true nature of the enemy, the breastplate of righteousness. If we are contaminated, we are ineffective. The sword of the spirit which is the word of God, our feet shod with the preparation of the gospel of peace—both are the instruments of personality rather than the physical instruments of destruction, and they alone have the promise of victory.

Enz (1972): 66-68

March 16

Living Sap
Andreas Ehrenpreis, Slovakia, 1650

*T*he fig tree was not cursed on account of bad or poisonous fruit. It was condemned to wither away because it could have borne good fruit and did not do so. Out of repentance and turning around must come good fruit. A new life that does not produce good fruit is not genuine. The Baptist tells us what this good fruit is: giving away your second coat and feeding those in need. Faith is power, the power that gives strength to bear fruit. Then we will provide food and drink and clothing, and our labor as well, for those who need it. Then we will put love for the brothers and for all men into practice. And then, if we are consistent in this service, we will become simple and modest in our own needs. This surrender will not let us become lazy or unfruitful. That is the fruit that God demands. That is the fruitfulness brought about by brotherly love, the living sap of the new tree.

In such a life, God and the brothers and sisters become greater than everything else. Whoever is not ready for this remains blind and unpurified. All talk of Christ remains aimless talk and idle opinion as long as our thoughts and longings are concerned with personal aims arising from our worldly condition. Only faith that brings forth love opens the door to that other Kingdom in which Jesus is Ruler. Jesus, our Healer and Savior, leads the way into this new life and Kingdom.

Hutterian Brethren (1978): 31-33

Actions Which Teach

Pilgram Marpeck, Switzerland(?), 1542

*T*he Evangelists, and especially John, indicate that the Lord, when He was gathered with His own in the evening meal, proceeded quite corporally and lovingly with both works as well as words. He stopped at nothing to demonstrate His great love (which He had toward His own) through service. It was inadequate for the Lord to address His followers with physical words, consoling and encouraging them, or even to indicate His willingness to give His life for them. Rather, He lowered Himself to washing the feet of His disciples.

*

If we intend to preserve the Lord's Supper correctly, it is vital that we, by loving each other, diligently study and seriously follow the example of our Master. After Christ had washed His disciples' feet, He said, among other things: "I have left you an example, so that you, too, do as I have done to you" (John 13:15). The meaning of Christ's words, beyond a doubt, is to give all His apostles, who were prepared to die with Him, a clear understanding that they should observe the holy communion in His memory, as a model of love. Let us remember that the Lord's communion can rightly be seen as a physical meeting. When Christians assemble, they are to be girded with love for one another, in the same way as Christ loved them, in order that they might thereby confirm and reveal the love of believers *in Christ*.

Marpeck (1978): 264

An Unparalleled Example

John M. Brenneman, United States, 1866

*J*esus Christ is "meek and lowly in heart." Behold, what an unparalleled example of humility he left us when he, the Lord of lords and King of kings, washed his disciples' feet! How condescendingly our Lord and Master stooped and humbled himself. Greater humility, it seems to me, could not have been manifested than Jesus manifested on the occasion, when he said, "If I, then, your Lord and Master, have washed your feet, ye also ought to wash one another's feet. For I have given you an example, that ye should do as I have done to you." Are we, then, all perfectly willing thus to stoop and to humble ourselves in conformity to the example of Jesus? Oh, how many Christian professors there are who refuse to do this!

We should not, however, when we wash one another's feet, expect thereby to gain our salvation, nor is it for the purpose of washing away outward impurity from the feet; but simply to show *obedience, love* and *humility*; and to show that we are not ashamed of Jesus and of his words. For if we perform merely the outward act of washing one another's feet and have not a genuine *humility of heart* and sincere love towards each other, we shall not in the least be benefited by it; but rather thereby bring on ourselves greater sin. In *lowliness of mind* we should each esteem another better than himself. The richest and most highly esteemed should not think himself too good to stoop and wash the feet of the least and the poorest member. If Jesus had bid us do "some great thing," would we not do it? How much rather, then, since he has said, "Ye also ought to wash one another's feet," inasmuch as he has given an example that we should do as he has done; and says, "Learn of me; for I am meek and lowly in heart."

"He humbled himself and became obedient unto death, even the death of the cross" (Philippians 2:8). Oh! consider, then. For if Jesus, the Lord of Heaven, thus stooped and humbled himself, took on him the form of a servant, was spit upon, scourged and crucified for us to reconcile us and to redeem us from the curse and from death, how it becomes us to imitate his example and to follow his footsteps in humility!

Brenneman (1866): 35, 36

March 19

A Much Higher and More Spiritual Meaning

Joseph Funk, United States, 1857

*F*rom this passage of the Word of God (John 13:1-17), it is evident that Christ Jesus washed his disciples' feet with his own hands, and also told them to wash one another's feet. But from certain circumstances, the writer is inclined to believe that there is a much higher and more spiritual meaning attached to it by Christ Jesus our Lord—and which he intended to convey to his disciples—than the literal washing of one another's feet with water.

When Peter said, "Thou shalt never wash my feet," and Christ told him, "If I wash thee not thou hast no part in me," and, "What I do thou knowest not now; but thou shalt know hereafter": these were figurative expressions and had allusion to Christ's sacrifice and his atoning blood, wherewith he would wash Peter (and of which Peter would stand in great need hereafter), and of which all believers and followers of Christ stand in need. And to this spiritual washing and the blood of sprinkling Christ alluded, when he said to Peter: "If I wash thee not, thou hast no part with me."

*

And may we not reasonably infer that Christ washed his disciples' feet that he might thereby signify the spiritual washing of the soul from sin? And is this not plainly intimated when Christ said unto Peter, "If I wash thee not, thou hast no part with me!" Here Peter was yet in the dark. He could not understand why Christ Jesus his Lord and Master should condescend so low as to wash his feet. He could not see the spiritual meaning of this. But there was something in it which he should hereafter know, as Christ said unto him, "What I do thou knowest not now; but thou shalt know hereafter." Thou wilt know how needful it will be for thee to be washed, after thou hast committed the heinous sin of denying that thou knowest me.

But see, when Christ told Peter, "If I wash thee not, thou hast no part with me," how ready Peter was to be washed: "Not my feet only, but also my hands and my head." But Jesus then said to him, "He that is washed needeth not save to wash his feet, but is clean every whit: and ye are clean, but not all" (John 13:10). This verse, we think, is the key to the whole meaning, purpose and aim, with reference to feet-washing. Christ said unto his disciples: "Now ye are clean through the word which I have spoken unto you. Abide in me and I in you. As the branch cannot bear fruit of itself, except it abide in the vine; no more can ye, except ye abide in me."

Funk (1857): 285-288

March 20

Committed to Participate
Hans Schlaffer, Austria, 1527

*T*he body of Christ is the faithful community of Christ. Whoever eats of this bread in the Supper of the Lord testifies that he desires to have fellowship with and to participate in all things with the body of Christ. That is, he commits himself to the community in all things: in love and suffering, wealth and poverty, honor and dishonor, sorrow and joy, death and life, indeed, that he is ready to give life and limb for the brothers, as Christ gave himself for him.

Similarly with the cup in the blood of Christ: whoever drinks of this cup has first surrendered himself and testifies with it that he is prepared to pour out his blood for the sake of Christ and his church insofar as faith and the test of love demands it.

Whoever gives his body and pours out his blood as indicated, he does not give his own life nor spill his own blood, but rather the body and blood of Christ. "For we are members of his body, indeed of his flesh and bone," says Paul. For this reason also Christ said to Paul when he called him on the way to persecuting the Christians: "Saul, Saul, why do you persecute me?" It is as if the Lord said: "Why do you kill my body and spill my blood?" Thus it is among the true Christians. If one of them suffers, they all suffer since they are all members of one another and of Christ the head. Thus also the head always suffers the most. Thus the Lamb has been slain from the beginning of the world and will thus be persecuted and killed. For as many of us as partake of the one bread and the one cup are all one bread and one body.

This is the test in which a man must persevere. Is he ready to be thus minded toward Christ the head and all his brothers and sisters as his members? Is he ready to be one member of this body and to remain and persevere to the end in all things that concern the body?

And this means discerning the body of Christ. But whoever eats and drinks alone has fellowship with Judas who also ate and drank with the other disciples from the bread and cup of the Lord. But he did not wish to participate in the common brotherly love but went and sought his own gain and sold the Lord.

Klaassen (1981b): 196, 197

March 21

In a Garden

Jan Philipsz. Schabaelje, The Netherlands, 1635

Simon Cleopas relates the account of Gethsemane to the Wandering Soul.

Simon Cleopas: With us the night was mostly spent in speaking of things divine, particularly at that time when Jesus prepared himself to leave this world. On yonder hill there was at that time a village called Gethsemane. There was a garden there, into which we often went to exercise ourselves in prayer; for it was a suitable, silent and solitary place.

*

On Thursday evening, when the passover had been prepared according to law, and after the same had been eaten, he with all the meek humility of a servant, subjected himself to his disciples, washed their feet, wiped them off, then again put on his clothes and in great solemnity broke the bread and divided it among us, and the cup likewise, and declared that in like manner he would offer up his body to be broken for us, which we did not at this time rightly understand. But when we saw his body hanging on the cross all torn and mangled, so that the blood streamed out of it like water, ah! then we understood what he meant by breaking the bread. Never before could we have imagined that the love of Christ was so great a mystery.

*

When he had secretly exposed his betrayer, who like a thief had been excluded, in order to accomplish his wicked design when he thought that now was the proper time to deliver him whom he had sold, Jesus, seeing that we were very sorrowful, comforted us like a father. O, I cannot describe how sweet the words were we heard at that time. When he went away we followed him, and he taught us on the road and told us of many future things, as he was wont to do, so that our hearts burned with love towards him and it seemed to us as if we could die for him. Peter, with a sword, went on before us as if he was willing to destroy all, but alas, it proved to be nothing but children's play, blindness and ignorance. In such cases other swords are to be made use of, such as this hero and captain of faith did afterwards use.

When we arrived in the aforementioned garden, he went away from us in great sorrow and prayed fervently, for anxiety and trouble had encompassed him. Life and death contended. His humanity placed before his view all the terrible sufferings, scourgings, shame and derision which the Jews would inflict upon him, and the dreadful agony of death. All these unjust judgments, pain and torments, which (had he been willing to avail himself of his power) he might have escaped, made his soul sorrowful unto death. However, his solicitude for our salvation and the saving of many thousands of souls by his sufferings, who would afterwards enjoy eternal happiness, bore him up amidst all this. Notwithstanding, he prayed to his heavenly Father that if it were possible, this cup might pass from him; and this he did three times.

O son, you may imagine what agony he suffered, when his sweat like drops of blood fell on the earth; and had not an angel from heaven strengthened him, his sufferings would have been still greater. At last he ceased to contend with death and resigned himself to the will of his heavenly Father who, by his eternal wisdom, had ordered these sufferings to befall him; and by this, his obedience, he regained what Adam, by his disobedience, had lost. Adam, contrary to the will of God, fulfilled the will of the flesh, and thereby inherited death. Christ, contrary to the will of the flesh, fulfilled the will of God and, as said, regained what Adam had lost. Both happened in a garden, and affected all mankind.

Schabalie ([1834]: 310-313

Falling Is Not Lying Down
Menno Simons, Germany, 1558

Certain sins may arise unpremeditately when we are unthinkingly surprised. Of this kind we have a good example in Peter. For when the Lord said to him, "Simon, Simon, behold Satan hath desired to have thee, that he may sift thee as wheat; but I have prayed for thee, that thy faith fail not; and when thou art converted, strengthen thy brethren," he replied with confidence, "Although all shall be offended, yet will not I. Lord, I am ready to go with thee, both into prison and to death, and to give my life for thee."

Peter was ready to go through thick and thin with his Master, he thought. But as soon as he stood alone, he could not endure a single question put to him by a simple maid. He openly forsook the Christ with whom the evening previous he had said he was ready to die. Yes, he was so disturbed and frightened that he began to curse and swear that he did not know Christ.

O God! there lay the confident, bold Peter, the firm rock, now broken. Although he had been taught by the heavenly Father just previously, and had been honored by Christ, the beloved Son of God, with the promise of the keys of the kingdom of heaven, yet he could not endure the trifling impact of such a flimsy arrow on his shield. Behold, so altogether little, poor, miserable, ill and impotent is that man (especially in great need) who is not strengthened by the Spirit of God. But what was it? Peter had to learn what that man is who depends upon his own strength, and not in the fear of God, on Christ and His grace. Besides he had to learn how to be compassionate and merciful toward his poor, fallen brother, who would repent heartily and rise without hypocrisy from his fall.

I do believe that this may justly be called a case of sudden surprise in Peter. For there had not been a single thought in his heart before to deny his Lord and Savior. And he also rose from his fall at once and went out and wept bitterly, and on the third day he was again comforted with the Gospel by the holy angels of the Lord.

Now notice what Paul teaches, Brethren, if a man be overtaken (observe that he says, overtaken) in a fault, ye which are spiritual (note this) restore such a one (notice again) in the spirit of meekness (notice once more) considering thyself (ponder this), lest thou also be tempted (notice this finally).

Elect brethren in the Lord, I would then admonish you in Christ Jesus by the words of Paul and by the fall of Peter, by all means to distinguish in the spirit of wisdom, between falling and lying. For he who lies down in sin, to which eternal death attaches, he is already condemned by the Scriptures. But he who falls into it by surprise, to him the prophet says, "Shall they fall and not arise?" And Paul says, "Restore such a one." Notice that. It is therefore helpful and proper that we be duly careful (I say, duly careful) and not depress such a poor surprised sinner who would so gladly be restored and rescued from his deplorable condition. But we must, in Christian meekness, extend to him the hand of love, lift him out of the mire and help him to bear his burden as much as we can, and as far as our consciences and the Word of God permit. Ah, take heed.

Be not too stern in such a case, lest you also be tempted, as Paul states. Let our high and holy Peter admonish you, in order that you may not lose yourselves in your proud minds. For if a man thinketh himself to be something when he is nothing, he deceiveth himself.

*

Let everyone examine himself carefully whether he has, since his conversion, sinned before God and become a broken vessel. He that thinks it is not so, let him cast the first stone. But he that knows it to be so, let him with Peter strengthen his weak brother, who perhaps has not sinned half so heinously as he.

Menno (1956): 984, 985

The Only Way
Jörg Wagner, Germany, 1527

Although not an Anabaptist himself, but a radical Lutheran, Jörg Wagner was esteemed as a martyr for the gospel by the Anabaptists. His story is told in the Martyrs Mirror, *and the following hymn is found in the* Ausbund.

He who would follow Christ in life
Must scorn the world's insult and strife,
And bear his cross each day.
For this alone leads to the throne;
Christ is the only way.
 Christ's servants follow him to death,
 And give their body life and breath
 On cross and rack and pyre.
 As gold is tried and purified
 They stand the test of fire.
Renouncing all, they choose the cross,
And claiming it, count all as loss,
E'en home and child and wife.
Forsaking gain, forgetting pain,
They enter into life.

Klaassen (1981b): 88

The Sacrifice of Freedom
Z. Marwa Kisare, Tanzania, mid-1900s

*P*eople take Jesus' death as a traditional religion. They do not realize that in his death is the power to set them free. So this is why nothing has changed in all these years since the gospel has been preached in this land. People think that those who preach the gospel are just doing it to benefit their own villages. 1 Peter 1:12 makes it clear that those who preach the gospel do it for the benefit of those on the outside who hear and not for their personal benefit.

I do not preach the gospel the way a farmer sells sugar cane. The farmer sells his sugar cane so he can get money to benefit himself and his village. Preaching the gospel is not this way. We preach in the hope that you, people for whom I would have no concern in the traditional way, will understand and accept the message and be set free to become part of God's new family. Even if only one person receives this message and is set free, then this land of Buturi is blessed.

God's people who have already died, millions and millions of them in heaven, are continually singing the praises of Jesus whose sacrifice set them free. At the moment of Jesus' death, at the ninth hour, there was a quaking of the earth. The soil itself and the trees cried out in joy. Why? Because from the time of Adam's sin, all of creation was under a curse. Now Jesus has set creation free and the earth, trembling, cried out, "Son of God, you have returned us to our former state!"

All of the religious things we do only box us in if we have not understood and appropriated Jesus' sacrifice for us. This I know is the truth, that through Jesus, those fences which held us in our traditional circles were torn down and we were set free to enter into a new and right relationship with each other and with God.

This work of Jesus is a miracle. How can I explain it? Take a cow. I do not know how a cow can eat grass and drink water and produce milk. It is not for me to know how that happens. All that is needful for me to have health is to milk the cow and drink the milk. The lake is full of water. I do not know how the water came to be there or of what water is made. To have life I do not need to know these things. All I need is to go to the lake with my vessel, draw and drink. This is how it is with Jesus' sacrifice. It is the power of God to save us. How it happens I do not know. What I know is that when I appropriate that sacrifice I am made whole.

Shenk (1984): 179, 180

March 25

Where To Find Jesus

Jakob Denner, Germany, ca. 1707

*T*hese women bought spices in order to anoint Jesus' body, for they thought he was still dead. From this we can see their pure and substantial love for Jesus. For they loved him not only in life but also in death.

*

They genuinely loved Jesus and remained true to him in life, in suffering and in death. So it is really no genuine love when or if we love Jesus only in good days when things go well for us, when we have much wealth and an overabundance of temporal things; but when crosses, need, misery, attacks, persecution, need and such like that come upon us and into our lives we turn away from him.

But it is the true kind of love when in all kinds of suffering and reproaches from within and from without we remain with him continually and dependably, when the love within us overcomes everything, so that "neither death nor life, neither angels nor principalities, nor powers, nor things present nor in the future, neither height nor depth, nor any other creature can separate us from the love of God, which is in us through Christ Jesus" (Romans 8:38, 39).

*

They wanted to anoint Jesus. Jesus is now in glory; so for this reason it is impossible for us to give him this kind of service of love. If we want to do this it must take place in his members. Fortunate are those rich persons who are in control of their earthly possessions that they can apply these things for the good of Christ's poor but genuine members: Those who feed the hungry or clothe the naked, give drink to the thirsty, minister to the sick and visit them, and show mercy and love to those who are within their reach.

Fortunate, I say, are those who together with these holy women anoint the body of Jesus. Jesus will raise them up on the day of judgment and they will hear the voice saying, "Come, ye blessed of my Father, inherit the kingdom that is prepared for you from the beginning of the world" (Matthew 25:34-36, 40), and if we cannot do this in deed, let us do it in word, in prayer, in giving comfort and in giving such help and service as we can in whatever way we can.

*

So let us then find Jesus here in this world of time so that we may also find him and be joined with him as well in eternity, that we may be eternally satisfied and made alive through him, that God, even our God may have eternal praise and honor for the eternal salvation of our souls. Amen.

Denner (1707): 359, 360, 374, trans. by Noah G. Good

March 26

Who Shall Roll the Stone?
Bernhard Harder, Russian Empire, ca. 1880

Who shall roll the stone from the closed tomb for us, when our soul languishes for Jesus, when no pleasure of this earth, when no gift delights the eye which weeps for Him? The heart which has broken with the world, which seeks Jesus and considers him only, and which has appropriated the forgiveness of sins—who shall roll the heavy stone from his tomb?

O see there! The stone has already disappeared. For Jesus lives; the One who died for you; the one who conquered victoriously the might of the devil—yours is the salvation which Jesus obtained. He died for you, and for you He rose again; for you He then took over heaven, and lovingly He now looks down upon you. Behold, where is the heavy stone?

Who shall roll away the heavy stone of sins? Who shall break in me the power of darkness? And even if I should find in Him forgiveness, who shall make me strong and steady my foot? O, will I not again fall daily and in the end nevertheless be lost? Who shall save me from all sins? Who shall roll away the heavy stone of sins?

O see there! The stone which pressed upon you so heavily is no longer there! After your Savior rose so victoriously the entire burden, if you believe it, has disappeared. He grants you righteousness and He imbues you with power to fight and to conquer. Awake, my soul! Rejoice in His peace and see—where is the stone of sins?

Who shall roll away from my breast the stone of the dark cares of life? Who shall still my sorrow? My Easter morning is overcast by sadness which my soul carried with it. Because of worries, grief, sorrow and misery my Good Friday will not end! Who shall help me? Who shall roll with strong hands from my heart this stone of cares?

O see there! Do not despair but believe! The stone is rolled away; it is gone. With courage leave the dust of this earth and trust the sure Word of God: He will not forsake you nor neglect you; He has prepared for you already the wind of Easter. Whatever still weighs upon you, He shall remove away. O see there! Where is the stone of cares?

Who shall roll away the stone from the grave of my hopes when base ingratitude seeks to hurt me? When I am hated, persecuted and cursed where I have loved and blessed? When with my childlike, believing trust my hope threatens to cave in? Where shall the eye look up in hope? Who shall roll away the stone of fearful doubts?

*

O risen Lord! Lead me poor sinner through your death to victory and life! Some day you, conqueror of death, shall roll away the last stone, the sleep of death. Then I shall stand transformed in your light, free from the pain of sin, cares and misery, singing that all of heaven shall resound! Halleluja! Deep down below the stone has rolled away!

Friesen (1978): 955, 956

March 27

Look to Our Risen Lord

H. Frances Davidson, United States, 1894

*E*very Easter brings to our minds afresh the blessed truth of a risen Lord. It tells us that our Mediator is seated on the right hand of the Father. If we observe the day at all, we should observe it with all the significance due unto the important event it commemorates.

*

Historians tell us that the early Christian church had no special days for celebration; it was a thought entirely alien from their minds. This is at least true among the churches of the Gentile Christians. Gradually, however, some of the festival days connected with the Jewish ceremonies were added to the Christian worship; not with their old formal significance, but with a newer and more spiritual meaning. In this manner Easter, so closely associated with the Jewish Passover, became the most noted among Christian holidays.

Chrysostom in commenting on the subject very aptly emphasizes the thought that "the whole of time is a festival unto Christians, because of the excellency of the good things which have been given." Every day brings with it many blessings, a fact which we are liable to overlook when we begin to set apart certain commemorative days.

Since, however, the anniversary of Christ's resurrection is so near at hand, I wish to emphasize a thought in connection with it. It is well for us to bow at the foot of the cross, to learn meekness and obedience, to crucify the flesh with the affections thereof, to die unto self. But Christ would also have us rise with Him. We are to leave those things which are behind and press forward. There is much greater enjoyment in store for us Christians than we usually permit ourselves to enjoy.

Let us look away from self to our risen Lord seated on the throne of His glory, and so shape our lives that they may be fashioned after His glorious one.

*

O, that we might arise, and shake off the lethargy which has fallen upon us and walk in newness of life! May the resurrection of our Savior have a higher significance to us than ever before. May we arise from the dead and receive the life of Christ in our souls.

Davidson (1894): 84

March 28

The Resurrection According to Matthew
James and Jeanette Krabill, Côte d'Ivoire, 1984

March 18: Today, just two weeks before the beginning of Holy Week festivities, death hit the village when our neighbor, Pita, left this world to join the next.

March 19: As Dida tradition prescribes, on the night before burial the body is placed outside on a spacious double bed in the courtyard of the deceased and the the entire community gathers around to pass the night in singing. Mama and Papa put Matthew and Elisabeth Anne to bed a bit early tonight and left them for several hours in the care of Lassina—a Muslim friend from Mali who sometimes helps with work around the place—in order to attend the "death watch."

March 20: This morning was Pita's funeral service and burial and Matthew accompanied his Mama and Papa throughout the entire affair, even walking the long distance in the scorching mid-day sun to the cemetery and back again. Most folks came dressed in black or dark blue, and before the service assembled quietly around Pita's bed to pay last respects. Pita's sister sat beside her brother on the bed, wiping his brow and chasing away a growing number of flies also drawn to the occasion. "Fight, fight the war for me!" the choir sang in muted voices and without the usual musical instruments. "It is you, my God, who can fight for me!"

When the body had been washed and placed in the casket, the mourners proceeded to the church in two long lines—men on the right, women on the left—on either side of Pita. "Women of Honor," dressed in black uniforms, led the way carrying bouquets of freshly cut flowers to be spread about Pita's grave. We paused for several brief moments at the church to offer final prayers. The middle row of benches had been removed to make way for the casket. Everywhere were signs of sadness. The sanctuary candles remained flameless, the flower pots flowerless, and the floor unswept. Across the altar was draped a large black cloth in place of the usual white one. Preacher Alphonse's comments were short and barely audible; from where he stood, only snatches reached us. Matthew, normally bubbling with questions, was caught up in the solemnity of the occasion. He remained silent and like the rest of us simply moved along with the flow of things until Pita had been lowered into the ground and we had headed for home.

April 1—Good Friday: The practice here on Good Friday is to reenact a funeral—the funeral of Jesus. And so today we did it all over again. Black dress, muted singing, the symbolic removal of the benches and freshly cut flowers (deposited this time at the foot of the altar). We explained the rerun to Matthew by telling him that Jesus had died and that on this day, all other activity ceased in order to think about His passing. "You mean Jesus is like Pita?" Matthew wanted to know. "He's like Pita lying there on his bed?" "Yes," we said, "Jesus is like Pita lying there on his bed."

April 3—Easter Sunday: Easter morning! We got up and began preparing for church. This day, we knew, would be one of great joy! There would be singing. Dancing. Bright flowers and palm branches decorating the sanctuary. And the musical instruments would be back in full force! We dressed the children in their little white outfits prescribed for the day. "Hey, why aren't we wearing dark clothing?" asked Matthew, confused by his revolving wardrobe. "Because Jesus isn't dead any longer," we replied. "He's come back to life!" Matthew stopped, reflected for a moment and then with a burst of inspiration added, "Jesus isn't on the bed anymore!" "No," we said, "Jesus isn't on the bed anymore!"

Krabill and Krabill (1984): 43

It Was Impossible for Him to Conceal His Love

Jan Philipsz. Schabaelje, The Netherlands, 1635

Simon Cleopas tells the Wandering Soul of the day Jesus appeared to a group travelling on the road to Emmaus.

Simon Cleopas: The sheep were bleating but the shepherd seemed not to hear them. The bride sought her beloved with tears, but he concealed himself. The children wept bitterly, and appeared to be forsaken of the father, because they heard not his voice. But pay attention to wondrous things. North of us is a desolate hamlet, called Emmaus. Thither went my father in company with others to his place of residence. There the fields were beautifully green with grain and grass, olive and fig trees lining the road on either side; the birds were warbling, chirping and basking in the mid-day sun.

But all this did not comfort them. Their hearts were heavy and full of sorrowing. They seemed to be in deep despair and all their hopes were blasted. They were reflecting on the promises made of the Messiah, who was to sit on the throne of David and rule the Gentiles and redeem Israel from the dominion of their enemies; who was to be, like Solomon, a peaceful king and rule them with wisdom and righteousness. They thought that Jesus was to do all this: but alas, their hopes were blasted. The Gentiles conquered him, and he was mocked by every one and shamefully nailed to the accursed wood, quite differently from what they anticipated.

In addition to this, their minds were also exceedingly perplexed on account of what they heard from the women. When their minds were thus perplexed, Jesus appeared to them as an unknown Joseph, to feed them with spiritual food. He appeared to them a stranger—as one ignorant of all that had taken place—and they told him all that had transpired. But he instructed them that they looked too prematurely for this kingdom, that they had not taken the cross into consideration, which, according to the prediction of the prophets, was to precede their anticipated joy. These words burned within them. They were convinced that he had spoken the truth; but they did not know whence he had this knowledge. Their hearts were most powerfully drawn to this pilgrim. He appeared to them a wonderful person!

The day drew to a close. It was time to bid each other good night, but this was impossible. They invited him to tarry all night with them. He was persuaded. Then there happened a greater wonder still: the table was set, and instead of holding a long conversation, he lifted his eyes to heaven in devotion and then broke the bread. After this they immediately recognized him whom they had with them; and as they were falling on his neck to kiss him, he vanished.

And then they thought on what the women had told them, and were exceedingly sorry that they did not believe what they said. For they now had seen him themselves, and their hearts were filled with the burning rays of the power of his words.

Schabalie ([1834]): 336-338

March 30

Testimony of Two Disciples
Yorifumi Yaguchi, Japan, 1987

On the Emmaus road
without realizing it
we spoke with Jesus—told him
what had happened in the capital
complained about the absence of God

We never recognized
this familiar figure
this familiar voice
When we arrived at the village
we sat down to eat, and then

our eyes opened
We saw the one we were with
was Jesus
So preoccupied with
human thoughts,

we never dreamt
the man who died
was walking with us
how often will he walk with us
on the road?

Perhaps not until the great banquet at world's end
will we know how many times he has walked with us

Yaguchi (1989): 47

The Emmaus Road

Joyce M. Shutt, United States, ca. 1980

*T*wenty-two years ago, my father had surgery for cancer of the colon. The night before his surgery he called us all together, talked with us and told us what he wanted done if he did not survive.

I've come to look back on that evening as one of the high points in my relationship with my parents. Dad's quiet acceptance of death, his lack of fear, his faith in God, his being at peace with himself and the life he'd lived with all its successes and failures struck a deep chord within me. Never again would I fear dying as I had before, for his modeling showed me something about what it means to live.

That evening in the hospital room, Dad asked that we read the Emmaus Road story at his funeral. When the time comes, we will.

*

The Emmaus Road story is a beautiful paradigm of life for all of us. Most of the time, we are like Cleopas and his friend who get too close to their own experiences and feelings to be able to understand what is happening to them and around them. They, like us, needed someone from the outside who could help them look through different eyes.

*

Living is a continuous experience in death and resurrection. As experiences impinge on us, the person we are is changed. A new me emerges, only to change and reshape. Our modern social patterns often make that natural sequence of death and resurrection difficult. We no longer allow each other the time that is often required to experience rebirth (or change). When the hard times come—and they are inevitable—we are encouraged to avoid confronting ourselves and the real issues. Instead, we are pushed to, or conclude that the only manageable option is to move on to new friends, new marital partners, new churches, new homes. . . .

*

In the 43 years that I've known my parents, there have been many ups and downs. I can recall violent arguments between them. I can recall days when they barely spoke to each other, days when the tension was so thick one became almost paralysed from it. Also, I recall days of infinite tenderness, of life-enriching love, of laughter, of quiet serenity, of fun and relaxation, challenge and affirmation. Like the night (in the hospital) Dad spoke of the possibility of his impending death and the modeling that offered. I remember, during my ten years at home, the difficulties Dad and Mother encountered in their own mid-life crises. What a pleasure now to see them enjoying each other, being affectionate, doing tasks together, reveling in shared activities, many of them newly discovered. Those memories—of the bad times, the pain and struggle, the anger, hatred, violence and despair—have known redemption through resurrection into renewed commitment and love.

Those memories, more than anything else, have kept me going during the long, dark nights of my own marriage and family trauma. For my parents modeled in the most dramatic way—through their own experience—that there are solid reasons for not separating when love, hope, passion and dreams seem to be gone. They modeled that commitment to a partner does not need to correspond with devaluing self, giving up personal interests or becoming less than one can become. In their own way, they have been the familiar stranger (unrecognized until later) walking the Emmaus Road with me (and how many others?), explaining the mysteries of life, marriage, fidelity, commitment, friendship through the lens of their own experience.

*

Along the Emmaus Road the stranger spoke to Cleopas and his friend of the mystery of life, of death and resurrection, of hope and promise in spite of fear and pain. Death and resurrection. How often must we die? How often do we need to go through the awful pangs of giving up what we've loved and valued to reach for the unknown and new? Just as often as our hopes, dreams, aspirations and needs interfere with the unfolding and growth of loved ones around us. As long as our insistence on one pattern prevents ourselves or others from experiencing newness and recreation of life.

Death and resurrection. The end and the beginning. One blends into another so smoothly that knowing where one stops or begins may be difficult. But one surety remains: death and resurrection, or buffeting and reshaping, is part of God's plan for our lives. As we daily die, may we rise to celebrate and affirm the wonder of God's world and life for each of us!

Nyce (1983): 145-147

April

April 1

A Time to Laugh
E. J. Swalm, Canada, 1969

*I*t has long been a subject of controversy as to whether or not a Christian should indulge in humor. Some outstanding church leaders and theologians of the last century have been generally opposed to any statements or attitudes that provoked levity. It should not be forgotten that in this generation we are likely to push the pendulum to the opposite position. Some observant people beyond middle life have been more or less perplexed theologically and otherwise by drastic swings. We learn so little from history.

The number of those already mentioned who insisted on rigid austerity has dwindled to a mere minority. A few religious kill-joys, however, are still with us. I confess I have difficulty in understanding them.

I am not sure their reactions are the result of physical, mental, super-sanctimonial or negative processes. I have wondered if some good people, who seldom see the funny side of anything, could be affected with an ultra bilious religion—a problem of the liver rather than of the heart or mind. I have prayed with people at public altars whom I felt needed a medical doctor or professional counselor as much as a preacher.

Jesus spoke of those who strain at a gnat and swallow a camel, people who would remove a sliver from their brother's eye when there is a whole saw-log in their own eye. Such proponents of super-sanctity only enjoy a joke when they tell one themselves. As a young Christian, my feet, like David's, "had well nigh slipped" as I was confused by such inconsistencies.

(None of the above, of course, refers to the mentally ill.)

I shall always feel grateful to God for the well-poised saints to whom I have been exposed throughout my life. They were people who could laugh and cry, pray and sing, work and play in well-balanced proportions.

One of the best definitions of humor I have heard is, "Humor is the ability to see yourself focused over against any unusual situation."

It is a great blessing to be able to laugh. We should be able to laugh at ourselves. Whether our laughing pleases God or not depends on when we laugh and what we laugh at. A healthy sense of humor helps prevent people from taking themselves too seriously.

Swalm (1969): 135, 136

God's Word Stands Sure Forever

Balthasar Hubmaier, Moravia, late 1520s

Rejoice, rejoice, ye Christians all,
    And break forth into singing!
Since far and wide on every side
    The Word of God is ringing.
And well we know, no human foe
    Our souls from Christ can sever;
For to the base, and men of grace,
    God's Word stands sure forever.

Jesus the Christ, of Mary born
    And of the Holy Spirit
What all the prophets promised
    We shall in him inherit.
"Hear him," the call of God to all,
    to save us his endeavor;
To him all praise and honor raise—
    God's Word stands sure forever.

Now hear, now hear, and mark with care
    What else for us is written,
And learn from his new covenant
    What more to do we're bidden.
And what of old has been foretold
    Of Christ our Lord and Savior;
To latest hour, in vaster power,
    God's Word stands sure forever.

Ah, man, blind man, now hear the Word,
    Make sure your state and calling;
Believe the Scripture is the power
    By which we're kept from falling.
Your valued lore at once give o'er,
    Renounce your vain endeavor;
This shows the way, no longer stray,
    God's Word stands sure forever.

O Jesus Christ, thou Son of God,
    Let us not lack thy favor,

For what shall be our just reward
>If the salt shall lose its savor?
With angry flame efface thy name
>In vain shall men endeavor;
Not for a day, the same for aye,
>God's Word stands sure forever.

Praise God, praise God in unity,
>Ye Christian people sweetly,
That he his Word has spread abroad—
>His Word, his work completely.
No human hand can him withstand,
>No name how high soever;
And sing we then our glad Amen!
>God's Word stands sure forever.

Hubmaier (1989): 569-571

April 3

Messages of the Risen Christ

Sally Schreiner, United States, 1982

We have a Risen Christ whose appearances are chronicled in six or more stories in the four Gospels and Acts. He spent the next forty days in a variety of ways, appearing to a variety of followers. Combining his messages into one is difficult because he was speaking to different needs and orientations of his followers. I am aware that you, too, are followers with different needs and different orientations. Therefore, as you hear my account of his messages to his diverse hearers, try to decide what messages the Risen Christ is speaking to you—in your distinctness, as you journey.

One message recorded in Luke 24:13-32 tells of the two disciples on the road to Emmaus. I characterize them as students of current events—observers and political analysts. They observe the events of the times and draw conclusions, but their understanding of these events is very limited. To them, Jesus says: You foolish men, "*See me.*"

You are so into your own interpretation of events that you don't recognize who walks beside you. You don't see God's will fulfilled in Christ's suffering. Your perception only goes so far—open your eyes.

*

Another message, John 20:24-29, reports one of Jesus' two appearances to the eleven disciples in the locked upper room. This is the first time Thomas sees Christ. Thomas is the down-to-earth type who dwells in the realm of the concrete physical detail, facts and evidence. I picture him as practical, solid, earthy and much given to saying, "I'll have to see it to believe it." To him, Christ says, "*Have faith in me.*" Take a risk, Thomas, a leap out into the unknown. I'm willing to meet you where you are right now and let you put your hands on the proof you seek. But, hey, how about growing in belief?

*

John 21:1-19 records what I think is the climactic appearance of Jesus. This account focuses on Peter, the man of actions, the impulsive, blunt and spontaneous fellow. He doesn't waste a lot of time thinking or analyzing. His motto might read, "If it feels right, do it. If it needs saying, say it." As we look at his conversation with Christ on the beach, what is going on?

Christ's central message to Peter is "*Love me.*" But why does he say it to him three times? One reason might be to give Peter three chances to clear his conscience of the three times he denied Christ. Another explanation is that Peter was thick-headed. If Jesus wanted the message to get through, he needed to repeat it. If you neglect someone you honestly care for, chances are you will be impressed by repeated calls to clarify your stance.

What then is the message? "Do you love me more than all else?" This is the fundamental question. He follows by saying, in essence, "Okay, then here's how you can show it to me: Feed my lambs. Tend my sheep. Feed my sheep." Loving always precedes doing. Authentic love persists in spite of the consequences. Jesus concludes: "*Follow me.*" This resembles his first recorded words to Peter. The journey continues. Motivation for following and feeding is love, all-out love for Jesus.

Matthew 28:16-20 expresses Jesus' great commission to all disciples. These are his final instructions, the marching orders, delivered to those who have been spectators in the stands as he has played out his battle with the forces of evil and death.

This group of disciples (which spans all time to include us as well) can be likened to the fans who left the game during the last quarter before the time clock ran out, because the team was doing so abysmally that there was no way they'd pull it out of the bag at the last minute...but hold everything! Even after all the fans had deserted the stadium, the home team won. Come back and see for yourself.

*

The Risen Christ's final earthly message is "*Witness about me.*" The Messiah has come. I've fulfilled the promise of the law and the prophets. All authority has been given to me. Death cannot hold me. You have nothing more to fear. Your sins are forgiven. Eternal life is yours. Celebrate. Don't hold this good news to yourself. Tell everyone. And one more thing, "I'm with you always." No more good-byes. I won't come to you in the bodily form you've been able to hear, see and touch. But I'll put my Spirit within you—thus spreading myself further than has yet been possible.

Nyce (1983): 70-72

The Winter is Past

Pilgram Marpeck, Germany, mid-1500s

The following meditation is steeped in the poetic imagery of the Song of Solomon.

*D*earest brothers and sisters in God, the desire of my heart, my prayer and my sighing to God for you and us is for that self-same love which fulfills everything in all. Yes, we may well say and pray with the Spirit in the Canticle: "Draw me after you, and we will follow." For truly, my dear ones, where love does not draw, our path is dangerous and hard. If love has not been placed over the vineyard of God to protect it, and if the vineyard does not bear the fruit of love, she does not protect it and allows it to be devastated.

However, where love is the protector of God's vineyard and brings fruit, and the friend lives behind us constantly, is behind all our action and looks for the fruit in the vineyard under the care of the keeper, the friend looks through the lattice, our flesh and blood, in which we are now imprisoned, into the heart. He replies to us and says to love who is our protectress:

"Arise, my friend, my fair one, and come to me. For behold, the winter is past, the rain is over and gone." That is, the previous destruction has been removed from us, so that now "the flowers appear in the land." They appear in his community through the protectress, which is love. Spring has arrived, the time to bring fruit to our God. "The turtledove," that is, the Holy Spirit acting through His Word and work in the hearts of the believers, "is heard in our land. The fig tree has developed buds," that is, the sweetness of the graciousness of God breaks out in his own. "The vines have sprouted blossoms and exude fragrance," that is, the planting of the heavenly Father which He has planted as the true Gardener in Jesus Christ, the true vine. The shoots from the vine which are planted are the true believers in Christ Jesus. Through the sap of grace from Christ the vine, they develop blossoms that they may see God's working in them through His plantings in Christ and give God praise, in Christ Jesus. As the Spirit says: "They give forth fragrance," and again the Spirit says in another passage: "Arise, My friend, My fair one, and come to Me."

Only that love is commanded which is the protectress of the vineyard and who brings the fruit of the vineyard of God with her as a sweet aroma. The Spirit speaks further: "My dove, in the clefts of the rock." This is only that love which is in Christ Jesus, the rock in whose clefts true love dwells. These clefts are his suffering, wounds, bloodshed and dying in which the believers in love have free security and rest from birds of prey, that is the devil and his seed which are enemies of love.

Again the Spirit says: "Let Me hear your voice, for your voice is sweet and your form is lovely." Here God demands the fruit as well as the voice from love, so that word and work agree. This voice is beautiful to God, and this form is lovely and pleasing.

Marpeck (1978): 518, 519

April 5

The Standpoint of Sojourners
Gilberto Flores, Guatemala, 1984

*I*t was of utmost importance to the apostles to remember that they were sojourners on earth and that their lives were to contrast with the surrounding world of that time.

This situation led them to speak to the reality of the world without losing their identity as children of God.

They proclaimed to the world the truth of the gospel of the kingdom, calling on all to use the ethical principles of Jesus Christ as a guide for all actions in life, not only with regard to sin in a subjective sense, but with the added urgency of also confronting social sins.

The apostles were moved by the desire to better the lives of people, demanding a personal commitment to Christ, inviting believers to live a consistent life characterized by equality, liberty, justice, forgiveness, reconciliation and a clear awareness of the realities of their surroundings.

They sought to have a church made up of disciples, for this was fundamental to the continuity of the church. For Peter, as for the rest of the apostles, the value of evangelism lay in a faith born of communion and strengthened by commitment, not necessarily in the number of believers.

They strove to maintain the vision of a church which understood its mission to be establishing a kingdom without manipulation, escapism or false hopes.

*

With regard to the role of the church in our time, one cannot speak of a message full of meaning or of a testimony laden with real compassion unless we as believers undertake a witness which responds to the needs of human beings today. The apostolic writings are full of a living witness, faith and steadfastness. We must remember that the task of witnessing was not easy. Wherever Christians went they were rejected as dissolute, atheist or depraved. They were labeled as "rebellious," and in some extreme cases killing them was seen as a service to God.

Their message had as its starting point the death of Jesus Christ, a criminal in the eyes of many. His death was nonsense for Greeks, a weakness for the Romans and heresy for the Jewish messianic understanding.

Surrounded by these attitudes, the disciples did not vacillate. They accepted the challenge of their age and triumphed with firm witness to this new faith born of the love of God, a faith which, although misunderstood, had to be accepted eventually as the only way of obtaining peace with God and the joy of a fulfilled life.

MWC ([1984]): 156, 160

April 6

"Give Us a Word of Love"
Helga Kremnitzer, Germany, 1948

"And this is his commandment, that we should believe in the name of his Son Jesus Christ and love one another, just as he has commanded us." —1 John 3:23

I should like to speak to you about some of the personal experiences I had back in Germany. There, right after the war, everything that had been built up without any Christian love broke into pieces. The results are hatred, jealousy and distress. German youth especially face a serious situation: all their ideals, for which most of them sacrificed all they had, proved to be wrong, to be delusion. Now many of them live without any goal to strive for, without any hope and very often without any faith. Many of them do not have a home or a place where they belong. They live in material and spiritual poverty. During those days right after the war they could not yet see a new way. But those days were a time of deliberation, too; in those days a German student sent a letter to America which expresses the feelings of most of the German young people. He wrote: "We all want to start a new life and you could help us with it. Give us a word of love." The youth of many foreign countries have heard that call and are willing to render their assistance.

A big help for German youth in accomplishing their conversion and in starting all over again is the work of the Mennonite Central Committee. In coming in contact with MCC workers many of our young people were surprised in the beginning to learn that there were young men and women overseas who came to the defeated country voluntarily to help and to try to heal the wounds of war. They were especially impressed by the fact that this help was given without any terms or political background, that it was given "In the Name of Christ."

Many of our youngsters were brought up without belonging to any church; many of them don't even know the Lord's Prayer. Now they experience for the first time the uniting power of Christian love which came to them through MCC. It is so new, so unbelievable, so overwhelming for them—and many start thinking seriously about that. An eighteen-year-old boy, for instance, said when he was invited to the school-feeding program: "Until now I did not believe in God. I had experienced human beings only as beasts and I thought that, therefore, there was no love in this world. Now I am starving and you came many, many miles across the ocean to feed me. Does that not prove that there is love, and that there is a living God in spite of all hatred and distress on earth?"

To me that is one of the best evidences in showing that the material help reaches much further, that it does not only cover material needs but spiritual needs, too. And it shows that there is not only hunger for bread in Germany, but that there is also hunger for the words of the Gospel.

Hiebert (1950): 311, 312

April 7

"Official Theology"
Hugo Zorilla, Colombia, 1989

We are faithful, committed and loyal to the truth of Jesus to the extent that our words and deeds are practiced here and now in the believing community. The liberating style of Jesus always makes sense in human history when it is applied in contexts of injustice and oppression. This reality demands that we abide in Jesus and in his love.

*

Today we must proclaim the God of life as the supreme cause of liberty and peace. The believing community should denounce all manipulation of the faith by governments and repressive systems that, in the name of God, kill and marginalize people. The contemporary "caesars" have also found an "official theology" that legitimizes and makes sacred any act that could be committed against human beings. Thus the state has been erected as a god that guarantees the privileges of the few, the "ruling" classes. The doctrines of the state are considered Christian, even though they serve to establish a repressive injustice. Perhaps that is why peace, life itself and existence as a human being appear as if they were a gift given by the oppressors.

Some insist that the hungry, the undernourished, the illiterate, the exploited and the unemployed should appreciate that at least they are alive—as if they should be thankful to the state for their inhuman miseries! The cynicism is greater on Christian lips which assure us that the poor are in that condition because they want to be, because they like to be poor, because they are accustomed to living with next to nothing or because their personal sin has kept them there. Social sin goes unquestioned, and the source of unjust prosperity goes undisputed.

Zorilla (1989): 169, 170

An Option for the Poor

Luis Elier Rodríguez, Puerto Rico, 1988

*J*ust as the Anabaptists of the sixteenth century refused loyalty to the feudal system that produced a society divided into classes of feudal lords and peasants, the Latin American neo-Anabaptists want to oppose divisions between rich and poor, and situations in which the poor suffer oppression and all its consequences.

The Anabaptist movement serves as an obvious model and inspiration for the Latin American Mennonite church. The Anabaptists refused to participate in the feudal government, presented the distribution of goods as an alternative to the feudal socio-economic structure, and did not swear oaths or go to war. They did so as a protest against feudal culture. Their refusal to baptize infants was a rejection of the official church and its feudal interests that legitimized the exploitation of the peasants by the feudal lords. Like their sixteenth century forebears, Latin American Mennonites are beginning to proclaim that Jesus and the Bible help to reorient the disciple and the life of the Mennonite church toward an option for the poor.

This is an option for those people tormented by sorrow, those martyred by suffering—that is, those who are marginalized. It is an option for people that do not cry necessarily for their sins but because of their condition as outsiders.

It is an option that the church faces in the context of dependency, underdevelopment and poverty in which Latin America exists. It is an option that brings the church to affirm that poverty is not innocent or neutral but that it is something fatal—destructive to life. The option for the poor should bring Mennonite believers to ethical and prophetic indignation, understanding that God does not want poverty because it is the fruit of great injustice that cries to heaven like the blood of Abel murdered by Cain.

Poverty is not something accidental. Moreover, the existence of the poor does not result from something missing on the part of a people, an inferiority or a lack of education. It is historically caused, the result of the rich countries that survive through political, economic and social structures that originate poverty.

Because of this, the question that arises among the Latin American Anabaptists for the Mennonites of the First World is, "What is the program of the Mennonite churches of the First World to be in solidarity with the poor?"

Rodríguez (1988): 20

A United "No" to Death

Dorothy A. Friesen, United States, 1980

*T*he story begins in Warman, Saskatchewan, where Mennonite farmers had dairies for a few generations. Eldorado Nuclear Corporation, a crown corporation in Canada, planned to build a uranium refinery on some of that dairy land. A development agency began buying options for the land. Some Mennonites sold, although they did not know what would be developed in their area. When they found out that uranium would be refined there, they began to raise questions.

*

Premier Blakeney of Saskatchewan told them that to withhold uranium for nuclear development in Third World countries was immoral. It doomed people in those countries to subsistence living. The people of Warman wanted to know what having nuclear reactors would mean for people living in the Philippines. They had heard that the Philippine and Canadian governments were talking about the sale of uranium for the newly-constructed nuclear plant in the Philippines. Because of their questions, we went to visit the little town of Morong just north of Manila, the capital city of the Philippines.

There we found fishermen, farmers and fear. The nuclear plant is being built between two earthquake faults on the slope of a volcanic mountain in an area where the tidal waves are pounding. Small bangus fingerlings, a favorite food, lived in the streams around the town. Because of the construction of the plant, the streams were muddied and the fingerlings died. Thirty-six families have already been moved off their land to make way for the plant, some without just compensation.

The people of Morong, like the people of Warman, were not told about the plant. They found out by accident. They raised questions and asked for public meetings to explain what this plant would mean in their lives. Sixty uniformed military men attended the meeting and intimidated the citizens. A Methodist pastor who raised questions about where the waste would be stored was told by a military officer at the meeting, "Why are you asking so many questions? You must be a subversive." A worker in the plant who asked too many questions was arrested, tortured and killed. Some of the core people of the opposition to the plant became very afraid and disappeared into the hills. One sympathizer, who had not been active in the organization, was picked up and killed.

We also found in Morong a basic Christian community. The base Christian communities are an exciting part of Filipino church life. They are essentially groups of ordinary people getting together to read the Bible, pray and take action together in economic or social projects.

*

In January of 1980 the Canadian federal government held hearings on placing a uranium refinery in Warman, Saskatchewan. The concerned citizens of Warman asked for some time within the hearings to discuss the moral questions. The federal panelists said that wasn't necessary. Though the hearings were supposed to be technical—on ecological and socioeconomic benefits—the people of Warman turned the hearings into a moral and ethical discussion. They wanted to say no to death.

Old men, housewives who had never spoken in public before, and small children stood to give their testimony of peace. Many of the people quoted the Bible and said, "We are a people of peace. We used to show our disagreement with war by refusing to send our sons. However, life has become more complex. Now the uranium we find in this area will be used for nuclear weapons to kill people. We say no to this."

Fathers talked about being stewards of the land, having received this land developed by their grandfathers and wishing to pass it on to their sons and grandsons in good condition. Students from the Swift Current Bible Institute and the Canadian Mennonite Bible College returned home, though they were in the middle of the semester, to support their families. One group brought a solar oven right in front of the chairman and through a one act drama proclaimed their willingness to change their lifestyle in order to find more peaceable ways to supply energy. One farm wife brought a tin of milk, a glass of wheat and strawberries, and placed them in front of the chairperson of the panel saying, "This is what grows on our land; we want to continue to raise it."

*

The community of Warman holds many traditional Mennonite values. They are a peaceable community. They concentrate on church life. They meet together, as do churches all over North America.

In the past they did not know they would be challenged by this uranium refinery. They simply tried to build a healthy church life which connected the demands of the gospel with their everyday social and economic life. Here were people who had thought about ethical implications of the gospel.

Nyce (1983): 84, 85

April 10

Enlightenment
Yorifumi Yaguchi, Japan, 1990

Why can't I be spiritually awakened to
understand that this world gets worse
as the inevitable result of evil
human nature? Why do I get angry with it so easily?

Why can't I retreat into a mountain
and enjoy the rest of my life, sipping wine,
looking at the moon and making haiku
like the one enlightened?

However hard and long I may raise
my insignificant voice of anger,
I know I cannot stop this stream;
but I cannot give it up.

Those who attained perfect enlightenment
yell at me from this world and the other,
"Hey! You have been a Christian for a
long time! How come you are not awakened yet!"

And I shout back to them, "Indeed, I haven't
attained enlightenment yet but I never
intend to! As long as I live, I will
continue to worry, get angry and shout!"

This is one of my recent poems. "Enlightenment" ("satori" in Japanese) is a
Buddhist term. I do not intend to attain enlightenment in a Buddhist sense. My
enlightenment is to follow Christ and go into the world. I do not want to separate
myself from the world. And in the face of mounting injustice and misery, I
would like to live with those suffering people, because Christ lives with them. I
often get lost, get angry, worry and make cries of protest, but Christ is with me
and soothes me.

Lichdi (1990): 39

April 11

I Beg Your Pardon
Jakob Waldner, United States, 1918

*Military conscription during the First World War wrought testing upon many young
men in Mennonite, Amish, Brethren in Christ and Hutterite groups. Some of the finest
testimonies of steadfastness (and even martyrdom) for the nonresistant faith were offered
by the Hutterites.*

*T*oday they called us to the office individually and asked whether we would
clean the hospital yard. Of the Hutterites, only the two Entz brothers were asked.
At 1 p.m. they called us together again and we walked two by two to the hill.

Peter Tschetter and I were at the head of the group. Thinking that this was supposed to be another march, we decided to go only far enough to see where it was leading. Then we discovered a major standing there on the hillside, who gathered around him about one hundred of us in a semicircle.

He made the following speech: "You are all registered soldiers according to the law. President Wilson is the highest authority in the United States. It has taken him six months to find noncombatant tasks for you. If you refuse now, you must know that you can be punished by death or life imprisonment in a penitentiary. Don't be such fools as to let this happen to you. Even a Christian can drive a car or take care of the sick or do something else. And now forget that I am a major and that you are soldiers and let us discuss this as friends. I am speaking today as the spokesman of our highest Army Chief. If anyone has anything to say, let him speak freely."

After that one man by the name of Moler stood up and said the following: "I beg your pardon for having to disagree with you, but you and I are two kinds of people. I am Christian-minded and you are worldly-minded. You cannot understand the situation as well as I can and I don't hold this against you. I have given myself to God on my knees, and He is the judge over the whole world. We must obey Him more than men. I now want to give a parable since you think that a Christian can help in the war without guilt. If one man buys powder or other explosive material, a second man transports the dynamite to the bridge, a third man sets the explosive, and the fourth man blows up the bridge, then tell me: Whom will the government arrest and punish? Only the fourth man, or all four of them?"

The major did not know what to reply and therefore said without thinking: "None of the men would be punished for this is wartime."

"Yes," Moler said, "if this were done to the enemy, the men would be praised for it."

The major left, quite bothered that he had made a slip. Thirteen signed their names for work in the camp and hospital. Today the major understood everything that we had to say. We were called five times today. May God continue to protect us as He has to the present. Amen.

Schlabach (1974): 97, 98

April 12

"I Have Always Felt the Support of a Loving Brotherhood"
Stephen Scott, United States, 1988

I had occasionally seen distinctively dressed people in town and was always impressed by their godly appearance. As a Christian I wanted to find out more about them. I wondered, could these people have the right idea? I read everything I could about these "plain people" and began subscribing to some of their magazines. This study resulted in more questions for those in my home church. Should Christians take part in war? Should we observe foot washing? Should Christian women wear a covering on their head? Would a uniform garb keep one from being caught up in the fashion world? The answers my church leaders gave me seemed weak and unconvincing. I began to seek fellowship elsewhere.

At first I attended a Mennonite church fairly close to my home. The people there were quite friendly and made me feel welcome. The a capella singing and kneeling for prayer seemed good to me. I felt especially attracted to the few members who wore plain garb. It bothered me that most of the people looked and lived little differently from those in the church from which I came.

My search took me further from home to the Amish and Mennonite community at Plain City, Ohio. Here I felt very much at home. I was able to attend church regularly by traveling with a family from Dayton who made the 60-mile trip every Sunday.

About this time Uncle Sam made his call. With God's help I secured a conscientious objector status with the draft board. This was somewhat difficult since I really didn't have church membership anywhere. I thought I would like to serve my alternate service in one of the larger "plain" communities. After an investigation trip to Pennsylvania, a 1-W job was quite providentially opened at Lancaster Mennonite High School.

*

After attending the River Brethren church for about six months, I asked for church membership and was taken into the fellowship in October 1969. In 1973 I married Harriet Sauder, daughter of Bishop John Sauder.

There have been many ups and downs in my Christian life over the fifteen years I have been a member of the Old Order River Brethren, but I have always felt the support of a loving brotherhood. I appreciate very much the church's effort to balance the current leading of the Holy Spirit with respect for the godly traditions and heritage of the forebears (although this has not been achieved without struggles).

My observation has been that people, especially young people, coming from the "world" into the plain churches have a similar recurrent conflict. The seekers have become repelled and disgusted with the world system and want to get as far away from it as possible. Many of those brought up in the plain faith have become bored with the old ways and want to get as close to the world as possible. So, while the convert sits humming an *Ausbund* tune and practicing fraktur with a quill pen by candlelight, the birthright child of the church polishes the mag wheels on his sports car to the tune of gospel rock.

The solution? Easy—from the convert's point of view. Teach the children of the church to appreciate their heritage. How exactly is this carried out? God help me to know. I now have three children of my own who are growing up as "insiders."

Stahl (1987): 99-101

Our Footprints Remain

Beth Witmer, United States, 1988

*L*ast winter the ground was covered with a very heavy snowfall. All the fields were buried beneath that winter wonderland. One day a man visited our farm to inquire about buying logs from our woods. He walked to the woods, which is situated on a hill several fields away from the farm buildings. Later that evening I pointed out the footprints to the children, and we admired the way they wound their way up the hill and disappeared into the woods.

We thought we had seen the last of those footprints when a week later we had another snowfall. But not so. Several weeks later it got warmer and gradually the snow melted from the fields. Each day a little more melted away, and bare spots appeared here and there. One day as I glanced toward the woods, there on the bare hillside were our footprints again, white and plain on the green and brown earth. The packed snow had not melted as fast as the rest and we had a perfect set of footprints winding up the hill. I again showed the children the footprints and tried to take a lesson from it.

Each thought, action and deed we do is a footprint. As they wind in and out throughout life, there are others about us who may look at them and notice the pattern they make.

Even after our life on earth is past, our footprints may remain. Perhaps the path we trod is the one our children choose to follow. Or maybe it influenced a neighbor who was looking for a guide to chart his course.

Where are our footprints leading? Do we follow the old paths established by the church leaders long ago? Or do we take our own way and thus lead others further away from that simple, godly life?

Witmer (1988): 9

Emotional Fanaticism

Abram Unger, Russian Empire, 1862

Connected with the renewal which gave birth to the Mennonite Brethren churches in the Russian Empire was a burst of emotional enthusiasm which led some into one-sided extremes and chaos. Wise leaders were able to keep the movement to a balanced and biblical pattern.

*D*ear brethren! become sober for a change! Is there not a wise person among you? Do not approach the Word of God from such a one-sided perspective!

Indeed, if the Bible were to contain nothing more than to say that one could dance, then one could quite frankly not reprove you; but it is also written: "Let us walk respectably or carefully before them who are without," or: "Work out your salvation with fear and trembling!" and many similar passages. You yourselves know the Holy Scriptures, and if you wish to use the whole of it with prayer and supplication to God, that He might lead you into all truth, then a sober, manly and at the same time lovely and happy Christianity will result, which will be pleasing before God and man.

When I think of the kind of dear souls there are among you, who love their Savior most fervently, I am obliged to weep that you are leading them into such an immoral, insipid way of life, in conflict with all orderliness. Do open your eyes for a change! Should the dear Savior Jesus Christ have achieved the kind of thing that is found among you through his indescribably severe suffering? Were you to take the entire Scriptures, you could not prove such a thing; for you would have to take it out of context, and that is not permissible.

Dear brother, please do not think that I am advocating a sad and morose Christianity—not at all! On the contrary, we can be heartily happy in Christ who redeems us only and alone through His grace, quite freely; we have been made free and need bring Him nothing but our sins. His holy name be praised in all eternity that He has saved us in this and no other way. We may come to him at any time with our sins and weaknesses, and always it is said: "For by a single offering He has perfected for all time those who are sanctified."

Hallelujah, honor, glory and praise be to the Lamb, who has loved and continues to love us! Let us not prepare Him any more shame through this extreme emotionalism, but neither by again returning to a dead church; no, we too want to establish an apostolic church, where Jesus Christ is cornerstone. Amen.

Friesen (1978): 267

April 15

Cheerfulness
Sallie Kniesly, United States, 1888

Sallie Kniesly's point of view was not typical of the Brethren in Christ of her day, and her article submitted to the church paper drew a critical reply in a later issue. But perhaps Sallie was ahead of her time, as the Brethren in Christ of today are noted as a cheerful people with a healthy sense of humor.

It is a sad mistake that persons are religious in proportion as they are sad and melancholy. There are professed Christians who talk and act as if it was a sin to be happy and enjoy life. They go about with a long face, correcting everybody's errors but their own, and making Christianity repulsive to everyone with whom they come in contact. In view of this fact is it any wonder we fail to win people, especially young people, for Christ, when they receive the impression from Christians themselves, that in order to live a Christian life, they must give up all that makes life pleasant and desirable?

But this is all a mistake; we should not burden ourselves with such a thought. Christ rebuked the lawyers for burdening the people with burdens grievous to be borne, and He said, "My yoke is easy, and my burden is light." This should be the experience of all true Christians. The practice of our holy religion is much easier than the servitude of sin. It is one of the offices of Christianity (while it takes away sin) to bring joy and gladness to the heart. When Jesus takes from us anything, He always gives something infinitely better. He takes away sin and gives salvation. And He says, "Rejoice, again I say, rejoice," and why should we not rejoice, knowing that all things work together for good to those that love the Lord? Who has a better right to be cheerful and happy than the true child of God? Who can rightly claim all the precious promises of the Bible? True Christianity makes us more cheerful and not more miserable; and, if cheerful and happy, we will not go about with a long face, but cheerfulness will shine out, illuminating our lives and making them rich with love to God.

There is vastly more Christianity in a smile than there is in a frown, and there is more true Christianity in a good hearty laugh than there is in a groan. I wish to be plain enough so as to be rightly understood. We should not be giddy and vain, but the point I wish to make is this: nothing can be more natural than for a happy person to laugh, and there can be nothing wrong about it, for Jesus says: "Ye shall laugh" (Luke 6:21). David says: "Then was our mouth filled with laughter" (Psalm 126:2). Oh, let us not be afraid to laugh. David laughed, and he was a man after God's own heart, and more than that, there will be laughter in Heaven, for the Bible says so. "He that sitteth in the heavens shall laugh" (Psalm 2:4). We may enjoy pure laughter, holy laughter, heavenly laughter.

O! the world needs more cheerful, loving, large-hearted, joyful Christians, who do not live for self alone, but who devote their lives to the comfort, happiness and good of others. And by so doing deny self and follow in the footsteps of the blessed Master, who while here on earth went about doing good. This blessed example of Jesus, although it cannot be equalled by any, should be imitated by all. And when faithfully engaged in the work of the Lord we may always say, "Her ways are ways of pleasantness, and all her paths are peace," sorrowful, yet always rejoicing, poor, yet making many rich, having nothing, yet possessing all things.

Kniesly (1888): 164

Has Claassen Become a Pharisee?
Johannes Claassen, Russian Empire, 1861

Johannes Claassen was among the founders of the Mennonite Brethren. In the fellowship's early years, the exuberance of spiritual renewal sometimes carried members to emotional excess. These dramatic expressions were then taken as signs of the Spirit at work. Claassen and other leaders were able to distinguish genuinely felt spirituality from mere emotionalism. Their efforts to curb extremism eventually succeeded.

*I*f one had the feeling that he could shout for joy with all his might but refrains from doing so out of consideration for one or another brother (but not because of human fear), and thus does him a service, should this always be sin? May the following verse have absolutely no application here: "All things are lawful for us, but not all things are helpful"? May one brother never say to another: Dear brother, if you were to shout or rejoice ten times harder than you already do—and if your voice were ten times stronger than it is, God's mercy would still be much greater, higher, deeper, longer and wider than you could ever shout it out. But since Christ, highly praised in all eternity, rather than shouting for joy, is our element, might we not, for this or that reason, perhaps acquit ourselves more quietly—should that always be considered pharisaism or sin?

Of course, I can understand that brothers and sisters filled with new wine cannot leave off shouting. Nor do I demand this of them, for I myself have felt and tasted how kind the Lord is when once in a dream I felt like throwing down my cap, tearing my clothes (which the Jews did for sadness), indeed even throwing myself down before the Lord, to be consumed, wishing never to rise again for joy. But even this would fall short and never express our joy adequately. God's mercy is too high, too glorious, too precious that we should be able to express it with our voice or gestures.

And so, since many things are the way they are, judge and be sober, and do not immediately think, if for some reason you sometimes shout less for joy, that Christ, our bridegroom, is therefore lowered one rung in heaven! That this my language will not at all please many of you, dear brethren, and you, indeed many of you will say Claassen has become a Pharisee, will not influence me in the least.

Friesen (1978): 269

The Soul's Natural Element

Jakob Denner, Germany, ca. 1707

*T*hat each being and creature lives in its own element is abundantly shown to us by experience. In the first place, gold, a choice metal, is very bright and stable, has its life in the fire and is purified in fire. A bird is cheerful by nature, is most blissful in the air, and is unable to exist without air. The fish is a water animal, so it is secure in water where it has its pleasure and life. A tree that is created of earth is earthy in nature; therefore it grows out of the earth, becomes green, blooms and produces fruit; but as it is taken out of the earth it is no more and dries up, or dies and ceases.

Now somebody may well be thinking, "What does this lead to?" The answer is that it may help you to understand the spiritual truth better. So we say then that just like a creature lives and rests in its natural element, so in a spiritual sense the spiritual person lives with a living soul, that is to say a true child of God and follower of Jesus Christ. His element is God, in whom he has his origin. This is also his highest source of enjoyment, life, joy, peace, rest, salvation and happiness in God, the ultimate of goodness, as his spiritual element.

And as we can see, the physical and the spiritual part of a creature cannot live out of its element, but instead just as soon as it is taken out of its natural element it must die and wither, so it is also in a spiritual sense with the soul; it can live only in God as its natural element, and just as soon as it is taken out of this element it has to go to nothing, die and wither.

*

So it would be my wish that we might see nature in its proper light; for through this we could learn many things that could be very useful to us in the spiritual realm, in that each one is a spiritual model. So I say once again that a true child of God, one who is born again, can be only one thing, that is to rest in God because this is his element. Outside of God he finds nothing, for it is here that he has his supreme enjoyment and peace.

For this reason also it is God who is his soul's longing, hunger and thirst. His entire being is directed toward God, his heart and emotion is toward God, and whether he is directing his efforts toward his natural sustenance he does this just as if in passing. With his heart he does not cling to anything that is earthly; he seeks no comfort or pleasure in it, but in God. God is his treasure, his rest, his joy, his solace and indeed his only life and quickening. What he does in a temporal sense is done by him as something of only small consequence. His controlling concern is to do for God, to have or possess God, to enjoy God and to be united with God, and to remain that way; this is his ultimate goal, this is his controlling purpose.

Denner (1707): 356, 357, trans. by Noah G. Good

What Is the New Birth?

David Beiler, United States, 1857

*A*ccording to the prophets the new birth is a work of God in mankind: in which the person by the grace of God is enlightened and sprinkled from above so that he can recognize his pitiful state and sinful condition; that in his poor state he comes in the spirit of humility, recognizing that in the flesh dwells no good thing, and that he with his carnal life, action and walk of life deserves only to be punished and afflicted. If the person is so touched and stricken down in his heart there will doubtless follow a sincere and genuine penitence, so that the person is fully broken and moved, so that he can say freely from the heart and with unrestrained lips: "Lord, have patience with me, I do want to pay my entire debt, but have patience with me a poor, miserable sinner, I mean to do better."

It may even come to the place where, as Christ said, "Then the lord of this servant took pity on him and forgave him all." When we examine this and go to the root of it, how that God is so gracious to us poor sinners when we turn to him with hearts full of faith, then God for Christ's sake will forgive us our entire debt and allow us to go free.

Beiler (1857): 222-224, trans. by Noah G. Good

April 19

He Requires No Hasty Decision

P. Cool, The Netherlands, 1854

A Dutch pastor responds to a young woman's inquiries prior to baptism.

*I*n your next to last letter you wrote to me you said: "I feel more and more that apart from Christ I cannot live in a higher sense. Through him only can I arrive at a forgiveness and deliverance from sin. Apart from him, the true vine, I can bear no fruit of true worth (real virtue). Christ has to stir up and nurture my spiritual life or I shall die morally and be lost." So minded you will experience baptism as a heart-felt commitment of yourself to the Savior. And then he will stretch out his arms to you full of holy love with joy saying, "Come and follow me!"

But also from those who feel such a need for him, he requires no hasty and rash decision. "Make an estimate before you begin," is advice he repeatedly gave to those who desired to follow him. And this was especially necessary in the early days of his ministry, when one often had to give up and forsake everything if one publicly declared his belief in the Nazarene. Because of this, then, the words to the scribe, "Foxes have their holes and birds have their nests; but the Son of Man has nowhere to lay his head."

There you see, Johanna, how Jesus wanted the scribe to consider what he wished to undertake. The scribe likely came to him in a moment of excitement and called out: "I will follow you wherever you go." There is something impulsive in this. Jesus certainly wished to communicate to him the need to think the matter over more carefully.

*

A life of vigilance, of prayer and battle against sin, inside and outside of us—yes, that is the life to which his disciples are called. Indeed, his yoke is easy and his burden is light compared to the unbearable yoke that the lawgivers of the time laid on the people; easy and light also compared with the oppressive burden of sin. But still, the utmost of our powers is required to attain to, to measure up to, the high calling of the Christian life. Inclinations have to be suppressed, customs forsaken—customs we thought necessary and dear to us. We have to work at habits we would rather ignore, often ignore what we desire to do; hold our peace when we want to speak, speak when we would rather be silent; yield when our pride wishes to assert itself, keep our heads up when we are disheartened.

The Christian cannot go along with the mainstream, but often has to diametrically oppose it; not praise the evil spirit of our times, but strongly oppose it; not bow down before the gods of our times, but—although the world consider one odd and peculiar—serve only the Lord. In the midst of a world full of distractions and amusements, the Christian has to aim at higher matters; to seek the filling of the Holy Spirit in the midst of a world full of contagious diseases, keeping oneself untarnished; to walk on the earth as a citizen of heaven. I realize this is asking a whole lot. Baptism is for those who come to the place where they consider these matters.

*

The Savior of mankind did not come to be served but to serve and to give his life as a ransom for many. Conscious of the command of the Father, he rejected crown and scepter, despised the enjoyments of the world, and stands before us in the humble clothing of a teacher, with nothing belonging to him except the garments he wore, poorer than the foxes with their own holes and the birds with their own nests.

Gorter (1856): 17-22, trans. by Irvin B. Horst

April 20

Real Devotion

Caleb Zimmerman, United States, 1985

*I*t would seem ironic that the same philosophy which promotes family devotions would fail to produce devoted families. Yet this can only be expected if we reduce to a 24-minute (or less)-a-day ritual that which God intended to be a 24-hour-a-day way of life.

This warped thinking and deception is evident also in other philosophies that may look very good on the surface, but which turn out to be only shallow counterfeits. Perhaps the most deceptive of all is that of the "New Birth experience" which many claim to have, but have little evidence of being new creatures in Christ, bypassing the principles of the blood of the cross. The "I will" spirit of Lucifer is still more alive than the "Thy will" spirit of Christ.

When one would question such philosophies, those that promote them would say that it is a mystery that we cannot explain or understand, but that we accept by faith. This again may sound fairly good on the surface, but the problem is that "faith" itself is reduced to a mystical state of the mind, which has no more stability than the chaff of a threshing floor—blown about by every wind of doctrine of man.

But just because we reject a few pietistic counterfeits, does not give us license to ignore the genuine. We must realize that there is a ditch on both sides of the road. And while the pietist may loudly proclaim that he is "of Christ," we dare not glory simply in the fact that we are "of Paul" or "of Apollos" (1 Cor. 1:12-13). But rather, let the Amishman and the Mennonite and the pietist give diligence to be baptized with the baptism that Jesus was baptized with, and to drink of that cup which Jesus told his disciples they would indeed drink of (Matt. 20:22-23).

This is the cup of the death of the cross (Luke 22:42) which says, not my will, but thine be done, and makes a realistic and voluntary surrender of the self-will in exchange for God's will, and by genuine repentance do God's commandments (Matt. 7:21, Rev. 22:14).

Zimmerman (1985): 5

April 21

Care for Creation
Albert Widjaja, Indonesia, 1978

"The Lord God took the man and put him in the garden of Eden to till it and keep it."
—Genesis 2:15

What kind of a world are we living in? Is our present global environment so different from that of our ancestors that we should reexamine our value system and scrutinize our theological perspective on what God requires of us in our world today? Before answering these questions, we should first ask whether the church has anything to do with the world issue. Should not the church talk about more spiritual things, and leave the problem of gasoline consumption to individuals, meat consumption to the homes, company profit to individual businessmen and corporate enterprises?

Some Christians may hold such a position. But it is certainly not the biblical one. Jesus said that His coming in the world is "to announce good news to the poor, to proclaim release for prisoners and recovery of sight to the blind, to let the broken victims go free, to proclaim the year of the Lord's favor" (Luke 4:18, 19). Hence the basic mission of the church is to proclaim the good news as well as to set men free from the shackles of social and economic injustices.

The teaching of Jesus was undoubtedly followed by the Anabaptists, whose heritage calls for transformation of personal life in relation to God, to himself, and to other human beings in order to conform to Christ's calling. The Anabaptist movement was said to be a radical break from the prevailing Christianity, unhampered by the Christian heritage of Catholicism and mainstream Protestantism of that day and unspoiled by the prevailing social and cultural condition. Based on their new experience with the grace of God, they were able to discern the signs of the times and regain authentic understanding of Jesus' teaching.

*

In that new type of relationship with God and with man, did it produce a new form of brotherhood or a new form of isolationism? Did it produce renewed disciples of Christ to witness to "all nations" or weary and withdrawn third-generation Christians with no vision of God's work in history? Whatever our answer might be, our global environment continues to challenge our faith and behavior, since the nature of our relation with God's creation increasingly determines its efficacy to sustain and enrich our life. Our care and attitude about it influences the quality of our life, our relation with other human beings, and ultimately our relation with and responsibility before God.

Kraybill ([1978]): 81, 82

Nonconformity and the Soil
Clarence T. Yoder, United States, 1987

"Your wrath has come and the time for judging the dead. . .and for destroying those who destroy the earth." —Revelation 11:18

The idea of the use of chemicals in farming is a comparatively recent one, and the most modern approach to tilling the soil. How can we practice these methods and be consistent in our belief of nonconformity to the world and its standards? Have we lost our convictions?

*

Not only do we transgress the Scriptures in accepting and adopting whatever modern technology has to offer—but how can we bypass all the warning labels like, "Wash hands thoroughly after use," and "Do not reuse empty container—destroy by burning and bury the remains." Yet the contents of these containers we apply to the soil as beneficial to life? The harmony in nature was established in the beginning, and God called it good. Who are we to disrupt so perfect a plan?

The reason for controversy on this subject is the very fact that the Bible does not directly teach against it. But neither does it say, "Thou shalt not use tobacco." Yet we are convinced that it is harmful to life, and therefore wrong. By the way, the warning labels on chemicals and tobacco are very similar, yet we are urged by advertisements to go ahead and use them both.

I realize that chemicals do away with a lot of work and sweat and health, and no telling what all else. My concern is that we might be held responsible for these and similar practices at the Great Judgment.

Clarence T. Yoder (1987): 5

The Covenant of a Good Conscience
Hans Denck, Germany, 1525

"Baptism. . .now saves you also—not the removal of dirt from the body but the pledge of a good conscience toward God." —1 Peter 3:21 NIV

Who would undertake to wash off the redness of bricks or the blackness of coal, whose very nature is what it is? It would be wasted labor indeed, because their nature cannot be softened and changed. By the same token, a person whose body and soul are unclean is washed in vain outwardly, if one does not begin to soften and change him from within.

The almighty word of God alone is able to descend to and penetrate the hardened abyss of human uncleanness, just as a driving rain can soften arid ground. When this takes place, a struggle begins in a person before nature is willing to make way. Despair grips him so that he thinks he will have to perish in body and soul; he will not be able to endure the work of God thus begun; just as one assumes, should there be a great flood, that the ground cannot withstand it and would be washed away. In such despair David cries out, "Lord God, help me, for the waters have reached my soul" (Psalm 69:2). Such despair—at times great, at times small—lasts as long as the elect is in this body. With it begins the work of Christ.

For this reason, not only John the Baptist but the apostles also baptized in water. The point was that whatever could not withstand the water, could tolerate fire even less, which latter is the baptism of Christ in the Spirit and the consummation of his work.

This water of baptism saves, not because it removes the filth of the flesh but rather because of the covenant of a good conscience with God. This covenant is that whoever is baptized is baptized into the death of Christ so that he might die to the old Adam even as Christ did and that as Christ was raised, he too may walk in a new life.

Denck (1989): 5, 6

April 24

The Baptism of Tribulation
Hans Hut, Germany, ca. 1526

"Are you able to drink the cup that I drink, or be baptized with the baptism that I am baptized with?" —Mark 10:38

*T*he outer baptism which follows preaching and faith is not the true reality by which man is made righteous, but is only a sign, a covenant, a likeness and a memorial of one's dedication, which sign reminds one daily to expect the true baptism, called by Christ "the water of all tribulation." It is through this baptism that the Lord makes one clean, washing and justifying him of all fleshly lusts, sins and impure works and life.

*

Thus the water of all tribulation is the true essence and power of baptism, whereby one sinks into the death of Christ. Nor was this true baptism first instituted at the time of Christ. It has been since the beginning, and every elect friend of God from Adam on has been baptized in it, as Paul says.

Christ also accepted this covenant from God at the Jordan and testified that, obedient to the Father, He would manifest love toward all men for an example, even unto death. Thereafter, He found the baptism of all tribulation poured over Him by the Father in great profusion.

Therefore, the sign and the essence of baptism must be sharply distinguished. The Christian church gives and administers the sign or the covenant of baptism through a true minister, as Christ received it from John. Thereafter follows the true baptism which God gives, first through the water of all tribulation, and second in the comfort of the Holy Spirit. God lets no one be swallowed up in this baptism. As it is written, He leads into hell and out again, He kills and makes alive again. Since even the Lord had to be baptized with this baptism, whoever wants to be His disciple must be baptized in the same way.

Armour (1966): 83, 84

April 25

The Narrow Gate
Pilgram Marpeck, Germany, 1542

*T*here is another understanding of the usage of baptism in the Scriptures, on which account we can refer to baptism, not unjustly, as a door or entrance into the holy church. Paul says in 1 Corinthians 12:13: "By one spirit were we all, Jews or Greeks, slaves or free, baptized into one body." Paul says here that there is one Spirit which has led us all to be baptized into one body.

Furthermore, we have been united into the unity of faith and the covenant of love, and are henceforth one body, for Paul says we have been baptized into one body. This one body is the holy church into which we have been baptized, that is, through one Spirit and in one faith; we must be united into one confession of God. But such unity does not happen through immersion or effusion of water; rather, it comes into being because we are united through the Spirit of Christ in faith.

*

Baptism is a door, an entrance into the holy church, and this is certainly the narrow gate of which Christ speaks (Luke 13:24); no one goes justified through baptism into the church or into the kingdom of God, except he who in baptism has taken off and laid aside the old life of sin, and has been raised up to a new life.

This portal without doubt is very narrow, for you cannot go through it with the old sinful man of the old life; everything must be laid aside and buried before one enters through this gate. For when the two sons of Zebedee asked to sit, the one at the right, the other at the left, Christ answered: "Are you prepared to drink the cup which I drink? Are you prepared to be baptized with the baptism with which I am baptized?" (Mark 10:35). Christ's is the baptism of death, to which the water baptism also bears witness. Through this narrow gate, Christ beckons His own and, since to enter is impossible for the carnal and those who have only little seriousness, Christ says, therefore, that only a few enter it.

*

Clearly, holy baptism is not to be lightly considered as an entrance into the holy church, and there is no other entrance to eternal life than the one Christ Himself prescribes: "Whoever would follow me, let him deny himself, take up his cross and follow me." That is to happen in baptism. We are then correctly consecrated into the Christian church, purified of sins, incorporated into Christ and clothed with Him; only then may we appear, without shame, at the wedding of the highest King in honorable clothing and adornment.

Marpeck (1978): 198-201

April 26

"Water Alone Will Not Do It"
Johannes Harder, Germany, mid-1900s

I continue to meditate on my relationship to the traditional community of faith by comparing it to the biblical tradition. My questions continually run into questionable circumstances in the relationship between our heritage and our reality. For example, baptism, which has gotten into a bad way no less than has nonresistance. Baptism was the confession of "mature" Christians; never a sacrament, that is, an act holy in itself, but always only a sign of obedience to Scripture. I can recall how in some Russian Mennonite churches baptism was given the adjective "holy" as though it was to be understood in a sacramental sense. Holy means "belonging to God": God himself is the Lord of baptism, his Spirit is the Baptizer. And so the transfer of the character of holiness to an act appears problematic to me.

It is something else when God speaks to persons in an act of the *Gemeinde* (community) through the Word or through images and symbols. The baptismal candidate can express himself only in a fragmentary and incomplete way as to what has happened to him, whether he uses his own or biblical language.

God himself, not a tradition, however good, has accepted the person; this adoption is beyond our asking or comprehension. That is why baptism is an exaltation out of indebtedness and at the same time a humbling before the rightful Lord. That is the way the Lord of baptism opens the door to the *Gemeinde*, which is his consulate (representative) on earth.

Baptism is a testimonial to the candidate of his decisive call. Through baptism in and of itself nothing is changed in the candidate, but it testifies that the Spirit has changed the mind of the person and directed him to others.

The teaching on baptism is a serious matter for me, but I want to inquire about the practice. I know of cases where it is "passed" as a kind of exam after a training process. Or it is considered a rite of passage out of childhood. Or baptism is seen to be part of a perfect life. Such misunderstandings lead "free" churches to become "state" churches, which set baptism as an entrance requirement for full membership. But already Luther knew: "Water alone will not do it."

Loewen (1988): 121, 122

April 27

Our Oath of Allegiance
Pilgram Marpeck, Germany, 1542

*S*acrament refers to anything done in connection with an oath or a similar obligation, and refers to an event that is special and holy or a work that has that kind of connotation. Similarly, the knight commits himself to serve his Lord by the raising of a finger in battle where, on his honor and with his oath, he commits himself not to yield in combat. Now, the raising of his finger is not the battle, nor a fight, nor endurance, nor is it victory. The action is a covenant, made in the firm hope that, according to the command and the desire of his Lord, he will diligently attack the enemy of his Lord, even risking his life until death.

*

Sacrament signifies all kinds of events which take place in the presence of an oath and are handled, or are dealt with, by an oath. Thus, sacrament is not to be understood as a single essential thing, but only as the act that is carried out. If the act is carried out with an oath or a similar commitment, then it can be called a sacrament.

The ancients called an oath a sacrament because the oath is a sign of something holy, that is, it is the divine truth in the same way that God is truthful and the truth. In this way, the oath must also be true and without falsehood.

When, now, the word sacrament is correctly taken in this natural meaning, it is not used incorrectly when baptism and the Lord's Supper are called sacraments, for they are, after all, instituted by Christ and, as mentioned above, are commanded with the same kind of force and binding quality as the oath.

Therefore, the sacrament must be practiced with the deep earnestness which Christ has ordained. How, and in what spirit, it happens are more important than any other considerations.

*

Paul, and all the other apostles, do not place a high value upon the elements and, indeed, attribute no special holiness to them; rather, as we shall see in a later time and place, they consider the total action and usage. Thus, you can see how both baptism and the Lord's Supper are called sacraments, namely, because both of them must take place with a commitment and sanctification, which is actually what sacrament is, for merely to plunge somebody into water or to baptize them is no sacrament.

You must baptize in such a manner that the one who is baptized dies to his sins in a sincere way and in the power of a living faith in Christ. From henceforth, he commits himself to a new life, and only then is baptism truly a sacrament, that is, when the content and action of baptism happens with the commitment to a holy covenant.

Marpeck (1978): 169-172

April 28

Committed to Mutual Care
Balthasar Hubmaier, Moravia, 1527

Now we see clearly whence the authority arises that one brother has the power and the right to admonish another. Namely from the baptismal commitment, which a person gave before receiving water baptism, in which he subjected himself, according to the order of Christ, to the church and all her members.

*

So all of those who cry: "Well, what about water baptism? Why all the fuss about the Lord's Supper? They are after all just outward signs! They're nothing but water, bread and wine! Why fight about that?" They have not in their whole life learned enough to know why the signs were instituted by Christ, what they seek to achieve or toward what they should finally be directed, namely to gather a church, to commit oneself publicly to live according to the Word of Christ in faith and brotherly love, and because of sin to subject oneself to fraternal admonition and the Christian ban. And to do all of this with a sacramental oath before the Christian church and all her members, assembled partly in body and completely in spirit, testifying publicly in the power of God, Father and Holy Spirit, or in the power of our Lord Jesus Christ (which is all the same power), and yielding oneself to her in hand-pledged fidelity.

Look to this, dear brethren, and not to water, bread or wine, lest our water baptism and breaking bread might also be only an appearance and a sleight of hand, nothing better than what the stupid child baptism and baby feeding have been before, if fraternal admonition and the Christian ban do not constantly accompany them.

In sum: Where water baptism is not given according to the order of Christ, there it is impossible to accept fraternal admonition from one another in a good spirit. For no one knows either who is in the church and who is outside. No one has authority over another, we are scattered to the winds, like sheep without shepherds, without a pasture, without markings, neither knowing nor being able to recognize who has let himself be marked as a sheep of Christ, or who chooses to remain as a wild buck outside the flock of Christ. May God help us all, that we might enter into the sheepfold of Christ through the right door (John 10:2), and not climb in elsewhere against the express ordering of Christ.

Hubmaier (1989): 383-385

What Infant Baptism Has Brought About
Melchior Rinck(?), Germany, ca. 1530

Would not a city soon be destroyed and a sheepfold soon laid waste if one would introduce the enemy of the city in his young years, raise him up in the city so that he would know all its customs, until he comes to his maturity; and thus would be able to attack the city not from the outside in (where it would not be possible to win over against her) but from the inside out (what no city can withstand)? Would it then be possible after the deed to get such an enemy out of the city, after he had bound to himself a major portion of the citizens, or someone from outside, to whom the city out of fear had become vassal? Or would it be possible to keep such a one within without surrendering the city?

Likewise if a shepherd were to take a young wolf or lion or bear into the sheepfold and raise it with the sheep, would they not finally, once they were grown, destroy both the shepherd and the sheep? Yea, they would themselves want to be both shepherd and sheep. Now the scribes are going about driving out of their congregations those whom they know are wolves, bears and lions, so they will well experience what infant baptism has brought about.

Yoder (1973): 136

The Baptism of Blood
Henry Funk, United States, 1744

So soon as the believer has the witness of the spiritual baptism, and has received the baptism with water, he should yield himself willingly to receive the baptism of the shedding of his blood for the name of Christ, if required, and take on him the witness of blood, according to 1 John 5:8, "And there are three that bear witness in earth: the Spirit and the water and the blood. And these three agree in one."

The believer, in his baptism, is baptized into the body of Christ, the church. And then he puts on Christ and unites himself to Him, to follow him truly and constantly, and bearing his cross after Him. And should the believer be called on to suffer for the name of Christ and to lay down his life for his name, he should be willing to be baptized with the same baptism of suffering and shedding of blood wherewith his Lord and Master was baptized, when he laid down his life to redeem man from death: and this is the allegiance of all the true disciples of Jesus Christ, in this world.

*

For it is evident that when believers, as members of Christ, will enter into heaven with Christ the heavenly bridegroom, to the marriage supper of the Lamb, and drink of the new and sweet wine in heaven (which is manifested in John 2:10 and Matthew 26:29), that they must first drink with him the bitter wine of affliction and tribulation, and be baptized with his baptism. But the drinking of *this cup* and being baptized with *this baptism* must be done and endured for the sake of Jesus Christ and for his name alone.

The drinking of this cup, and being baptized with the baptism of affliction, tribulation and shedding of blood unto death, fell manifoldly on the apostles and followers of Christ; all of which they underwent for the sake of Jesus Christ, and in testimony of his adorable name. The first of these witnesses was Stephen. For as Stephen, by the Spirit, was testifying with power that Jesus was the Christ, the just One, and the Jews heard it, they were cut to the heart, and gnashed upon him with their teeth. And when he said, "Behold I see the heavens opened, and the Son of Man standing on the right hand of God," they cried out with a loud voice, and stopped their ears, and ran upon him with one accord, and cast him out of the city and stoned him, calling upon God and saying, "Lord Jesus, receive my spirit." And he kneeled down and cried with a loud voice, "Lord, lay not this sin to their charge." And when he had said this, he fell asleep. Thus did Stephen—the first after Christ—drink the bitter cup, and receive the baptism of suffering and shedding of blood.

Moreover, James, the son of Zebedee, and John his brother, whom Jesus told before that they should drink his cup, and be baptized with the baptism that he is baptized with, did also drink this bitter cup of their Lord and Master, and so did the other apostles.

Funk (1851): 98, 100, 101

May

May 1

Eating the Flesh of the Poor
Pieter Pietersz., The Netherlands, 1638

*T*he individual tight-fistedly seeks to beat the laborer out of his remuneration even though he very well knows that it is impossible that the laborer can properly subsist from such a miserly wage. Nevertheless he sharply squeezes the laborer and says, "Do you not want to work for the price? I can obtain someone else for that price." Then the poor working man reflects to himself, "Is it not better that I labor for half a wage than that I go away empty?" And he must grasp for what he can.

Those who increase their empire of wealth in this manner are eating the flesh of the poor. And in chapter five, the apostle James speaks and laments with respect to these when he says, "Go to now ye rich men, weep and howl for your miseries that shall come upon you. Your riches are corrupted and your garments are moth-eaten. Your gold and silver is cankered, and the rust of them shall be a witness against you and shall eat your flesh as if it were a fire. Behold, the hire of the laborers who have reaped your fields, which is of you kept back by fraud, crieth: and the cries of them which have reaped are entered into the ears of the Lord of Sabaoth."

However, those who throw this speech of the apostle James into the wind are assuring unto themselves that they might do well, namely, to ruthlessly exploit a laborer as much as possible, for they are counting only on their own advantage. How much can they consume in their household in one year? How much will their income be and how much can they save? In addition to this they think to themselves that the less they need pay out for the wages of the laborers, the greater their profit in and from the yearly rentals. But they do not consider that they are also to be economical with respect to their lavish household expenditures: for their huge houses which are constructed like temples, and also with respect to their costly clothes and feasts, household embellishments, paintings and other magnificence. Oh a most unfortunate empire of wealth which is assembled in this manner!

And in addition to all of this, when they have to pay their laborer they frequently do so with bad coinage, which has been shaved down in weight, or which is not even legal tender, which the employee cannot even readily pass on. And of course the laborer should not complain of this, in that he must be scared

---

to be treated sourly or actually to be fired. But his wife at home quickly becomes conscious of the situation as she cannot even offer him the equivalent of the crumbs which fall from the table of the rich man.

Plett (1985): 348

May 2

Sunday on the Island of Chortitza
Kornelius Hildebrand, Sr., Russian Empire, late 1800s

A glorious May day breaks out! Nature is bathed in beautiful sunshine. The mountains and valleys are ornamented in gleaming green of their renewed existence. The thrilling song of the lark calls out the joy of life in its long waves of song. "Life has returned, fresh blooms beautify the earth. You too awake, O child of mankind, from your incomprehensible sleep of indifference to all the beauty and splendor that is revealed daily in the divine creation."

The surface of the Dnieper River glitters and shines like an immense mirror, wonderfully illuminated by the just-rising sun. Here and there a gay little fish in its youthful exuberance darts out of the water's black depth through the faultlessly smooth surface and sets up a series of constantly larger circular waves. One lone gull skims over it and from time to time cools its breast in the cool stream of water.

From the chimneys of the houses on the little island village, which are arranged in a direct line from the edge of the bank right up to the mountain in unbroken straight lines as if aimed, there rises a fine, blue smoke going straight up like a candle in the windless air, almost as if celebrating mass with the scented smoke of incense of the altars of worship in the houses.

There is not a wagon in the streets, no laboring person, not a bit of sound to disturb the worshipful silence. It is Sunday, and a Sunday day of rest. The joy of Sunday clothes nature and creature and envelops at least for a little time the uneasy breast of the person.

Thanks be to God for giving us Sunday!

Just now there is the peal of the church bells coming from the opposite shore across the water to this side, calling the pious to quiet worship at the dedicated site.

Reverential sincerity is mingled with musically harmonious beauty in the charming, clanging sound that marks Sunday in creation and nature. And the islanders would not want to think of Sunday morning without this metallic sound. It comes so gently through the open window to the ear of the infant child in the crib, and wakens the young lad and lass to the joy of Sunday, and leads the churchgoers on their way to worship. So it has always been; and so it will always continue to be.

Peters (1965): 48, trans. by Noah G. Good

A Change for Unity

Dirk Philips, Germany(?), 1558

*O*ne may observe that as Christ accepts the believers, he unites himself with them, so that he is the head and the believers are his body. He pours his eternal life into them, gives them his Spirit, and grants them all his good and makes them partakers of it.

This is the spiritual fellowship of Christ and the believers which they have with each other.

*

Through the bread and through the wine of the Supper, the unity and the agreeableness and fellowship of believers is portrayed and testified. However, in order to signify this fellowship, the Lord has taken and ordained such symbols in the Supper which over all merge back and forth and with their forms arouse and motivate to such fellowship. For just as the bread is made of many grains, poured together and ground, and the many grains become one loaf in which each individual grain loses its body and form, and similarly with the grapes with the changing of their form become a common wine and drink's body, so also all Christians must be united with Christ and with each other.

In the first place they are united with Christ, whom they receive through faith and are nourished with him. But there is now none greater, more firm, and can no more be separated one from the other than the unification of the food with the one who is fed by it. The food goes into and is transformed into the nature and becomes one being with the one who is fed. So also true Christians are through faith in Jesus Christ completely united in him, incorporated in him, yes, transposed and changed into his nature and character. Therefore, Christ also accepts them more firmly so that whoever harms them harms Christ himself, and again whoever does them good does it to Christ himself, as he himself said, "What you have done to one of the least of my brothers, that you have done to me."

However, through this fellowship and love of Christ, Christians must thus again be enkindled in love, so that they regard all Christian need to be common, take their form and need upon themselves, and so become united through the true love which bears the burden one for the other and so fulfills the law of Christ.

Oh, that is a great sacrament and a great mystery, says Paul, that Christ and his congregation are one flesh and bone. That is also a marvelous and blessed union that all Christians are one body and bread in Christ Jesus. They are one bread from the good seed which the heavenly Father has sown in the field of this world. Baked through the fire of love, they are one body of many members of Christ; baptized through one Spirit into one body, and must, according to the example of the natural body, be of one heart and soul and serve each other, be helpful and comforting, just as the members of the natural body do.

Dirk (1992): 121-123

May 4

Heaven Is My Home
Eusebius Hershey, Liberia, 1891

Eusebius Hershey became the first Mennonite foreign missionary from North America at age 67, after a long career as a home missionary. He died in Africa after less than six months of service, and before this letter reached its destination.

God revealed himself to his people through the Old and New Testament dispensation, by visions and revelations years back. The Lord revealed himself to me as follows: I crossed the ocean, landed safely. The colored people came around and rejoiced, saying, "The white man has come." Hear this all ye honest Christians. All this was filled out between me and my honest Master in 1890.

The vessel which left New York Nov. 1st, bound for Liberia, Africa, landed in thirty-eight days, the 9th of Dec., at Freetown, where I preached the gospel three times while the vessel layed over Sabbath. You should have seen the friendly faces and the shaking of the white man's hand. I am very thankful to my heavenly Father who kept me, now in the fourth month in Africa, not one day in bed sick. During the month I have preached Jesus in the Gail churches and to the naked and half-naked heathens under the open heavens, with weeping eyes beholding Ham's posterity so deeply sunken in lack of Scriptural knowledge.

My mind and heart is mostly drawn towards the Mohammedans where I commenced my labors of love by preaching by my interpreter, and teaching their children the ABC's from the books which I bought in Philadelphia on my way to Africa, not thinking that God would lead me to preach Jesus to them and not Mohammet. I tell the children that Alla is God in their language. When I kneel down to pray in their terms under the open heaven, I say, "O Alla, thou eternal God."

*

O ye honest Christians, I often weep by day and night, knowing that many prayers are sent to God for me, both in America and Canada. That is right. Do not forget me. I believe that God will give me the great blessing to celebrate my fiftieth spiritual birthday in Africa next Aug. 17, 1891, and then tell me clearly how soon I will be justified to return to America and spend my few remaining days, using my influence to awaken up the sleeping millions of so-called Christians, who do not walk as they should.

*

I saw no person I knew since I left New York. I am the only white person within ten miles. Well I am contented with my lot; therefore I murmur not. Heaven is my home.

Hershey (1891): 179, 180

May 5

The Garden of the Lord
Jakob Hutter, Moravia, 1535

*T*he brothers and sisters are growing in godly righteousness and flourishing like lovely tulips and sweet-scented lilies. As a garden bursts into leaf and flower after rain in May, so they are budding and blossoming in God's sight, flourishing in the fear of God and in His love and peace. Their hearts burn with God's pure love and are constantly kindled by His light and fire.

I cannot praise and thank Him enough for this. I truly rejoice before God; my heart leaps for joy when I think of their obedience and the love and faithfulness God has given them. How richly the Almighty has blessed them! And even though they have all just started on God's way and have heard very little of His Word, still they have made a good and wholehearted beginning. May God help them to reach the end. They are a joy to my heart and deserve the name "garden of the Lord," as Scripture says. For them I praise and thank God with all my heart.

It is my heartfelt request to God that he will water His garden with rain from Heaven, with the comfort of His Holy Spirit and the oil of His compassion. May He anoint all our hearts, pouring heavenly blessing upon His garden, so that it is fruitful and bears many good works. This garden is the Church of the living God. He raised a fence around His garden to guard it from wild beasts. May He also protect it from bad thunderstorms and from evil blights so that the fruit may ripen, for the Lord's Eden is now in full bloom. May He himself keep watch over it and bring it to a bountiful harvest.

Hutter (1979): 112, 113

May 6

God-Consciousness
Levi P. Miller, United States, late 1900s

*W*e find Job a man of a strong God-conscious character, being perfect and upright, fearing God and shunning evil. In the first two chapters we find some insights to his testings. In chapter one God asks Satan, "Whence comest thou?"

implying Satan was accountable for his doings. Satan knew God is sovereign and in control of circumstances affecting Job's life (Job 1:11).

Monotheism sees Satan only as an instrument in Job's testings. Job sees God as taking away and not Satan. Job's possessions, family and life were surrendered to God. In the remainder of this narrative we see a strong God-consciousness in Job's speech. He did not focus on the evil side of his trials but said, "God knoweth the way that I take: when he has tried me, I shall come forth as gold" (Job 23:10). Had Job focused on evil he probably never would have come to understand God's greatness or lovingkindness, or learned humility. God's people have lost something very precious when they no longer see God always in control and testing them for their own good and for his glory.

There is a strong monotheism in the *Martyrs' Mirror* and *Ausbund*. In our "Dortrecht Confession of Faith" we find very little mention of Satan. Why? Because the writers found no need of spending much time speculating about demons and the devil. Theirs was a strong, positive faith, founded upon the Bible, conducive to the building of a sound and scriptural church.

*

Reading books on demonology, listening to talks and lectures on the subject, are dangerous and hinder Christian growth. Some may say we should study evil to refute it. "But, can a man take fire in his bosom, and not be burned?"

*

It is an apostate belief to attribute too much power to demons and to fear them. Christians are entitled and called to live in peace without the fear of demons. Demons seem very real to those who focus on their power, but the person whose life is hid with Christ in God has been lifted into a sphere of life where demons have no practical effect.

Where the fear of God is absent, and God is no longer central in life, demons may become overwhelming and fearful. To portray the devil and demons too strongly as though the devil were a second God hinders wholesome Christian living. This is as great a detriment as humanism and liberalism who portray God too small.

Miller (n.d.): 8, 9, 16

May 7

Long-Range Hope
Takio Tanase, Japan, 1984

I will admit that sometimes in our witness in Japan we have experiences that make us wonder if God is in charge of history. Is there any hope in this kind of world?

Just this spring a young Mennonite congregation in eastern Hokkaido had such an experience. Three twenty-year-old men who were new Christians left after the morning worship service to go to the beach, saying they would return at 3:00 for the youth meeting. In April, huge chunks of ice break away from the Siberian coast and float down past Hokkaido in a scenic fashion, creating a tourist attraction.

These young men have not been seen since. Their car was found at the beach and their footsteps led to the water's edge. It looked like they climbed aboard some ice chunks and were carried away.

Naturally the young congregation was devastated to lose these brothers who were potential workers and leaders. The surrounding community read in the newspapers that the incident happened after Sunday services and asked, "Does the God of Christianity let such a thing come to pass?"

But even in the days of recent sorrow there is hope, the biblical kind of long-range hope and assurance that comes from genuine witness.

These young men had joined the church without the full blessing of their families. But in the one case, the Sato family came to church to exchange memories of their son. They listened to church members talk about Sato San's contribution. They looked at photos of him among the young people. They saw him smiling and relaxed and joyful. The beauty of that *kalos* (goodness) has begun to witness to them. "Yes," they said, "after all, church was the place where our son was truly himself and was truly happy. We can be glad about that." Now Mr. Sato is considering joining the church. May our witnessing produce more such fruit and more of that kind of hope.

Mennonite World Conference ([1984]): 146-148

May 8

Love, Examples and a Bit of Religion
Kornelius Hildebrand, Sr., Russian Empire, late 1800s

The author recreates a Sunday morning scene from the Ukraine in 1840.

Dressed in Sunday attire father and mother step along toward the church. And the growing children come along with them. The sons who have already reached their 17th and 18th year of life, since they are the children of well-to-do parents, are dressed in ruffled Schirkassin coats of an uncertain gray color. The younger lads walk along on Sunday in white shirtsleeves instead of the blue workday shirts. The grown daughters match their mothers in dress, except that their eyes peer out mischievously from under their loosely buttoned calico and they are quite ready to laugh "just like the baking, frying and other fish of this day." But everything has to be "duse" [using the thee/thou form of address in speaking], especially when on the way to worship. (To go to church dressed in a bright red jacket would be a quite serious violation of the Ordnung and approved custom, indeed almost sacrilegious.) The still-very-young boys and girls run along barefoot, just as the first swallow can be seen.

Thus the old and the young move along in reverent stillness and with constrained voices to church. Very silently the mother admonishes her youngest offspring during the sermon (of up to two hours in time) by all means not to fall asleep, lest with her snoring she might disturb others; but also not to engage in any kind of distracting conduct or folly. Her very smallest one she has assigned to the care of the maid or one of the older sisters at home in the house. These little ones celebrate their Sunday morning hour in the pure white sand of the beach playing with mussel shells.

My parents, too, were of the opinion that children must have a lot of love and good examples, but only a little bit of "religion." The dear Lord Jesus welcomed and blessed the dear children but did not command them to follow him. That takes care of itself if the parents go in this way and instruct the little ones with great care.

Peters (1965): 49, 50, trans. by Noah G. Good

May 9

The Bird School of the Cyevaers
Peter Jansz. Twisck, The Netherlands, 1622

"Honor your father and your mother, so that you may live long in the land the Lord your God is giving you." —Exodus 20:12 (NIV)

In Egypt there is a certain bird named Cyevaers. When an Egyptian person wants to describe a child who loves and honors his parents, they will compare him to this bird. When this bird's parents become old and cannot fly and feed themselves, the younger bird will land on the back of the older bird to feed it until it dies.

The Greeks also use this example to teach their children responsibility toward their parents. These birds are different from most others and do not let their parent birds down. They help and feed them. It seems difficult for some children to do as much as this bird. This bird provides a valuable lesson for many whose parents have brought them up in the world. We who have and we who do not have should say to father and mother, "Come to us, you shall have it as good as we." But many object to helping their parents. They should go to the bird school of the Cyevaers.

The prophet Jeremiah said we should learn from the birds: "The stork in the sky knoweth her appointed time. The turtle dove, crane and the swallow observe the time of their coming, but my people know not the judgment of God." Should not then the children know their duty toward their parents? Instead they neglect and dishonor their parents which even these birds do not do.

*

Two of these birds lived upon the house of the widow Torentin. One day when one of the young was trying to fly, it fell and broke a bone. The widow took care of him until the bone healed and he could fly again. A long time after this, the bird brought a pearl and dropped it in her lap as the widow was sitting near her door. It is even more important that children be good to their parents since they have received so much from them. Children are created so much higher than the birds for they can think and talk.

Twisck (1982): 46, 47

May 10
"God, Help Mother"
Family Life, United States, 1989

I try to teach our preschoolers the "art" of prayer by kneeling down by their bed with them each night. Besides letting them voice their own childish prayers, I also mention a few things like, "Thank you, God, for letting us hear about you in church." Or, "God, help me be a good boy tomorrow," and so forth. Then I have them repeat it.

One particular evening, after an especially trying day of straightening out childish squabbles, getting preschoolers out of mischief, and thinking I didn't get much work done because of their misconduct, I phrased a prayer thus, "God, help me that I will not act so bad tomorrow."

Instead of repeating it word for word like he usually does, my four-year-old son prayed, "God, help Mother that she will not act so bad tomorrow."

Speak of being humbled! Quite a meek and contrite mother rose from her knees, and did much thinking the rest of the evening.

Ever since, when the children begin to be somewhat unhandy, I examine myself. Does the fault lie within me rather than with the children? And that child's prayer has become my own, "Lord, help Mother not to act so bad."

"When Children Pray" (1989): 22

May 11
My Last Adieu
Maeyken Wens, The Netherlands, 1573

An Anabaptist martyr writes from prison to her son.

*M*y dear child Adriaen, my son, I leave you this for a testament, because you are the oldest, to exhort you that you should begin to fear our dear Lord, for you are getting old enough to perceive what is good or evil. Think of Betteken, who is about as old as you are. My son, from your youth follow that which is good and depart from evil: do good while you have time and look at your father, how lovingly he went before me with kindness and courteousness, always instructing me with the Word of the Lord. Oh, if I had so followed after him, how light would be my bonds! Hence, my dear son, beware of that which is evil that you will not have to lament afterwards: "Had I done this or that"; for then, when it is as far as it now is with me, it will be too late.

*

Join yourself to those that fear the Lord, and depart from evil, and through love do all that is good.

Oh, regard not the great multitude or the ancient custom, but look at the little flock, which is persecuted for the word of the Lord, for the good persecute none, but are persecuted.

*

The doctrine of Christ is mercy, peace, purity, faith, meekness, humbleness, and full obedience to God.

My dear son, yield yourself to that which is good; the Lord will give you understanding. I give you this as my last adieu to you. My dear child, heed the Lord's chastening; for whenever you do evil, He will chasten you in your mind. Desist then, and call to the Lord for help, and hate that which is evil, and the Lord will deliver you and good will come to you.

*

My dear son, I hope now to go before you. Follow me thus as much as you value your soul, for besides this there shall be found no other way to salvation. Thus, I will now commend you to the Lord; may He keep you. I trust the Lord that He will do it, if you seek Him. Love one another all the days of your life; take Hansken on your arm now and then for me. And if your father should be taken from you, care for one another. The Lord keep you one and all. My dear children, kiss one another once for me, for remembrance. Adieu, my dear children, all of you. My dear son, be not afraid of this suffering; it is nothing compared to that which shall endure forever. The Lord takes away all fear. I did not know what to do for joy, when I was sentenced. Hence cease not to fear God because of this temporal death. I cannot fully thank my God for the great grace which He has shown me. Adieu once more, my dear son Adriaen. Ever be kind, I pray you, to your afflicted father all the days of your life, and do not grieve him; this I pray all of you, for what I write to the oldest, I also mean to say to the youngest. Herewith I will commend you to the Lord once more. I have written this after I was sentenced to die for the testimony of Jesus Christ.

*

Adriaen Wens, aged about fifteen years, could not stay away from the place of execution on the day on which his dear mother was offered up. Hence he took his youngest little brother, named Hans (or Jan) Mattheus Wens, who was about three years old, upon his

---

arm and went and stood with him somewhere upon a bench, not far from the stakes erected, to behold his mother's death.

But when she was brought forth and placed at the stake, he lost consciousness, fell to the ground and remained in this condition until his mother and the rest were burnt. Afterwards, when the people had gone away, having regained consciousness, he went to the place where his mother had been burnt and hunted in the ashes, in which he found the screw with which her tongue had been screwed fast, which he kept in remembrance of her.

—Thieleman Jansz. van Braght, The Netherlands, 1660

van Braght (1979): 980-982

May 12

A Joyful Find
Klaus Felbinger, Germany, 1560

I was asked further why I separated myself from the holy Christian Church and joined a sect that is tolerated nowhere and is obnoxious to emperor, king, princes and to all the world. I told them that I did not separate myself from the true Christian Church. On the contrary, I only really joined the Church by entering into the true community of saints through true Christian baptism. There is no doubt in my mind that this is where we find forgiveness and remission of sins, where we find the power given by the Holy Spirit to loose and to bind so that this will be valid both on earth and in Heaven.

I know in my heart that no other teaching could have helped me to find true inner peace with God. For as soon as I heard God's voice in my heart and obediently answered, "Here I am," my soul was restored, and now I wait in hope and joy and quiet confidence for His salvation.

Praise and thanks be to God for the love and compassion He has shown me, His unworthy servant. I am certain that God has removed my sins from me farther than night is removed from day. He will no longer remember my sins or hold them against me if from now on I walk faithfully in His sight. He has promised to remit all my sins and blot them out in the innocence of Christ Jesus. Of that I am certain.

Could I ever have found such faith and certainty to God through my blind, unconscious infant baptism?

Hutterian Brethren (1978): 116, 117

I Desire to Remain

Pilgram Marpeck, Germany, 1531

*T*he true saints of God and children of Christ are those whose ruler is the Holy Spirit in the Word of truth. Where two or three are gathered in His name, He is among them. He alone rules in faith through patience and love in His own. I pray God my heavenly Father that He will not allow me to be separated from such a gathering and fellowship of the Holy Spirit; it makes no difference who they are or where they gather in the whole world. I hope to be in their fellowship and to submit myself to the rule of the Holy Spirit of Christ in the obedience of faith.

But I will have nothing to do with any other sect, faction or gathering, no matter what they are called in the whole world. I will especially avoid those who use the bodily sword, contrary to the patience of Christ, who did not resist any evil and who likewise commands His own not to resist tribulation or evil, in order to rule in the kingdom of Christ. I avoid those who institute, command and forbid, therewith to lead and rule the kingdom of Christ.

I also avoid those who deny the true divinity, Spirit, Word and power in Jesus Christ. I avoid those who destroy and deny His natural, earthly humanity which was received from man, of the seed of David, born without man's seed and sin, born of Mary the pure virgin. He was crucified and died a natural earthly death, from which He arose again, and has now seated Himself at the right hand of God.

I also avoid those who, living in open sin and gross evil, want to have fellowship in the kingdom of Christ but without true repentance, and I avoid all those who tolerate such a thing. I avoid all who oppose and fight against the words and the truth of Christ. With all such, regardless of what they are called in the world, I will have no part or fellowship in the kingdom of Christ unless they repent.

My salvation depends alone on Christ's, the Lord's, dying and the shedding of His blood. In Him alone have I received the remission and forgiveness of sins from the Holy Spirit in the fellowship of His saints. Into this fellowship I have also been baptized according to the witness and truth of my heart in the Holy Spirit, on my own testimony and confession of the truth. I also reject all ignorant baptism which happens without true, revealed, personal faith whether in children or adults. For this reason, I also was baptized with external water and external word, in confession of my faith. I was gladly baptized into this fellowship of the Holy Spirit, visibly gathered, for the remission and forgiveness of sins. In it I sincerely desire to remain until my end. Amen to all who desire this with me. That is briefly the testimony of my heart in Christ Jesus

Marpeck (1978): 331-333

A Home for God's Children

Nanne van der Zijp, The Netherlands, 1957

*S*hall the congregation be thought of as the true and holy church, administering the Word of God and directing the faith of its members, who as obedient servants accept the authority of the congregation and submit themselves to its ministers as the ministers of God? Or shall the emphasis be placed upon the operation of the Holy Spirit in the heart of the believer, in this way opening the Scriptures and making known to him the will of God, and giving to the believer the direct experience of peace restored and of sins forgiven?

Those holding to the former view regarded the congregation as all-important, striving for the realization of a church without spot or wrinkle. Much attention was given to the objective holiness of the church. The ban was rigorously applied even in the case of minor sins and the need for a uniform creed, a confession of faith, was emphasized. An ordained ministry, also, was a strict necessity under this pattern of church life. It is self-evident that much support for this type of church life can be found in the New Testament, especially in the pastoral epistles, as well as in the practices of the apostolic church.

Spiritualism, on the other hand, also goes back to the Bible, although it is usually not inclined to rely upon proof texts from the "outer word" for the support of its position. Like congregationalism, spiritualism also has its pitfalls, always being exposed to the danger of disdaining the visible church. Emphasis upon inner security ("My grace is sufficient for thee," 2 Corinthians 12:9) often includes the rejection of an objective formulation of doctrine or confession of faith. The experience of faith as a purely personal relationship between God and the individual soul can be the source of a vigorous religious and moral life. Frequently, however, it also tends toward a low view of the communion service and even of baptism; and occasionally it runs off into an unsound mysticism.

*

The spiritualist view which considers it sufficient to believe that God's Spirit will move and act in the hearts of men without the aid of a visible church is a glorious vision, but it has small chance of realization in the actual world. This vision will survive only with the aid of an eschatology which expects the absolute reign of Christ to be realized upon the earth in the imminent future.

As soon as it is believed that the kingdom of God will be realized only in His time, and that this can be in the far as well as the near future, the building of the visible church in this world becomes a necessity. Believing that without such a visible house of God His children would be homeless in this world, Dirk Philips and Menno Simons proceeded to organize the church.

Hershberger (1957): 74-76, 78

Forms Are Not Irrelevant

Abraham Friesen, United States, 1988

Nearly from the moment we began attending an American evangelical church in Santa Barbara it became apparent to me that the people who attended had little loyalty to any given church. Their loyalty was essentially to themselves. As long as the minister suited them, they stayed. When ministers changed, so did the congregation. There was virtually no concept of what the church was. To be sure, there was talk of the "body of believers," but when it came to problems among members of that body, there was rarely any reconciliation. What happened most often was that people simply left to go elsewhere. Furthermore, salvation was considered to be a very personal matter with few, if any, social consequences.

To most, talk of a "Social Gospel" was a Liberal abomination. Adult and infant baptism, too, were practiced at the same time with virtually no awareness of the different concepts of the church each involved.

*

As I began to teach classes on the Reformation in the various churches of the city, it quickly became apparent to me that few, if any, even knew why they believed what they did. They had little, if any, knowledge of their spiritual heritage, never mind the changes that had taken place in that heritage since the time of its inception. In effect, they were rootless. And because they were rootless they were easy prey for every new evangelical fad and wind of doctrine that blew across the bows of their rudderless vessels.

It was at this point that a passage in Conrad Grebel's September 1524 letter to Thomas Müntzer became increasingly significant to me. There Grebel argued that the Christian insights arrived at earlier by Zwingli and passed on to them were to be used to transform and reshape the church and society. He therefore wrote:

> In respecting persons and in manifold seduction there is grosser and more pernicious error now than has been since the beginning of the world. In the same error we too lingered as long as we heard and read only the evangelical preachers who are to blame for all this, in punishment for our sins. But after we took Scriptures to hand too, and consulted it on many points, we have been instructed somewhat and have discovered the great and harmful error of the shepherds, of ours too, namely, that we do not beseech God earnestly with constant groaning to be brought out of this destruction of all godly life and out of human abominations, to attain to the true faith and divine practices. The cause of all this is false forbearance, the hiding of the divine Word, and the mixing of it with the human. Aye, we say it harms all and frustrates all things divine.

The faith of the apostles, they argued, had led to apostolic practices, apostolic ordinances and institutions. There had, in those early years of the church, been a congruence between theology and the way it was expressed, be that in a transformed life, in certain kinds of practices, ordinances, and yes, even in the way the church itself had been constituted. It was for this reason they were so determined to reestablish the apostolic form of the church. For if the New Testament faith was normative for all time—and everyone said it was—then the forms in which that faith had expressed itself were to be normative as well.

It was this struggle to integrate not only faith and action in a new discipleship, but also apostolic faith with apostolic practice, that was critical. In the past ten years or so this latter aspect has become of central importance to me. The American evangelical churches, heirs to the Magisterial Reformation in this respect, have never done this. Therefore, if we as Mennonites move in their direction with respect to the external forms of Christian practice—and to a certain extent we have already done so—we must inevitably fall prey to their theological tendencies. Rather than move in an evangelical direction, we need rather to return to the Anabaptist model, remove from it those elements that still need removing, and clarify those where they saw only dimly.

In their central concern, however, I regard them as having been right on target. Theological content and the forms in which it is expressed must be congruent. Disastrous consequences will occur if they are not. Discipleship is the personal integration of faith in one's life; that same integration must take place on a corporate level in the experience of the Christian life of the church. The Anabaptists recognized this and church history confirms their judgment. That is why being a Mennonite is important, and that is why I am a Mennonite.

Loewen (1988): 85-89

May 16

Having Roots
Luis Correa, Colombia, 1990

I remember a few years ago that several other members and I decided to leave the church because of some arguments in the local congregation.

*

I was gone from the church for two years, during which time I visited several churches and congregations trying to find a place where I felt comfortable and that would meet my needs. I had spent twenty years in the Mennonite church, first in Cachipay and later in Bogotá, two years at the seminary in Montevideo, later as pastor in a small congregation in Cachipay, and eight months in the new church in Bogotá (1967).

*

I loved my church so much that when practices and liturgy in worship that went against our customs were introduced, we preferred to leave the church. At first glance this could seem like a negative reaction, but fortunately, with time, those of us who had left that congregation again gathered (all ex-students of the school in Cachipay). Although our original purpose was not to form a new congregation, perhaps God's plans were different.

*

Why did I not join another church? Well, it could be that it was because I was born into and grew up in the Mennonite church, but actually it was more than that. For me history is very important: it is said that a people without history is a people without a future. The Mennonite church is a historical church. Having a history, having roots, having been part of the process, has a lot of value. The Mennonite church is not the result of disputes or misunderstandings among people; it represented instead a new concept of the Christian faith, a more authentic and real vision of the word of God, of a life more in touch with that word.

Its liturgy or form of worship is balanced and participatory. It is not tied to tradition, but neither does it go too far toward the Pentecostal-like forms of disorder or improvisation. The worldwide Mennonite family is quite large, but it has known how to keep its identity and brother/sisterhood over time.

*

In all the Latin American countries we live in a very difficult period: unjust political structures, external debts that extremely limit the minimal services to which the citizens are entitled, violence on all sides, propagation of religious sects through false messages that distract people from their reality and oppression. It is important that the Mennonite church recover the biblical message of peace and justice and preach God's plan for humanity, which is no other than life itself and, more specifically, abundant life. My worry is that the Mennonite church would quit participating in the building up of the kingdom; that it would quit being the church of the rural people, of the artisans, of the homemakers; that it would quit preaching and living the gospel within the reality of a liberating gospel.

It is very hard to leave or abandon a Mennonite congregation. I appreciate the Mennonite theology and, as I said before, the history. I appreciate the General Conference's vision of the world and their progressive ideas. I really like the friendship and fraternal ties between foreigners and nationals. I believe this last aspect has determined the success of the work. I hardly remember any serious conflicts between Colombian workers and foreign missionaries. Even when the missionaries have returned to their countries, we remember them here with much love. I like that family warmth in the Mennonite church.

Lichdi (1990): 49, 50

Neither Mine Nor Thine

Ulrich Stadler, Moravia, ca. 1537

*T*here is one communion of all the faithful in Christ and one community of the holy children called of God. They have one Father in heaven, one Lord Christ. All are baptized and sealed in their hearts with one Spirit. They have one mind, opinion, heart and soul as having all drunk from the same Fountain, and alike await one and the same struggle, cross, trial and, at length, one and the same hope in glory.

But it, that is, such a community, must move about in this world, poor, miserable, small and rejected of the world; of whom, however, the world is not worthy. Whoever strives for the lofty things does not belong. Thus in this community everything must proceed equally, all things be one and communal, alike in the bodily gifts of their Father in heaven, which he daily gives to be used by his own according to his will. For how does it make sense that all who here in this pilgrimage look forward to an inheritance in the Kingdom of their Father should not be satisfied with their bodily goods and gifts?

*

They have also yielded themselves and presented themselves to him intimately, patiently, of their own free will, naked and uncovered, to suffer and endure his will and, moreover, to fulfill it and thereafter also to devote themselves in obedience and service to all the children of God. Therefore, they also live with one another where the Lord assigns a place to them, peaceably, united, lovingly, amicably and fraternally, as children of one Father. In their pilgrimage they should be satisfied with the bodily goods and gifts of their Father, since they should also be altogether as one body and members one toward another.

Now if, then, each member withholds assistance from the other, the whole thing must go to pieces. The eyes won't see, the hands won't take hold. Where, however, each member extends assistance equally to the whole body, it is built up and grows and there is peace and unity, yea, each member takes care for the other.

In brief, equal care, sadness and joy, and peace are at hand. It is just the same in the spiritual body of Christ. If the deacon of the community will never serve, the teacher will not teach, the young brother will not be obedient, the strong will not work for the community but for himself, and each one wishes to take care of himself, and if once in a while someone withdraws without profit to himself, the whole body is divided. In brief, *one, common* builds the Lord's house and is pure; but *mine, thine, his, own* divides the Lord's house and is impure. Therefore, where there is ownership and one has it, and it is his, and one does not wish to be one with Christ and his own in living and dying, he is outside of Christ and his communion and has thus no Father in heaven.

*

But the wickedness of men has spoiled everything. For as the sun with its shining is common to all, so also the use of all creaturely things. Whoever appropriates them for himself and encloses them is a thief and steals what is not his. For everything has been created free in common. Of such thieves the whole world is full. May God guard his own from them.

Williams and Mergal (1957): 277-279

May 18

Bear With Each Other
Andreas Ehrenpreis, Slovakia, 1650

*S*ome people are not without light and recognition of the truth, yet they do not want to step completely into the light. They hinder others from seeing the full light because they still love wealth and its benefits. They have enough recognition to see that on the day of reckoning, self-seeking will not be justified and praised. But to excuse themselves they claim that community living is an endless source of dissent and strife, as if Christ who is the Lord, the apostles and the Holy Spirit did not know what they were doing when they brought community life into being. They may be taking certain unhappy marriages as a parallel: man and wife live together in disunity, and of them it is unfortunately said that they love each other best at a distance. But in a good marriage it is different. Each one bears with the weaknesses of the other. Both together bear joy and sorrow as they come.

How much more does that apply to the new life of community, in which a whole people of God should bear with one another in love and forgive each other everything! They make allowances for each other. They can never forsake each other because of human weakness. They do not desert each other. We know very well that Jesus turned sharply on Peter. We know of disputes among the first disciples. Did they therefore desert one another? Could the unity of the Spirit be lost on this account? Or shall the communal life of Christ and His apostles be despised or rejected on this account? That is impossible. Now we can understand why Christ who is our Lord, insists so much upon reconciliation and forgiveness.

Even at the time of the early Christians there was plenty of unpleasantness among the believers. Was the unity of the Spirit lost because of that? The Church remained united in spite of it—that one Church to which we must listen if we do not want to be outside. It would be wonderful if a people of God could live in uninterrupted peace, completely without blemish or defilement or any hateful thing. But because of our human weakness, such disturbances happen all the time. One ought never, on account of such shortcomings and weaknesses, to reject a whole people. "Don't throw the baby out with the bath water."

These things will not be an obstacle to anyone who is intent on building up church community for the sake of love and salvation. He will be filled with a burning zeal to build up a living organism and to make the sacrifices demanded by the Spirit. That includes the surrender of all his possessions and all his strength in true service to God. He surrenders his whole self. That is how he finds true *Gelassenheit*. If a light is to burn, it must consume itself. That is the only way it can give light.

Hutterian Brethren (1978): 15-18

May 19

Questions on a Spring Evening
Anna Baerg, Soviet Union, 1918

*T*hey say that the Prussians were surprised that we Germans in Russia had remained so German. I was happy about this observation, even if the idea seems a little offensive to me. That one should think otherwise! What are we but Germans! Naturally there are sorry exceptions; but the real Germans, the ones who feel it from the heart, have never been able to adapt themselves to the Russian way of life. Two such contradictory metals do not allow themselves to be alloyed. And if during the war people here supported the Russians, it was, after all, because of their duty towards the Fatherland rather than out of love and sympathy. It is hardly to be wondered at that the Germans were so warmly welcomed here and that so many people are enthusiastic about Germany in spite of the fact that half of the Ukraine is already ruled by the Bolsheviks.

One thing will certainly result from the German takeover: Mennonite pacifism will become a thing of the past. Now everyone will have to take up weapons, and many are also in entire agreement with this. For me this seems to be a breach of faith. But then I am just a simple girl whose opinion isn't worth much and, I must say right off, I can hardly begin to answer the hundred and one clever arguments for it. Often even I have wondered why it is that other peoples pay tribute to the military—even Israel went into battle on God's orders. Why then do we Mennonites picture ourselves so different from the rest? Are we better than other people? Certainly not. And what of the charge of cowardice that so many people lay on us? All I can say is that often there is more courage in patience and endurance than in retaliation. But enough of that.

As I sit at the open window breathing in the fresh evening air, the song of the nightingale greets me from the garden. After this afternoon's rain the air is still and mild. The garden is particularly beautiful now when you walk along the avenue of blooming chestnut trees and lilac bushes and when you feel surrounded by a symphony of sounds. Beautiful too, this garden in the moonlight, when the world lies couched in such a peculiar magic, captivating the heart.

Baerg (1985): 21, 22

May 20

I Completely Abandoned Myself to the Lord

Michael Sattler, Germany, 1527

On his return from the historic meeting at Schleitheim, where the Brotherly Union of the Swiss Brethren was agreed upon, Michael Sattler was arrested for his Anabaptist beliefs. The following are excerpts from his farewell letter written from prison to his congregation.

Dear fellow members in Christ, you should be admonished not to forget love, without which it is not possible that you be a Christian congregation. You know what love is through the testimony of Paul our fellow brother. He says: "Love is patient and kind, not jealous, not puffed up, not ambitious, seeks not its own, thinks no evil, rejoices not in iniquity, rejoices in the truth, suffers everything, endures everything, believes everything, hopes everything." If you understand this text, you will find the love of God and of neighbor.

If you love God you will rejoice in the truth and will believe, hope and endure everything that comes from God. Thereby the shortcomings mentioned above can be removed and avoided. But if you love the neighbor, you will not scold or ban zealously, will not seek your own, will not remember evil, will not be ambitious or puffed up, but kind, righteous, generous in all gifts, humble and sympathetic with the weak and imperfect.

*

You have probably learned from brothers how some of ours have been taken prisoner and then, when the brothers had also been taken prisoner in Horb, how we were taken to Binsdorf. During this time we underwent all sorts of attacks from the adversaries. They menaced us with a cord, then with fire, then with the sword. In such dangers I completely abandoned myself to the Lord in His will and readied myself for death for the sake of His testimony, with all my brothers and my wife. Then I thought of the great number of false brothers and of you who are so few, yea, such a small band; and how few faithful workers there are in the vineyard of the Lord. So it seemed needful to me to urge you by this exhortation to follow us in God's combat and thereby to console you that you might not become weary under the discipline of the Lord.

*

You know, my beloved fellow members, how it is fitting to live godly and Christianly. Look out, watch and pray, that your wisdom might not bring you under judgment. Persevere in prayer, that you might stand worthily before the Son of Man. Be mindful of your predecessor, Jesus Christ, and follow after Him in faith and obedience, love and longsuffering. Forget what is carnal, that you might truly be named Christians and children of the most high God; persevere in the discipline of your heavenly Father and turn not aside, neither to the left, nor to the right, that you might enter in through the gate, and that it might not be needful of you to follow an alien path, which the sinners, sorcerers, idolaters and everyone who loves and does lies must take.

Be mindful of our meeting and what was decided there, and continue in strict accordance therewith. And if something should have been forgotten, pray the Lord for understanding. Be generous toward all who have need among you, but especially for those who work among you with the Word and are hunted and cannot eat their own bread in peace and quiet. Forget not the assembly, but apply yourselves to coming together constantly and that you may be united in prayer for all men and the breaking of bread, and this all the more fervently as the day of the Lord draws nearer.

Yoder (1973): 59-62

May 21

Ready to Suffer

Wilhelm Reublin, Germany, ca. 1527

The following is from an account of Michael Sattler's trial and execution. He was martyred on May 20 or 21, 1527.

To these accusations Michael answered himself with mild Christian speech, about each and every article, grounding and supporting himself only upon the one eternal Word of God in Old and New Testaments.

*

Insistently he called for Scripture to be judge. But this was not to be.

To which the Lord Advocate, the *Stadtschreiber* of Ensisheim, said: "The hangman is the one who should debate with him." Drawing his sword half out of its sheath, he said, "If he does not, then I myself will execute you with this sword. And thereby would do God a service." With which he rested his case.

But Michael would not argue the case, but was rather ready to suffer in a clear Christian way, and commended himself to God and His will.

The judgment which was given: that Michael should be led to the market, his tongue be cut off, and then gripped six times with red hot tongs, be thrown alive into a fire and burnt to a powder.

Whereupon [immediately after the pronouncing of the verdict] he joyfully addressed and consoled his wedded sister in the presence of the lords and princes.

Then he was put back in the prison from Saturday till Monday. (What anxiety, combat and strife his flesh and spirit had with one another is inconceivable. What he in his love must have meditated.) And then on the said day, according to the content of the verdict, he was led out and they began by cutting off his tongue and tearing his body with red hot tongs. But he praised God at the place of execution, hard and strong. As he was being tied to the ladder with cords, he admonished the *Schultheiss* that he should meditate on the words which he had spoken with him in love and secretly, and that he should willingly render himself to God the Lord.

A small sack of powder was hung around his neck and thus he was thrown into the fire. When then the powder went off and one despaired of his still being alive, he cried with a clear voice often and constantly to God in heaven. When he had been crying thus for a long time, he became unbound in the fire and raised his arms high with the first two fingers on each hand outstretched and cried with a powerful voice: "Father, into thy hands I commend my soul!" And thus ended his life. The Lord be eternally praised. Amen!

His right hand could not be burned up, nor the heart, until the executioner had to cut it into pieces, and then the blood at first spurted high heavenward. In the night, many observed the sun and the moon standing still above the place of execution, three hours long, with golden letters written within. Such a bright light went out from them that many thought it was midday. Which the rulers undertook to forbid and suppress with oaths. Which, however, was no help.

Yoder (1973): 77, 78

May 22

God Will Not Force Anyone
Klaus Felbinger, Germany, 1560

Does Christ make people accept His teaching by threatening them with prison and torture as many do who are called Christians? O no! He speaks to those who thirst for His righteousness, who have ears to hear, whose hearts are heavy, who want to be freed of their sins—those who are called and urged by God.

In truth, faith is not for everyone. It is a gift, given to those who love God. God will not force anyone to serve Him. He loves free and willing hearts who serve Him with gladness of soul and joyfully do what is right. For it is written: "Those who believe will obey God out of love." And again: "Those who fear God will seek to please Him and keep His commandments." For the Spirit promised by God to those who believe in Him is not a timid and slavish one, but a childlike, enthusiastic, free and willing Spirit, through whom we cry to God the Father with faith and trust. He is our powerful advocate before God. John has said, "We have confidence before God; and we receive from him whatever we ask, because we keep his commandments and do what pleases him."

Hutterian Brethren (1978): 101, 102

May 23
Becoming a Mennonite
George Shillington, Canada, 1988

A question frequently put to me at Mennonite gatherings is, "How did you, an Irishman, become *involved with* the Mennonites?"

*

Initially I was convinced that Mennonite identity centered primarily on theological and practical implications of Christian faith, and only secondarily on language, food, heredity and ethnicity. In a secondary position these latter factors of Mennonite self-consciousness are not threatening to those of us whose ethnic and sociological ancestry resides elsewhere. Regrettably, however, the parameters of Mennonite self-definition seem to have been shifting in recent years in the Mennonite Brethren setting with which I am more familiar. Perhaps the same is happening in other settings as well.

The shift is not simply that primary and secondary features of Mennonite self-awareness are being inverted. That would be serious enough. But the situation as I see it happening in my own Mennonite conference is even more disconcerting. The primary elements of historic Mennonite faith are being replaced with a modern and conspicuously popular form of Christianity that poses as "the truth" for all. This mode of Christian self-understanding, promoted aggressively in the United States but found widely in Canada as well, tends to define Christian faith in terms of a number of fundamental formulations to be *professed*, resulting in a good feeling and material well-being. Adoption of this way of thinking is certain to break down authentic piety, characteristic of historic Anabaptist Christian self-understanding.

*

Moreover, the shift that has been taking place in the Canadian Mennonite Brethren Church is more than inversion of the primary and secondary aspects of Anabaptist-Mennonite faith and life. It is a shift away from the center of the Anabaptist heritage of faith, leaving the other aspects, the secondary culture ones, as the *only* marks of Mennonite identity. This condition concerns me, because I am not and cannot be personally committed to this vestige of Mennonite identity by virtue of another cultural heritage and heredity from which I am not prepared to extricate myself.

Coming back to the question frequently put to me, "How does it feel to be among the Mennonites?" I have come to understand, I think, the reason for the structure of the question. To be a Mennonite, to actually be one, a person has to be born of Mennonite parents and enculturated in Mennonite customs. The fact is, I feel just fine among the Mennonites. I feel accepted, respected, loved. And yet I still have the feeling of not being a Mennonite. What saddens me about that "feeling" is the fact that while I treasure the Anabaptist-Mennonite heritage of faith I am not completely free to call myself "Mennonite."

*

In conversation with an administrator of a Mennonite institution I learned that he was seeking someone to fill a position in the institution. A "Mennonite name" was mentioned. But that person had joined a non-Mennonite church, had been a member there for years, drove past a Mennonite church to attend the non-Mennonite one. I asked if the position in the Mennonite institution was open to a non-Mennonite, to which the administrator replied: "But he *is* Mennonite: I have known his parents for years." Immediately I wondered if I had the right to think of myself as Mennonite, coming as I did from a non-Mennonite home, not having a Mennonite name.

Loewen (1988): 285-289

May 24

Forward to Full Discipleship
Conrad Grebel, Switzerland, 1524

The emerging Swiss Brethren in Zurich had read two booklets by Thomas Müntzer which encouraged them in their radical reform. On behalf of the Zurich circle, Conrad Grebel drafted a letter to Müntzer in order to learn more about Müntzer's ideas. The Swiss mistakenly believed that Müntzer advocated nonresistance.

March forward with the Word and create a Christian church with the help of Christ and his rule such as we find instituted in Matthew 18 and practiced in the epistles. Press on in earnest with common prayer and fasting, in accord with faith and love without being commanded and compelled. Then God will help you and your lambs to all purity.

*

There is more than enough wisdom and counsel in the Scripture on how to teach, govern, direct and make devout all classes and all men. Anyone who will not reform or believe and strives against the Word and acts of God and persists therein, after Christ and his Word and rule have been preached to him and he has been admonished with the three witnesses before the church, such a man we say on the basis of God's Word shall not be put to death but regarded as a heathen and publican and left alone.

Moreover, the gospel and its adherents are not to be protected by the sword, nor should they protect themselves, which as we have heard through our brother is what you believe and maintain. True believing Christians are sheep among wolves, sheep for the slaughter. They must be baptized in anguish and tribulation, persecution, suffering and death; tried in fire; and must reach the fatherland of eternal rest not by slaying the physical but the spiritual. They use neither worldly sword nor war, since killing has ceased with them entirely, unless indeed we are still under the old law, and even there (as far as we can know) war was only a plague after they had once conquered the Promised Land.

Harder (1985): 289, 290

May 25

Is He Not Our Lord and Master?

Menno Simons, The Netherlands, 1535

Christ did not want to be defended with Peter's sword. How can a Christian then defend himself with it? Christ wanted to drink the cup which the Father had given Him. How then can a Christian avoid it?

Or does any person expect to be saved by other means than those which Christ has taught us? Is not Christ the way, the truth and the life? Is He not the door to the fold, so that none can enter into the fold but by Him?

Is not He the Shepherd of His sheep, whom the sheep should follow? Is not He our Lord and Master? And who is it that would be above his Lord? Is it not he that would not suffer as Christ suffered? Who is it that would be above his Master but he that is not satisfied with his Master's doctrine? Let everyone take heed. It is forbidden to us to fight with physical weapons.

*

And if we are to take prophets as an example to suffer persecution, then we must put on the apostolic armor, and the armor of David must be laid aside. How can it be harmonized with the Word of God that one who boasts of being a Christian could lay aside the spiritual weapons and take up the carnal ones? For Paul says: "The servant of the Lord must not strive; but be gentle unto all men, apt to teach, patient; in meekness instructing those that oppose themselves."

*

All of you who would fight with the sword of David and also be the servants of the Lord, consider these words which show how a servant should be minded. If he is not to strive and quarrel, how then can he fight? If he is to be gentle to all men, how can he then hate and harm them? If he is to be ready to learn, how can he lay aside the apostolic weapons? He will need them. If he is to instruct in meekness those that oppose, how can he destroy them?

Menno (1956): 45, 46

May 26

Is It Surprising?
Samuel Gerber, Switzerland, 1948

*I*n a wonderful way our country was spared from the war. However, we young men were obliged to carry out boundary patrol duty during these years. When hunger threatened our country, the farmers were called upon to do almost superhuman work in their fields. Strenuous general coercive measures and restrictions were not spared. Nevertheless, the utmost trials—the actual horrible war—we did not live through. By far the majority of our Mennonite youth did their service in the medical corps. Some, however, allowed themselves to be enrolled in the regular military forces. Our position in regard to bearing arms became a lively topic of discussion when a young minister from the Sonnenberg congregation enrolled in a training school for officers. In all of the discussions concerning nonresistance there is with us up to now a piercing note of discord.

*

The winter of 1942-1943 was especially severe in our region. So much snow fell that one could hardly venture forth except on skis. One Sunday during this time there was to be a worship service. My father was sick. The above-mentioned minister already was in the service as an officer. Another minister, who was to substitute for my father, was very critical of the minister-officer. However, on this Sunday he was otherwise busy and stayed out of the bad weather. Then we telephoned the officer. He received a Sunday leave, came by train and on skis walked up the mountain from the depot to the church through the deep snow. He preached the Gospel to the little group who had gathered there despite the storm, in a clear, fresh and joyous manner.

Similar examples could be related. Is it surprising that the congregation of Sonnenberg elected the young officer as their elder? Is it surprising that he is at the present time the secretary of our conference? Is it surprising if we at the present reject the nonresistance of those brethren who in their daily lives are everything but nonresistant? And are you surprised that we young people became skeptical of all nonresistance? We recognize thankfully that you brethren in America have shown us a different kind of nonresistance. There has awakened here and there in our Swiss congregations a new insight and thinking on this question.

Hiebert (1950): 214, 215

May 27

A Changing Attitude

Margaret Greenwalt, The Netherlands, 1948

I would like to take you back to Holland in the year 1943 when our country was overrun and occupied by the Germans. You will understand that our feelings toward them were not too friendly. When we heard of the invasion in France, how we desired and wished that the French and the British would fight on to liberate us. We admired the glorious armies. We were militaristically minded. One day I had a chance to see the glorious army. That was in the hospital where I was employed. There before me I beheld soldiers badly injured physically, and often spiritual wrecks. Then it began to dawn upon me that I had desired results such as these in my attitude toward the war.

This was revolting to think about. I could not feel easy. I began to realize the cruelty and sinfulness of war which was impossible to harmonize with the life and teachings of Christ. However, I think that you will all realize that a complete change did not happen in one day. It took a lot of time and a lot of prayer before I could change my feelings and faith to the point that I can love my enemies. That is my continuous prayer. Dear Lord, help me to love my enemies. Amen.

Hiebert (1950): 171

May 28

Leading the Way

Maria Quiroga de Alvarez, Argentina, 1990

*R*esistance to the mandatory military service became a subject for study and discussion among the youth. New phrases such as "conscientious objectors," "alternate service" and "voluntary service" were introduced into my vocabulary and mind. I discovered then that our group surely had a definite place among other groups. Yes, and today when conscientious objectors are calling at the steps of the House of Representatives of the nation, our people are in the front line. They write and sign petitions so that the government may study these options and create legal provisions for our young people who, because of their conscience, do not want to bear arms or train to bring death.

In spite of sixty years of the Mennonite presence in Argentina, in spite of raising our voices against the military draft, the goal has yet to be accomplished. During the war between Argentina and England over the possession of islands in the south Atlantic, some of our youths came face to face with the problem. One eighteen-year-old who had been called up for military service, son of a pastor of one of our Mennonite churches, asked his father, "Dad, what will I do if I am faced with a battle and have to kill?" His father answered him, "You will have to decide for yourself. I can tell you that I would rather have a son who died in peace with his Lord than a son who has had his peace disturbed because he killed a fellow human being."

The Mennonite church in Argentina has not renounced that objective. On the contrary, in the organization of the evangelicals it is the one that leads the way because of its pacifist history that has brought so much pain and so many blessings to this world. A clear and definite law has still not been passed, but the presentation of that request continues, each time accompanied by a larger group of people in favor of peace. Now I can say that "I am a Mennonite," but I still cannot fully understand all those deaths in our history, unjust deaths of our forebears in Europe. How much blood was shed, how much pain and how much torture, all in the name of faith and in defense of life in Christ and obedience to his teachings.

My personal temperament leads me to reject all dogmatism and, even more as I perceive the ample and generous spirit of our history, to understand the forgiveness and goodness that come from Christ himself.

Lichdi (1990): 46, 47

May 29

Please Let Me Refuse
Bui Quang, Vietnam, 1975

I would like to refuse one ready-made heaven. . . .
Because that heaven parallels hell,
But hell is actually my home:
It's a long weary war,
It's a hundred years of slavery,
       a thousand years of oppression.

I would like to refuse that heaven
       displaying its merchandise
On the city street of Freedom,
With all the "Freedoms" listed
On bills of lading from England, America, and France.

I would like to refuse
The heaven and the god
       of cold glittering church buildings
And of cold air-conditioned restaurants
Belonging to coffin contractors
       for those killed in combat.

Slogans promising full stomachs and warm clothes
    by tricky traitors
Hang on barbed wire fences around schools
And on iron bars and shackles of beastly prisons.

I would only like to be the smallest gentle lamb
In the flock which the Lord leads.
. . . and I will go together with Him.

Klassen (1986): 241, 242

May 30

The Greatest Warriors?
Jacob S. Lehman, United States, 1903

We hear it said that the Christian nations are the greatest warriors and that the best Christians make the best soldiers. This may be so according to the popular acceptation of these terms, but if christian nations were nations of Christians, this would not be so. But if simply accepting Christ as the Messiah, and so much of His Gospel as is convenient, and organizing into church order under sectarian rule is sufficient to entitle a people or nation to be termed Christian, then those assertions may be accepted by those who consent to them.

This class no doubt has no trouble to believe that the officer who prays most will fight the best. And no wonder that a popular preacher could speak in praise of Cromwell—who it is said had his men sing a doxology, and while they sang they marched, and as they marched they fought, and as they fought they gained the victory.

Popular Christianity has great faith in the warrior who prays much, and it has for his deeds only words of praise which it hangs as laurels upon his brow. It seems to delight in immortalizing the memory of such, but seems to forget that the avowed infidel is deserving of as much honor for the same service in the same cause as the other. His efforts are as unselfish, his devotions as marked and his services as beneficial.

But we must not forget that they are both God's ministers, but only ministers under the world-power, and stand upon one common plane; and that their reward is in their work, without any promise in the kingdom of Christ. And however morally good and of exalted character, no part of their work bears any comparison with the loving and forgiving spirit that must ever characterize the soldier of the cross. The work of the one is to waste and destroy, even the lives of helpless and often innocent men, while the other is to love and to save.

But some assert that they can engage in litigation or go to war without hating those who oppose them, and think they can even love them. But it would be hard to convince a man that you love him when you are thrusting at him with a sword or bayonet. At least you could not convince him that you were "walking in love," as the apostle teaches. Even if some could fight and kill and not be angry, that still does not prove that for Christians to do so is right.

Lehman ([1903]): 124, 125

May 31

Pentecost in Exile
Alexander Ediger, Soviet Union, early 1930s

*I*t is Pentecost and towards evening I walked into a Russian church and attended the festive service. The singing in the high vaulted room was beautiful and the quiet reverence which permeated the large assembly was especially soothing. I thought of the song, "He is always there if one desires Him." What a comfort it is that we can always have Him, regardless if we are in the North or South, free or captive, together or all alone.

*

Not long ago I met a dear Lutheran brother here in the far north, whom the Lord had led into deep ways. We greatly strengthened one another through mutual encouragement. He let me read a poem which has remained in my memory. A tired pilgrim is on the way to his eternal home. He has been en route for a long time: the sun is hot and his limbs ache. The large cross which he carries on his shoulders presses upon him. "Oh, if only the cross was not so heavy," he sighs. As he walks along, he suddenly sees a saw lying beside the road. "Wait a minute," he thinks, "I can make my cross lighter by cutting off a good-sized piece." No sooner said than done.

He continues on his way with his shortened cross and finally reaches the city towards evening. Oh no, a deep wide moat surrounds it and a bridge is nowhere in sight. The pilgrim takes his cross and tries to lay it over the moat but it is too short. He needed exactly the length which he had sawed off. How sad, so near and yet so far from his goal. So, tired pilgrim, do not saw off your cross. Patiently carry it further, for your Savior himself will help you. You will soon reach the eternal city and then you will rest with God. Thank God, there is still a rest for the tired people of God.

Then I met a dear young brother from Konteniusfeld who, in spite of difficult circumstances, has remained firm in the faith. He has been separated from his family and church for years. I often have to think of Elijah and his feeling that faith no longer existed. Yet I am convinced that God has many thousands even here. Yes, the Lord knows His own and the hour is nigh when He shall come and call them by name.

*

As far as I am concerned, I know I had to walk this path. The Lord had to lead me this way; it meant only good for me. They were often difficult times and I have seen hunger, cold and nakedness in abundance. And yet, looking back on my pathway I can honestly say, "Bless the Lord, Oh my soul, and forget not all His benefits."

I have often had to think of a text on which I once spoke: the Lord does not protect from suffering, but protects in suffering. You know as long as one does not suffer one fears suffering and thinks one will not be able to bear it when it comes. Yet when one is suffering one begins to experience the comforting and helping hand of God. How meaningful that Word from Psalm 23 has become: "Yes, though I walk through the valley of the shadow of death I will fear no harm, for Thou art with me; Thy rod and Thy staff, they comfort me."

Toews (1990): 75, 76

June

June 1

The Significance of Signs
Hans Denck, Germany, 1527

*H*oliness means to have separated oneself once and for all from the evil world and from all filth of the flesh to serve God the Lord only. This is signified and testified by water baptism through which one declares the old life to be wicked and desires henceforth to walk in the new life. Righteousness is to give everyone his just due.

*

Now, one owes God the Lord everything one has and is capable of in body and soul, honor and possessions. For his name's sake therefore, everything must be risked and given up, even to the ultimate surrender, so that all children should experience what the first-born son experienced, that he might be transformed into our nature. Therefore, we should become and break bread, one for the other, as he has become our bread—ground and baked into one food. All this we are to recall and remind one another of in the breaking of bread.

Therefore one breaks bread frequently, but is baptized only once. For the beginning of the new covenant happens but once, even though it may be transgressed and sought after again. As a child is born of its father but once, even though it may run away and return; it remains nonetheless the father's child and is in no need to be born once more. But the fulfillment of the covenant which is righteousness must be continuously practiced and carried out.

These customs have not been introduced so that one who fails to keep them cannot be saved, but rather that they be kept in true earnestness wherever they are observed. However simple and foolish this may appear to the world, the Lord will not have it despised. He himself set an example for us therefore, so that he might fulfill all righteousness from the least to the greatest. By this he also intended to show that nothing is so bad that something precious could not be recalled from it.

Denck (1989): 277, 278

By the Spirit

Henry Funk, United States, 1744

*I*n the regeneration and renewal of the mind by the word of the Spirit is great gain. Thereby man becomes a fit subject to be baptized with water in the name of the Lord Jesus as a member of his body the church. He will thereby also be prepared to receive the Spirit in a greater measure and to dispense the gift of the Spirit as the Lord may impart to every one the manifold gifts. By the Holy Spirit we can call Jesus "Lord."

*

By the Spirit, and from the Spirit of God, grow the good fruits and the generous grapes of the living vine: the rich pearls and the ornaments of a holy life which adorn the people of God—the Spiritual Bride, his church.

By the Spirit we are brought to believe in God with a firm faith, to love him ardently with our whole heart. Above all things to put our hope in him and trust him patiently in all the afflictions and tribulations that may come over us in his providence. By the Spirit we live in peace and love with all men, exercising mercy and forbearance with their infirmities and walking in truth and honesty with all. By the Spirit we mortify our members which are upon the earth, and live a life of chastity; by the Spirit pride and arrogance are subdued; and to sum up all: by the Spirit God directs and guides mankind into all good and into his everlasting kingdom. And without the divine Spirit man can do nothing to merit his soul's salvation—much less to work it out and accomplish it.

This Holy Spirit is a watchful sentinel in the believer, or in those that are his, so that when the enemy attempts to surprise the believer to tempt him to sin, he withstands and warns him of his danger of sin.

*

We see the goodness of God in the invaluable gift of his Spirit: for all that man can do in working out his soul's salvation is done by the operation of the Holy Spirit; and whatsoever is not done by the operation of the divine Spirit of God will not benefit man in the blessedness of his soul's salvation.

Funk (1851): 34-38

A Taste of Paradise

Jan Philipsz. Schabaelje, The Netherlands, 1635

In this imaginary conversation, Simon Cleopas describes to a Wandering Soul the life of the apostolic church in Jerusalem following the sending of the Spirit on the day of Pentecost (see Acts 2: 44-46).

Simon Cleopas: The three thousand were of one mind, even so as bread is baked of many thousand grains that one cannot be known from the other; or like a great fire made by laying together many sticks, so that the more sticks the greater the fire, and would in reality be but one fire. Thus were these hearts melted together by the fire of the Spirit, that they were one heart, one soul, one will, one love, one hope, one joy! A work that God performed—such a grand reformation among the people.

It appeared as though paradise was again restored. The golden period appeared to be ushered in; all what Cain and Nimrod had undone was again restored. The lambs fed with the wolf, the young child handled the serpent, and the weaned child put his hand into the mouth of the basilisk; there was neither contention nor any one to molest on the mountain of the Lord.

*

Simon Cleopas: The avaricious became liberal, good hearted, free-givers. They distributed their surplus moneys among the needy that they also might have to live upon. They destroyed their indentures by which the poor were oppressively held; were ashamed to take usury, sold their possessions and had all things in common. Nay, they did not say that those possessions were theirs, for they knew that the poor stood more in need of them than they, whom they had so long oppressed. Here it was demonstrated that charity is the bond of perfection—charity that is impartial, uniting all.

*

Wandering Soul: The poor must have been exceedingly glad of this, who were formerly so much oppressed by these avaricious persons.

Simon Cleopas: They rejoiced as though they had been released from a dismal dungeon and placed into a royal palace. They assembled nearly every evening. A table common to all was prepared. One came with his basket of bread; another with his basket of meat; another with a flask of wine or some other drink. Their language was, "Praise, brothers, praise ye the Lord, who gives us all things bountifully. None shall want: be not solicitous on account of your poverty; all that you need shall be given you freely." And they spent their time in praising and conversing of the Lord and comforting each other. Exercising in acts of devotion, their hearts were filled with joy—with the joys of the Spirit of love, and hence these feasts were called *love feasts*.

Wandering Soul: O the paradise upon earth! But did not the wealthy regret to depart with their goods and possessions when they saw how they diminished? Or did not the poor become voluptuous and overbearing, as is often the case when they see that the rich are humbled and they share part of the goods (for many of the poor become very impolite and profligate when they get to rise in the world)?

Simon Cleopas: Touching the first, because the rich were enlightened of God, they did not care for more than what was sufficient for the common comforts of life; therefore they had no occasion to be solicitous about many things. Besides that, they saw the hand of God work powerfully in this communion, so that everywhere there was abundance. And because there were none idle, but all industriously employed, they could therefore readily conclude that the joint labor of many, properly managed, would support a greater number than for a few to labor and others to spend it.

Besides, everything was brought under an economical management, and many living together, there was a great saving in that respect. But the most remarkable was that they dedicated themselves and their possessions unto the Lord, whom they served and who promised to provide for them in all things necessary. And they also bore in mind how Jesus, their master, spoke against the riches of this world. To be like him, they preferred to be poor, as being the more secure condition for them.

Respecting the poor becoming voluptuous or proud—I have to reply that the wholesome doctrines and the fear of God, of which they always conversed, both at their feasts and in their meetings, kept them within due bounds, so that nothing of the kind was heard or seen, lest they would be excluded. And they did delight to be in the church—for the ungodly have no pleasure in meeting with the pious. And there was such a power of the Spirit among them that all these things were completely suppressed, so that the Holy Ghost formed them as of one lump, into one harmonious whole.

Schabalie ([1834]): 347-351

June 4

The Most Powerful Picture of Community
Andreas Ehrenpreis, Slovakia, 1650

*T*o this first church, the Lord's Supper was given as a uniting and sharing in *one* loaf and *one* body. The grain had to die for the sake of the unity of the loaf. Only by dying was it able to take root and grow in the field and withstand all the storms. Only in this way could it bear fruit. Similarly, each individual must give himself up, must die to himself if he wants to follow Christ on His way. Then in turn the harvested grain had to be crushed and milled if it was to become bread. Our own will undergoes the same for the sake of community. It must be broken if we are to belong to the community of the Supper and to serve in communal work. Furthermore, the grains had to be brought together into *one* flour and *one* loaf. Not one grain could preserve itself as it was or keep what it had. No kernel could remain isolated. Every grain had given itself and its whole strength into the bread.

In the same way, the grapes have to be pressed for the wine. Every grape gives all its strength and all its juice into the one wine. In it no grape can stay as it is. This is the only way wine can be made. Grapes or kernels that remain whole are only fit for the pigs or the manure heap. They are far from being bread and wine. In keeping their own strength and individuality they lose everything and remain lost.

Here we see the most powerful picture of community. That is how Christ presented it to those who were with Him at the Supper. But even this uniform loaf is broken, just as Christ let His Body be broken. For us this means that the stubbornness of self-will is broken and that we must be ready to suffer and die, even in community. God himself brings this about by letting His power break in upon us, and that is what we pray for. His power streams out over us as love, as the love that brings all God's truth to fulfillment.

As Christ has loved us, so love reigns among us. By this His flock will be known. This is the only way we can hold the Lord's Supper and community of the table. Everything we were or had, all strength and energy and property were given for common use. Like the loaf and the wine, we have become one. Whoever wants to be a brother, whoever has a longing to share in the breaking of the bread and in prayer, cannot reject community.

We never ask in the Lord's Prayer for *my* bread or *thy* bread. We ask for *our* bread, *our* daily bread, the opposite of private property. Each time Christ distributed bread, He gave to many, to all, to each alike, no matter how small the supply was. He did not want to give to any one person alone. So the small became great, the little became much.

Hutterian Brethren (1978): 22-25

June 5

God Still Has a People
Klaus Felbinger, Germany, 1560

God still has a devout people on this earth, who have been shocked and startled out of sin through His living Word. He has called them out from the world and gathered them to His Name through the Holy Spirit. He has chosen them to be His own, to praise His glory, to walk in His ways, and to proclaim His power and goodness.

They say we are a sect that is obnoxious to princes and lords and all the world, and that everybody objects to us. That cannot intimidate me or any true lover of God; it strengthens our certainty and deepens our faith in the proofs of God's working wherever word and deed go hand in hand. When Simeon held the little Baby Jesus in his arms in the Temple, he foretold to His mother Mary that He would be the light of the world and the salvation of all peoples to the ends of the earth—and His sign will be that men will reject Him. That means not only Him but all those who follow Him, who believe in Him and walk in His footsteps.

*

A devout heart that fears God cannot remain silent but must speak up and protest the wicked ways of those who do not please God, much less find salvation. That arouses their hatred, and the cry goes up: "Away with the scoundrels! They think they are better than we are! They have no right to live!" And so the godly have to flee as Jacob, whom God loved, fled from the wicked Esau and his children to Mesopotamia to stay with his relatives and fellow believers.

*

Nowhere is a sincere believer happier than in the presence of his brothers and fellow believers. They show each other love, reverence and faithfulness and do good to each other. It is the divine nature of love that makes us feel we are in our neighbor's debt and urges us to serve him joyfully wherever we can. Brothers and sisters refresh each other by sharing the gifts God put into their hearts for the good of the Body of Christ, His holy Church, which is the gathering of all the believers who have made a common bond in God's love.

*

And God still has such a Church on earth, that gathering of those who live and work in true community, sharing all blessings of the Spirit and all temporal goods. God wants His children to be like Him, not false but ruled by His Holy Spirit, who gathered them and therefore keeps them as one.

Hutterian Brethren (1978): 118-121, 124

June 6

A Sweet Satisfaction
C. Henry Smith, United States, 1925

The author, from Amish-Mennonite background in Illinois, was the first American Mennonite known to have received a Ph.D.

*F*ew of my relatives sympathized with me in my life ambitions. Some thought I was lazy; all were sure that I was foolish. Uncle Joe, especially, who thought of values largely in terms of dollars and cents, after finding out some years later that I was earning less money with all my college preparation than his Henry, who had quit country school as soon as he was able to hold a plow handle, once told me he hoped none of his children would ever waste their lives like that. Of course I did not tell him that I left the farm not to make more money elsewhere but to live a more satisfactory life. He would not have understood. I believe Henry's sister expressed the family estimate of the value of an education when she said, "If I know enough to count my eggs and figure up the amount of my butter I have all the education I need. What more does anybody want?"

But while most of my uncles and aunts may have thought me foolish in wasting my time in an occupation that brought such meager financial returns, I think I retained their respect and affection through all these years. I deliberately set myself the task of avoiding any break in the ties of affection that bound me to my family and my relatives. Although the world of my chief interests was far removed from theirs, that did not prevent me from sharing with them our far more important family heritage and traditions. For years I never returned home from college or from teaching in the city without a visit with them. They were always glad to see me and especially pleased that I was not "stuck up" as college boys were supposed to be when they visited the folks back on the farm. On such occasions I simply stepped out of my world and lived with them in theirs, forgetting for the time being that I had ever been anything but an unsophisticated farm boy.

With Uncle John, I argued the futility of waiting for the right sign of the moon to plant potatoes; with Uncle Pete, who remained a staunch Republican to the end, I talked politics, and to his delight usually agreed with him; while to Aunt Lena, who had taken up the collecting fad in her declining years, I would bring a rock or fossil from some strange place I had visited. This bit of recognition of her pet hobby on my part always gave her great pleasure, even though the contribution may have been nothing but an ordinary pebble picked up from a creek bed in a neighboring state.

These visits I continued for years, until one after the other had all silently passed into that better land where neither wise nor foolish, high nor low, are known. It has always been a matter of sweet satisfaction to me that I was able to keep alive this spirit of comradeship and fellowship to the end with the brothers and sisters of my father and mother.

Smith (1962): 157, 158

June 7

Flesh and Blood Cannot Be Sin
Pilgram Marpeck, Switzerland, 1542

*F*lesh and blood in and of itself cannot be sin. Rather it is a good creation of God and became a dwelling of sin only after or through the sin of Adam, as Paul indicates when he says that no good thing dwells in his flesh. He means not that flesh and blood are sin but that they are the dwelling of sin—which came in, was born and became rooted in the flesh in the fall of Adam and Eve through the serpent, the devil.

Even as today the mind of the true believer may be moved from the simplicity of faith in Christ through the serpent, so the serpent with his instant cunning seduced Eve to eat from the forbidden fruit. Adam followed and thus the mind of both was moved from its created innocence. Thus their human flesh was ruined and became a dwelling of sin by the entry of sinful lusts and appetites.

Were flesh and blood in and of itself sin, the flesh and blood of the blessed virgin Mary, the mother of the Lord Jesus, indeed the flesh and blood of Christ himself, yes, and the flesh of John the Baptist, the prophets, apostles and all the saints would also be sin. How then could they be saved? Indeed, how could any single man today or in all eternity be saved if flesh and blood were sin? And how could a man get rid of his sin or separate it from his flesh or cleanse his flesh from sin if it were sin itself, the wages of which is eternal death which follows? Then also the error would follow that in the resurrection the godly would be clothed with another flesh to their eternal joy and not the flesh with which they have been clothed in this time.

Marpeck (1978): 183, 184

June 8

The Breadth of Grace
Dirk Philips, Germany(?), 1558

Since Christ has now set the children as an example and said that we should become as children and humble ourselves, it follows from this without any contradiction: first, that children (so long as they are in their simplicity) are guiltless and reckoned as without sin by God; second, that there is still something good in children (though they have, indeed, become participants of the trespass and sinful nature of Adam), namely, the simple and unassuming and humble nature in which they please God (yet all out of pure grace through Jesus Christ), so long as they remain in it. For this reason Christ also set the children as an example for us that we, in this regard, must become like them.

But now many arrogant persons dispute about the salvation of children and become fools before the Lord over such disputations, no matter how wise and intelligent they are regarded by the world. For they dispute and chatter much about the salvation of children, but where this concern is of the greatest necessity for themselves—that is, to learn true simplicity and humility from the children, as Christ admonishes us—that they do not even think of a single time.

Since then infants are saved and included in the hand and grace of God, and the kingdom of heaven belongs to them, therefore it is a great lack of understanding that one should baptize children so that through this they might be kept and saved, and besides this condemn children who die without baptism. This is an open diminishing and denial of the grace of God and merit of Jesus Christ. For since the sin of Adam, yes, of the whole world, is paid for and taken away through Jesus Christ and sin may not be ascribed to children except what comes from Adam, how then may children be condemned on account of Adam's sin? Yes, who may condemn the children for whom Christ shed his precious blood? Who will condemn the children to whom the Lord in his boundless grace has promised the kingdom of heaven?

*

No one may either accuse or damn young children on account of original sin except he denies the death, blood and merit of Jesus Christ. For if children may be damned through Adam and on account of his transgression, then Jesus Christ has died in vain for them, and the guilt of Adam that has come upon us has not been paid for through Jesus Christ. Then grace has not become mightier than sin and life has not overcome death through Jesus Christ.

*

So now we conclude with the apostles and with the entire Holy Scripture that original sin has been paid for and removed through Jesus Christ, to the extent that children may neither be judged nor condemned on account of Adam's transgression.

*

It is a sure and undoubted word that the children as well as the adults—the children in their innocence, but the adults in faith—are saved through the grace of our Lord Jesus Christ.

Dirk (1992): 91-93

June 9

Safe

Philip Osborne, United States, 1989

When Jeff was a baby, I was feeding him with a bottle one day while visiting with a neighbor. The neighbor's philosophy of parenting was the conservative Christian philosophy, so when Jeff forced the nipple out of his mouth and refused to take it again, he said, "Look at that! His sinful nature is showing up already." Although I didn't argue with my friend, I perceived the event from a different perspective.

Persons taking the position of my neighbor tend to place the human race into two classes of people—the lost and the saved. Children are thought to be born into the former because of their sinful human nature. The implication of this position for parents is clear—children should be moved from the category of the lost to the category of the saved as soon as possible.

One means of meeting the spiritual obligations of parents, from the point of view of those who emphasize the evil nature of children, is to see that children are baptized. According to this view, baptism saves children (or signifies their salvation) and marks the end of their vulnerability to eternal damnation.

*

Some of those who reject infant baptism replaced it with child evangelism and retained the sense of urgency about converting children from their naturally evil condition.

*

Another group of reformers rejected infant baptism on the basis that Jesus' call to repentance and a life of discipleship was a message for adults, not children. Those taking this adult-believers position argued that children cannot make the kinds of decisions required for membership in the kingdom of God, nor can anybody else make the decisions for children.

*

Those who hold the adult-believers position today maintain that the New Testament calls for the Christian nurture and teaching of children, but not for their conversion or baptism. Children are neither lost nor saved, but "safe" under the atonement of Christ until the "age of accountability," at which time they will be responsible for making the decisions of faith for themselves. Although the age at which their status changes is not specified, it is assumed to accompany the physical, intellectual and social changes which mark the passage from childhood to adulthood.

*

My friend was convinced that Jeff's willful, sinful nature revealed itself when he pushed the nipple out of his mouth and wouldn't take it anymore. But the assumption from an adult-believers position is different. Jeff may have been distracted, full or even stubborn. But there is no reason to interpret what happened as a struggle between good and evil. Jeff was developmentally immature and was responding to his world within the limits of his capabilities. And even though he was just an infant, he was a separate individual with his own will and a set of characteristics which made him different from all other persons, including us his parents.

As Jeff grew older his will sometimes led him to misbehave and he needed to be corrected. But that same will sometimes led him to run across the room, jump on my lap and give me a hug. And what makes those moments special is that they are voluntary, not automatic. Even God prefers such acts to be voluntary, according to the Genesis account of the Creation, because he made Adam and Eve with the capacity to make decisions.

Human nature was created with potential for both good and evil, and this is the way God wanted it.

Osborne (1989): 46-48

June 10

Nurture Toward Salvation
Andreas Ehrenpreis, Slovakia, 1650

We must constantly endeavor to find the best ways of bringing up our children. Not only in the later teens but even from earliest childhood, what is corrupt in human nature begins to stir. From an early age it threatens to grow. We can compare it to iron that tends to rust, or soil which by its very nature encourages weeds to grow. Only with constant effort can they both be kept clean.

*

Many parents are by nature soft with their own children. They have not the strength to fight seriously against what is wrong in them. Therefore there is double cause, indeed thousandfold cause, to seek Christian community for the sake of the children, so that they can be kept clearly separate from the world. The value of such separation is that children can be prevented from falling into godless ways and bringing shame to their parents, who are otherwise good and honest people. The burden of children's disgrace falls on the parents, for it is they who should have brought up their children properly. If children fall into evil ways, into pride and arrogance, drunkenness, loose living or other wickedness, as long as these children live it will be said of the parents that they brought up their children to their own dishonor and shame. They neglected discipline.

*

The guidance of young people is threatened by yet another danger, arising out of poverty. Many who know the good way and try to follow it give their own flesh and blood into the service of men who have no faith. It even happens that children are allowed to work in taverns and inns. Children are the highest and most precious treasure, the noblest and best of all that is entrusted to us. We must look after them with holy zeal. On the great Day of the Lord we will have to account for what has become of them.

That applies also to those who are ambitious for their children. They hand them over to the world so that they will get to know the things that are important in the world. As a result, many such children have turned away from the faith of their parents. The salvation of these young people is taken so lightly, so little value is set on it, that these defenseless young people are handed over to beasts of prey. They are practically pushed toward their ruin. They are delivered to the worst and most godless influences, which in the end must spell their ruin. Who can answer for that before God?

Hutterian Brethren (1978): 70-73

June 11

Jesus Has Done Enough For Them
Henry Funk, United States, mid-1700s

So long as man continues in his childhood in his first born state of soul in Christ, he is a child of God and an heir of the kingdom of God, and needs nothing of man to improve or assure his saved condition, because he has been redeemed with the best of all—the blood of Jesus; neither can any man take from him this salvation wrought by Jesus. "Suffer the little children to come unto me, and forbid them not; for of such is the kingdom of heaven. And he took them into his arms and blessed them."

Where Jesus opens, no man can shut; and where he shuts, no man can open. Likewise no one has power to give this life to the firstlings of God, for it is already given them by Jesus; neither has any one power to take it away from them. For the Lord, from whom they have this life, carries them as lambs in his bosom.

Thus Jesus is the High Priest, Redeemer, Preserver of the firstlings of God, and all efforts made by man to bestow salvation upon them is misspent effort, for Jesus has done enough for them. And whosoever receives a child in the name of Jesus, receives Jesus. If then a person receives a child in this name—as one that is redeemed by Jesus—receives Jesus as the Savior and Redeemer.

*

When man grows up from infancy to the age of intelligent speech, desire is universally found in him, and out of these desires are born sin and death, through which man departs from redemption and the sonship of God and falls into the kingdom of sin and spiritual death, by his own actual sin, out of which man can never help or save himself. "A man can receive nothing except it be given him from heaven" (John 3:27).

But the High Priest sits in the throne of his glory, robed in his glorious priestly raiment and official capacity, with the breastplate of the new testament full of light, love and righteousness upon his robes, in his heart—in which he in the spirit of his wisdom speaks from heaven through his ministers and admonishes the fallen sinner through the gospel to come unto him and be reconciled to God, not according to the Mosaic law, with the offering of bulls and of rams and the like, but with a broken heart and a contrite spirit, with which God is well pleased.

In this condition shall a man come to the High Priest Jesus, in living faith, in penitence and amendment of life, in the putting away of the works of sin, and the putting on of righteousness. In short, Jesus is authorized to forgive and is the only High Priest in and by whom alone man can be reconciled to God.

Funk (1915): 168, 169

June 12

"I Take the Responsibility"
Washington Brun, Uruguay, 1988

*H*ugo Donatti and his family have been members of the La Paz Mennonite congregation in Uruguay since 1982. They came to this community in a severe personal and family crisis. Alcohol was ruining Hugo's life, and consequently the lives of his loved ones.

After a crisis conversion—both at a fixed point in time and as a continuing process—the Lord worked miracles of liberation in Hugo's personal and family life.

Two years ago, Hugo took a position with a state-owned electrical energy firm. For this reason and as a Uruguayan citizen he has to be subject to certain laws of the state.

*

Although required military service exists in law, it is not enforced in practice. Nevertheless, article 28 of the Law of Military Instruction is still enforced. It states: "Every citizen is obligated to swear loyalty to the national flag in a public, solemn ceremony."

The law goes on to provide for penalties. These can include being barred from working for any state organization or losing such employment, not being able to study in any public educational institution or being forced to work one month without any salary.

*

June 12—the birthday of our nation's founder—is the day the nation swears to the flag. Public employees who haven't sworn allegiance before must do so.

When Hugo learned that he must take a loyalty oath, he went to his superiors to ask if he could be excused. The response was, "There is no alternative, it is an order of the management. If you don't present yourself for the oath-taking you will be penalized with a month without salary and the risk of losing your job altogether."

As the national holiday neared, the conflict within Hugo grew. His family depends on his work and it is not easy in Uruguay to find another job. The temptation to lie about an illness or to justify an absence with a falsified medical certificate was very seductive. What to do? Could it be there was really no alternative?

A search in his Bible confirmed Hugo's decision. Texts such as Matthew 5:33-37 and James 5:12 were decisive. According to Hugo, "This was the revealing light. In spite of everything, I made my decision: I would not take the oath."

Prayer and the commitment of the community accompanied Hugo in his decision. Many brothers and sisters, on learning of the case, came to him with moral and material support. They committed themselves to sharing their goods with him for whatever time he would be without work, if indeed he would lose his job or his salary. His family would not suffer.

In reflecting about the biblical texts, the community found that they were given within the context of community relationships in which brothers and sisters look out for each other and remain in a permanent attitude of prayer. This was another affirmation for Hugo.

Just two days before the swearing ceremony, Hugo went to the office of the head of the firm.

"I have Christian principles, for which reason I refuse to swear to the flag," Hugo said.

"What do you mean you aren't going to swear?" the boss replied. "Do you realize the risk you're taking? What is your religion?"

"That which Christ preached."

The boss was visibly uncomfortable.

"I respect you," he told Hugo. "Why don't you come, but stand outside during the ceremony. When the public act is over, step inside and say that you were present. There will be many people milling about."

But Hugo refused to accomodate himself to such deception, tempting as it might have been.

"But my friend!" the boss said. "Don't you realize they can dismiss you from your job?"

"I take the responsibility," Hugo replied. "I am subject to whatever you decide, but I will not swear to the flag."

Then he was able to give his testimony. He shared of his former life in bondage to alcohol and the liberation that Christ gave him. Coincidentally, his boss was also an alcoholic and began to get interested. He listened sincerely to Hugo's testimony. Finally, he made a statement:

"Look, Mr. Donatti, we need people who have convictions and who stand up for them the way you do. Be firm, and if anyone questions you, say exactly what you said to me. Nothing will happen to you."

After the national holiday, Hugo returned to work. His fellow employees commented about the discomfort they had felt about the authoritarian way in which they were treated in the oath-taking. Hugo was summoned, his absence was noted and again he had the opportunity to share his conscientious objection. The final response was, "We won't bother you any more."

Within a few weeks, Hugo was promoted to a position of greater responsibility. His testimony was made known among the workers, who consult him and respect him. He has taken on the role of a critical conscience and reconciler between the labor union and the management.

Brun (1988): 18, 20

When Christ With His Teaching True

Michael Sattler, Germany, 1527

This hymn is found in the Ausbund, *an Anabaptist hymn-book still in use by the Old Order Amish. The translation which follows is literal.*

When Christ with His teaching true
Had gathered a little flock
He said that each with patience
Must daily follow Him bearing his cross.

And said: You, my beloved disciples,
Must be ever courageous
Must love nothing on earth more than Me
And must follow My teaching.

The world will lie in wait for you
And bring you much mockery and dishonor;
Will drive you away and outlaw you
As if Satan were in you.

When then you are blasphemed and defamed
For My sake persecuted and beaten
Rejoice; for behold your reward
Is prepared for you at heaven's throne.

Behold Me: I am the Son of God
And have always done the right.
I am certainly the best of all
Still they finally killed Me.

Because the world calls Me an evil spirit
And malicious seducer of the people
And contradicts My truth
Neither will it go easy with you.

Yet fear not such a man
Who can kill only the body
But far more fear the faithful God
Whose it is to condemn both.

He it is who tests you as gold
And yet is loving to you as His children.
As long as you abide in My teaching
I will nevermore forsake you.

For I am yours and you are Mine
Thus where I am there shall you be,
And he who abuses you touches My eye,
Woe to the same on that day.

Your misery, fear, anxiety, distress and pain
Will be great joy to you there
And this shame a praise and honor
Yea, before the whole host of heaven.

The apostles accepted this
And taught the same to every man;
He who would follow after the Lord,
That he should count on as much.

O Christ, help Thou Thy people
Which follows Thee in all faithfulness,
That though through Thy bitter death
It may be redeemed from all distress.

Praise to Thee, God, on Thy throne
And also to Thy beloved Son
And to the Holy Ghost as well.
May He yet draw many to His kingdom.

Yoder (1973): 141-145

June 14

"Farming Is Good"
David Kline, United States, 1990

Probably the greatest difference between Amish farming and agribusiness is the supportive community life we have. Let me give an example. When we cut our wheat in early summer (we cut about half of a thirteen-acre field in one day) the whole family, after the evening milking, went shocking. It was one of those clear, cool June evenings. Simply perfect.

*

Row by row we worked our way across the field, the girls talking and giggling while they worked and Michael explaining in excited detail some project he had under way in the shop. When we reached the top of the hill we stood together and watched the sun slip behind a brilliant magenta-colored cloud and then sink beneath the horizon. From far to the south came the mellow whistle of an upland sandpiper. Tim said, to no one in particular, "Shocking together with the family is fun." He spoke for all of us. Then we heard voices from the next hill and saw three neighbors shocking toward us from the far end of the field. One of the girls excitedly remarked, "Seven rows at a time. That is speed." Soon all the bundles were set up in shocks and everyone came along to the house for ice cream and visiting.

The assurance and comfort of having caring neighbors is one of the reasons we enjoy our way of farming so much. Eight years ago I had an accident that required surgery and a week in the hospital. My wife tells me the first words I said to her in the recovery room were, "Get me out of here; the wheat has to be cut." Of course she couldn't, and I need not have worried because we had neighbors.

While Dad cut the wheat with the binder, the neighbors shocked it. When our team tired my brother brought his four-horse team, and by supper time the twelve-acre field was cut and shocked.

This year the neighbor who had been in first to help us needed help himself. Since a bout of pneumonia in July he hadn't been able to do much. So last Thursday six teams and mowers cut his eleven acres of alfalfa hay. Then on Saturday afternoon, with four teams and wagons and two hay loaders and fifteen men and about as many boys, we put the hay in his barn in less than two hours. We spent almost as much time afterward sitting in a circle beneath the maple tree with cool drinks and fresh cookies, listening as one of the neighbors told of his recent trip west.

*

I couldn't help thinking of my young friend who got married last September and then bought his dad's machinery and livestock and rented the farm. He and his wife really worked on that debt. Milking by hand, selling Grade B milk, tending a good group of sows, cultivating corn twice, sometimes three times, using no herbicides, they are nearing the end of their first year of farming on their own, and most of their debts are paid off. He didn't tell me this, he's much too humble, but he did say to me while threshing, "You know, farming is good."

Kline (1990): xxiii-xxv

When You Get Old

Peter Jansz. Twisck, The Netherlands, 1622

I have often been asked, "Why can a father and mother raise twelve children but twelve children cannot take care of their father and mother?" When such things become needful they should care for their parents. Many times there is grumbling, strife and trials. One will say they had the parents long enough and another will say they didn't have them long enough. So they correct each other, each concerned that they need not support father and mother too long.

Each one should try to do the most instead of the least. God will not let the deeds of mercy remain unpaid with outward spiritual blessing. When parents are unwelcome and feel that they are a burden, it grieves their hearts and they cry unto the Most High to deliver them and shorten their life that they would no longer be in the children's way.

*

It is recorded that a son had driven his father from his home forcing him to live in a guest home. The father asked if the son would bring him two small blankets for his bed. It touched the son's heart and when he arrived home, he told his little son to take two of the smallest bed blankets to the guest house where his grandfather was staying. When the little son returned home, his father noticed that he had only taken one blanket. He admonished the little son who answered, "I wanted to save one so when you get old like grandfather and live in a guest house you will have a blanket too."

*

When their parents become old, many children disregard them saying, "Father does everything wrong." "Mother doesn't know what she is doing." "They both don't understand." "It is best that way," they say and so they please themselves in a luxurious life. It often happens that parents' minds weaken, yet the children should be careful not to despise them, esteem them too little, shame their speech or laugh at their faulty suggestions. Don't mock them as you might a child even if they are childish in their thoughts. They are your parents and the Lord wants them to be honored.

If their conversation lacks understanding, we should not make light of it but provide good judgment for them. It is expedient and Christlike that you give them no reason to be angered. If they become dissatisfied because of their childish reasoning we should bear with them since they have become as children in their thoughts. They have overlooked unpleasantness in you. Both scripture and nature teach that you have a duty to overlook unpleasantness in your parents.

Twisck (1982): 48, 50, 51, 57

June 16

Parents and Teachers

Christopher Dock, United States, 1750

He called a child, whom he put among them, and said, "Truly I tell you, unless you change and become like children, you will never enter the kingdom of heaven. Whoever becomes humble like this child is the greatest in the kingdom of heaven. Whoever welcomes one such child in my name welcomes me." — Matthew 18: 2-5

Now all the duties of parents to their children are also the duties of the teacher to whom the children are entrusted. And as he is in this sense head of these children, so Christ is his head, according to whose command we must act. When Christ came to this world to seek and to save, he called the children to him in especial love, caressed and blessed them and promised them the kingdom of heaven. For this reason we will not be blessed if we are tyrannical with them, however much they must be raised in discipline and in the fear of the Lord.

*

If we would enter heaven and be happy forever we need not imagine that the way is to glare at these children or even scold and punish them if they do not show us enough honor or pay us enough compliments. Ah no, this is not the way to the kingdom of heaven.

But if we turn from such selfish pride to Christ's teachings and humble ourselves to the level of children, it not only leads us to the kingdom of God, but gives us a community with the children that is much more useful than all this keeping aloof. For who exalts himself here will be humbled, and who humbles himself will be exalted.

Martin (1971): 31, 32

Moriah

E.J. Swalm, Canada, 1969

"Take your son, your only son Isaac, whom you love, and go to the land of Moriah, and offer him there as a burnt offering on one of the mountains that I shall show you."

"Because you have done this, and have not withheld your son, your only son, I will indeed bless you. . .because you have obeyed my voice." — Genesis 22: 2, 16-18

I was fortunate in having been exposed to the Biblical teachings of nonresistance from my earliest memory. On approaching maturity I endeavored to rethink these positions for myself. This resulted in a staunch decision that I could not participate in any form of army service.

Early in the summer of 1918, the last year of World War I, I was drafted into the Canadian Army.

*

Father and son walked solemnly the two miles to the railroad depot where we took the train to Hamilton. Our conversation was punctuated with periods of silence. At one point Dad finally spoke.

"I feel this morning something like Abraham must have felt on his way to Mount Moriah."

Certainly, I would not be so immodest as to elevate my parent to the status of "father of the faithful." I cannot escape, however, remembering his bravery and Christian fortitude as he faced the whole ordeal. One instance of this heroism may suffice.

While doing the morning chores shortly before my departure, he directed the following conversation. "My boy, you will soon be leaving me, and we cannot tell what the consequences will be. I want to ask you: if the worst comes to the worst, how is it with your soul?"

To this I took a rapid retrospective of my past and recalled the two crises in my spiritual life of which he was aware. They were my conversion at twelve years and my entire commitment to Christ at nineteen years.

All I said in reply was, "It holds good this morning."

What followed was a bit dramatic. He put that bony left arm around my neck and said, "My boy, I do not know how I can get along without you here on the farm with only one arm, but I want you to stand true to God and your convictions at any price. I would rather get word that you were shot than to know you compromised your position and disobeyed the Lord."

Such rugged faith and staunch belief produced a buoyancy in my soul that I needed. I can never forget it. We then went into our granary and had a season of prayer together. What a prayer-meeting that was!

Swalm (1969): 23-25

I Still Can't Understand It

Family Life, United States, 1974

*I*t was the summer I had just turned nineteen, the age at which young boys are apt to notice a lot of things and have a lot of questions. I had my own horse and buggy; it was a beautiful sunny Sunday afternoon and I was on my way home from church. The peaches were hanging thick for harvest as I was going past my uncle's place, whom we shall call Ike Schmucker. I decided to stop in for a visit with my cousin. Just as I drove in, a young man whom we shall call Bob Walters came driving in too, accompanied by his wife. Bob had a blacksmith and general repair shop in a nearby town.

My uncle was standing in the yard. Bob said, "Hello there, Ike. It's sure a nice day."

"Yes, it is," said my uncle.

"Say, Ike, I brought my wife down to see about getting some peaches. Looks like you've got a lot of them now."

"Well, yes, we do," Ike answered slowly. "But today is Sunday and we don't sell peaches on Sunday."

"All right, all right," Bob answered. "I just thought we would like to look at them so we would know if we wanted any or not."

"Well, I would rather not show them on Sunday either," my uncle said, trying hard to be nice to Bob.

"But you know it is hard for me to get away from the shop during the week," Bob coaxed. "If we could take a look at them now maybe we could make arrangements to pick some up next week."

My uncle didn't budge. From here the conversation turned from peaches to the prospects for a good corn crop. It was unanimously agreed that a good rain was needed.

"Oh, yes," my uncle said, "that reminds me. I have a piece that's broken on my manure spreader. I have it off already so maybe when you come to look at about the peaches you can take it along and weld it. Then I will pick it up the first time I am in town."

"Oh, yes, I'll be glad to do that," Bob answered.

They visited awhile and then Bob said as he got ready to go, "Why don't I just take that piece along for the manure spreader now? Then I can fix it and bring it back to you when I come to see about the peaches next week?"

"I will run and get it right away," my uncle said.

There I sat in my buggy. I saw and heard the whole episode and I could hardly believe what I was hearing. I tried to get Ike's attention as he hurried past me toward the shed to get the broken piece for his manure spreader. But he never noticed me, nor the big question mark which was on my face. I couldn't understand it then and I've often thought about it since, which has been a good many years. I still can't understand it. What did Bob Walters think of this man who refused to let him look at the peaches on Sunday but saw nothing wrong with sending a broken piece of machinery with him on the same day to get it fixed?

"No Peaches on Sunday" (1974): 15

June 19

No Idle Faith

Menno Simons, The Netherlands, ca. 1541

*F*or a genuine Christian faith cannot be idle, but it changes, renews, purifies, sanctifies and justifies more and more. It gives peace and joy, for by faith it knows that hell, the devil, sin and death are conquered through Christ, and that grace, mercy, pardon from sin and eternal life are acquired through Him. In full confidence it approaches the Father in the name of Christ, receives the Holy Ghost, becomes partaker of the divine nature and is renewed after the image of Him who created him. It lives out the power of Christ which is in it; all its ways are righteousness, godliness, honesty, truth, wisdom, goodness, kindness, light, love, peace.

It sanctifies the body and heart as a habitation and temple for Christ and His Holy Ghost; it hates all that is contrary to God and His Word; it honors, praises and thanks its God with a faithful heart. There is nothing that can dismay it, neither judgment, nor wrath, nor hell, nor devil, nor sin, nor eternal death. For it knows that it has Christ as its Intercessor, Mediator and Atoner. It acknowledges with holy Paul, "There is therefore now no condemnation to them which are in Christ Jesus, who walk not after the flesh, but after the spirit" (Romans 8:1). The Spirit of the Lord assures it of being a child of God and a joint heir of Christ; therefore it takes itself to be property of its Lord and Savior, Christ, who called it by His grace, drew it by His Spirit, enlightened it by His Word and purchased it with His blood.

Behold, such a living faith it is, one which has such a constraint, power, Spirit, fruit, emphasis in life, that it can avail with God and has the promise in the Scriptures. Happy is he who has it and keeps it intact to the end!

Let me repeat, test yourselves, whether you are in the faith or no, in Christ or outside of Him, penitent or impenitent. For in the mirror presented you may view the whole face of your conscience and life, if you but believe that the Word of the Lord is true and right. Notice how the true Christian faith, thanks to grace, is the only living fountain whence flows not only the penitent, new life, but also obedience to the evangelical ceremonies, such as baptism and the Lord's Supper, and that they will have to take their origin and come forth, although constrained by the law. For the rod of the taskmaster is broken already by the bold and submissive spirit of love which is out of a Christian nature, prepared unto all good works and obedience to the holy, divine Word.

For all the truly regenerated and spiritually minded conform in all things to the Word and ordinances of the Lord. Not because they think to merit the atonement of their sins and eternal life. By no means. In this matter they depend upon nothing except the true promise of the merciful Father, given in grace to all believers through the blood and merits of Christ, which blood is and ever will be the only and eternal medium of our reconciliation; and not works, baptism or the Lord's Supper, as said above repeatedly. For if our reconciliation depended on works and ceremonies, then grace would be a thing of the past, and the merits and fruits of the blood of Christ would end. Oh no, it is grace, and will be grace to all eternity; all that the merciful Father does for us miserable sinners through His beloved Son and Holy Spirit is grace.

Menno (1956): 396, 397

June 20

Surrender
Hans Denck, Germany, 1526

*T*he Lord is trustworthy and merciful, more than any human or angelic being could ever utter. But what kind of conversion takes place is plainly evident every day. People seem to get increasingly worse or else where there is improvement it is for appearance only. The tree does, indeed, look good in all its foliage but it bears nothing but crab apples. We show as much regret for our sin as one who slaps his brother's face and says, "Forgive me, I did not mean to do it."

Dear brothers, there is a great deal to be desired. Conversion must be from the roots up if we are to come into the presence of God and prevent a sinner from turning into a hypocrite who surpasses all sinners. Whoever desires to be a new being but cannot leave behind the old life is like a pig that has just been washed and returns promptly to the mud puddle. Anyone who speaks of some future conversion and relies on it must take heed where he stands with such designs. The reason is that one who loves God does not intend to remove himself from him. Yet one who has never been close to him and longs to come to him will not impose any limits of his own. For anyone who postpones the good shows that he does need it badly.

*

What God has made one, he can restore again after someone has broken it. But if he does not want to restore it, it is and shall always remain broken. Whatever he has restored suffers no damage from having been broken. For a damage mended is no damage at all.

God the Lord of heaven and earth has established a salvation by which satisfaction is made for any damage. The penance must be as hard on the flesh as the breaking may have been easy; it must be as much in keeping with the Spirit as the other was against it. The amount of which God and the law had been robbed by the one must be restored by the act of satisfaction. Blessed is the person who finds such work within and yields to it.

*

No one can receive anything from God unless he be prepared to receive it from God against his own desires, when it pleases God. Whoever prays God for wisdom and cannot suffer God to grant him folly, does not ask that God's, but rather that his own, will be done. As long as a person is not prepared to surrender salvation out of his own grasp he will not achieve it. As long as one fights condemnation, he cannot get it off his neck. Should a perverse person truly say, "I will gladly forfeit salvation because it is God's will and willingly accept condemnation for God's sake," God would indeed show himself none other than good; he would have to give him the best and most precious he has, which is himself.

Denck (1989): 228-230

June 21

False Wisdom
Christian Lesher, United States, 1849

*T*here will be false and incorrect conversions, as God complained through the prophet: "They convert themselves, but not correctly, they are like a false bow" (Hosea 7:16). Does this mean a loose bow? As in archery, a false or weak bow could not drive the arrow to its target, as it would fall to the ground. So are the false conversions, that are not drawn and filled by the power of God. The depth of their conversion is not deep enough. They see themselves too much, and don't behold God and the power of His grace.

*

Because they still feel sinful, they then persuade themselves, or have others persuade them, that they should participate with an outward society and be baptized, believing this would forgive or wash away their sins. They also partake of the communion and all outward ceremonies their church or society does practice. In this they feel they are living a virtuous life and have peace! peace! But as yet God has not promised peace in the heart through His Holy Spirit. Those that don't have more than this have an incorrect, false conversion, and can with all this be lost.

*

As the prophet says, "For they shall see eye to eye, when the Lord shall bring again Zion" (Isaiah 52:8). Jesus also says: "For that which is highly esteemed among men is abomination in the sight of God" (Luke 16:15).

Now such people that follow Jesus Christ do deny themselves and withdraw from the pleasures of this world—they will learn from Jesus to be meek and lowly in heart.

Lesher (1971): 140-142

June 22

Two Kinds of Obedience
Michael Sattler(?), Germany, 1520s

*T*here are two kinds of obedience: servile and filial. The filial springs forth from the love of the Father even if no other reward should follow; yea, even if the Father should wish to damn the child. The servile springs out of love of reward or of self.

The filial ever does as much as it can, apart from any command. The servile does as little as it can; yea, does nothing unless it be commanded. The filial can never do enough for Him; the servile thinks it is always doing too much. The filial rejoices in the Father's chastisement even if it has transgressed in nothing. The servile wants never to be chastised by the Lord even though it does nothing right.

The filial has its treasure and its righteousness in the Father whom it obeys solely in order to manifest His righteousness. The treasure and the righteousness of the servile are the works that it does to acquire righteousness. The filial remains in the house and inherits all that the Father has; the servile is driven out and receives its justly prescribed reward. The servile looks to the outward and prescribed command of his Lord, the filial is attentive to the inner witness and the Spirit. The servile is imperfect and therefore his Lord has no pleasure in him; the filial strives thereafter and becomes perfect, and therefore the Father cannot reject him.

The filial is not contrary to the servile, as it might appear, but better and higher. Therefore let him who is in the servile, seek after a better obedience which is the filial, which needs the servile not at all.

Yoder (1973): 121

Saved By Grace

John S. Coffman, United States, late 1800s

"For by grace you have been saved through faith, and this is not your own doing; it is the gift of God—not the result of works, so that no one may boast." — Ephesians 2: 8-9

As man sees and learns more of God, he gets faith, and the more he knows of God the stronger will be his faith in God. A want of faith in God is the result of ignorance of God. But when we are convinced of God and His mighty workings so that we now have faith in Him and His Son Jesus Christ, does the faith we have within ourselves turn upon us this saving power? No, it is grace that saves. Yet we remember that the Savior on one occasion said to one whose sins He had forgiven, "Thy faith hath saved thee." It was faith in Christ that brought this sinner to Him and enabled her to accept the gift of salvation, but it was not the faith that was within her that accomplished the saving work. It was grace, the working of God. We must understand faith aright and not ascribe to our faith the power of salvation. It is by grace through faith.

Faith is the medium by which we get to God. It is the vehicle on which we are carried to Him and brought into His presence. It is the electric wire that connects us directly with Him, and through which we converse, as it were, face to face with Him. But when we are in His presence He does not turn the faith we brought to Him upon us in saving power; the grace that is in Him is the saving power that He applies to us.

Jesus said to the impotent man who had lain many years at the pool of Bethesda, "Wilt thou be made whole?" The poor sufferer understood not the power that was standing in his presence, nor the power that was in his reach to heal his helpless body. But he would have been willing to get into the pool by his slow process, at the troubling of the waters and be healed. The Savior then said to him, "Rise, take up thy bed and walk." The healing power was in God. It was grace, the working power of God, that saved him.

It was faith in the man sick of the palsy and those that bore him on his bed that induced them to bring him into the presence of Jesus; but it was grace in the Son of God with its blessed working that forgave his sins and enabled him to take his bed and go to his own house.

It was through faith that the suffering woman in the throng about Jesus said, "If I may but touch the hem of His garment, I shall be whole." Jesus turned about in the press and said, "Who touched my clothes?" His disciples answered, "Thou seest the multitude thronging thee and sayest thou, who touched me?" But he had perceived that virtue had gone out of him. Was it the faith in the woman that constituted the saving power? Certainly not, but it was through faith that she came to Him, and by grace that was in Him that she was saved. So every regenerated, pardoned soul is yet saved by grace through faith.

Steiner (1903): 82-84

June 24
Our Father
John Smyth, The Netherlands, ca. 1611

Mennonites have frequently been criticized by Calvinists, who teach that humans are totally depraved and without free will, and that God alone chooses who will be saved and who will be damned—the doctrine of predestination. The author of this piece, once an English Puritan, associates Calvinists with the ancient Manicheean sect which also taught predestination.

To fashion, predestine and ordain a creature for destruction is very far removed from the divine nature. God by nature is a father.

*

Because He is the creator and father of souls, God does not create them for destruction. He does not create, does not ordain, does not predestine to destruction, unless someone wants to ascribe contradictory works and intentions to God.

*

If indeed men love their own children and from the heart want whatever is best for them and care for them, how can we fashion God as a most cruel father who longs for sons for this reason, so He can hate them, cast them off and scourge them forever? This novel predestination, which fashions God as a savage father and murderer, is ignorant of the divine nature.

*

Therefore, away with that savage god of the Manicheeans, the most cruel tyrant who creates countless creatures and predestines them to ruin. Our God is full of mercy, most ready to pardon, slow to anger. That god of the Manicheeans is wholly wrathful, merciless, swift to vengeance; indeed, he damns countless innocent creatures from eternity regardless of any merit of theirs. The god of the Manicheeans casts men down into sin since he is a judge.

Our merciful God judges men since they cast themselves down into sins and despise his mercy. The former forsakes his own before his own forsake him; ours forsakes no one unless he first forsakes Him. The former is primarily a judge, never a father to the damned; ours is primarily a father, secondarily a judge. The former first pronounces a sentence of death against the innocent, then mocks the accused and tries his case for sport; ours first longs from the heart to benefit the criminal, treats the matter seriously and at last reluctantly punishes the one who perseveres in sins.

Coggins (1991): 179, 180

June 25

A Call to All
Peter Burkholder, United States, ca. 1837

What is the cause that but few are chosen? Is it not because they *will not* obey the call and come? For the invitation was as urgent to those who did not come as to those who came. And even those who were *first bidden* refused to come: for when the Lord sent out his servants at supper-time to say to them that were bidden, "Come, for all things are now ready," they all with one consent began to make excuses and refused to come.

*

"Now when this was shewed unto the Lord, he said to his servants, 'Go quickly into the streets and lanes of the city and bring in hither the poor and the maimed, and the halt and the blind.' And the servant said, 'Lord, it is done as thou hast commanded and yet there is room.' And the Lord said unto the servant, 'Go out into the highways and hedges and compel them to come in, that my house may be filled'" (Luke 14:21-23). The highways and hedges may denote the whole world; and this accords with the commandments given to the apostles by our Lord Jesus Christ when he ascended to heaven saying, "Go ye into all the world, and preach the gospel to every creature" (Mark 16:15). This call extends to *all*—both Jews and Gentiles—all nations, of every language and tongue—free grace for all those who *will come* and accept it. Now if the greater part are reprobated and rejected, why are they all called?

*

It is in the *free will* of man to accept the call and invitation of the gospel, and come to Christ and live; or to reject it and perish. For it is the will of God our Savior that all men should be gathered under the wings of his mercy and be saved, and come to the knowledge of the truth. This is evidenced by many passages in holy writ. For God has no pleasure in the death of the wicked, as he saith by the prophet, "Say unto them, 'As I live,' saith the Lord God, 'I have no pleasure in the death of the wicked; but that the wicked turn from his evil way and live. Turn ye, turn ye from your evil ways; for why will ye die, O house of Israel?'" (Ezekiel 33:11).

*

If all that are athirst shall come, and if whosoever will may come and take the water of life freely: can it yet be said that God—that Holy, Just and Good God who is no respecter of persons—should, in his foreknowledge, have reprobated

214

and abandoned some of his rational creatures—unavoidably on their part—to eternal death and misery! Would it not be inconsistent with the above scripture texts and in opposition to them? And, moreover, would it not be inconsistent with the divine attributes?

Conversation *(1856): 292-296*

June 26

Whosoever Will, Let Him Come
Jacob Kleinsasser, Canada, 1988

*A*s Jesus passed by the pool of Bethesda he saw a poor man lying there who had been ill a very long time. Thirty-eight years he had been in pain and suffering. He could find no cure for his disease. Could not the troubled waters cure him? Yes, they might. But he was too ill and weak to step into the pool.

*

Jesus looked kindly upon the sick man and asked, "Do you want to get well?"

The man wanted to be made well but he had waited so many years in vain that he was almost in despair. So he told Jesus all his sorrow. The kind Savior said, "Get up, pick up your mat and walk."

And the man was made whole immediately. He took up his mat and walked. Jesus is the all-powerful cure. In this man he proved his strength and power.

Soon afterward Jesus found him in the temple and spoke to him, saying, "Sin no more, or something worse may happen to you." The man was now healed of his bodily disease but Jesus was reminding him of a worse disease. "Sin no more!"

Jesus in his mercy does give us healing, yet by this we must also learn that the sickness of sin is worse, that maybe all of us lie sick in sin. If we ask for anything, we should ask for healing from the sickness of our sin. If this sin is not taken away we must suffer much more after death. The suffering does not come to an end.

*

Throughout the teachings of Jesus forgiveness of sins is mentioned. This is the real preparation for the coming time in everlasting life. If we have received his forgiveness for our sins, it will be glory in everlasting life. If we haven't been cleared, God forbid it, it will be everlasting torment.

We have reason to be thankful to God for the gift of forgiveness. God has healed us from the sickness of our sin. Physical sickness becomes less important. It is only the deteriorating of our bodies, a wearing out which isn't so meaningful before God because in time we all turn to dust. We can suffer anything else in joy if we appreciate that we have been cured from a greater ailment, a sickness which no man on earth could ever heal.

There is no pool of Bethesda now. Sometimes we hear of healing springs to which people flock, anxious to be cured, like the poor man who lay at the pool of Bethesda. But the pool of Bethesda reminds us here of something more important: Jesus, the healing fountain upon whom we rely. Jesus can heal us in body *and* soul.

Who else can heal our perishing soul? Nobody. But sinners may come to that fountain every day and be cured. We read, "None need to perish." And none need wait for thirty-eight years. "Whosoever will," Jesus says, "let him come."

Kleinsasser (1988): 7-9

June 27

The Jesus Fire
Heinrich Dirks, Sr., Russian Empire, ca. 1890

*T*he Lord Jesus wants to kindle His fire on the whole earth. The whole earth is meant, not a part of the earth, when He says: "I came to cast fire upon the earth, and would that it were already kindled!" Everyone who is called man—all the descendants of Adam, all peoples and nations, the white and the black, the brown and the yellow—all, yes all, shall be set aflame by His fire; all shall become a reward of His sufferings.

In order that this may be accomplished, sparks must fly from where the fire already burns, to where it does not burn as yet. Missionaries have to be sent out who will go to the non-Christian peoples. Missions must be propagated, for the very purpose of missions is to kindle the Jesus-fire on the whole earth among all the peoples and nations. The work of missions is not in vain in the name of the Lord; it will accomplish that which it is supposed to accomplish, namely that it will lead to the burning of the Jesus-fire on the whole earth.

*

When the Savior says: "I came to cast fire upon the earth, and would that it were already kindled," He does not doubt at all that some day His fire will burn upon the earth; He only deplores somewhat that it takes so long till this is accomplished. He desired very much that it should happen quickly. This desire we may share with Him—yes, and do whatever we can, that it may come more speedily.

The word of the Savior, "I came to cast fire upon the earth, and would that it were already kindled!" is not mere wish that his fire might soon burn upon the whole earth, but a prophecy that it will actually happen, that His fire will burn upon the whole earth—a prophecy that in no way has found its complete fulfillment, but which will surely be fulfilled. The prophet Isaiah in spirit has seen this fulfillment when he says, "And nations shall come to your light, and kings to the brightness of your rising."

It will come to that; it will be fulfilled that on the whole earth the fire of Jesus Christ will burn. Heaven and earth will resound with the jubilation and the hallelujah song of the redeemed of the Lord, and He uses mission to bring about this glorious consummation. Therefore my beloved in the Lord, let us joyfully take part in the work of missions, and in this way help to fulfill the word of the Savior: ". . .and would that it were kindled!"

Friesen (1978): 672

June 28

Advice Well Refused
Family Life, United States, 1990

*T*he little man with the gentle brown eyes was in no hurry as he stopped and picked a few green beans which he tossed in my bucket. He chatted quietly of such things as his Irish ancestry and the potato famine of the 1800s in Ireland. It was a while before I even knew what he wanted.

He had two buggy wheels he wanted repaired and he also wanted to buy two sets of shaft pieces. So I fixed him up, took his check and continued picking beans.

About a month later a letter from the bank arrived. My first reaction was, "Oh no, an overdraft." Upon opening the letter, I found the little man's check inside. It was stamped, "Account Closed."

This was the second time that had happened in the three years we were in business. The other time I wrote a polite letter and promptly got results. So I decided the first step was to write the man. Then I would have to trust that he would make it right. Days passed into weeks and I didn't get a reply.

Then the battle started. What should I do? Here I was, a hard-working man with a wife and five children scratching to make a living, and this man who had probably never worked a whole day in his life wanted to live off me yet.

Friends advised me to turn it over to the law, saying that would take care of it since there was a law against writing bad checks. Somehow though, this didn't quite blend with Jesus' words, "But I say unto you that ye resist not evil, but whosoever shall smite thee on thy right cheek turn to him the other also. And if any man will sue thee at the law and take away thy coat let him have thy cloak also. And whosoever shall compel thee to go a mile, go with him twain. Give to him that asketh thee and from him that would borrow of thee, turn not thou away."

I decided what I would do while I was in church one Sunday. I would simply write him one more nice letter, then forget about it. Why was I making this fuss over a measly seventy-three dollars anyway, when I considered all the spiritual riches that were at stake!

So I wrote him explaining that I was disappointed that he hadn't answered my other letter, but I had decided not to turn his check over to the law, hoping to settle this like two men should. If I did faulty work or charged too much, I would compensate for it.

A few days later I was down in a hollow not far from the house, fixing a fence, when a movement caught my eye. I recognized the little man immediately who came slipping and sliding down the muddy hill toward me, clutching some papers in his hand. The paper turned out to be my latest letter which was the only one he got, he explained. He said he had no idea the check was bad and was sorry that he had upset me so. He got out his billfold and paid me in cash, even offering to pay extra for the trouble.

I blubbered and stuttered around like a child who had gotten his way after throwing a temper fit. I sincerely thanked him for the one hundred mile round trip he had made just to pay me.

I want to continue asking my friends for advice, but this was one time I'm glad I didn't take it.

"The Little Man's Bad Check" (1990): 15

June 29

Mute Pious Expectancy
Kornelius Hildebrand, Sr., Russian Empire, late 1800s

We join Mennonites of the Ukraine just before a Sunday worship service in 1840.

*T*he school stands right next to the great stream. Only the street, actually just a driveway, and a bit of bank lie between. For the newcomer the view from out of the windows of the high-standing schoolhouse to the enormous stream is impressive; but the islander, on the contrary, pays little attention anymore to the picture of nature, just as today when he gives his entire attention to the worship service. In the space of a half hour all the inhabitants of the island are assembled.

Religious disagreements were not known then yet among our ancestors and failure to attend the common public worship service was unthinkable even though a minister was available to come over for the service only every third or fourth Sunday. And if some person in good health and at home was missing at his or her place in the schoolhouse it aroused such a great stir and concern that the reason for it had to be searched out and learned and in an hour after the worship service the whole village knew why the person in question was absent.

The schoolroom is not large. People sit closely crowded, the men to the right and the women to the left of the improvised pulpit. Reverent stillness is the rule in the meeting. No conversation is conducted. Only in the softest whisper the new arrival bids a "Good morning" to the person sitting nearest him—beyond this nothing at all. In this way some time passes in gravest silence. The hum of a hungry buzzing bee that mistakenly came in through the window sounds like loud music. One can hear this distinctly beside the chirping of the sparrow outside and the song of the blackbird in the bushes nearby.

Suddenly there is a simulated cough by one of the men in front whose ears begin to ring because of the long silence—which is followed by a scarcely audible scraping with the foot. For one of the women it comes in the form of a gentle sneeze, and ever so cautiously she pulls out her stiffly-starched pocket kerchief with the sprig of marjoram or thyme and passes it gently a few times by the dry nose, and by this movement releases among the neighboring women a cloud of herbal aroma, like from the fragrance of some sweet spikenard.

Once more soundless silence—mute, pious expectancy. Even the movement of the lungs in breathing seems hypnotic, and on the smooth forehead of the girls are drawn delicate lines of worship.

Peters (1965): 50, trans. by Noah G. Good

June 30

I Had the Stronger One on My Side
Jacob Hershey, United States, 1825

*T*here were many things which I was ashamed to do, such as putting on the plain apparel, letting my hair grow, doing good to my neighbor who is living in sin, opening with prayer in the congregation and in my house, and humbling my proud heart. Here I found the way was narrow; here I found a hard struggle that I cannot describe. Sometimes I obeyed, sometimes not.

*

Then a voice came unto me saying, "Slay Old Adam, namely, the Old Creature." In this I began, and found that daily I had both hands full. Now at this time I was well nigh recovered from my bodily afflictions being able again to come among the people. Here Satan again assaulted me with all his hosts so I had a hard struggle: now I had need to use the sword of the spirit earnestly; I had also need with diligence to watch and pray. Then I could well feel that I had more power to overcome evil within myself, and was more inclined to the good. And I began to notice that those that were mockers began to avoid me, though they still laughed at me behind my back. This I could easily bear, even with sympathy for them, because I believed it was Satan that prompted them to do it.

*

Here I could often weep from my heart for my neighbors who still lived on so satisfied in their condition. Now I was to begin to lay off, and I believe when we are convicted by the grace of God from the heart to lay off anything out of love to God and we do not obey, our souls will suffer loss.

At the same time I believe if we are taught in our heart by the grace of God to obey in anything commanded us by the book of life, namely, baptism, communion, supplication and prayer for friend and foe, and we neglect it through carelessness, our souls will likewise suffer—because the Scripture, namely, the Book of Life, emphatically tells us that faith without works is dead (James 2:17, 26). I am a witness that out of weakness in love for my Jesus, I have at least fulfilled a small part of the same, thereby feeling unspeakably happy; how would he feel who had done all?

Thank God, I now had it good in my journey. Here I had strong evidence that Satan was against me, but I knew that God was for me. Now I had a hard struggle with self: Satan tried to hinder me, but I had the Stronger One on my side and this time I smote him.

*

So again I went on in my journey with great joy for a long time, though not making much progress—still depending somewhat on my own strength: here again Satan with craft deceived my heart and I went on for a time not knowing it. Finally I came to a place where a heart hung on a brittle thread, whereupon I saw the appearance of a man in bodily form revealing to me that underneath this heart there was a horrible pit. Here was great danger: world and money, idleness, laughing and jesting was all offered to this heart. Being in sympathy with this heart I offered my assistance but could not.

Here I began to realize that this heart that I saw was my own. Here I was in a miserable condition—realizing this, I first humbled myself to my neighbors beseeching their assistance for my rescue ere the brittle thread would break. Here I could do nothing but pray for pardon for my foolishness.

Thank God, finally the grace of God once more revealed unto me my condition; I realized that in all my former prayers I forgot to pray, "Father thy will be done and not mine."

Hershey (n.d.): 11-14

July

The Gospel of Peace
Menno Simons, Germany, 1552

*T*he Prince of peace is Christ Jesus. His kingdom is the kingdom of peace, which is His church. His messengers are the messengers of peace. His Word is the Word of peace. His body is the body of peace. His children are the seed of peace and His inheritance and reward are the inheritance and reward of peace. In short, with this King, and in His kingdom and reign, it is nothing but peace. Everything that is seen, heard and done is peace.

We have heard the word of peace, namely, the consoling Gospel of peace from the mouth of His messengers of peace. We, by His grace, have believed and accepted it in peace and have committed ourselves to the only, eternal and true Prince of peace—Christ Jesus—in His kingdom of peace and under His reign, and are thus by the gift of His Holy Spirit, by means of faith, incorporated into His body. And henceforth we look with all the children of His peace for the promised inheritance and reward of peace.

Such exceeding grace of God has appeared unto us poor, miserable sinners that we who were formerly no people at all and who knew of no peace are now called to be such a glorious people of God, a church, kingdom, inheritance, body and possession of peace. Therefore we desire not to break this peace, but by His great power by which He has called us to this peace and portion, to walk in this grace and peace, unchangeably and unwaveringly unto death.

Peter was commanded to sheathe his sword. All Christians are commanded to love their enemies; to do good unto those who abuse and persecute them; to give the mantle when the cloak is taken, the other cheek when one is struck.

*

O beloved reader, our weapons are not swords and spears, but patience, silence, and hope and the Word of God. With these we must maintain our heavy warfare and fight our battle. Paul says, "The weapons of our warfare are not carnal; but mighty through God." With these we intend and desire to storm the kingdom of the devil; and not with swords, spears, cannon and coats of mail. For He esteemeth iron as straw, and brass as rotten wood.

*

True Christians do not know vengeance, no matter how they are mistreated. In patience they possess their souls. And they do not break their peace, even if they should be tempted by bondage, torture, poverty and besides, by the sword and fire. They do not cry, "Vengeance, vengeance," as does the world; but with Christ they supplicate and pray: "Father, forgive them, for they know not what they do."

According to the declaration of the prophets they have beaten their swords into plowshares and their spears into pruning hooks. They shall sit every man under his vine and under his fig-tree, Christ; neither shall they learn war anymore.

Menno (1956): 554, 555

July 2

The Love of Christ Extends to All
Christian Burkholder, United States, 1792

The love of Christ, which is a general and eternal love, extends to all men, as well as to his enemies and friends. He suffered his blood to be shed for the sins of the whole world, and also prayed for his enemies: "Father forgive them, for they know not what they do."

*

Endeavor to love every human being and abhor all sin and sinful actions; and be also no partaker of other men's sins, but endeavor to convince the world rather by your life and conduct than by your words. In your words also be careful, and speak nothing contrary to the foundation of truth. In short, be wise as a serpent, and harmless as a dove.

*

Now as Christ commanded us to love our enemies, so he also showed by his course of life that he truly loved his enemies. To love our enemies and not to resist evil are the fruits that grow out of the vine of Christ. But quarrels and wars grow out of the lusts of our sinful members. The doctrine and deportment of Christ do not allow us to go to war or to use violence towards our enemies. As John spoke to the soldiers: "Do violence to no man" (Luke 3:14). Under such circumstances then, no true Christian can be engaged in military service; not being allowed to do violence to any one. Now the prophet did already prophesy of a kingdom of peace—the kingdom of Christ—in which they shall "beat their swords into plough-shares, and their spears into pruning hooks: nation shall not lift up sword against nation, neither shall they learn war any more" (Isaiah 2:4, Micah 4:3).

*

What a great difference there is between the doctrine and deportment of Christ and his apostles—as well as that of the doctrine and deportment of all true

Christians—and that of the professed followers of Christ at the present day. The former loved the brethren, left their lives for each other and loved their enemies according to the doctrine and example of the Son of God. Whereas, on the other hand, the Christians of the present day go to war with one another by thousands, kill and destroy one another in the most horrible manner—and this even such as are of the same religious faith, who boast as holding the true doctrine and who are united by the sacrament into the same body. But it is not to be believed that the true body of Christ will injure itself.

Further there are, alas! many amongst all religious denominations, who show by their fruits that they are not true branches of the vine of Christ, inasmuch as one brother belies and defrauds another and does violence and injustice to him.

*

Now to walk in love, as Christ walked therein, is something rare, as well as something important. So Christ also further says: "Continue in my love."

Conversation (1856): 211-216

July 3

I Live With the Peace-Makers

Pieter Pietersz., The Netherlands, 1625

Where I live, I (Christ) make the poor rich in their poverty, give joy to the suffering, give peace to the afflicted and comfort to the abandoned; open the door for those in bondage and give a free heart to those who are dying. To him who is downtrodden by everyone I am as a loving Father and embrace him in my arms. Therefore, he who possesses and retains me will remain secure even though the whole world shall pass away. For where I am there is blessedness always and anything which overtakes those who possess me serves them in every way for the best.

*

I live with the Peace-makers for they are my children. I reside with the humble who are of a contrite spirit. I dwell with those who love me for they keep my sayings. I reside with those who count all things but injury and dung for the sake of the excellency and knowledge of me. I live with those who want nothing other than what God wants. I dwell with those who would want to say with truth, "Lord, if only I have You, I desire for nothing else under heaven or on earth."

I gladly live with those persons who lament their own transgressions before me with earnest repentance and who seek my grace with firm trust. I reside with those who are poor in spirit and who consider themselves the least of all the blessed ones and at all times in humility esteem each other higher than themselves. I dwell with those who receive all things from my hand with thanks, poverty as well as wealth, suffering as well as joy, reproach as well as good favor. I reside with those who are pure in heart for they shall eternally look upon me with joy.

These are the ones in which I dwell, this is the true Israel of God, these are the new creatures. This is the poor wretched people which I have preserved for myself, and they trust in my name. These are those who hate injustice, including covetousness. These are the ones that I show my hidden treasures. These are the ones who have left everything for my sake. And therefore they find in me eternal peace.

Plett (1985): 82

July 4

We Have Dedicated Ourselves to Serve
Benjamin Hershey (?), United States, 1775

In the gathering storm of the American Revolution, Mennonites feared their freedoms as conscientious objectors to war were being increasingly threatened. Mennonites had willingly paid taxes for government, but did not want to pay for war. Neither were they willing to assemble for military preparations. Consequently, together with the Dunkers (now Church of the Brethren and related groups), they petitioned the Pennsylvania Assembly for toleration. A portion of the petition follows.

The advice to those who do not find freedom of conscience to take up arms, that they ought to be helpful to those who are in need and distressed circumstances, we receive with cheerfulness towards all men of what station they may be—it is our principle to feed the hungry and give the thirsty drink. We have dedicated ourselves to serve all men in everything that can be helpful to the preservation of men's lives, but we find no freedom in giving, or doing or assisting in anything by which men's lives are destroyed or hurt. We beg the patience of all those who believe we err in this point.

We are always ready, according to Christ's command to Peter, to pay the tribute, that we may offend no man. And so we are willing to pay taxes *and render to Caesar those things that are Caesar's and to God those things that are God's,* although we think ourselves very weak to give God his due honor, he being a spirit and Life, and we only dust and ashes.

We are also willing to be subject to the higher powers and to give in the manner Paul directs us—*for he beareth the sword not in vain, for he is the minister of God, a revenger to execute wrath upon him that doeth evil.*

This testimony we lay down before our worthy assembly and all other persons in government, letting them know that we are thankful as above-mentioned, and that we are not at liberty of conscience to take up arms to conquer our enemies, but rather pray to God who has power in heaven and on earth, for *us* and *them*.

We also crave the patience of all the inhabitants of this country—what they think to see clearer in the doctrine of the blessed Jesus Christ, we will leave to them and God, finding ourselves very poor; for faith is to proceed out of the Word of God, which is life and spirit, and a power of God, and our conscience to be instructed by the same. Therefore we beg for patience.

Our small gift which we have given, we gave to those who have power over us that we may not offend them, as Christ taught us by the tribute penny.

We heartily pray that God would govern all hearts of our rulers, be they high or low, to meditate on those good things which will pertain to *our* and *their* happiness.

MacMaster, Horst and Ulle (1979): 267

July 5

Have We All Been Dreaming?
Anna Baerg, Soviet Union, 1919

*D*usk has arrived; the day's work is finished. The moon has already greeted us with his smiling friend, the evening star. How is it though that even the most beautiful pleasure carries with it a bitter aftertaste, so that nothing is ever really satisfying? Mobilization is about to begin here again. People were already afraid of the conscription when the Reds were in charge. But then the Mennonites only had to sign up—they weren't yet trusted to carry weapons. With time this may have changed. But now the situation is completely different.

"Your men have courage." So said a Cossack to one of the local Mennonites. And truly, it's quite amazing to see: our people, who have had so little to do with war, now seem to have made a name for themselves. The skill and effectiveness of the *Selbstschutz* [self-defense] should not go to people's heads, however. We should thank God for our safety. I spoke of the great "evil"—and are not the war and conscription evil? A necessary one, perhaps, for the sake of survival, but an evil nonetheless, for it has brought with it so much sorrow already. That our pacifism has gone to shambles is only one of the consequences—and now there is no turning back.

Heinrich Koop, who also served in the *Selbstschutz*, says that he would no longer go voluntarily as he did then, but when I hear him talking about his exploits last winter, which he does constantly with such enthusiasm and pride, I realize what strong Germanic blood flows through the Mennonite veins.

Sleeping Beauty has been roused from her slumbers and the prince who has awakened her is, in this case, the war—this civil war, this evil. Even a lean, hungry peace would be better than not being able to sleep at night for fear of being murdered. Sleep? Have we all been dreaming until now? Are we not pacifists? Is not pacifism the whole idea behind Christianity? Yes, and one day it will be not only an idea but a reality! At least that's the way it should have been, yet it has turned out to be nothing but a dream, a beautiful dream. In any case, everything is quiet now. After great losses, the Red Army has been beaten back to the Dnieper. Thank God we have been spared the terrorism of Makhno.

Baerg (1985): 42, 43

July 6

Oaths and Promises
Hans Denck, Germany, 1527

Oaths and solemn promises are not within human power to keep. Rather, whatever a friend of God knows to be right, he is to do without an oath or solemn promise, as much as is within his power. Whatever he lacks in order to accomplish it, he ought to ask the Lord in prayer that he might grant it to him; but he should not vauntingly promise anything, as if it had to be granted to him. For whenever a person vows to do what he is incapable of (and he is not capable even of adding a tiny hair), it has to be either presumption without any understanding or else hypocrisy with understanding (i.e., one pretends to be able to do something when in one's heart one does not understand at all).

*

But no one should really be too hasty with "yes" and "no" just because this is permitted. For anyone who assures and convinces another with "yes" has already sworn, in that he thereby seeks to anticipate the will of God. Otherwise, one would become guilty of swearing a false oath if one were incapable of keeping the promise. But this is not the case when done rightly, as for example, when Paul apologized to the Corinthians (2 Corinthians 1:23), upon finding that he could not come to them again, contrary to his earlier assurance. All this is said about the swearing of oaths concerning future events.

Anyone who wishes to testify to something that has already happened, in keeping with the teaching of the Lord, should do it modestly and with as few words as possible (i.e., by yes or no). Anything beyond that has to be accounted for before God. Someone who has God for a witness of what he says, that it is yes, may go with it, as Paul also did. Only he ought to be aware that God's name must not be used in vain, for this too is forbidden by the law as well as in the New Testament where it is prohibited to swear by anything. To use God's name as such is not forbidden and has never been evil. Indeed, love bids all her children use it so that he alone be known, loved and praised in all eternity.

Denck (1989): 280, 281

A Dilemma

Menno Simons, Germany, 1552

We are aware that the magistracy claims and says that we are allowed to swear when justice is on our side. We reply with the Word of the Lord very simply. To swear truly was allowed to the Jews under the Law, but the Gospel forbids this to Christians. Since Christ does not allow us to swear, and since the magistracy, notwithstanding, proceeds according to their policy, although contrary to Scripture, and since the Scriptures may not be set aside by man, what shall the conscientious Christian do? If he swears, he falls into the hand of the Lord. If he swears not, he will have to bear the disfavor and punishment of the magistracy.

*

Therefore, worthy reader, if you fear the Lord and if it should happen that you are asked to swear, then pray the Most High for wisdom, courage and strength. Do not listen to the glosses of the learned ones, for they deceive you. Do not look to the numbers lest you follow in their evil ways, as Moses says. Give way to no flesh in this matter; it makes no difference who, what or where they be, but admonish them in a becoming manner and in love when they ask of you more than Scriptures command.

Continue in the Lord's Word which has forbidden you so plainly to swear, and let your yea and nay be your oath as was commanded, whether life or death be your lot, in order that you by your courage and firm truthfulness may admonish and reprove unto righteousness the useless, empty, vain world (which respects nothing less than the Word of the Lord) by your truthful yea and nay; if perchance some might be converted from their unrighteousness and thereby be led more deeply to study the truth and be saved.

Even at that it is better to incur the disfavor, scorn and slander of men and remain in the truth, than to be the friend of men and sin against God. The good John Hus declared when he was pressed to swear saying, "I am pressed on all sides. If I swear, I have eternal death; and if I do not swear, I will fall into your hands. But it is better to fall into your hands without swearing than to sin in the sight of God." Thus highly did this worthy man evaluate the oath.

Menno (1956): 519, 520

We Decided to Forgive Them

Simon Schrock, United States, 1978

*T*his time they were caught in the act. Some young people were failing to respect the property of others. There had been some problems earlier, but it was hard to find out who was really doing the dirty work. One blamed the other and the other "didn't know" who it was. However, this time they were caught in the very act.

On this hot Sunday afternoon they strayed into our yard and picked some precious Golden Delicious apples from the tree. Since the apples weren't ripe, they didn't pick them to eat. They took them to the next door neighbors to throw at the huge hornets' nest near the peak of the roof of the garage. Of course the hornets' nest was damaged and the ventilator was bent from being hit with hard green apples.

We confronted several of the offenders and asked them to round up the others who were involved.

*

Here were my terms. Since our Choice Books headquarters is located at the entrance of our street, I requested that each one meet me there the following morning. The penalty was going to be stiff. It would be two hours of work. Part of it was going to be cutting and trimming weeds around the building. There was another alternative. They could return to see me with their parents. In the event their parents would not support this action they would be relieved from the penalty. So they had the choice—work for two hours, or see me with their parents.

Since this happened in the afternoon, I had some time to think through the incident and how I responded to it. I wondered whether my action was a proper response for a Christian to take. Since I am not the owner of things, but a steward, how would God want His children to respond to destruction of His property?

*

After serious thought and discussion with other Christians who heard the incident I changed my mind and decided to forgive them with no strings attached.

*

This would be an opportunity to illustrate to them what forgiveness really means.

We prepared for the arrival of the group. I outlined Scripture verses and made enough copies for each to have one. My partner who had witnessed the ordeal picked up a box of donuts. The young people arrived, anxious to see what their penalty would be. We sat around a table, passed the donuts and discussed the incident. Most of them showed signs of regret and saw the point of respecting the property of others.

We had a good discussion on stealing and principles for living. Then we looked at the Scripture verses together. After telling them that Christ has forgiven us we explained that because of His forgiveness to us, we decided to forgive them.

*

Forgiveness opened other doors. To maintain relationships with them, we invited them to our house for a game of volleyball that evening. We had a good game, followed by devotions and refreshments. On another night the young people stayed around and asked questions about God, hell and other important subjects that opened the door to sharing God's way of life.

Because we decided to forgive, they went free and later I pulled the weeds and trimmed the grass. Forgiveness to another means he is released from further demands. That is what Christ did for us. He paid our price for sin so we could go free.

I think it was the right thing to do. It healed relationships and opened doors to further friendship and discussion of God's Word. I trust God's Spirit will lead them to seeking God's forgiveness through our Lord Jesus Christ.

Hertzler (1983): 170, 171

July 9

A Time to Yield

Johannes Risser, Germany, 1827

I am thoroughly convinced that the men who tried to organize and lead our discussions were wholeheartedly seeking the welfare of our churches. To achieve it they had as their sole basis the Holy Scriptures with the purest intention, and they placed their trust on God's aid. When we have expressed our reasons for the resolutions, as we can and should, and it happens that the majority of the votes are convinced that the opposing position is right—it is our Christian duty to yield our opinion and admit that the error may be on our side. This we owe to our faith in the leading of the Holy Spirit. Such an attitude is in agreement with the doctrine of lowliness and humility of the Christian. "Do not consider yourself wise" is pertinent here.

Granted that we are outvoted and the better idea is on our side, we are absolved of any guilt even in our yielding. First, we have the consolation that we have the verdict of God to King Saul that obedience is better than sacrifice. And second, when it is evident that the better view was outvoted, as must become evident in all truth in the consequences, we are justified also before the world and before men. Because we can always refer back to our words and our vote.

When the Israelites, in imitation of the heathen, wanted a king, Samuel opposed them; and it was obvious that he had voted for the better course.

Nevertheless, it was God's will that he yield to the voice of the people who had outvoted him. That is a rule in all common *external* matters—that God's Word has clearly put into our hands and that should therefore always be observed and fulfilled, especially by Christians.

In *inward things*, however, in matters of faith, it is different. There we cannot, and dare not, subordinate our conviction—if it is based on the Word of God—to any majority or authority. In such cases we must say, "It is better to obey God than man." It is therefore very important to distinguish correctly in such instances whether the matter is in the category of outward or inward matters, lest we err and sin by our persistence, where we ought to yield and learn to obey. Likewise, we should not sin by yielding when we ought to show steadfastness and faith in God.

I ask you to give this comment, which is surely right, serious consideration because these general (also sacred) conferences can yield their true usefulness and proceed smoothly only if they eventuate in deeds. Divisions occurred among Mennonites only because secondary or outward things were made into principal things.

Risser (1827): 8, 9, trans. by Elizabeth Horsch Bender

July 10

A Bishop's Kiss
H.B.M., United States, 1889

I can hardly remember the time when I did not pray. Especially when there was a heavy thunderstorm, I prayed with fear and trembling. When I came to the age of thirteen, I gave my heart to Jesus. I just had one sin that pressed me very hard, and that was telling my father a lie and denying it three times. This came to me when I promised and it seemed to go very hard before I could give it up. It took me a whole day before I became willing to confess my sin. I expected nothing else but a complete whipping but I found no other way than to go to father as the prodigal son did and confess all. I went and told him all about it. I told him to chastise me hard for it, for I felt I deserved it, but father said, "My beloved son, you are chastised enough," and advised me to obey the Savior. Oh then what a blessing I received, and I felt my sins were forgiven.

Then I thought every person, all my companions, should realize this, so I talked to them, but they could not see it. I would have carried them to the Savior if I could. At the evening meetings I still tried to get them along with me to the meetings, and to go in; but they were not ready. By that I was induced to remain with them, but the longer I remained, the more influence they got over me.

So one evening in particular I remained with them, and Bishop Gish must have seen us through the window. He came out and went around, and gave each one the hand and when he came to me he drew me to him and gave me a kiss, and then left us. Now the Spirit of the Lord came with power and said, "What way are you going?" I then asked my companions to go along in the house, but they refused, so I told them if they would not I must leave them. I then and there left my young companions and with them my good name.

I then again received a blessing and went on my way rejoicing. Now right here I would say to the older brethren; remember the lambs of the flock. I do believe that many could be kept on the way by the older members obeying faithfully the good spirit to feed the lambs.

M. (1889): 109

July 11

Peace Among Us

Kusangila Kitondo, Zaire, 1987

*T*he Apostle Peter says we pastors must be examples to our flocks. Frequently when conflict develops between individuals or groups opposed to each other it is because one of them refuses to yield or forgive the other one. We pastors must teach about forgiveness. Then we can help resolve many conflicts among church members. It is also important that *we* live with the spirit of humility and forgiveness. I believe that forgiveness is the most worthy thing to give in a conflict situation.

I want to emphasize tolerance as another good quality for committed Christians. The opposite, intolerance, is the main source of conflict in our churches. Are we really tolerant? Another thing that Jesus Christ underlined is that reconciliation between members depends first of all on their willingness to listen to the reconciler.

We find two methods in the Bible for dealing with conflict. 1) Cain's method consisted of retaliation—a bad action for a bad action. The aims are division, killing, hatred, jealousy and confusion. 2) The other way is that of the cross—of Golgotha. This approach has opposite goals: love, unity, nonviolence, truth, fraternity and harmony. As Christians we need to follow this method. It may help us to face various difficult situations. But it is not easy; it costs a lot. I want us as brothers and sisters to use the Golgotha method for solving problems in our churches.

*

In the Bible peace has various senses. It signifies the opposite of war as well as the state of the soul which is in harmony with God. Jesus said, "By this will all men know that you are my disciples if you love one another."

It is true that every person, every family, every Christian community and people all over the world wish for and like to live in peace. On the other hand, throughout history there have been men and women from our Christian communities who have caused troubles, divisions and cold wars because of their ambitions and human tendencies. According to the Bible and following Jesus' example, a Christian must necessarily have the elements of the new world (the church of Christ): love, unity, forgiveness, gentleness and peace. We note that the church preaches but hasn't always put it into practice so that the members experience this peace.

In the Beatitudes Jesus said, "Blessed are the peacemakers, for they will be called the sons of God" (Matthew 5:9). May we not only preach the Gospel of peace, but practice the elements of Christ's peace in our churches.

Kitondo (1987): 8

July 12

Who Am I?

Z. Marwa Kisare, Tanzania, 1984

*T*oo often a leader is like a small child who takes a pencil and, not knowing the proper use of it breaks it; or he is like a child who, not knowing the function of a knife, cuts himself. When a leader treats God's grace lightly and goes about his activity roughly behaving like those who don't know God, it shows that he is immature in his understanding of grace. Grace then turns again to harm him and he is empty, forspent. God's intent in gifting us with grace is to empower us so we may face each issue and task with confidence in peace.

When it has been my duty to confront another person, maybe even a pastor in the church, I take Galatians 6:1-2 as my guide. "Brothers, if someone is caught in a sin, you who are spiritual should restore him gently. But watch yourself, or you also may be tempted. Carry each other's burdens, and in this way you will fulfill the law of Christ." I cannot help someone if I have disdain in my heart for him. If I despise someone, then all I do when visiting him is to trade insults. No good comes of it.

Once, after I became a bishop, I needed to go to a pastor about sin in his life. He was not from my tribe. I was very afraid to go to him because he could take my coming to him ethnically. He might think I was picking on him. But more than this, I feared to go because he was my age-mate. As human beings we were equal.

I took with me another pastor, a brother with whom I had peace, a man of wisdom and grace. We went then, after much prayer, in a spirit of humility and gentleness. We did not go to him like holy people, but like fellow pilgrims. He received us with great fear. I asked myself, "Who am I that I should come to this man with this word?" I honored him in how I approached him and he in turn honored me in how he received my word.

Shenk (1984): 97

A Leader's Integrity
Z. Marwa Kisare, Tanzania, 1984

*T*here is a Bantu saying that a person is like a thicket. You do not know what is in a thicket. If you throw a rock into a thicket, you don't know what will come out. Maybe a rabbit will come hopping out or maybe a lion will leap out, roaring, intending to kill you. A thicket hides what it contains.

But with a Christian leader it must not be so. What is seen on the outside must be a true reflection of what is there on the inside. This is especially important for a leader's family. A man's wife and children know his inner life. If there is a split between his public and private life, he creates a great wilderness for his family.

*

In order to stand firmly against evil in society, a leader needs to be seen by the people to be in a right relationship with God. His relationship to God cloaks him, as a garment covers the naked, giving him power to speak the truth. His relationship to God gives him power so people don't take his leadership jokingly. People are afraid to take him lightly or to brush his teaching aside.

*

But if a leader is gossiping to others, then his garment of right-standing with God is stripped off him and he is defenseless prey to any who choose to attack him. His ministry is powerless.

A wrestler has power as long as his two feet are firmly on the ground. Here in Africa you conquer your wrestling opponent by tripping him so he falls. A gossiping leader is like a wrestler with only one leg. His opponent may pick him up any way he likes and toss him where he pleases.

It is good for a leader to cultivate the presence of God's grace in his life, a serenity born of the presence of the Holy Spirit. When I am in harmony with God, it is as though I am in an ocean of peace and joy. This serenity gives power to my witness in the world. It opens my life to God's activity on my behalf because I am within the stream of God's active will on earth.

This serenity is sometimes broken. Maybe my wife comes suddenly, breaking into my thoughts of God, reminding me of some problem or issue which needs my attention. Maybe the children come shouting through the house, slamming the doors. Maybe someone comes with a complex bit of administration which he is pushing me to quickly decide on or do something about. Then I answer roughly in frustration. I lash out angrily at my detractors. It is then that the vase of grace slips from my hands, shattering on the floor.

When this happens, a light goes out in my soul. That grace of God's presence cannot be recovered without great effort and cost. I can't just pick it up again and be at peace. No. Recovery requires repentance and cleansing and a return to that attitude of mind which again welcomes God's presence. What I should do is to respond to the daily barrage of detractions with equanimity, in a spirit of grace. Then the day's work and activity go forward blessed always by God's presence.

Shenk (1984): 94-97

July 14

I Cannot Conscientiously Interfere
Menno Simons, Germany, 1553

When Leenaert Bouwens was chosen to be an elder and a co-worker with Menno Simons, Leenaert's wife wrote to Menno asking that Leenaert be excused from serving due to the danger of persecution he would face. Menno's reply is sensitive, but he is committed to heeding the call of God through the congregation.

Worthy and faithful sister in the Lord, my inmost soul is grieved in your behalf more so than I can write. For I understand from our dear brethren that you have difficulty reconciling yourself to the request of the poor, afflicted and pastorless church in regard to your beloved husband. I cannot reprove you severely if it be considered in the light of natural considerations rather than spiritual. I also understand from the words of Leonard and Helmicht that you hoped that Leonard would be excused by me from serving.

*

Dear sister, who am I that I should resist the Holy Spirit? You are aware, are you not, that not I but the church, and that without my knowledge, has called him to this service? Since the church so urgently desires him and since he cannot conscientiously refuse, how then shall I oppose it? I can find nothing in Leonard for which I could with Scriptural warrant oppose his call.

Dear sister, I am sorry that I cannot give you your way in this matter, for the sorrow and sadness of your flesh pierces my heart as often as I think of it, but the love to God and our brethren must be considered first of all. You are called to this of the Lord and by the operation of your faith you have yielded yourself to the service, not of your own self but of Jesus Christ and of your brethren as long as you live.

*

Inasmuch then as the merciful Lord has gifted our beloved brother with knowledge of divine things, has enlightened him with His Holy Spirit, and gifted him with speech and wisdom so that the brethren are pleased with him, sincerely love him, and desire his talent, therefore if you for the sake of flesh and blood should oppose this and not acquiesce therein, it would seem to me to be identical with seeing your brethren in danger, in fire or water, and then for your own comfort's sake refusing to help. Dear sister, do love your brethren as Christ Jesus has loved us, even if for the sake of your brethren you should be robbed of your goods. Remember that Christ has for a time left the glory of His Almighty Father and the company of angels that He might obtain an eternal inheritance in heaven. So long as we live we shall have enough of the necessities of life if we fear God, depart from evil and do the right.

*

If you are solicitous for your husband's natural life, then remember and believe that our life is measured by spans, that life and death are in the hands of the Lord, that not a hair falls from our heads without the will of our Father. He protects us as the apple of His eye.

Elijah and Elisha, David, Daniel, Shadrach, Meshach and Abednego, Peter and Paul have all escaped the hands of the tyrant and none could injure a single hair on their head so long as the appointed day and hour were not come. So long as the Lord has more pleasure in our life than in our death they cannot injure us; but when our death is more pleasing to the Lord than our life, then we shall not escape from their hands.

O dear sister, if our beloved brother should not serve our brethren, yet still he has years ago already committed himself to danger of death, tribulation, misery, scorn, persecution, anxiety, robbery, water, fire and sword. And even if he had not committed himself to the cross by baptism, and could pass through all cities and populations unmolested, you know not at what moment he would have to put off the tabernacle of clay and appear before his God.

*

Behold, worthy and true sister, as the church calls our beloved brother to the office and service, I cannot conscientiously interfere unless I should love flesh, your flesh, more than Christ Jesus my Lord and Savior and my sincerely beloved brethren. May the Almighty merciful Father act in this matter according to His divine good pleasure and guide the heart of my beloved sister so as to be resigned to His Holy will. I sincerely thank my beloved sister for the gift of your love that you have sent me. The Lord repay you in heavenly riches of eternal glory. My wife greets you with the peace of the Lord. The Lord Jesus Christ be forever with my most beloved friend and sister. Amen.

Menno (1956): 1038-1040

True Leadership

Uli Ammann, France, ca. 1720

A minister and leader of the congregation—at whatever place he may be, whether an ordained person or a completely confirmed minister who bears the name of being an elder—can keep himself clear of guilt and of accusations of others in no better way than by taking counsel in those matters of consequence that occur in the congregation. It is our opinion that he ought to do this whenever a matter causing contention or something else of importance arises in the congregation; he should first of all take counsel with his fellow ministers and then also with the congregation.

It is our understanding that an elder or confirmed minister does indeed have authority in the case of such incidents to give his view first and thus establish a model, based on his best understanding of the matter; and then he may present it to his fellow ministers and to the congregation, and commit it to them for possible correction from the Word of God. He shall not assume that his view must be the valid one, or that no one has the right to find fault with it.

*

If it should happen—as it easily could—that the general counsel does not turn out for the best, then the minister who made the initial statement does not bear the sole responsibility, but the entire congregation shares with him in bearing the blame, in which case the congregation has no authority or right to put the blame on him.

If it should happen that the minister's or elder's initial presentation on some important matter was not generally understood to be the best and dissension then follows, some people favoring the elder and his initial presentation while the opposing party thinks they could not accept it, it is our opinion that they should not argue about it to the point where love is lost, nor should the minister assume that the opposition must yield to his understanding and that he would like to rule over them contrary to their conscience.

*

The elder and those who accept his initial statement, and the opposing party who feel that they cannot accept it, should come to an agreement and refer the matter to other elders and ministers in other congregations for consideration and express themselves on it with their best understanding; then both sides should be content to adapt themselves to it as far as is possible so that peace may be furthered on the part of the elders as well as the other side.

*

The Savior said, "Ye know that the princes of the Gentiles exercise dominion over them, and they that are great exercise authority upon them. But it shall not be so among you. . .even as the Son of man came not to be ministered unto, but to minister, and to give his life a ransom for many" (Matthew 20:25-28). From these words one cannot draw the meaning that freedom is granted a minister in the Lord's church to dominate; nor on the other hand can these words be understood to imply that an elder or minister shall be badly and unlovingly treated, as can easily happen at times.

Bender (1977): 2, 3

July 16

Church Machinery
Edward Yoder, United States, 1931

*T*o me it would seem a sorry day when General Conference will step down from its position as a spiritually edifying body to that of a supreme court of church politicians with pretended powers to direct and regulate the work of the Spirit of God. Our little denomination has so far in history been rather consistently known for the quiet, peaceable and pietistic living of its members. We have had little connection with the streams of the world's thought, activity and customs. But during the past decades we have been minded to get away from the simple unworldly way of living.

One line of worldly conformity that is never mentioned in this time when many complain of the worldward drift in our group is that of our aping after the spirit of our age and time in our feverish craving for organization, the multiplication of boards, committees, etc., etc. The question is inevitable: Is it still possible to hear the still small voice of the Holy Spirit and of conscience in this new era above the clanking of the church machinery and the rumbling of its steam rollers made to flatten out differences and to crush the individual personality?

The generation now growing up is being taught to think of Christian activity and of witnessing for Christ solely in terms of organized boards and authorized committees, a conception that is sure to be deadening to the idea and conviction of personal responsibility. Can it be a good sign for the perpetuation of our ideals of simple obedience to God and the simple guidance of His Spirit when even church leaders seemingly think of problems and their solution in terms of special committees and conference legislation rather than in terms of prayer and the leading of the Spirit?

Some simple organization is doubtless necessary even in church work, but I am personally convinced that for our small group our multiplication of machinery has now become a genuine menace to our ideals that will smother and strangle the Spirit's efforts to use us as a witness to the world.

Yoder (1985): 6, 7

Dividers

Paul Hostetler, United States, 1980

When we first attended the Sippo Church, it had two outside entrances—one for men and one for women. Since the doors were not marked, visitors would sometimes wander in at the wrong door to the great amusement of us children. When they did this, the only way to get to the correct side (except for crossing in front of the first pew) was to go back outside and come in the other door.

The reason people couldn't rectify their mistake once they were inside was because a partition had been built into the center of the church. This barricade was very effective in keeping the men and boys on the right side and the women and girls on the left side.

The first time I heard the sheep and goats parable referred to in the Bible I immediately concluded that the men and boys were the sheep and the women were the goats. But Dad quickly debunked that chauvinist thinking by pointing out that from his place in the pulpit the distaff people were on the right side.

Dad was opposed to that dividing partition. He was also tired of the much too low and narrow benches which caused him to ache long before a service was over. So he proposed at one of the annual congregational councils that the partition be removed, the pews raised and the seats widened. After the proposal was batted around negatively for a while, Dad sensed that it was going to be benched. He therefore offered to do all the work himself. And with that, the proposition was approved.

By the ingenious method of offering to do things himself, Dad was able to bring about a number of changes at the Sippo Church.

*

He got into serious trouble, however, on another improvement venture. The Sippo Church had no indoor plumbing, just two outdoor toilets. These small privies had no protecting walls to provide a sight barrier to an open toilet door. One day Dad decided to remedy this immodest situation without checking with the congregation. He supposed that everyone at church would pronounce blessings on him for his thoughtfulness and industry.

He purchased new lumber and built the screens which the law, even then, called for in public rest rooms. On Sunday he waited for the plaudits of the people. To his amazement the money-minded members first asked what the cost was going to be. When assured that both labor and materials were gratis, they then wondered by whose authority he had cast out the evil situation. Since Dad had to admit going ahead on his own, the displeasure of all too many brothers and sisters was given center stage.

One brother who liked to wield power to make up for his lack of common sense suggested that the walls be torn down. Fortunately, wiser heads prevailed.

Yes, Dad should be scolded for proceeding without proper clearances, but the walls would stay because they were needed.

We boys were indignant and thirsty for revenge. When we arrived at home, we had a plan. "Let's go right over to church tomorrow morning, Dad, and tear those walls down. Then all those mean people will be sorry for the way they treated you today!" But Dad shook his head, smiling sadly.

"Just remember the lesson you learned today, boys," he advised. "You can't even improve an outdoor toilet at the church without a ballot vote at the annual congregational council." In all the years I attended Sippo Church after that incident, I never saw the offending walls without remembering the hubbub and Dad's wry comment.

Paul Hostetler (1980): 68-70

July 18

The Price of Popularity
Edward Yoder, United States, 1932

*H*ave reflected frequently of late on what it apparently costs one to attain standing and repute in our Mennonite Church circles. The price set for such a desiderata is high enough, in fact, quite too high for some to be able to pay it. Among the things included in this price that is set for popularity, is that of saying about what people desire to hear, saying these things in the generally accepted words and phrases, and saying them with the precise relative emphasis that is conventional and orthodox at that moment. A certain modicum of adaptation of oneself to the psychosis of the group that one desires to lead is undeniably essential. But it may be questioned whether the mere aspiration to be a well-liked leader of people is a legitimate ambition. My ideal rather is to serve.

*

I have made a rather interesting observation from my own experience. In 1928, at the time we were planning to move back to Hesston, some months before we actually came on the scene after an absence of five years, I received notice that I was to serve on the program of the Workers' Conference in connection with the Missouri-Kansas Church Conference. The topic was one of those rather stereotyped kinds that have been in great favor in this district for some time, something about one's individual responsibility in upholding the faith of our fathers. I gave an informal talk as I could, treating it as I sincerely thought of it myself. I was scarcely aware that what I said was not according to the usual pattern with the precise vocables and niceties of emphasis that those desire who are especially interested in that line of thought. Three brethren took the pains and trouble later to speak to me in commendatory wise on what I had said. They were men whose opinions I value much because they think for themselves. One of these also volunteered the information that some had expressed themselves as having been disappointed in what was said on the topic. At any rate the ideas I gave out on that occasion were evidently entirely and completely satisfying, so much so that I have not been called upon to speak on such a conference program since. I congratulate myself on my efficiency, so far as that goes, for I always find it more or less an ordeal to speak before a large audience.

One is made to wonder whether this psychosis that makes many good folks reduce orthodoxy and religious truth to certain set and fixed formulae is not an escape mechanism to conscientiously avoid the hard and exacting task of thinking for themselves. I recall reading a statement years ago to the effect that there is scarcely any length to which people will not go to avoid the hard labor of thinking. One could write a long satire, I imagine, on the complacent smugness of large numbers of church people in their churchgoing and religious performances.

Apparently many go to church and to conferences, not to get new knowledge and truth and vision, but to have their ears tickled periodically by the very familiar music of time-worn words, phrases and ideas given out with that soothing and comfortable emphasis which they somehow feel is orthodoxy and good form religiously. Any slight shift of emphasis, all new and unusual terms or suggestive ideas strike upon their ears as terrible discords. It frightens them seemingly to be even slightly jarred out of their comfortable and unthinking security, and faced with the prospect of thinking something out for themselves.

While many doubtless are incapable of thinking things through in their religion, yet it is unquestionably true that numbers could do so if their spiritual leaders would force them to it instead of merely patting them on the back for the sake of their own popularity.

Yoder (1985): 68, 69

July 19

A Heretic I Cannot Be

Balthasar Hubmaier, Moravia, 1526

Hubmaier was among the first to take up his pen to defend freedom of religious belief during the Reformation. Already in 1524 he declared that "the inquisitors are the greatest heretics of all, because counter to the teaching and example of Jesus, they condemn heretics to fire." Hubmaier was burned at the stake for his beliefs in 1528.

I may err. I am a human being—but a heretic I cannot be, for I constantly ask instruction in the Word of God. But nobody has yet come forth who has showed me a different word, save one sole man with his party, and that contrary to his own prior preaching, word and publications. His name I will protect on account of the divine Word. He wanted to teach me the faith by means of a public law and trial before his own government, before the confederates, also before the emperor himself, by means of capturing, imprisoning, torture and the executioner. But faith is a work of God and not of the Heretics' Tower, in which one sees neither sun nor moon and lives on nothing but bread and water.

But praise be to God, who protected me from this lions' pit in which the dead and living people remain lying next to each other and must thus perish. O God, forgive me my weakness. "It is good for me," as David says, "that you have humbled me. The son whom you love, you chasten. I am well satisfied with you. You have given and taken, praised be your name. You know what I say."

Hubmaier (1989): 308

July 20

Bright Blinding Lights
Charles Christano, Indonesia, 1978

*H*ow all of us need to repent because we have been so much concerned about the right structure(s), analyzing and scrutinizing words in hairsplitting manners. We spend hours and thousands of dollars theologizing them. We print well researched books which fill up our study rooms only to be used as references for writing thicker books.

I am speaking on behalf of the billions—people who are hungry, simply for the truth. The Lord of the Kingdom is recruiting more laborers for a great harvest because the hour has come. I am making an appeal for those who are craving for justice, for righteousness, needing very badly the down-to-earth truth, the "pedicab drivers' theology" and not pie in the sky.

I have nothing against higher and contemporary theology. It has its rightful place. But I am afraid that many of us have already been drawn as moths to bright blinding lights. The glamor of things which are big, attractive, new and sophisticated has become a fad. In spite of the big leap in technology and theology so to speak, we come up with calloused man who has come of age.

I acknowledge that the good news of the Kingdom of God is also for the wise and the rich, but I can not overemphasize too much that our Lord gave His time to the poor and oppressed, people who lived on the margin.

Many have attempted to elevate the poor to higher and better levels. We believe that the Christian utopia will come one day. But Isaiah said, "Every valley shall be filled, every mountain and hill shall be brought low" (Isaiah 40:3-5). And it was not by accident that John, the forerunner of Jesus, used that very verse in preparing for the coming King! And I believe that all of us are recruited to be the voice in the wilderness of our modern day to prepare the second coming of the great King.

Might it be that we had read those verses differently or misunderstood them completely? We are given the mandate by the King, not to "push up" the lowest of the low but the very opposite, to "bring down" the highest and the mighty. That is how we are to understand the incarnation.

I affirm that instead of having the right theology of evangelism, or a theology of the church, we ought to have the biblical theology of the Kingdom. But no matter how good and comprehensive our theology of the Kingdom is, unless we live what we preach, and incarnate it, the rich will still be getting richer and mightier and the poor, poorer.

Kraybill ([1978]): 100

July 21

A Personal Affair
Edward Yoder, United States, 1932

Religion has been to me essentially a personal affair, the quiet inner fellowship with the personality of God, the contemplation of God's character and his work, the yearning and striving to conform more nearly to His will. The features of formal and militant Christianity which include any forms of display, noise, blatant ballyhoo and the like have always been more or less distasteful to me.

I think it is necessary to witness for one's faith, to exercise the expressional side of one's religion. But for me, living day by day in the strength that comes from intimate fellowship with God is as potent as any form of religious expression, to my mind. However, to be dogmatic in insisting on any specific pattern of experience or any set formula or slogan in such matters, even if it be a latitudinarian formula, is still one degree worse than a noisy expression of religion.

My notion is that varieties of religious experience are as numerous and seemingly infinite as the forms and shapes of the leaves and flowers that the Creator has fashioned. The cloistered monk and hermit saint of past ages did undoubtedly honor and glorify their Maker as often as the Christian today who runs hither and thither to conventions, conferences, meetings and whatnot. Even the contribution of the former type to the advancement of religion can easily have been as great and as significant as that of moderns who are so completely sold on the slogan of "service."

A favorite motto of mine has long been St. Paul's admonition: "Make it your ambition to be quiet and to attend to your own business." At the same time God needs active propagandists and I rejoice that He can find them for His work.

Yoder (1985): 108, 109

It Was On the Same Road!

Agrippa V. Masiye, 1967

I was on my way from Salisbury to Bulawayo. It was a Saturday afternoon in 1962.

*

Two men stopped me and asked for a lift to Hartley. They looked innocent and without a moment's hesitation I picked them up.

A little later I stopped for a drink at a roadside store. I left the two men in the car, but before I had finished my cold drink they also came into the store to buy bread and sugar.

Soon we were on our way again. We had not yet reached Hartley when the two men asked to get down. I stopped the car and let them out, never stopping to think that I might have reason to wish I had not picked them up. I left.

Before long I was in Gatooma. I stopped at a petrol station for fuel. I reached for my brief case to get the four pounds I had there for petrol. I stared into it with fear. My brief case was empty!

*

On 5th February, 1967, I was on the same road from Bulawayo to Salisbury. Three men stopped me at Gwelo and asked for a lift!

My memory was not short! Was I going to let the sad story of 1962 happen again? "No," I said to myself.

But they were persuasive and I was not hard-hearted. "I shall take them, but I shall lock my brief case," I decided.

Off we went. At Que Que two of the men got off the car, but the third man went on to Salisbury with me. It was 9:30 p.m. and it was raining heavily.

"Do you smoke?" my passenger asked, offering me a cigarette.

"No, thank you," I replied.

"Do you drink?"

"No," I said again.

"You are blessed," he said.

"Maybe I am blessed, but I miss the fun that you fellows have," I said to my friend, trying to make him feel unembarrassed.

"Yes, you miss the fun and the heartaches too!" he answered. My friend was clever. He was not like the people who are in trouble and yet do not know that they are in trouble.

*

Before long we were deeply involved in a discussion about Christianity, a discussion that went on for 166 miles. He summed up his stand in this way:

"I am not a Christian because I have not found a church that will treat me as a human being. I do not believe that the whole Bible is the Word of God. To me, only the ten commandments are the Word of God. I do not believe that Jesus is God. He is the Son of God in the same way that all men are Sons of God. The Bible has no real message for Africa. If it had, there would have been African writers who took part in the writing of the Bible."

*

"It is a pity that no church has seen fit to treat you like a human being," I said. "But I know that God does. Leave people alone. Face God squarely and listen to His demands upon you.

"The Bible says that all Scripture is given by the inspiration of God. I cannot understand why you think that the rest of the Bible is not God's Word when the Bible says that the whole thing is God's Word.

"In John we are told, 'In the beginning was the Word, and the Word was with God, and the Word was God. . . .' This verse shows clearly that Jesus is God.

"I agree that no African took part in the writing of the Bible, but the African is not the only race that did not write. The Russians, Americans, English, Poles and many others did not write, and yet the Bible is as much for them as it is for the Jews."

Finally he said, "You surpass me because you know the Bible verses, whereas I do not know them."

The 166 miles were eaten unnoticed. Our conversation ended with these words from my friend: "May I have your address? I should like to come to your church on Sunday! I see now that some of the problems that I have are caused by the fact that I do not know the Bible. I want to begin to read the Bible now."

I promised to send him some literature and a New Testament. Then he gave me his address.

It was on this same road. Where I lost four pounds, Christ can win a man. What are four pounds compared with a human soul?

Masiye (1967): 8

July 23

Mr. and Mrs. Normal
Marvin Hein, United States, 1980

What kinds of images come to mind when you think of a typical American family at worship? The pictures on most church bulletins likely show Mr. and Mrs. Normal and their three normal children, sitting devoutly in the front pew of a nice, clean church. They are nicely dressed, properly coiffed. They are singing a hymn or bowing their heads in prayer. In short, they are a beautiful normal American family.

*

Of such, thinks the person in the street today, is the kingdom of God.

The church has helped foster that kind of impression. We have helped paint the picture of a church whose pews are filled with normal families whose smooth passage through life just needs a little weekly boost from the church. We give the impression that the vast majority of church members fit into the conventional pattern of normality, neatness and well-being.

But what happens when somebody "out there" believes and tries to join our ranks? They are left frustrated and discouraged, convinced they can't really be a part of the church because they really don't belong in a button-down society of thoroughly healthy, normal Christians.

Even within the church we keep giving each other the impression we are normal Christians without any grave problems. In fact, we go to a lot of sham and costly pretense to keep the person beside us thinking we are Mr. and Mrs. Normal. And when we don't fit the pattern exactly we feel guilty and insecure, and if we brood long enough about the whole matter we may even despair and head for the psychiatrist. Or, we may just buy a new suit or dress, sprinkle on the latest lotion, borrow some money and try to pass ourselves off as well on the way to being normal Christians.

How much better (and more biblical) if we just kicked Mr. and Mrs. Normal back into limbo where they belong and frankly faced the fact that we are all sinful, struggling, hopeful, half-fulfilled, half-frustrated men and women, each with our own quirks and oddities, and each troubled by the fact that we fall so desperately short of what we ought to be in Jesus Christ.

While the world thinks of the church as a group of religious-minded, happy families, what we really are is a fellowship of misfits being shaped and molded by the grace of God. Our Lord made this perfectly clear. He said, "I came not to call the righteous, but sinners to repentance" (Mark 2:17). What we don't always hear in that verse are the quotation marks around the word "righteous." Jesus was saying the "righteous" are like the mythical, normal American family. They don't really exist, but some people act as if they do. God didn't send his Son to confer a blessing on people whose lives were flowing smoothly, and for whom no problems loomed larger than a cold in the sinuses. He came "to seek and save what is lost." And the lost are precisely those who know that they are not normal. The lost are those who do not automatically belong in the company of the smooth and the satisfied.

Would Christ have gone through the agony of crucifixion on behalf of normal people who only need an occasional pat on the back to keep them on their smooth path of happiness and success? It was "while we were yet sinners," twisted, maimed and abnormal misfits in God's world, that Christ died for us. The gospel is good news because it is pointed straight at those who know they are off base. The gospel is good news because it offers to bring people into the company, not of the normal, but of the crooked who are being straightened out—or, as the Bible says, sinners who are being saved.

Those who know they are sick go to the doctor, Jesus said, and it was the sick he came to cure. You might say that the only people excluded from the church Jesus came to establish, from the kingdom he announced, are those who think they are too normal to require the healing grace of God.

Hein (1980): 37-39

July 24

Diary Martyrs
Viktor G. Doerksen, Canada, 1980(?)

*T*here is one overwhelming difference between the fate of the Anabaptist martyr and the eighteenth century "soul" that must be noted here. Put bluntly, the earlier heroes' souls are attached to their bodies, with very drastic consequences. Unfortunately, it was not possible for them, the Felix Mantzes and George Wagners of the sixteenth century, to declare that they were prepared for martyrdom in "attitude" or "spiritually," and the martyr songs depict the physical consequences of this fact in excruciating detail.

But by the eighteenth century, when a relatively high degree of toleration had developed, the protagonists are sophisticated enough to separate these two areas, and so it is possible for the "soul" to undergo a series of dramatic adventures, no less spectacular than those of its more primitive forerunners, without so much as being singed or getting wet.

This process of internalization, for example, allowed Goethe's progressive Faust to recognize the devil as nothing more than a negative potential within himself, and thus permitted him to be saved ultimately, unlike his hapless sixteenth century counterpart, whose body was literally splatted about when his soul became the devil's due.

Through the process of separating body and soul (to the detriment of the former, while the latter is emphasized) it is possible to redefine all of the old terms: persecution, suffering, martyrdom, as well as others, so that the individual could be a spiritual adventurer and indeed, a martyr, without necessarily losing his often lofty stature in society and, indeed, at times, without anyone else knowing about his sufferings at all—this being revealed only to himself and his God in his secret diary.

Plett (1985): 77, 78

July 25

Overcoming From the Depths
Johann J. Toews, Soviet Union, ca. 1932

"Thou hast put me in the pit of the lowest, in dark places, in deep regions." —Psalm 88:6
(from Luther's translation)

My recent period of suffering is beautifully yet very realistically portrayed in the verse in Psalm 88:6. The three steps of the intensifying phenomena are typical and classic of my own accumulative experiences.

First came the pit—my Gethsemane: the prison with its interrogation and thousand fears, though I was always able to find tranquility. Two processes: becoming quiet, and intense struggle, went hand in hand in this pit. When in desperate hours the flood tide of surging waters in the prison cell reached a breaking point, I was still able to speak of grace in that I called to others: "Whoever can conquer himself is strongest among us," or "Who can imprison himself fears no prison," or "He who has become his own stinking prison is the most wretched," or "Who himself brings a noble prisoner into prison, for him prison is no prison."

Then came the dark place, my Gabbatha in the life in the concentration camp: with all its mockery and scorn, with the indignity of being placed on exhibit, with its trial in Pilate's court where acknowledged innocence is cruelly misjudged. Established authority reconstituted submissive victims into dedicated "criminals."

Then came the deep, my Golgotha: the free exile with its rape of all innocence and all nobility of spirit, where broken strength was fastened upon martyr wood of hard labor with irons. Oh the hours of forsakenness by God and men—what deep furrows you have left in my heart. This was my highest schooling in the practice of my faith and suffering, a final exam upon the sacrificial altar of my love for Jesus. This was the supreme test. Here everything had to mature, everything had to come into the open; every mask, like any pious garb, gave way before the weighty hammer-blows of spiteful, scornful laughter over weakness and illness, over age incapable of work and intelligent mental power.

My life ascended to such a fruitful "Sursum Corda" ["Lift Up Your Hearts" from the Latin liturgy]. I cannot help it if others felt it less intensely. Overcoming my life was never as difficult or as clearly necessary, nor as precious. Here it was a question of becoming and becoming until one overcame.

Not a breeze, not anywhere
Deathly silence, fearfulness
And amid the endless vastness
Not a single wave bestirs.
That has become the deep experience of my soul. And the beauty of it was:

"It happened!"

When I was completely overcome, then I overcame: then the overcome became the overcomer.

Toews (1990): 236-238

July 26

Teach Him First to Know God
Hans Denck, Germany, 1526

One who is sure and without worry must take heed so as not to be found exposed at an inopportune time. Let every one who can, make peace with his enemy on the road—the sooner the better. Woe to him who waits for the judge to settle a quarrel. Dearly beloved, do not start any unnecessary quarreling. Let each one suffer as much wrong as can be endured without harm to the Kingdom of God. I am greatly worried that we sin grievously in uttering so many unnecessary words on both sides. What value is there in shunning all outward things at once? What value is there on the other hand, were you to retain them all?

If you notice your brother treasuring something which he should not, teach him first to know God, then he will treasure him alone. Should he not do so, leave him alone and lose few words over it. For if you destroy everything he has and he heeds you, he will set another treasure in its place which will be like the former or even worse. If, on the other hand, you hear your brother say something that is strange to you, do not refute it right away, but listen first to determine whether it is right for you to accept it.

If you cannot accept it, do not judge him. Even if you think him in error, be mindful lest you be found in still greater error. Let no one look to the mighty in this world, be it for their strength, art or riches. Let the one whose heart is set toward heaven turn it toward the despised and lowly in this world whose Lord and Master is Jesus Christ. He became the most despised of all people and was therefore exalted by God the Father to rule over all creatures that can be named or thought.

Woe to anyone who looks to another goal but this. Whoever thinks he belongs to Christ must walk the path which Christ walked to reach the eternal dwelling-place of God. Whoever does not walk in this path shall err eternally; whoever points to or walks on another path, "is a thief and murderer." Such are all who love God and his Son for the sake of their own advantage, which is the case with the entire world. God knows who is not of this world and one to whom God has revealed it may rejoice that his name is inscribed in the Book of Life.

Denck (1989): 217-219

July 27

Lessons From Medicine
Pilgram Marpeck, Germany, 1531

This selection illustrates the "gospel of the creatures" (introduction, pp. 12-13; also pp. 306-311) as applied to matters of congregational discipline.

Does not a physician who undertakes to heal someone command those who care for him to have patience with his illness? He does not, however, command them to become ill as well; otherwise, one ill person would poorly serve the other. Thus, it is always the strong who is the servant of him who is ill, in order that his illness may be cured and his weakness become strong while there is breath left in him.

No one buries someone who is still alive, nor does he expel from the house someone in the last stage of illness. Rather, one waits with patience and endurance for him to get better. Nor does one give him strong food which would only make him become weaker. For this reason, Paul commands that overseers and bishops be chosen who will uphold the weak and bear with the wicked.

*

I testify before my God, through the Lord Jesus Christ, that whoever charges with sin and burdens the conscience where there is no sin, he accuses the innocent blood of the Lord Jesus Christ, through which all of us are bought and released from all sin. He makes sin where there is none, which is equivalent to charging someone with murder when in fact he is innocent. And if he thus accused another, he would be guilty of that other's life and innocent death. Much graver is the murder of conscience and soul, both of which belong to God alone.

Whoever murders, wounds and burdens an innocent conscience with his own commands and prohibitions, outside of God's commandment and prohibition, robs God of His honor, murders souls and tramples the Son of God with his feet. He derides and makes a mockery of the sacrifice of Jesus Christ, with which he is bought.

*

Even the world does not judge anyone on the basis of hearsay, suspicion or appearance, but only on the words of the accused and of reliable witnesses. Christ also commands His own that all testimony must be substantiated by two or three witnesses. Only when evidence has been presented before the church and he will not hear, does the judgment begin with tribulation, anxiety, sorrow.

The other members of the body of Christ experience great pain and suffering for at stake is a member of the body of Christ the Lord. They must lose a member in order that the other members, who are well, are not hurt and the whole body destroyed, be it eye, foot or hand. It should be pulled out or cut off according to the commandment of Christ, our Head: "If your eye offends you, or your hand, or foot," etc. The other members of the body of Christ will not be able to do this without great pain and tribulation. If the member is honorable and useful to the body, the tribulation is so much greater. It cannot possibly happen easily or simply.

The natural body cannot lose a member without pain. Nor does it immediately cut it off, even if it is failing and weak; rather it uses all kinds of medicines. As long as it is not dead and is only painful, the body bears it with patience and long-suffering, and delays the penalty to allow for improvement. If, however, it allows the body no rest, nor does it improve by means of any medicine from the Lord Jesus Christ, through suffering and pain, it must be cut off in order that the other members of the body of Christ remain healthy in the fear and love of God and the neighbor, to whom alone the judgment to retain and to forgive sin has been committed.

My fervent prayer to God and my hope is that no truthful heart should be excluded from the true members of Christ. Indeed it does not happen. My conscience also bears me witness that I am grafted into the body of Christ and, even though I am weak, I hope that God's power and strength will be revealed in my weakness.

Marpeck (1978): 354-357

July 28

The Purpose of Excommunication
Menno Simons, The Netherlands, 1541

What does it avail to go by the mere name of a Christian brother if we have not the inward, evangelical faith, love and irreproachable life of the true brother of Jesus Christ? Or what does it profit to eat of the Holy Supper of our Lord Jesus Christ with the brethren if we have not the true symbolized fruits of this Supper, namely, the death of Christ, the love of the brethren and the peaceful unity of faith in Christ Jesus? Similarly it profits nothing to move about in the outward communion of the brethren if we are not inwardly in the communion of our beloved Lord Jesus Christ.

Wherefore brethren, understand correctly, no one is excommunicated or expelled by us from the communion of the brethren but those who have already separated and expelled themselves from Christ's communion either by false doctrine or by improper conduct. For we do not want to expel any, but rather to receive; not to amputate, but rather to heal; not to discard, but rather to win back; not to grieve, but rather to comfort; not to condemn, but rather to save. For this is the true nature of a Christian brother. Whoever turns from evil, whether it be false doctrine or vain life, and conforms to the Gospel of Jesus Christ, unto which he was baptized, such a one shall not and may not be expelled or excommunicated by the brethren forever.

But those whom we cannot raise up and repentingly revive by admonition, tears, warning, rebuke or by any other Christian services and godly means, these we should put forth from us, not without great sadness and anguish of soul, sincerely lamenting the fall and condemnation of such a straying brother; lest we also be deceived and led astray by such false doctrine which eats as does a cancer; and lest we corrupt our flesh which is inclined to evil by the contagion. Thus we must obey the Word of God which teaches and commands us so to do; and this in order that the excommunicated brother or sister whom we cannot convert by gentle services may by such means be shamed unto repentance and made to acknowledge to what he has come and from what he is fallen. In this way the ban is a great work of love, notwithstanding it is looked upon by the foolish as an act of hatred.

*

In every respect use it and practice it with godly wisdom, discretion, gentleness and prudence, toward those who have gone aside from the evangelical doctrine or life, not with austerity nor with cruelty, but rather with gentleness; with many tears because of the diseased and infected members whom we cannot cure, and in whose case pains and labor are lost.

*

May God, the merciful Father, save all His chosen children who have entered into His holy covenant and communion from such a fearful fall, obduracy, and excommunication. Amen.

Menno (1956): 413, 414

July 29

Are We Living Simply?
Esther Bowman, Canada, 1987

*A*s plain people, we profess to have a simple lifestyle. We are not part of the world's rat race. The complexities of modern technology have barely reached us. Even so, are we living simply? Do we practice a lifestyle that is relatively free from stress?

Living simply means reducing tension. When we strip life of some of the frills and ornaments we also remove some of the stress. In the simple life, we have no need to pressure ourselves physically and financially to compete with others. We are not constantly yearning for the unusual, the expensive or the faraway. Instead we find simple pleasures and are content with what we have.

Sometimes we long for a trip away from home to relax our nerves or broaden our vision. The usual trip frequently leaves us with fatigue and headaches from the stress of meeting people and creating extra expenses. As an alternative, why don't we make full use of all that lies readily at hand?

Visits to local factories, museums or the county courthouse can be educational and enjoyable. A leisurely drive or stroll along scenic roads is fascinating, especially if we take a small child by the hand and travel at his speed, viewing our surroundings through his eyes. We should not be too hurried to closely examine a leaf, watch ants struggle with oversized burdens or imagine unusual objects in cloud formations. We find ourselves surrounded by intriguing subjects when we slow down and wake up.

Beauty lies everywhere about us if we only take the time to really see it. The vast variety of sounds, smells and textures makes an exploration of our environment a rich experience. Our taste buds, too, provide us with much pleasure if we stop to consider. Yet how often do we fully use and appreciate these senses?

We should practice the art of enjoying the immediate, the nearby. We need to cultivate simple tastes, and learn to be content in our present circumstances. In so doing, we will discover that the simple life brings us the greatest satisfaction.

Bowman (1987): 24

July 30

What Does It Mean To Be Amish?
Monroe L. Beachy, United States, 1982

*T*here are many churches. For example: Church of God, Assemblies of God, Baptist, Church of the Brethren, Christian and Missionary Alliance, United Church of Christ, Church of the Nazarene, Quaker, Mormon, Lutheran, Methodist, Moravian, Presbyterian, Salvation Army, Unitarian, Christian Scientist, Episcopalian, Catholic, Jew, Muslim and so on.

It is interesting to notice that most of these came into being after 1525, which is usually considered as the year when ours started. Now, of course, we dress differently and our lifestyle is different, but are they the only differences between the Amish and all these other churches?

Well, let me tell you a story: Some time ago a group of fifty-two people chartered a bus and came to Holmes County to see the Amish. They had arranged to have an Amishman meet them and answer some of their questions.

The first question was: "We all go to church," and they named some of these churches, "so we all know about Jesus, but what does it mean to be Amish?"

The Amishman thought a bit and then he asked a question of his own. "How many of you have TV in your homes?" Fifty-two hands went up. "Now, how many of you feel that perhaps you would be better off without TV in your homes?" Again fifty-two hands went up. "All right. Now, how many of you are going to go home and get rid of your TV?" Not one hand went up!

Now that is what it means to be Amish. As a church, if we see or experience something that is not good for us spiritually, we will discipline ourselves to do without.

The world in general does not know what it is to do without!

Beachy (1982): 18

July 31

This Is Entertainment
Eli Stoltzfus, United States, 1969

*T*ourists often ask me how many children we have. I tell them we have seven and my mother had seven and her mother had seven. It is a perfect number, or a symbol of completion. Sometimes they ask me stupid or laughable questions. One time I was driving in a nail with a short piece of pipe, because I didn't have a hammer handy. Then a lady asked me if it was against our religion to use a hammer.

One time I was hitching up three mules and one horse together. Then a man asked me why I hitched up three mules and one horse together. I told him "to make four." I didn't know what else to say. I guess he was dumbfounded. My landlord said the man came into the shop laughing so much that he asked what it was all about. The man replied, "If you ask a stupid question you get a funny answer."

Somebody asked me whether our goat was a baby horse. I am surprised sometimes to hear gray-haired city people tell me they were never on a farm in their life, and I pity them. They missed half their life.

A man asked what we do for entertainment. I just say, "We farm." He understood what I meant. He was intelligent. You see, it is a beautiful sight to see our Creator's nice brown earth being smoothly turned upside down in long strips back and forth through the field with the anticipation of producing good food for some hungry person. This is entertainment.

It is thrilling to turn nine horses and mules and a pony out into the pasture when they haven't been out for a while and to see them burst forth at full speed and kick and snort and carry on. This is entertainment.

It is charming to see our smiling fifteen-year-old boy jump on the pony and go and round up the cows at ease and bring them in. This is entertainment.

It is a beautiful sight to see my wife and daughter out in the garden hoeing weeds and picking some fresh mouth-watering organic vegetables. This is entertainment.

Stoltzfus (1969): 40-42

August

Christ the Teacher
Cornelis Ris, Poland, 1766

After the Son of God had been solemnly anointed and had passed victoriously through sundry hellish temptations, He presented Himself at once to the world as the great prophet who had been promised of God, in that He taught the way of God in truth as one who had authority and with a wisdom which no one could withstand; preached the gospel of the kingdom of God, repentance and faith; testified likewise how one must walk to be pleasing to God; foretold also things to come; and confirmed it all with many wonderful miracles. Moreover, He lived just as He taught and has thus left us both in His teaching and His life an example which we are to follow.

Further, as the Lord Christ taught and led His people under the old covenant as the angel of God's presence, through Moses and all the prophets, in whom His Spirit was, and as He now did the same in His own person, so He continued His teaching office through His apostles and evangelists, whom He called, instructed, endowed with the Holy Spirit and sent forth to be His witnesses to the ends of the earth. And these were faithful even unto death and kept back nothing that is profitable, but declared the whole counsel of God unto salvation, to which God also bore witness by signs and wonders and by manifold gifts of the Holy Spirit according to His own will.

The Lord Jesus also continues His work as teacher by means of His holy Word, seeing He has given a short yet sufficiently complete account of His holy life and divine teaching as well as of those of His holy apostles to be transmitted in the books of the New Testament, in which, together with the books of the Old Testament, there is included everything needful to a rule of faith and life. Through the teaching, reading and hearing of this Word He continues to bring about conversion and sanctification, for it is the power of God unto salvation to every one that believeth.

Finally the Lord Jesus teaches also through the Spirit according to His promise, both convincing and winning the unbelieving, and leading the believers into all truth. In this work the Spirit never contradicts the true meaning of the written Word, but enlightens the believer's mind to a right understanding of the Word, gives them assurance of its truth and brings to remembrance the things that the Lord has spoken.

Loewen (1985): 88, 89

The Spirit and Humanity of Christ

Pilgram Marpeck, Germany, 1531

*O*ne does no wrong if, out of the deepest conviction of the heart, out of belief and out of the inward living Word, one submits oneself to the work, teaching and deeds of Christ, and appropriates them, not according to the letter, but according to His Word and command. The Scriptures are also a witness to the true teaching of the humanity of Christ and the teaching of the apostles; through Christ's humanity, the inward must be revealed and recognized.

*

Down with those prophets who say that the drawing of the Father and the unknown hidden Spirit of God have been manifested and recognized without the revelation and knowledge of Christ. Down with the spirits who say that one is able to believe in the Son of God, His human voice and speech, teaching and works without being drawn by the Father. This breath or Spirit of God would have remained an eternal secret without the humanity and the physical voice of Christ. Where this physical voice of Christ—which Christ even today channels through men and the Scriptures, which are preserved for us and are still a witness to him—is believed sincerely, our spirit is free and the drawing of the Father revealed.

The Spirit of Christ, our assurance in all works, deeds and gifts, possesses all power and authority, even until the end of the world. I defy those false teachers who teach that a really good work of faith can occur apart from the working of the Holy Spirit. Whoever believes that Jesus is the Christ of God has the Spirit of God. "This, flesh and blood cannot reveal," as Christ says to Peter: "Upon this rock I will build my church" (Matthew 16:18). Therefore, every command is made in faith, and all authority comes forth from faith. Concerning this faith, Christ says to His disciples: "What I say to you, I say to all" (Mark 13:37); "Who because of your word believe in me" (John 17:20). With such a promise and the consolation of Christ, I comfort myself, as do all believers, who are unprofitable servants that do not work, but simply receive the physical words and voice of Christ in order that we may confess them and thereby testify to His physical works, leaving the effect to God the Father, Son and Holy Spirit who have worked until now and have reigned from eternity and will reign in eternity.

Marpeck (1978): 76, 77

Knowing Christ Inwardly

Jacob Denner, Germany, ca. 1707

*I*f we know Christ physically according to the flesh, what good does that do for us if we do not know him inwardly in our soul? This is why it did not help the Scribes and Pharisees to know Christ according to the flesh since they were missing the true living and spiritual acquaintance with him. For this reason also Saint Paul says in 2 Corinthians 5:16, "Therefore from now on we know nobody according to the flesh, and even though we have known Christ also according to the flesh, from henceforth we do not know him in that way anymore." If we know Christ outwardly to the letter and we are able to talk knowingly about his holy birth in the flesh—if we are widely and broadly informed about these things, all this can help us nothing at all if we do not know him according to the Spirit. For the person who has experienced only the physical and not the spiritual in his soul—when Christ is not born there; where there is no union with him so that his presence is openly evident—it helps nothing. All-important is that inner experience. Therefore Paul says very emphatically in Galatians 1:15 and 16: "But since it pleased God when he separated me from my mother's womb and called me by his grace that he should make known to me his Son through the new birth in me, that I should preach the gospel among the heathen." There we see how Christ is to be made known in us in our souls, and how no person can truly proclaim Christ or even speak about him until he is known to him in his soul.

Therefore it is important for all those who desire to make Christ known to others that they first know him in that inner self, that he is to them a living reality in the Spirit. Alas! what poor mortals they are who know Christ and proclaim him only according to the letter, and talk about him to others when he is not a living reality within, when they have had no experience in their souls with his Word, Spirit, power and working in their lives, so that they know nothing about the spiritual outworking, but are still living in sin and unrighteousness.

Denner (1730): 64, trans. by Noah G. Good

August 4

Grace in Nature

Anna Baerg, Soviet Union, 1918

The following two excerpts from Anna Baerg's diary were written on August 4 and August 7, 1918.

*A*fter coffee Mr. Dick held a Bible study here. To be sure, there is not always much opportunity here for pleasure and enjoyment, but to be able to hear God's Word, even when one often yearns more for the former, is worthwhile. For "the world passes away in its passions, but whosoever does the will of God lives on in eternity." Of course, a person doesn't become holy by merely listening; it is in belief and deed that one attains eternal life.

*

I am lying next to the river which is bordered on either side by willows and flows on between the garden and the forest. The river bed is dry now. There is a stillness all around, except for the muted humming of the threshing machine drifting out from the farm yard. Occasionally one hears the sounds of cattle in the distance. The last golden rays of sunset are breaking through the trees. The wind whispers quietly in the treetops as if it had something to tell. Do you understand, child, that voice in the trees? Do you not know God's grace is at work in nature and that it too has a soul that yearns for freedom? A soul that often speaks in the silence if you only listen for it. Oh, my heart is so full at times, but there are no words to express what I feel.

Baerg (1985): 29

August 5

Note To Conrad Grebel From Mt. Pilatus

Jean Janzen, United States, ca. 1986

Conrad Grebel came to his Anabaptist convictions from a humanist education. The rediscovery of nature for its own sake, so characteristic of the Renaissance, had influenced Grebel too. He had been a member of the first expedition to climb Mt. Pilatus in the Swiss Alps.

We take the easy way up, Conrad,
a tram on greased cogs and unbreakable cable.
You would laugh to see us, soft-bellied
and swinging in the blue air. But you too

had your luxuries and an appetite
for the eternal—Greek poetry, Luther's ferment,
and your youthful passions all wrapped into
a brief life. This is your view, the first
to climb and chart its peak. Four hundred sixty
years ago, and yet, against this granite,
only yesterday.

An alphorn sounds against the stone,
its deep tones ricochet from face to face
and fall into the rich valleys. Towns
with towers like the dark tower where your
health broke, where Zwingli, once your friend,
held you for your lofty contradictions,
and you escaped to teach again and to die.

What is the measure of our love?
Is it risk, or endurance? Should I regret
the way I came, a follower, a view unearned?

The air is thin, the edges sharp and clear.
Snowfields deep and glistening around me
are giving themselves away in small streams
and in vapors lifting off. Nothing you
can really measure. Below is the misty valley
with its muddy river where we love, where we
make our choices—you, dropping from the tower
hand over hand, your face luminous in the dark,
and me, holding the rope in my hands.

Janzen, Yaguchi, Waltner-Toews (1986): 23

August 6

A Christian Should Be a Pacifist
Gan Sakakibara, Japan, 1990

I was baptized at the age of twenty as a Presbyterian and then became a
Mennonite when I was sixty-two years old. During those intervening forty-two
years I was very dissatisfied with the positions the Protestant church of Japan
held on the issues of war and peace. My dissatisfaction with the Protestant
church in my country increased greatly during Japan's preparations for war.
During that time the weak Protestant church had no choice but to acquiesce to

the government's request for support of their efforts to prepare for war in the face of commercial attacks from all over the world. My Christian conscience wanted to express its opposition to the warlike governmental policy; but as a weak, private man, that was impossible for me to do. I was very ashamed. I thought: "A Christian should be a pacifist; I should be a pacifist; stand up to the government and be counted."

*

I rationalized away my conscientious way of life. Of course, this was in direct opposition to my true beliefs and I was always living in the midst of shame. The military defeat forced upon the Japanese people feelings of shame and humility. All the Japanese Christians became Christian pacifists, including me. But I found it difficult to be born again as a pacifist just because of a defeat in war.

*

In 1960 my wife and I visited the United States for the first time. We spent one half year visiting Hutterian communities and similar communal groups such as the Reba Place Fellowship in Evanston, Illinois, and others. At first these communities interested me as a student of political economy, but later the religious character of the members greatly attracted me.

*

My true conversion to Christian pacifism was brought along by the historical Hutterian logic used in their resistance to a military tax. This logic had been applied when the Hutterites were still living in Moravia. The emperor wanted to collect a military tax in order to establish a military force to fight the Turkish invasion. In those days, the Hutterian people were the most obedient and hardworking people and were always willing to pay their taxes. Therefore, the tax collectors expected the Hutterites to pay the tax obediently.

But the reaction of the Hutterites surprised the tax collectors. The Hutterites resisted the tax using the following logic: "We are blacksmiths who can make swords and kitchen knives. But we do not want to make swords because the sword's primary purpose is to kill, and to kill people is a sin. If we did make swords and those swords killed men, then we would also be responsible for the killing. So we do not want to commit a sin by making swords. But we blacksmiths also make kitchen knives for the purpose of preparing food. There might be people who would kill or wound others with a kitchen knife that we had made, but under those circumstances we would not be responsible and therefore would not have committed any sins." The same logic worked for paying the military taxes. Therefore, their Christian pacifism did not allow them to pay the military tax. This logic taught me about Christian pacifism.

Lichdi (1990): 41, 42

Our Weapons

Menno Simons, The Netherlands, 1539

I tell you the truth in Christ: the rightly baptized disciples of Christ—note well—they who are baptized inwardly with Spirit and fire, and externally with water, according to the Word of the Lord, have no weapons except patience, hope, silence and God's Word. "The weapons of our warfare," says Paul, "are not carnal, but mighty through God to the pulling down of strongholds, casting down imaginations and every high thing that exalteth itself against the knowledge of God, and bringing into captivity every thought to the obedience of Christ" (2 Corinthians 10:4, 5).

Our weapons are not weapons with which cities and countries may be destroyed, walls and gates broken down, and human blood shed in torrents like water. But they are weapons with which the spiritual kingdom of the devil is destroyed and the wicked principle in man's soul is broken down, flinty hearts broken, hearts that have never been sprinkled with the heavenly dew of the Holy Word. We have and know no other weapons besides this, the Lord knows, even if we should be torn into a thousand pieces, and if as many false witnesses rose up against us as there are spears of grass in the fields, and grains of sand upon the seashore.

Once more, Christ is our fortress; patience our weapon of defense; the Word of God our sword; and our victory a courageous, firm, unfeigned faith in Jesus Christ. And iron and metal spears and swords we leave to those who, alas, regard human blood and swine's blood about alike. He that is wise let him judge what I mean.

Menno (1956): 198

Mercy

Peter Burkholder, United States, 1837

*B*lessed are the merciful for they shall obtain mercy. Mercy is that disposition of mind which excites us to pity, and to relieve those who are distressed and in trouble, by using every means in our power to alleviate their calamity and to make them more happy.

In allusion to the words of our Savior, "Be ye therefore merciful, as your Father also is merciful," this temper will show and exert itself not only towards those of our friends, acquaintance and benefactors, but also over the whole human family, be they friends or enemies. For our heavenly Father is merciful over all, as Christ saith, "For he maketh his sun to rise on the evil and the good, and sendeth rain on the just and on the unjust; and he is kind unto the unthankful and to the evil." From these words we learn that God extends his bounty to all: for he sends rain, and moistens and maketh fruitful the fields of the ungodly and wicked, as well as those of the just and pious; and letteth his sun shine over the unrighteous and sinners, as well as over the righteous and godly. Here we see that God exercises his mercy over all, both good and bad; and if we are born of him and have partaken of his nature, we must be followers of him, as his dear children, and aim at perfection in holiness.

"But," saith Christ, "If you love them which love you, what reward have ye? Do not even the publicans the same? And if ye salute your brethren only, what do ye more than others? Do not even the publicans so? Be ye therefore perfect, even as your Father which is in heaven is perfect." Though this may not be understood that it is in our capacity to be perfect as God is perfect in holiness, power and the divine attributes; yet it is our unbounded duty to desire and aim at perfection, and therein to study to be more and more renewed after the image of God, and to conform ourselves to our heavenly Father's example, and to be governed and guided by his divine Spirit, to love our enemies and do good to the evil and to the unthankful and those that hate us, and in forgiving injuries: and thus to imitate and copy after our heavenly Father and to keep his commandments. For the apostle Paul saith, "If thine enemy hunger, feed him; if he is thirsty, give him drink: for in doing so thou shalt heap coals of fire on his head.

Sauder (1945)

August 9

How I Got Involved
Yorifumi Yaguchi, Japan, 1990

*T*he first Americans I saw were the soldiers. There was a navy camp in our town and they located themselves there. And they were the first Christians I saw. Because I was a child then, I thought at that time that all American soldiers were Christians. There were two chapels in the camp. I remember that I visited one of them, which was full of soldiers, and a chaplain preached with eloquence.

But the soldiers I saw in the street or in cabarets spat, smoked like chimneys, got drunk, danced and used abusive words.

*

Christianity was not an admirable religion in our town. As a matter of fact, it was a despicable one. Many of our townspeople laughed as it. "It is a brute's religion!" some said behind the American soldiers' backs. I felt the same. I did not realize then that the Japanese soldiers had done far worse things in neighboring countries.

When the war was over, I lost interest in the Japanese religions. Both Buddhism and Shintoism had been behind the Japanese government during the war. I could not trust those religions which had supported the war and which had told us lies, saying that Japan was a divine country and that Japan would never lose. And I thought that Christianity was not trustworthy either.

So when I first met some pacifist Christians, it was a big shock for me. They turned my world upside down. They said they had not fought but had obeyed God. They had been critical of their own government and had been praying for the Japanese people during the war. It was a revelation for me. Scales fell from my eyes and I could finally see the work of Christ. And I joined the Mennonite church.

Lichdi (1990): 37, 38

August 10

Faith Over Fear
David Beiler, United States, 1857

Why did Nicodemus come to Jesus by night? I note that it was because the Jews had agreed that if anybody confessed Jesus that person was to be cast out (banned). It appears that he had the desire to engage in conversation with Jesus, for which he chose the night time; it can well be supposed that the fear of man was one reason. It would seem that by the time of the burial of Jesus this fear had disappeared. This was true because the love he had for Jesus caused him to bring a hundred pounds of myrrh mixed with aloes with which to anoint the body of Jesus.

And we have this example with Saul who was very zealous for the law of Moses according to the knowledge he had at that time. But since he was faithful to what he knew, God was patient with him till the time when he wanted to use him as a preacher of the gospel. Then he gave him a real understanding of Jesus Christ, and the great grace of God and the love of God shown to us through Jesus Christ showed also that he became zealous for the gospel of Jesus Christ to proclaim it where the name of Jesus Christ was not known. He undertook many arduous journeys in order to plant and build Christian churches, and again visited them often and strengthened their faith. Through this he often came into danger of death, of which he himself said this, "I do not value my life highly in order that I may finish my course of life." And as he also said to those who were concerned for him, "Why do you weep and break my heart? I am prepared not only to be bound, but also to give my life as an offering in Jerusalem for the sake of the name of Christ."

Christ did not answer Nicodemus' question, but told him a most important thing in response, "Verily, I say to you that a man must be born again, otherwise he cannot come to the kingdom of God." I do believe that if a person is enlightened by God from above and infilled by the Holy Spirit, he will see with the divine eye of faith, in hope and childlike trust, the kingdom of God, and will rejoice when he sees the blessed state of the children of God as it is promised in the Word of God.

And in this faith we will have the strong assurance that at that time through the great grace and mercy of God for Christ's sake we will be raised to such splendor as no eye has ever seen nor ear heard and beyond anything that has ever come into the heart of man, the glory and splendor that God has prepared for those who love him, as the highest of all goodness.

Beiler (1857): 218-220, trans. by Noah G. Good

August 11

Strength Over Weakness
Abraham Godshalk, United States, 1838

Men give up their infirmities too much, saying, "We are poor weak creatures and cannot live so perfect as the Lord would have us live," and thus stand still or give up, instead of looking unto Jesus, the author and finisher of our faith who, for the joy that was set before him, endured the cross, despising the shame, and is set down at the right hand of the throne of God.

*

It would be hard to tell where regeneration begins in every one, or from whence it comes to every one (otherwise than the certainty that it comes from God). As our Savior said unto Nicodemus: "The wind bloweth where it listeth, and thou hearest the sound thereof, but canst not tell whence it cometh, or whither it goeth: so is every one that is born of the Spirit." Here we see that even he who receiveth the birth out of the Spirit does not exactly know whence this came upon him; it is like unto the wind which men can hear and feel, but cannot exactly tell from whence it cometh or whither it goeth.

So it is with him that receiveth the birth, or is born out of the Spirit of God. He feels the power, but doth not directly know from whence this comes unto him, or what is its end—even as men do not exactly understand the nature of the wind. But it commonly comes to a man while hearing the word of God, by which, according to Paul's doctrine, faith comes, and by this also the will to receive it; for by faith Abraham obeyed, and by faith man is yet made willing to receive Christ, and to be obedient unto him.

Godshalk (1838): 36, 37

Nicodemus of Patna

Leoda A. Buckwalter, United States, 1950

One day a man of influence came. He was shown to the office and Dick Sahib was called. As the latter confronted the stately educated Mohammedan dressed in long coat and fez and possessor of a well-kept black beard, he thought, "Intellectual; interesting also; no ordinary Mohammedan. I wonder what he wants."

The man facing Bro. Dick had come from Patna where he was teaching in a Mohammedan school. He had attained to the highest education which Mohammedanism had to offer, for he had memorized the Koran, taken certificates in medicine, mathematics and other related subjects, and had received a degree in Mohammedan law. And yet he was not satisfied. Intensely he asked the Sahib, "What is the Christian doctrine concerning the forgiveness of sins?"

"Why?" asked Bro. Dick.

"I know what Mohammedanism has to offer," he answered, "and yet I cannot feel satisfied for it does not meet the need of the human heart on this point."

The Sahib spoke up gladly. Here was a real opportunity. "Friend, through the sacrifice for sin, paid by Jesus on the cross, *every* sin may be forgiven. By faith in Him, we are made righteous."

And so they continued to talk, the one seeking, the other pointing the inquirer to the Lamb of God. That was the beginning of many visits. Like a modern Nicodemus, he came at night. Having become dissatisfied with his own empty form of religion, he purchased a Bible in Arabic and immediately started memorizing such portions as John's Gospel and Romans. Studying continuously, he would come to some Scripture which he could not understand and would then make a hurried trip by night to Saharsa to obtain the answer.

Finally, the day came when Bashir was convinced of the truth of Christianity. He found it impossible to any longer teach the Koran and hold it up before his students as "The Book." He must accept the Lord Jesus Christ publicly, or betray Him, for no longer could he remain a secret disciple.

It was not hard to detect the change. The Sahib could tell it as soon as Bashir walked into the room. The Mohammedan garb was gone. Simple European dress took its place. He was clean shaven, and his face radiated joy. His good news told itself. Having been publicly baptized, he received such persecution that he had to flee. His becoming a Christian raised a storm of protest. It was termed unthinkable, low, disgraceful, base! But Bashir had found his Christ. His sins were forgiven and he was content. Fleeing from place to place, he found that his Christ never forsook him. In the years that followed, he found many occasions to return to Saharsa, and always he was able to give a clear, definite witness to the saving and keeping power of the Lord.

Engle, Climenhaga and Buckwalter (1950): 297, 298

Where the Question Mark Belongs
Eberhard Arnold, Germany, 1924

*O*ur words about "God" are nothing but weak human stammering. The charges constantly made against the word "God" have a certain justification. To say that the name of "God," when we pronounce it, is utter blasphemy has a deep, divine justification. For what we say about God, what we think about God, what we address as divine, the way we abuse the name of God in our preaching—all that is downright blasphemy. The very claim or presumption to speak of God, which I have taken upon myself here as destiny and guilt—this very claim and presumption is an enormous burden for man's weak shoulders. It is clear that all we utter about God is not God. Whatever we speak about God comes no closer to Him than the dust on our streets can come to the furthest star.

And yet when we are gripped by the God whom we cannot express or think, when we are seized by the majesty of His actual existence, by the tremendous might of His coming, by His intervention in temporal history and the physical world, then we cannot be silent. Woe to us if we withhold the tidings about Him!

In mankind's history the tidings of God have emerged over and over again. This religious history of the concepts and proclamations of God must not be confused with God himself either. We must not think that this development of words about God and feelings men have had about God are the same as that which only God himself can be. He is the Unchangeable. "I am who I am" is His name. The concepts we have of Him, the thoughts we entertain about Him, the feelings impressed on us by Him change and pass, but God remains. It is not God who is in question. There is no question about God. But everything we say and think about this God, everything we confess to feeling God to be, all this is what is questionable; here is where the question mark belongs.

Arnold (1967): 223-225

Religion?
Eberhard Arnold, Germany, 1923

*I*t is not true when people think that everything religious is a unity and that everything irreligious belongs to the other side. It would correspond to the truth in a much deeper sense if one were to draw a dividing line of an altogether different evaluation cutting right across the religious and the nonreligious.

Everything that goes by the name of religion is related to a power that carries on its activity independently of men. The question is whether all relationships relate to the same world center, the same life content. With many who call themselves Christians and confess to the name of Jesus Christ, it is questionable whether their religion really has to do with the Father and God of the Messiah, of the coming Kingdom. The question is whether their religion is not that of the Antigod. The question is whether religion, including Christianity, is not permeated by the demonic powers of the abyss that cause the disintegration of mankind's solidarity. The question is whether the great world organization which names itself after Christ is not serving a god other than the God and Father whom Jesus confessed, the God of a totally different order. The question is whether the world church, which in practice has sided with wealth and protected it, which has sanctified Mammon, christened warships and blessed soldiers going into war, whether this church has not in essence denied Him whom it confesses with words. The question is whether the Christian state, despised as it is by the Hindus and Chinese, is not the most antidivine institution that ever existed. The question is whether a state that protects privilege and wealth as well as the organized church is not diametrically opposed to what is to come when God comes and Jesus establishes the order of justice.

We are faced here with the most revolutionary question, whether that greatest and holiest thing, reverence for church and state, does not contain within it homage to Satan; whether the justification of large landed property is not intrinsically Satanism; whether this Satanism has not led to the acme of covetousness—the murderous slaughter of fellow men. Can this Moloch possibly be identical with the God and Father of Jesus Christ? Only from the Mammon spirit do wars come; only out of the Mammon spirit does purchasable love, the defiling of bodies on the street, arise. You cannot serve God and Mammon.

Arnold (1967): 83-85

August 15

Genuine Believers Will Be Baptized
Jakob Ammann, Switzerland(?), 1693

Jakob Ammann, an elder serving Mennonites in the Alsace, differed with the elders in Switzerland over the status of the "true-hearted"—persons who assisted or even sympathized with the harassed Mennonites, but did not separate themselves from the state church and commit themselves to Anabaptist practice. Could they be given the hope of salvation? The Swiss were more generous in this matter than Ammann was.

There is but one Way that leads to life. There is but one faith that counts with God. There is but one people who are the bride of Christ. Are we not among this people? Have we not this faith? And are we not traveling the narrow path?

We cannot enter life otherwise. But let it be far from us to judge or condemn anyone out of season, for we are well aware that the Scripture says: "Condemn not and ye shall not be damned."

There is one who shall judge all people in due season, every man according to his works, namely, the Father, who has provided judgment. We also are unaware what grace the sinner may attain before his death. We have therefore condemned no one. We may well comply with the Word of God, however, in this conclusion, by saying: If the miser does not repent of his greed, or the fornicator of his fornication, or the drunkard of his drinking, or other offenses which cut them off from the kingdom of God, and does not fully repent by complete amendment of their lives, that person is no Christian and will not inherit the kingdom of God.

*

Without a truly regenerating faith it is impossible to please God. But whosoever has received this faith from God will be baptized in spite of all opposition, otherwise it cannot be the real faith, as Christ said: "He that believeth and is baptized shall be saved." Whosoever has this true faith will forsake the ways of the world in spite of opposition, as the Apostle John says in his Revelation: "Come out of [Babylon], my people, that ye be not partakers of her sins and that ye receive not of her plagues."

*

Christ said: "Whosoever doth not bear his cross, and come after me, cannot be my disciple." Whosoever will not leave his home, farm, father, mother, wife and children for my sake cannot be my disciple.

Anyone believing in the heart, but unwilling to confess with the mouth endeavors to serve two masters, and no one can simultaneously serve two masters who oppose each other. Christ said: "He that is not with me is against me; and he that gathereth not with me scattereth abroad." Paul said, "Ye cannot drink the cup of the Lord and the cup of devils: ye cannot be partakers of the Lord's table and of the table of devils" (1 Corinthians 10:21). And: "For if I yet pleased men, I should not be the servant of Christ" (Galatians 1:10). James also says: "Know ye not that the friendship of the world is enmity with God? Whosoever therefore will be a friend of the world is the enemy of God" (James 4:1).

Mast (1950): 35, 37, 38

August 16

Inconsistencies
Magdalene Redekop, Canada, 1988

We were taught, of course, that people who were not "saved" would go to hell. Did that mean that Billy Graham's wife would go to hell for wearing lipstick? I can remember the intensity of my fear for myself and for those millions and billions and trillions of others—all going to hell, helter-skelter, without so much as a hint that there was a way to avoid it. Cowering under the huge prairie sky, we sensed always the approaching end times. When my father burned the stubble fields, I could smell the acrid smoke of hell in my nostrils and I wondered who would be taken and who would be left. If I believed in a literal hell of that sort, the conclusion was inescapable: I had to be a missionary.

The annual "Missionsfest" was a glorious event. There was the big tent, flapping loudly in the warm wind. The choirs sang with a thrilling intensity. The congregation sang lustily of the day when we would all "come rejoicing, bringing in the sheaves." Then there were the missionaries, the people who had put their lives where their mouths were. Never mind that after they had stayed at our house all summer (on "furlough") eating *Schinkefleisch*, we ended up eating bologna in winter. Never mind that the American missionaries were sometimes patronizing. They were exotic emblems of self-sacrifice. The inglorious side to this glorious occasion, however, was the pleasure that came from the complacent knowledge (surrounded by comforting multitudes) that you were not one of those perishing and in need of rescue. Surely not. Surely not, at least, if the Lord would only come quickly *now*, just *now*, while you were eating your *klik* and lettuce sandwiches made on store-bought bread (such a treat after roast beef and homemade buns).

The image of hell was hard to reconcile with the quiet pace of life in the community. I sensed in my father an aversion for the flaming rhetoric of the non-Mennonite evangelists who came around, implying that the Mennonites needed saving.

Loewen (1988): 233, 234

August 17

Grant To Us a Gracious God
Hans Umlauft, Germany, 1539

You write further that we have no faith, word nor sacrament, and that we cannot pray nor be saved. Even if this were true—and may the kind Father preserve us from it—you should nevertheless not judge or condemn anyone, nor deny him salvation. Consider rather, that we are people and human as you and those of your kind, created in the image of God, a creation of God, having God's law, will and word written in our hearts. Therefore you should grant to us a gracious God as well as to yourselves, since God is also a God of the heathen. He is no respecter of persons, but whoever among all nations fears him and does right, is acceptable to him.

From the beginning until the end he has scattered his church among all the nations. At his appearing he will gather in the dispersed, true Israel from the four winds and corners of the earth. Ruth, the Moabite woman who was a heathen, was included in the genealogy of Christ. Therefore I believe that many children of Abraham are to be found among the heathen, carved in stone. Similarly, this unpartisan God took pleasure in Adam, Abel, Enoch, Noah, Job, Abraham (who was a heathen before his circumcision), Naaman, Cyrus the Persian king, the Babylonian king Nebuchadnezzar, Nathanael, the Ethiopian eunuch and Cornelius before and without the external circumcision in baptism. So little has God bound his grace and people to the external elements and ceremonies. We really ought to take this to heart and refuse to condemn anyone.

We should allow God to remain unpartisan and accessible to all as one who is no respecter of persons. Certainly we should not, in a sectarian way, claim God as our own as the Jews did, implying that all others, who do not agree with us or belong to our sect, are simply heathen. God can make children of Abraham out of stones. We must listen to Christ when he says that many, who are today called Turks and heathen, will come from east and west and eat with Abraham in the kingdom of God. By contrast, the children of the kingdom, the so-called Christians and Jews who presume to sit in the front and who believe that God belongs to them, will be thrust out. We heathen should be careful about such presumption since we are bastards and aliens in this Testament and covenant of grace.

Klaassen (1981b): 294, 295

August 18

You Must Have Seen Glorious Things
Jan Philipsz. Schabaelje, The Netherlands, 1635

An imaginary conversation between the Wandering Soul and Adam.

Adam: O, when I think! When I remember!

Wandering Soul: Father, I entreat you, be not grieved to instruct me, your junior. You must have seen glorious things, and to think upon those things of which you are deprived makes you so mournfully sad.

Adam: No human tongue can describe how pleasingly God addressed me when I was in favor with him.

Wandering Soul: Did you see God?

Adam: He approached me according to my weakness, in the most pleasing manner, so that I can never forget it; especially since I see that his love towards me is not so great ever since my disobedience. Therefore, O son, beware of disobedience, be the matter ever so small, lest the love of God depart from you.

Wandering Soul: Tell me at present a little more of Paradise; of disobedience, we will speak hereafter.

Adam: I am not able fully to tell you how pleasant and agreeable everything appeared—the trees were regularly arranged, of variegated foliage, bearing every kind of fruit. I went from tree to tree and did eat of each I desired—the birds were warbling and chirping on the boughs, caroling the sweetest music: for every creature was more sprightly, while I, their head, was in my first glorious state and had sweeter fellowship with God than afterwards. But now they appear to groan with me, their lord. I gave them their names, each according to its quality and nature: for God gave me wisdom, that I had a knowledge of every thing under my care. The fields yielded abundantly; I had whatsoever I desired—I had neither cares nor sorrows, nor fears. Besides, God gave me a helpmate—I loved her dearly, for she was flesh of my flesh and bone of my bone; this I knew as soon as she was brought to me. We had much pleasure in Paradise; we never had an angry word—we lived as innocent lambs, without care or toil.

We were blessed in Paradise: when we had a desire to eat, we did eat—we drank of the crystal streams. The powers of our souls were glorious—we were in burning love to God as he approached us—implanted love was our very life. We knew nothing of deceit and fraud—we were not subject to frailties—we knew of no evil in the world—we lived upon the good things which God gave us. We communed more with heavenly things than we were aware of: even as a child is not so fully sensible of the love and friendship of his father while with him as when he has lost him, neither were we so sensible of the privileged blessings we enjoyed till driven from Paradise.

Schabalie ([1834]): 8, 9

August 19

The Spiritual Paradise
Jan Philipsz. Schabaelje, The Netherlands, 1635

The conversation continues.

Wandering Soul: Which is the most noble part of man?

Adam: The heart; for out of it are the issues of life. Man was first placed in this paradise to cultivate and to keep it; for God let the stream of life flow into it, to irrigate the whole, which divides itself into four principal streams, making everything fertile; so that it produced all manner of fruit.

Wandering Soul: I perceive that it is of the utmost importance that this garden be well cultivated?

Adam: If I and my wife had taken good care of this spiritual paradise, we should never have been driven from the earthly paradise. But my wife was deceived by the lust of the eye and was induced to eat of the forbidden fruit, and we did eat spiritually of the forbidden tree of the spiritual paradise.

Wandering Soul: What is the forbidden tree of the spiritual paradise?

Adam: The tree of the knowledge of good and evil, of which many have eaten so much that they can never come to the tree of life. For life does not consist in knowledge; but man attains it in simplicity, that he may enjoy the goodness of God. Therefore, my son, when the subtle serpent cunningly comes to you, recommending that tree, and telling you that by tasting of it you can become as God, be not deceived by his cunning, but be humble and fear God.

*

Adam: Whenever the serpent has raised or started evil, it is necessary also to know the good, so that a person be not deceived by evil. But there is something more precious than knowledge.

Wandering Soul: What is that, father?

Adam: Love, charity.

Wandering Soul: How can I love that of which I have no knowledge?

Adam: Love is within you, and if you never commit or do any thing evil, then it will not be necessary for you to learn to know love.

Wandering Soul: I must certainly increase in love.

Adam: God, who is the author of love, will increase it in you, provided you cultivate with care and attention the inward garden.

Wandering Soul: How does that take place?

Adam: You will have to close well the hedge, so that all manner of wild beasts, such as lions, bears, the wild boar, etc., etc., be kept out of it. These are wild, unclean and destructive thoughts which arise out of impure desires. These you must lop off close, and not suffer them in the least to sprout in your precious and noble soul, for they would destroy and choke every thing, destroy the tender germs which put forth spiritually—nay, root them up and convert the pleasant garden into a wilderness.

But on the contrary, if you be vigilant and keep secure every entrance, the pleasant plants, and especially the tree of life, will increase more and more within you; for the melliferous dew of Divine grace will continually moisten the spiritual field and make it fertile; so that it will become a glorious and pleasant garden.

Wandering Soul: I thank you, father, for this wholesome instruction. But, tell me, is there also another Paradise?

Adam: There is also a heavenly paradise, with which this is intimately connected. The one of which we spoke last is only earthly: this is spiritual; it is a Paradise into which Enoch expects to enter. Touching myself, I cannot say that I have a perfect knowledge of it, but when God will send the promised seed of the woman, he will give full instruction concerning it. I hope that he (though I will not live to see him) will make amends for all; heal the wound which the serpent occasioned, and convey me and you, my son, after we have suffered tribulation and affliction, and bring us safe into eternal life, out of his great mercy and goodness.

Schabalie ([1834]): 36-39

August 20

Equal to Christ
Hans Denck, Germany, 1526

One should not deny the word in one's heart, but listen diligently and earnestly to what it intends to say to us. Nor should one simply discard external testimony, but rather hear and test everything and compare all in the fear of the spirit. Thus our understanding would from day to day become increasingly the purer, until we are enabled to hear God speak with us in the clearest manner and are certain of his will which is to surrender all selfness and to yield oneself to the freedom which is God. Then a person takes after God, takes on the traits of divine nature as one who is a son of God and co-heir with Christ.

For this reason he then lives as Christ lived, according to his measure. But it is not he who lives, but Christ within him who does not consider it robbery that he is in some measure equal to God. Rather, though he is Lord of all creation, he must humbly submit himself to all creatures, not that they serve him, but that he might serve them, according to his measure, in order to fulfill the will of the Father.

You might say: "By this reasoning you make all Christians equal to Christ and it appears almost as if they are in no need of Christ." Answer: In some measure all Christians are equal to Christ. For as he offered himself to the Father, so they, too, are ready to offer themselves. Not, I say, that they are as perfect as Christ was, but that they seek the perfection which Christ never lost.

*

To sum up, all Christians, that is those who received the Holy Spirit, are in God one with and equal to Christ, so that what pertains to one pertains to the other. As Christ does, so do they also. And they have Christ as their lord and master because he is the most perfect mirror of his father who could not have been more perfect except if he had not become a human being. And had he been a touch more perfect so as not to do it, he would not have been the true Savior; we would have had to wait for another. Far be that!

That he was the most perfect he proved by offering up his life on his own without any objection and by receiving it again through the power of the Father without any boasting. In all this he never wavered for an instant, but accomplished it all in the best fashion in due season—neither too early nor too late. No one has ever done this. And insofar as anyone has done anything, he has taken it from him alone which is righteousness out of grace. And he himself received it from no one but from the Father which is grace out of righteousness.

Denck (1989): 196-198

August 21

The Word of God Speaks Clearly
Hans Denck, Germany, 1526

You might say, "There may well be someone speaking within me, but I cannot hear anything since I am deaf on account of sin. A light too may shine within me, but I cannot see it because I am blind." Answer: This is a lame excuse as are all such excuses which try to put oneself in a good light while blaming and condemning God. For the word of God speaks ever so clearly that everyone—the deaf, dumb, blind, yes, unreasoning beasts, even; leaf, grass, stone, wood, heaven and earth and all that is within them—is able to hear it and do his will. Humankind alone, not wanting to be nothing, yet being more than nothing, resists it. O what perverse ways! Did God promise eternal life to unreasoning beasts and not much more to humankind? But continue doing what you do as long as nothing else strikes your fancy. But if you would know what shall still befall you, you would be anxious enough. At that point you would gladly surrender to suffer everything, if he would only comfort you with a single word.

You might say: "If then the word is in every human being, what need is there of the humanity of Jesus of Nazareth; is it not capable otherwise of carrying out the will of the Father?" Answer: It was in human beings that it might deify them, as has happened with all the elect, for which reason Scripture calls them gods.

*

The word had to be incarnate in Jesus so that humankind might have testimony in spirit and flesh, internally and externally, from behind and before and in every place. To the elect it served toward their advancement and salvation. To the others, so that they might no longer say that God allows a person freely to lay hold of whatever he desires that he might sin and die—which would be God's secret wanton pleasure, though he might give us the impression as if he found no pleasure in it. The perverse speak like this to this day. In fact, so common is such talk that many an elect person agrees with them, though not as satisfied as these.

That such a lie has been exposed and disabused by the humanity of Jesus should be perceived as follows: Since God created all humankind in his image but no one except for one, namely Jesus, remained in it—who loved all others in such a way as to offer his life to the Father in place of their death. He must surely have learned this from the Father, for he is wholly like the Father and obeyed him in all things—so God had this love from eternity which Jesus demonstrated under Pilate. He always loved his son like the apple of his eye. Yet, he took a sincere delight in his death which he would have preferred to endure himself had this not been contrary to order and had human beings been able to perceive the spiritual. For he is Spirit whom no fleshly eyes can see or ears hear.

Denck (1989): 199-201

August 22

Knowledge Through Suffering
Hans Hut, Germany, 1527

*I*f a man is to come to the knowledge of the living Son of God, he must await the work of God through the cross of Christ, which we must carry and follow in the footsteps of Christ. At those places Christ shows us the seriousness and righteousness of God the Father which the Father exercises through Christ. And all who desire to grow in the body of Christ, in which the Son of God is known and through which we become God's children and joint heirs with Christ (as Paul witnesses to the Romans), must also suffer with him and grow into the image of the Son of God through the justification of the Father.

And whoever will not follow the footsteps and ways of Christ and will not carry the cross of Christ: he does not have or know the Son. And whoever does not have or know the Son does not have or know the Father, and cannot be illuminated by the graciousness of the Holy Spirit who dwells in us.

In [the crucified Son of God] we must be incorporated to participate in the unity of the Trinity. This is revealed to us in the deepest suffering.

*

A man must endure in himself *all* the articles [of faith] if he is to come to a knowledge of the highest good. The Word must be received in him with a true heart through the Holy Spirit and become flesh in us. That happens through great terror and trembling as with Mary when she heard the will of God from the angel. The Word must be born in us too. That can happen only through pain, poverty, and distress inside and out, etc. And where the Word has been born and become flesh in us so that we praise God for such a favor, our heart has found peace and we become Christ's mother, brother and sister.

Those people who are now satisfied with God become a derision and stumbling block to the whole world. With Christ they are called enthusiasts and

Beelzebub. Everything one of these says is stamped as a lie by the world, and he himself is called a lying spirit because he admonishes the world about its ways and will not conform to them.

Klaassen (1981b): 89, 90

He Suffers In Me
Leonhard Schiemer, 1527

*A*s soon as a man wants to begin to live as a Christian he will experience exactly those things that Christ experienced. That is the lot of all Christians for the disciple is no greater than the master. For it is grace if someone for the sake of conscience suffers godly sorrow. For it is grace with God when you patiently suffer for doing good. For to this you were called, since Christ also suffered for us and left us an example that you should follow in his footsteps. He committed no sins, neither was deceit found in his mouth. Christ suffered in the flesh. Arm yourselves with the thought that whoever suffers in the flesh ceases from sin.

It is given to you that you not only believe in Christ but also suffer for him and fight the same battle. Paul says that you are heirs of God and joint heirs with Christ if you suffer with him, in order that you may be exalted with him in glory. For we must be conformed to the image of his Son. It is true: Christ's suffering destroys sin, but only if he suffers in man. For as the water does not quench my thirst unless I drink it, and as the bread does not drive away my hunger unless I eat it, even so Christ's suffering does not prevent me from sinning until he suffers in me.

Klaassen (1981b): 90, 91

It Is Possible
Andreas Ehrenpreis, Slovakia, 1650

*M*any thousands regard it as impossible to surrender all property and self-will. But Christ knew that it was possible. He stood before God. He could demand it. Historic examples stand as mighty proof that this way is actually feasible. Abraham showed it to be feasible when he left his rich homeland. And Moses was able to leave his comfortable court life. So we should not be surprised that it was possible for apostles of Jesus Christ to leave family and work, boat and net, in fact everything they had. Quite unexpectedly, even Paul was enabled to throw away high rank, personal greatness and prestige, as if they were dirt.

For Christ himself had proved something a thousand times greater. He had left the greatest to become poorer than animals in their holes and birds in their nests. These have their own place of rest. He had none. He opened up the new way on which He held all things in common with His disciples, in shared poverty. *One* kept the purse for *all*. And furthermore, as Jesus had foretold, the Spirit of unity came with such power over this company that suddenly thousands found the will to community, in the face of which they could no longer be concerned about their former possessions. They adopted just that attitude which so many now look upon as impossible.

From then on in the course of the centuries there were many thousands who gave up completely not only a considerable fortune, but what is more, their self-will. Many of them came with empty hands to the Church they had been searching for; for the rest of their lives they were thankful for it.

Hutterian Brethren (1978): 20, 21

August 25
No Back Door
Theo Loosli, Switzerland, 1962

*I*t is the desire of Jesus that our life should conform to His will. It is possible to deceive ourselves: to surrender the invisible but to retain the visible for ourselves. Therefore, God commands that our body as well as our mind and spirit be given to Him.

No back door remains open in this question. The beauty of life is destroyed when one of the members of the body refuses to surrender. James speaks clearly of this. In our life, for example, surrender is lacking when the tongue is not surrendered. What possibilities for enjoyment of the flesh does the eye not provide if it is not surrendered to the Lord? What paths of evil do not open to our feet if we do not surrender them? What does an ear that is not surrendered to God hear daily by way of gossip, rumor and idle talk? In our surrender to God, therefore, everything is included: our body, our mind and our spirit.

"Do not yield your members to sin as instruments of wickedness, but yield yourselves to God as men who have been brought from death to life, and your members to God as instruments of righteousness" (Romans 6:13). Note the "you." Yield yourselves, your members: everything is included. This surrender includes our entire life. Everything within—spirit, soul, heart, will, emotions. Everything external—life, children, house, possessions, vocation; as well as everything that stands in relation to us—friendships, time, money, recreation, life's planning. This surrender also includes our past, our present and our future. Nothing can be held back. The Lord wills that everything be surrendered to Him and be made subject to Him.

Frequently we desire to surrender only that which causes us difficulty—that which we cannot control—but retain our will, our heart and our mind for ourselves. We are like the man who brought the hand of his watch to the watchmaker and asked him to repair it. The watchmaker replied, "Bring me the entire watch. The trouble does not lie with the hands." "No," said the man, "you will take it all apart and this will cost too much. Only the hands are not functioning properly." Surrender means the whole of life. If we refuse to surrender every aspect of it, our life will not know fulfillment. To follow Jesus means complete surrender. It means to stay with Jesus regardless of cost.

Dyck ([1962]): 109

August 26

The Name of God

Jan Philipsz. Schabaelje, The Netherlands, 1635

More conversation between the Wandering Soul and Adam.

Adam: When I was two hundred and thirty-five years old, and my son Seth one hundred and five, he begat a son whom he called Enos. About that time my son Seth and my other children began publicly to preach the name of the Lord.

Wandering Soul: Father, why was it necessary to preach? Was not God generally acknowledged? Did he no longer speak unto man? Was the creation not sufficient evidence that there was a God?

Adam: O son, you have a profitable question; it is well worthy of an answer. God made his name known by his works: the creation could be seen everywhere. And it is true, He spake with men, at times through visions, and especially through the inward monitor, the conscience. But they disregarded that with which they had become familiar; for the generation of Cain, existing upwards of a century, was so depraved through the fall, that their consciences were apparently completely seared.

*

Adam: Therefore the sons of Seth began to preach the name of God with zeal, showing the excellency and eternal duration of the name of the Lord.

Wandering Soul: Inasmuch as the generation of Cain was so blinded and hardened in heart, and disregarding the voice of God, and not knowing God by the creation of every creature, what would preaching under such circumstances avail?

Adam: Son, do you not know that like produces like? Do you not know that children are induced sooner to give heed to strangers rather than to their parents? Although God teaches powerfully, and the conscience is convinced by the things of creation, nevertheless, the voice of man may frequently cause more attention, especially with those who have been inattentive; and with those who live prudently, it cannot be in vain to establish more and more the name of the Lord, through an abundance of evidence. And furthermore, if man testify the same which God witnesses in the conscience, or through other means, it may be called the voice of God being spoken by the impulse of the Spirit.

Finally, that which God teaches by the creation in the conscience, and through other means, such as visions, speaking through men who are moved thereunto, the same is to all word and doctrine, though each have its particular signification, whereby men are drawn. For it often happens that one means is auxiliary to another, and when connected, they make a harmonious concord.

Wandering Soul: You have given me much satisfaction in this matter; but, tell me, had God a name whereby he is known, since your children preached the *name* of God?

Adam: You ought to know that God has such a name as he is; therefore, to preach God is nothing less than to preach his name. He is called Almighty, because he is *almighty*; Holy, because he is *holy*; Eternal, because he is *eternal*; Love, because he is *love*; Righteous, because he is *righteous*, etc.,etc. All his attributes are his names. Therefore, his name is profaned and denied when the image of his being is defaced in man through sin. God wills that his name be glorified and praised in man; therefore, it is necessary to preach the name of God, to build it up when we see his name made nought by the sins of men.

Schabalie ([1834]): 22-24

August 27

The Divine Life
Jan Philipsz. Schabaelje, The Netherlands, 1635

The conversation turns to the life of Enoch, who "walked with God" (Genesis 5:24).

Wandering Soul: Father, I perceive by your words that if one does not reform he increases in wickedness, and finally comes into a state of hardened impenitence.

Adam: Certainly, that is my opinion.

Wandering Soul: On the contrary, can a person, if he regard himself and give heed to the things of God, attain to such a degree of virtue that he will always do the things of God, and never turn unto sin?

Adam: To be sure, if he believe steadfastly in God: for by faith a man is acceptable to God, and he overcomes the world.

Wandering Soul: O this is something precious—important!

Adam: There is a man now living who lived many years in the divine life, and has come to such a state of perfection that he is more like an angel than man.

*

Wandering Soul: What might be the name of this blessed and pious man?

Adam: His name is Enoch.

*

Adam: He has ever, from his youth, been amiable, and feared God; especially after he begat Methuselah he resolved to be wholly dedicated to God and devote all his powers of body and mind to the service of God. He visited me frequently, and interrogated me concerning many things; for he took particular notice of the creation—of the revelation of God—of every thing that had any the least tendency to the reformation of life, and of Divine Being. And when I told him of the joys of Paradise, what we saw and heard there, and the friendship God manifested towards us, he was ardently excited to know more concerning it; and it grieved him exceedingly that we were so indifferent to divine things.

O, were I to tell you of the many nights we spent together, forgetting to eat, drink or sleep—how he called upon God his Creator, loved the immortal Being, and had a confident hope to enjoy him. The faith of this young man is certainly not in vain: for by faith we accomplish things that appear to be impossible to be done. For the things he expects appear impossible to follow; for, if I am allowed to express my views, he has always had quite a different way from ours; for he depended wholly upon the power of the Almighty, to whom all things must be subjected.

*

Wandering Soul: I well perceive that this man also had the spirit of prophecy and knew to foretell remarkable things. But I have heard of those stiff-necked sinners. How am I to understand that, father? God is mightier than sinners; what can their stiff-neckedness harm him?

Adam: God is a precious and amiable Being, who wishes to dwell with friendship in their hearts, and implant the seeds of virtue. Because the ungodly are obstinate, quarrelsome, haughty and proud, that peaceable Being departs from their hearts, so that they through their blindness cannot cherish the word in a meek heart, whereby they might be saved.

*

Wandering Soul: Tell me, father, how was the posterity of Cain pleased with this man's manner of life, and his doctrine; could they in any way agree with him?

Adam: This generation is so much engaged in temporal things, and so bent upon becoming wealthy, since Tubal Cain discovered how to extract gold—and being engrossed in agriculture—building—so that the greater part of them take no time to hear him preach. The voluptuous hate him; others count him as

279

worthless, because he lived in a mean cottage, like the one I have, and his clothes were not made fashionable, serving only to cover his nakedness, to protect him from heat and cold. Others considered him as melancholy, because he spent much time alone in meditating in the field; so that his preaching did but little good among his generation.

But among the posterity of Seth, he is a great comfort to the believers; he encouraged them, he admonished them to do good; he set them a good example by his life, and was very serviceable to them in many things. When he preached, he was surrounded by a great multitude of men, women and children, that it was a pleasure to behold them. Frequently he preached in their houses—oft in the groves—upon the mountains—at the waterside—according to the exigencies of circumstances; yet he was, withal, much for retirement, endeavoring how he might serve God most acceptably.

Schabalie ([1834]): 28-33

August 28

First, Surrender

Jacob Denner, Germany, ca. 1707

*F*irst of all the person needs to fully surrender to God and turn around completely before he can take any comfort in the grace of God through Christ, and taste Christ living in his soul and experience this saving faith. And I say it once again, each one is indebted to exercise faith in God and to receive the grace of God, without which no person can be saved, even though he is converted, so that he can be a partaker of the grace of God.

Oh, where is there genuine penitence and complete reversal of the way of life, true change of thinking, and then faith after that? Most people continue right on in sin in their inner life as well as externally, but claim to have faith in God and think by this they can lay claim to God's grace. Alas, not so, not so at all!

Conversion and the change in life style must come first, after that one can take comfort in the grace of God. This is according to God's plan: first penitence, then forgiveness of sin. This does not mean that we achieve salvation through penitence and conversion, and become reconciled with God; but rather that this is the divine order—Jesus has paid for the grace of God on our behalf and has reconciled us with God, but it is faith that serves as the hand by which we take hold of this contracted grace which Christ has provided for us, and it is penitence that serves for us as the way and route which we must go to become partakers of it. Oh, would that we could only experience and taste this as a reality!

Denner (1730): 67, trans. by Noah G. Good

Rest Through Obedience

Tennessee John Stoltzfus, United States, 1885

The newcomers (converts) responded to the call of our Redeemer to all the weary and heavy laden to come to Him to accept His yoke, that is to say, the sweet heavenly doctrine in which blessed rest for souls is promised in obeying the commands of God. Rebecca Miller and Susanna Schaffer and Kate Neuhauser are the three who gave themselves up to this heavenly calling, but I hope that their associates, or more of the young people will take on the example of these women and be won without words because of their quiet and submissive obedience, as the Apostle Peter writes. Rebecca is, so much as I know, a quiet, retiring, respected woman, both in walk and conduct, and the woman's example of the apostolic teaching made a warm impression on me when I saw, as it appeared, that she was in earnest about filling the lamps with the oil of obedience, through which, along with prayer, we can partake of the divine nature, which has the precious and greatest promise, if she flees from the fleeting lusts of the world, and so on.

O beloved friend, there would be so much to be written about faith without works, and then faith with works, and that faith without works is dead. So I said yesterday that I now want to turn away from the argument about the truth of faith without works and faith with works and note that it is the fear of God which is the beginning of wisdom. Wherefore, by maintaining obedience to God's Word, holy rest is promised.

Through obedience and fear of God, Abraham traveled until the third day to offer up Isaac. The obedience of children to their elders is the first commandment that carries a promise. Samuel said disobedience is as the sin of witchcraft and stubbornness is as iniquity and idolatry.

Oh beloved friend, how much can we read through the holy Scriptures where obedience was blessed and disobedience was punished? The call of the prophets from God was to proclaim what He said to them; and if they did it they had rest and peace with God, even if it cost them their earthly lives. Jonah, however, because he did not want to proclaim the destruction of Ninevah, experienced anxiety and chastisement. And all that which was formerly written was written to teach us, on which we through patience and comfort have the scriptural hope.

Paton Yoder (1987): 168, 169

Tobacco

Eli Z. Zimmerman, United States, 1982

*T*obacco farming was, and still is, a regular occupation for a lot of farmers in Lancaster and Lebanon Counties (Pennsylvania), not considering what might be farmed more beneficially for the inhabitants of the earth. According to statistics, the cigarette has caused the death of many, including some that I well remember.

A young, thin, friendly neighbor lady of ours is a cigarette smoker. She wishes she could quit. When I inquired how she ever got started, she blamed society. When she first started, she disliked them and wanted to quit, but she was urged to try longer—then she would like them. And it came to be so. She now wishes to stop but seems helpless to do so.

I do not want to talk of my resisting power, as I also smoked. I accepted a cigarette as they were passed around, smoked it to a small butt, and flipped it away. That was the first and the last one I ever had in my mouth. I am also grateful for the one chew of tobacco I experienced in my youth when an old joker (I thought he was a gentleman) got me to take a chew of his good tobacco, when I was about fourteen years of age. I don't want to go into detail about the results, but that chew was satisfactory for the rest of my life!

I have heard, and I believe it to be true, that Bishop Moses Horning, when ready to go to the store for groceries, said to his wife, "I have trouble with my stomach, I guess I will get me a pack of chewing tobacco. Maybe that will help."

His wife said, "I have the same trouble. Would you bring me a pack also?" So Moses went to the store and came back without any tobacco.

Raising tobacco is a lot of hard work. Some farmers quit farming it because of the hard work involved and the shortage of help. Others quit for conscience' sake, raising food crops instead because they heard say, or have seen, the undernourished, innocent children starving from want of food. Still others stop farming tobacco because they feel they might be responsible for so many losing their lives annually, for tobacco causes cancer.

Many take these things into consideration but decide that they almost must farm it so they will be able to pay off the farm.

Zimmerman (1982): 70-73

My Two Faiths

Elizabeth Soto, United States, 1990

*I*t was in Puerto Rico while I was a teenager that I first learned to know about the Mennonites. Why Mennonites and not Baptists, Methodists or Pentecostals? As I became a committed Christian coming from the Catholic tradition, I recall making a conscious decision to move away from the faith of my forebears. I was just a teenager, but I needed a change: and this small Mennonite church, two houses away from my house, looked as good as any.

*

In this small church I began to understand discipleship. In the midst of this evangelical church among many in Puerto Rico, I was given the opportunity to learn about Anabaptist history. I began owning the Mennonite faith. This church met my needs. It confirmed my pacifist attitudes and my yearning for a sense of community.

*

As a child I grew up Catholic. Once I made my move to the Mennonite church in Puerto Rico, I, like almost all Latino evangelicals who come from Catholic background, was taught to deny that I was a Christian before. This I see as one of the big misconceptions the evangelicals in Latin America have. They believe that Catholics are not Christians. This is quite ironic considering that one moves from one Christian faith to another.

The intensity of self-denial and self-awareness opened my eyes to an internal need to express fully the richness of my two faiths. I became aware that I was a victim of the fundamentalist interpretations of Christianity that the evangelicals in Puerto Rico have. It was as though my past had been stolen from me and I needed to rescue it.

My journey was mixed with pain and joy as I began to celebrate the Mass and to sing lively choruses in the Mennonite church in Puerto Rico. I was able to reconcile or celebrate their differences and rejoice in the similarities. I was not on a lonely journey; I had community and special friends who heard me during moments of need. Today I own a Mennonite Catholic faith. Is this possible? Yes, all is possible when we walk with our Savior.

*

Today, because of this, I am a better Christian. I am open for new ways of expressing my faith through the gift of owning two faiths, two cultures and two languages. This has a lot to do with why I am a Mennonite today. For this and many more reasons, I can say in a proud and humble voice: "Yo soy Menonita."

Lichdi (1990): 31-33

September

An Amish Baptismal Service
John A. Hostetler, United States, 1980

*I*t is a beautiful September morning. The sun shines brightly into the faces of the audience through large, swinging, red barn doors. The huge doors are propped open with sticks on the barn's sloping banks. The rows of benches on the barn floor are almost filled—men on one side and women on the other—except for two rows in the middle.

*

As the *Vorsinger* ("song leader") begins to sing the first song, the ministers, bishops and deacons retire to a room in the house for consultation and to meet with the baptismal applicants for the last time. Here they will also agree on the order of service for the day.

Between hymns there is a deep silence in the audience. The aroma of the haymow and sounds of the birds and insects pentrate the consciousness of the audience. One can hear the horses munching hay below. While waiting for the next hymn to begin, the farm owner notices that it is too warm, and with some difficulty opens a second barn door on the side where the women are seated. The ventilation taken care of, he returns to his seat.

Several hymns are sung and the applicants for baptism—on this occasion six girls aged eighteen and upward—file up the barn bank and take their seats in the center section near the ministers' bench. Both young and old intently watch the six young women who are ready to make their vows to God and the church, to say "no" to the world and "yes" to Jesus Christ and his *Gemein* here on earth. Each sits with bowed head, as though in deep meditation and prayer for the lifelong vow about to be taken. None dare to risk a glimpse at the audience or to gaze about, for it is a solemn occasion. Their clothing is strictly uniform: black organdy caps, black dresses, white organdy capes, long white organdy aprons, black stockings and black oxfords. The fabric of the dresses and the color of ribbon bows at the left shoulder, faintly showing through the organdy capes, are the only evidence of personal taste.

The ministers now enter, quietly removing their hats.

*

As soon as the ministers are seated the assembly stops singing.

Sitting silently in anticipation, the audience listens to two sermons. Two hours of intense waiting finally give way to the climax of the day as the bishop turns to the applicants with a personal admonition. The deacon leaves the service and returns with a small pail of water and a tin cup. The bishop reminds the applicants that the vow they are about to make will be made not to the ministers or to the church but to God. He requests the applicants to kneel if it is still their desire to become members of the body of Christ. All six kneel. The bishop asks a few simple questions and each gives an affirmative answer.

After the applicants respond to the preliminary questions, the bishop asks the assembly to rise for prayer. He reads one of the simple prayers from *Die Ernsthafte Christenpflicht*, a prayer book of the Swiss Anabaptists.

The assembly is seated, but the applicants continue to kneel. The bishop, a deacon and the deacon's wife proceed with the baptism. The three stand at the head of the line while the deacon's wife unties the ribbon of the first applicant's cap and removes the cap from her head. The bishop then lays his hands on the girl's head and says: "*Auf deinen Glauben den du bekennt hast vor Gott und viele Zeugen wirst du getauft in Namen des Vaters, des Sohnes und des Heiligen Geistes, Amen*" ("Upon your faith, which you have confessed before God and these many witnesses, you are baptized in the name of the Father, the Son and the Holy Spirit, Amen"). The deacon pours water into the bishop's hands cupped above the young woman's head, and it drips down over her hair and face.

Overhead, the pigeons flap their wings and fly from one end of the barn to the other. A gentle breeze from the open door of the straw shed stirs up a cloud of fine particles of chaff and dust. An airplane roars in the distance.

When the rite of baptism is completed, the bishop takes the hand of each kneeling applicant in turn and greets her: "*In Namen des Herrn und die Gemein wird die Hand geboten, so steh auf*" ("In the name of the Lord and the Church, we extend to you the hand of fellowship, rise up"). The applicant stands up and the bishop then gives her hand to the assisting wife, who greets the new member with the Holy Kiss. All applicants remain standing until the last one is greeted, and then the bishop asks them to be seated. A few tears are brushed aside as they retie their covering (cap) strings. They will now be considered members of the church and will enjoy full privileges as members of the *Gemein*.

Hostetler (1980): 81-83

Jesus Worked With His Hands

Peter Jansz. Twisck, The Netherlands, 1622

*T*hrough the words and example of Jesus, all lazy people who spend their time in idleness should turn their faces in shame if they have shame. Look how zealously Jesus worked with his hands. He did not look for a handout but tried to support his dear mother. These are lasting examples that teach us that we should not be lax but go to work with our hands so that we have food and raiment. It is not enough that we care for ourselves but also for those who are in need, those who cannot work and earn an income. We should stretch out our hands and labor that we may give to him that needeth. We should be received into the eternal dwelling as those who have not wasted their time with idle and lazy ways.

Solomon said, "Go to the ant, thou sluggard, and watch how they work. They have no guide, no overseer, no ruler and yet they still prepare their bread in the summer and gather their food in the harvest. How long wilt thou sleep, O sluggard? When wilt thou arise out of thy sleep? A little sleep, a little slumber, a little folding of the hands in rest, and poverty will come upon you like a robber, want like a ruffian."

*

He that would not work should not eat, according to the words of Paul. There is nothing more harmful in a Church than a lazy person who needs much but helps little. What more is laziness than the grave of a lazy person? God looks with displeasure on the lazy person. This is why he said we shall work six days and rest one.

Those who desire abundant blessing and well-being should be zealous to work and have a trade. This is the order of God for a happy life. Dear children, it is then needful that you are not careless, but do your tasks right and to the honor of God. This way you will have a good life and inherit the blessings of God. It is well with him who fears God and walks in his ways.

You shall support yourselves with your work. In labor there is profit but the talk of lips tendeth only to need. He who supports himself by his labors and is satisfied has a fine and peaceful life. He has found treasures above all treasures. Experience teaches that the rich sluggard oftentimes eats and drinks more but the taste and appreciation is oftentime missing. The man that works but is poor has not much to eat and little time to waste. This man is usually blessed with good taste, sweet sleep, peace and rest. Sweet is the sleep of a laboring man.

Twisck (1982): 108-110

September 3

For Those Who Work For Us

Menno Simons, The Netherlands, ca. 1541

"A centurion there had a slave whom he valued highly, and who was ill and close to death. When he heard about Jesus, he sent some Jewish elders to him, asking him to come and heal his slave."—Luke 7:2-3

*T*he centurion was moved with compassion toward his poor servant, and was so concerned for him that he spared no pains to trouble the elders of the Jews to send Christ and entreat Him to come and heal his sick servant. This is to the disgrace and shame of all false Christians and especially to many rich, some of whom are more merciless and cruel toward poor servants and hirelings than they are to their dogs and animals (pardon the expression). For as soon as they get so ill that they cannot perform mule's labor, then they are unmercifully turned out of doors and sent to this or that institution, or to their parents and friends who sometimes have scarcely a bite of bread or an old cot in their houses.

Again, others with great damage to their little earnings have to get a substitute while they are sick. And even if they do serve their time in health with hard and severe labor, some of these unmerciful, cruel, bloody folk put forth efforts to deprive these poor lambs, who have to watch when they sleep, labor when they rest, run when they command, and stand when they sit, of a goodly portion of their grievous toil. Now they complain that a spoon is lost; then it is a dish that is broken; always they have ruined this or that. Yes, some of them would feed them with water and straw, and pay them with the whip and chaff, as they do their laboring oxen and horses, if they were not ashamed before men. They would not be ashamed of such things before God whom alas they know not. Oh, woe upon such heathenish tyranny and unmerciful cruelty!

The centurion called his servant his child, by which he manifested his fatherly love and humility toward his poor servant. Although he was lord and held in high honor, nevertheless he did not exalt himself above his humble servant, knowing well that they were created both of them by one and the same God, that they were born of one stock. But what virtue and love some heathen Christians often manifest toward their miserable servants, their actions, alas, openly show.

*

But let it not be so with you, dearly beloved. Take this faithful, pious centurion as an example so that you may resemble him in his faith, love, humility and virtue. Be as solicitous for your servants as he was for his servant. Teach them, admonish and reprove them with a fatherly spirit as often as they do wrong. Set them an unblamable example in all righteousness and piety. Sympathize with them a bit in their severe and heavy labor. Comfort them in their poverty, comfort them I say, and grieve them not. Give them decent support and their earned pay and do not dock them in their wages. Protect them in all honorable things. Do not chide them without cause lest they become discouraged; do not discharge them before the agreed time but let them serve out without loss their time as agreed, lest the name of the Lord be blasphemed. Be friendly toward them at all times. And if they are weak and sick, assist and serve them. Get someone else to serve in their place without loss to them until the Lord takes them or restores them to health. Be sympathetic and compassionate toward them. Assist them in their need. Do not exalt yourselves above them, nor despise them in their humbleness, for they are your brethren according to the flesh. In short, take the attitude toward them that Christ Jesus takes toward us. Always remember that we also have a Lord in heaven before whose judgment seat we must all appear and render an account of all our works.

But if they are willful and obstinate and refuse to hear your word and command, if they do not follow your admonition and counsel, if they want to rule rather than serve, if they waste their time and labor in laziness, if they are unfaithful, rebellious and troublesome, wickedly corrupting your family and children, etc., then come to an agreement with them as to wages earned, before two or three witnesses, so that the fault may not be on your side, and the Word of the Lord be not disgraced. In this way let them move on, that your conscience be not troubled on their account and your house and children be not ruined. Yes, my brethren, do to your poor servant even as you desire that it should be done to you, if you were called as they are. This is the law and the prophets.

Menno (1956): 364-366

September 4

For This New Day
Leenaert Clock, The Netherlands, ca. 1625

O Lord God, heavenly Father, not only have you created us as human beings, formed us and given us life and placed us into this world to obtain our sustenance with grief and toil (because of our transgression), until we return to the earth from which we were taken, but you have also set a period of time how long and where we should live, so that we may seek, feel, fear and love you and wholeheartedly follow you.

As you have given us the day for work you have also ordained the night for us to rest (through your divine kindness). This night's rest we have enjoyed, dear Father, under your gracious paternal protection and preservation. For this it is fitting that we thank, praise and glorify you from the bottom of our hearts and the depths of our souls.

*

And now that you, dear Father, have let this day dawn, grant for us, O God, an awareness that it is your gracious gift. And teach us to understand gratefully why you are again giving us this glorious gift, and as a merciful Father letting the beautiful sun rise over us, that we may spend not only this day, but also all the coming days of our lives according to your divine will—that because of this day we may be reminded of the eternally long, unending day that you are preparing for us, and that we in turn may prepare ourselves to that end through your grace.

Grant that we may thereby understand and be taught to forsake the night of darkness and sin and be liberated from it, and may walk henceforth in the clear light of your divine grace, that we may discard the works of darkness, put on the armor of light and walk honorably as in the day.

To this end, O God, let us illuminate the light of your divine mercy, that we may constantly keep you, O God and Father, foremost before our eyes in all we do, and do not do, believing you to be present—you who see everything with your fire-flashing eyes, even what we are planning and thinking.

*

Also, dear Father, may we enjoy with moderation all the gifts that you have supplied for our needs, using them solely for their intended purpose, and not misusing them through extravagance, greed or wanton delights: give us hearts that are willing to share.

May our hearts not be burdened with eating, drinking or worries about food, but teach us to place our trust in you and to await your providence. To this end give us a broken, lowly and contrite heart, a penitent spirit and true gentleness, and a genuine hunger and thirst for your righteousness, together with a merciful, sympathetic heart that is clean and pure—that we may see you, O God, upon which all our salvation and eternal life is based.

God of love and peace, grant us your eternal peace and grace that we may at all times show ourselves to be peace-loving, avoiding all strife and quarreling.

And all the calamities we may encounter in this life, whether cross or grief, disgrace or other misfortune, help us to bear them patiently with gentle spirit and quiet heart, without too much complaining or grumbling.

Lord, since you are our God and Creator, shape the order of our lives according to your holy and divine will. For all our works and acts are in your hands as we commit ourselves, with body and soul and all that we have, to you. Rule us and encourage the work of our hands, O God, according to your divine will.

Gross (Forthcoming)

Ascending the Mountain Together
José Ortíz, United States, 1989

*T*eachers perform different roles in different places. At times they are prophets of the future, pointing toward utopia or proclaiming the virtues of the emerging order. At other times they are the curators of history and the defenders of tradition. In some places they are pillars of the status quo, in others catalysts of change.

Modern education has borrowed from both Hebrew and Greek models. The rabbinical schools that emerged out of the Old Testament emphasized the transfer of information from teacher to disciple. In this way, traditions were perpetuated. Today this approach is known as the "banking" system of education. Though no longer considered the ideal, it remains influential.

In Greek education, the emphasis was on dialogue between student and teacher. Teachers such as Socrates and Plato tried to nurture good relationships among teachers, students and the public. They believed that knowledge would lead to practice and to wholesome living. Of course, not all Greeks saw knowledge and morality as congruent.

*

Jesus' approach to education was more active than that of either the rabbis or the Greeks. His disciples were more than students; the New Testament term *mathetes* means a follower who honors the cause of the teacher. Jesus did not merely transfer information or engage his disciples in dialogue. He taught his followers by living with them and leading them into action. He became a *dunamis*, a force by which the disciples changed their communities.

*

Jesus' method of student recruitment was a simple "Follow me." He warned would-be dropouts that without him "nothing can be done." That radical call to discipleship produced a network of followers that turned the New Testament world upside down.

*

Jesus' teaching approach could be described as one that emphasizes "being"—being with people, being present-oriented, being an agent of liberation for others.

This cannot be accomplished by a computer or programmed learning system. I can't envision a descendant of Pac-Man serving as a role model for my future grandchildren, nor parents conferring with a tube about a student who has a learning disability.

Flesh-and-blood teachers, on the other hand, can have an influence that goes beyond their own lifetimes. As the Old Testament Hebrews secured immortality by having children and the Spaniards by writing books, so teachers have a sort of immortality through the ideas and examples they present to their students.

In education, teacher and student ascend the mountain of transfiguration together to see alarms and visions, then test those visions in the valleys of history. Whether on a darkening road or a radiant summit, learning occurs when teachers are alert to their students' context and seek the good of others.

Ortíz and Graybill (1989): 57-60

September 6

Entrusted to Me

Christopher Dock, United States, 1750

*I*n my dealings with youth, this is of all my duties the heaviest burden upon my heart, and it outweighs everything else, call it what you may, namely this: How I may rule and conduct my household that I may some day receive a gracious testimonial from the great Shepherd of the sheep, who entrusted the young lambs to me through twenty-six years? They were really entrusted to me thirty-six years, by an occupation that no one knows better than I. But in this country I neglected that profession for ten years, for which I often felt the smiting hand of God, which before then had served me well. May the Lord graciously overlook my neglect of the youth during that time.

*

After I had, as stated above, given up the school at Skippack which I had taught for ten years in the country, doing farming according to my limited ability, various opportunities for teaching presented themselves, until finally I began teaching again, in the two townships of Skippack and Sollford, three days weekly in each school. But I was already acquainted with keeping school in this country, and knew that it is very different from methods in Germany, where the schools stand upon such pillars as the common man cannot well overthrow.

Then when I considered the duties of the profession and firmly determined to carry out all these duties, I also saw the degenerate condition of my youth, and the many wrongs of this world by which adults spoil and distress youth. And I saw not only my own unworthiness, but also the unequal ability of parents in the training of their children, for while some seek the salvation of their children in precept and example, and do all in their power to promote the glory of God and the good of their children, others are quite the opposite. They teach their children evil by their own example, and thus the teacher must counteract this influence and be stern toward such unruly pupils. This readily gives a teacher the reputation of being partial. It is said that he is more severe with one child than with another. This indeed he must be, for the children's sake, that good children may not be ruined by bad ones. Otherwise it is of course a teacher's duty to be impartial.

The poor beggar child, scurfy, ragged and lousy, if otherwise it have a good disposition and willingness to learn, should be as dear to the teacher, though he never receive a penny for it in this world, as the child of wealth from whom he expects good remuneration. The rich reward for the poor child will come in the next world. In fact, it would take too long to enumerate all the duties of a schoolmaster. But it would take still longer to enumerate his troubles. Considering all this, I early discovered that if I wished to accomplish good among children I must daily with David lift up my eyes to the mountains for help if I wished to do good work in the world as it exists, and so I reentered this work and have thus far remained in it. I often wish I could have accomplished more, but I thank God for helping me to do as much as I did.

Martin (1971): 17, 18

September 7

Education for Mediocrity
Edward Yoder, United States, 1935

The more superficial our American culture becomes, the more pressure, psychological and otherwise, will be applied to make the mores, the habits, the ideas of every mother's son alike. We will probably increasingly and of course unconsciously compensate for our subconscious sense of inferiority by imposing our ideas and our practices, or trying to impose them, upon all our neighbors. We are so poverty-stricken in spirit, soul and heart that we can find no better employment for our energies than trying to reform our countrymen through laws, ordinances, constitutional amendments and what not. We have not the mental energy and the stamina of soul, not the patience and the faith to work on fundamental things in the formation of human character.

Many times have I wondered to myself whether it might not be true that men are being rendered weaker and weaker through the benefit of all our solicitous and painstaking educational efforts. Is not everyone being tended and nurtured with such high-pressure hothouse methods that true stamina of character has no real chance to develop, that the innate spiritual and mental fiber of many is not actually being weakened and destroyed?

More freedom for children, not freedom to follow their own devices, but a true freedom to get at the real values in life, a true freedom to experience the best in life; more freedom for parents to direct their children's development would surely be a good thing. But no! Every infant must be regimented early and smeant to goose-step with the multitudinous herd. Every parent must surrender to the public school system the growth of the child; just because some parents are stupid, unintelligent, basically unfit to guide their children's education, for that reason must parents of culture, intelligence and good judgment also deliver their progeny to the processes of mass leveling! The reply of American democratic stupidity is, "Yes," with great emphasis.

Does not nature all about emphasize the infinite diversification and variation of all living forms? Only man plans to subvert the Creator's wisdom and design by striving to bring about uniformity. In the sermon we heard this morning, the subject was referred to, as to why well-meaning and conscientious Christian brethren cannot see matters alike and agree more fully. The suggestion was offered, that in this life people are rarely or never fully sanctified and consecrated, surrendered to the Lord, and so differences must be expected. Personally, I think Christians should be trained and instructed to see the harmony, the beauty, the divine design there is in diversity. It can be only little minds that see in diversity of practice and thought anything evil, wrong or undesirable. I'm for variation and liberty.

Yoder (1985): 257, 258

September 8

Duty Toward the Teacher
Peter Jansz. Twisck, The Netherlands, 1622

*D*ear children, be alert to accept all good instruction that is placed before you so that it may be planted within you and pressed upon the tablet of your heart. This will lead to correction, profit and well-being for you and your father's house and all men. A child's duty is to study, not to gather honor or riches. The full measure of his study shall be to become wise so that he can better teach others and learn to know himself. He will work for the good of the land, spreading the praise of God, enlightening those in the dark, and multiplying unto a blessed end. Take interest in the teacher's lessons, his examples and instruction.

A poet carried a note in his pocket which he read each night before he went to sleep. Even so you should preserve useful instruction and Christian doctrines of your school teacher as well as the teachings and books of your father. Especially love to read the Holy Scriptures of your Heavenly Father. Consider, search and meditate with love for the truth. Spend your life thus and you will guide your feet to life everlasting. Do not fly so high in your learning that you forget the humble life of the Lamb of God so that you are not cast away in outer darkness.

When the fruits of knowledge are blended with edifying love they are sweet, precious and pleasant. Knowing that the root of knowledge is bitter but the fruit sweet, gives you reason to love those who instruct you and teach you a trade which is essential to a godly life. Let them help you unto salvation.

*

Learn to be submissive and progressive in the manner of those who instruct.

Twisck (1982): 81, 82

We Must Once Separate

Jaques Mesdag, Belgium, 1567

The following selection is from a letter which Jaques Mesdag wrote to his wife, two months before he was burned at the stake along with three other Mennonites.

O my dear chosen sister whom I love so greatly with all my heart, I should not be able to describe to you, I think, with what true, unfeigned godly and brotherly love I love you. Oh, adhere always valiantly to the true, pure truth and doctrine of Christ, as I, through the grace of the Lord, most confidently trust that you will do, though I thus write.

O my dearest sister, I also trust, through the great grace and mercy of the Lord, to do myself according to my weak ability, all that I have written you; for it is still my unwavering mind and purpose rather to lay down my life, though it be tomorrow, than to forsake the truth. For I am still willing to resign my life for Him who gave it me, if it shall come to this; and again, if it be His divine will, that I am to remain in iron bonds yet for a long time, I will also gladly suffer it for His holy name; for He suffered so much for us. And I cannot fully thank or praise the Lord for the great grace, mercy and the benefits which He has shown me in prison; and for patience, that the lying in bonds has so little affected me—it seems to me that you could hardly believe how little it has affected me. I am not conscious, it seems to me, that I was imprisoned, or that it lasted too long, or that I was thus imprisoned; eternal praise, glory and thanks to the Lord, for His abundant grace and mercy.

However I have sometimes wished, if it could have been, to be with you, if it had been for the good of my soul, and the Lord had permitted it; and this chiefly because of the love which I have towards you, and you to me. My dear lamb, the Lord be praised, I have never grieved much on account of it, since it was for the name of the Lord, and I know that we must once separate here. Though we should be together here a hundred years yet, the time of separation would nevertheless come, and it is better to die honorably than to transgress the law of God and live in disgrace, as is written in the second book of the Maccabees (6:19). And Christ also said: "Whosoever shall seek to save his life shall lose it; and whosoever shall lose his life for my sake and the gospel's, the same shall preserve it. But whosoever loveth father or mother, or sister or brother, or wife or children more than me, the same is not worthy of me" (Luke 17:33; 14:26).

Therefore, my dearest, when it comes so far that we are apprehended and put into bonds, everything must be forsaken for the sake of His holy will and name, if we wish to be of His number; for he that does not forsake all that he has cannot be His disciple.

van Braght (1979): 720, 721

Stand Still For a Moment

Peter M. Friesen, Russian Empire, 1911

*T*hough I am not really an "Old" Mennonite, I have for years been tired, tired, tired of the foreign influences and would like to urge all reformers ("Old" Mennonite and Brethren), especially the leaders: Stand still for a moment and ask yourself this question from the perspective of church history: What is Mennonitism? Have we perhaps forgotten to relearn that which is good, as a balance to the endless new, new, new?! Are we not losing a large and essential part of our Mennonite psyche, in the good sense?

What does God want of us as a group, a fellowship: that we, while calling ourselves Mennonite, become a conglomerate of Lutheranism, Baptist and Plymouthism, etc. (we mean in the understanding and manner of expressing our Christianity)? What is the specific direction that God has assigned to us through our original doctrines, history and present situation? Certainly we should now more seriously begin to study our own background, examine the newly acquired for its values, throw away the ballast and deliberately, discreetly, bring the good old and the good new—for "every scribe fit for the kingdom" brings forth old and new from his treasures—into proper relationship.

Friesen (1979): 309, 310

September 11

Dissimilarity

David Beiler, United States, 1862

Bishop David Beiler's conservative influence held most of the Lancaster County (Pa.) Amish to the Old Order during the 1860s and '70s, when the Amish in America were separating into progressive and Old Order groups.

*T*he old order has fallen into disuse more and more among some people and in some respects it has no longer been interpreted and followed so exactly. In this way hatred and dissimilarity of interpretation have arisen. Some did not wish to consent to the ordinances which the fathers had any farther than could be shown by the letter of the Scriptures. In this way hairsplitting (or subtle) questions arose, one may well believe. And along with this a presumptuous spirit to meddle in that which was not commanded to all has found entrance and place among some through the secular education which is in high esteem among worldly minded people. In this way one thing after another has crept in so that confusion and strife have arisen.

Now as one hears and experiences, there is so much difference of opinion among ministers and brethren and sisters that one can scarcely see or believe. This is as Paul mentions, "We are baptized by one spirit into one body." We know this well that the members in one body are united and peaceful and there is to be no division in the body. If we look at our present-day Christianity, the dissimilarity in our conduct, our customs and way of life we would have reason to conclude that we are not driven by one spirit if the inside is so dissimilar. For as the spirit which rules and directs man so are his manners and customs, his words, his looks and his outward appearance.

Through lack of uniformity in opinion it has come so far that divisions and vexations have arisen. The split appears to be becoming almost irreparable. So that if God does not stop this destruction and does not chastise the people in one way or another by cross or tribulation, it will be perhaps with war and strife and bloodshed, of which there appears already to be a beginning. And we know not when or how it will become otherwise.

Umble (1948): 105

September 12

Thoughts on Prayer
Noah E. Byers, United States, 1911

*R*educed to its simplest terms, religion is the true fellowship of man with God and this is promoted by prayer. It is important therefore, above all things, that we understand prayer and emphasize it in our daily lives.

The two essential conditions for prayer are: (1) a definite sense of the presence of a wise, all-powerful, personal God, and (2) an honest purpose to live in harmony with His will. I believe that many honest souls fail in their prayer life because of the difficulty of realizing the presence of God. Some hesitate because they cannot get a satisfactory picture or mental image of His form; others are skeptical because they can not comprehend His nature and attributes. Now what is needed is not the imangination of the artist nor the explanation of the theologian, but a practical experience of His spiritual presence.

*

But there are many more, no doubt, that are definitely conscious of a prayer-hearing and answering God—they believe in Him and tremble—but they are not on speaking terms with Him. The consciousness of sin and the unwillingness to forsake it make it impossible for them to address Him, in faith, for the least of blessings. God hears the cry of the sinner, but not until he is willing to come to Him and submit to his Father's will.

The real prayer is the attitude of the heart toward God. "If ye abide in me, and my words abide in you"—this is the condition in which we "pray without ceasing." Our whole attitude may be constantly that of dependence and trust, gratitude and praise, and of strong purpose in line with His will. This is more important than the words we use at special times. And yet it is important that at special and regular times we give our whole attention to Him and for the sake of concentration and definiteness of thought put our heart's desire into words.

The object of prayer is not so much to change God's purposes and plans as it is to make it possible for Him to accomplish His work through us. He always purposes that which is best and is "more willing to give than we are to receive," but not until we come to Him in the prayer, unuttered or expressed, "not my will but thine be done," can He give us what we need. As soon as we are willing, the answer is sure to come.

But at times it seems desirable that the regular order of nature should be interfered with for a special purpose. Can God oppose nature? No, God's regular habits of doing things constitute nature and so if for sufficient reason He desires on occasions to change His regular way of doing as a free, willing being He can so change. However we do not believe that He will do this often enough to seriously interfere with the uniformity of nature.

Hertzler (1983): 25, 26

September 13

A Plan for Prayer
Samuel K. Landis, United States, ca. 1912

*I*f praying is talking with God, and it is, then surely any one that can talk can pray. But for the benefit of any one who may feel weak in prayer I will suggest the following plan:

Steal away to some quiet, secluded place where no one but God can see and hear you. It may be some private room in the house. It may be in a field, or woods or along a country roadside—select the best time of day for this purpose; that is, the hour in which you can obtain the best results. Some find the morning hour the best for praying, but as for me I prefer the impressing scene of the evening, just as the shadow of night begins to fall and I am encouraged to select and mention this time because "Isaac went out to meditate in the field at the eventide" (Genesis 24:63).

When you have come to your selected place for prayer, turn your back toward the world and its cares and your eyes toward the "Holy city, the New Jerusalem."

*

Sing a verse or two of some suitable hymn, so that you may get your heart in proper condition for prayer. Then tell God what you desire and what you need, and ask Him in the name of Jesus to grant your request. But because it might not be well for you to have all you ask for, don't forget to add to your humble petition these words, "Nevertheless, not as I will, but as thou wilt." If you do not know what you need, then ask God to give you what He sees you need and what is good for you. If you cannot do this, then I believe you do not want to pray. If you have a will to pray you will find a way.

Prayer must be the sentiments of the heart; the end in view must be right as well as the means employed by which to reach it. We must not only pray because we have made it a rule or practice, but we should be intensely interested in our prayers. Too many of our prayers are, as Beecher says, like driving a wedge into a log.

I do not mean that we should not pray until we feel like doing so. We should make it a rule, as Daniel did, to pray three times a day, and then stick to that rule. I mean to say that if we are Christians indeed, even though it may require a little effort to direct our minds from our particular interest and employments while busily engaged in the midst of them, yet we will not have prayed very long until it will become a pleasure and a blessing.

Landis ([1912]): 54-56

September 14

Everything By Prayer
Joseph Klopfenstein, France, early 1800s

As the Lord himself has promised in the Gospel of St. Luke 11:9-10: "Ask and it shall be given you; seek and ye shall find; knock and it shall be opened unto you. For every one that asketh receiveth; and he that seeketh findeth; and to him that knocketh it shall be opened." With these words the Lord teaches and comforts us that no believing prayer is made in vain and disregarded. He taught us by his own example, for he frequently persisted all night in prayer, not for his own sake but on our behalf; for all of his words and works are our medicine and were done for our benefit and salvation, my beloved.

Therefore consider well those who have prayer hours and certain days for prayer, that these days and hours of prayer may be days and hours of repentance, if you desire to be heard. For although all spiritual gifts have again been attained and gained in Christ, still no one will be a partaker in them except by faith, by which one must seek to pray and knock. In short, everything must be acquired from above, by prayer, as the Apostle James says in his epistle, first chapter: "Every good gift and every perfect gift is from above, and cometh from the Father of lights, with whom there is no variableness, neither shadow of turning."

Oyer (1984): 312

The Lord's Prayer

Samuel K. Landis, United States, ca.1912

I believe they do well who repeat the "Lord's Prayer" verbatim; that is word for word, especially if they have studied well so as to understand it thoroughly, thus making it in a sense their own sentiment. Yes, I believe we should make more frequent use of this prayer than many of us do. Christ taught us these words, and if we use them right we will never pray amiss.

*

God loves to have us pray as though we would remind Him of the relation between Him and us since God and sinner have become reconciled, and the tender relationship which began when we became the sons and daughters of God. He will have us acknowledge Him as our Father and ourselves as His children: "Our Father, which art in heaven."

He would have us know that He is high and holy, wise and good, powerful and mighty. We should regard Him with godly fear mingled with affection, and strive to honor and glorify Him in all things: "Hallowed be thy name."

He would have us seek first the kingdom of God, and his righteousness, and pray for the joyful flourishing of Christ's kingdom on earth, and longingly look forward to His second coming: "Thy kingdom come."

In heaven the will of God is done always, gladly and perfectly; therefore all are infinitely happy. God would make earth the counterpart of heaven, but His will must first be done: "Thy will be done in earth as it is in heaven."

Bread is the staff of life, a necessary food. It is not luxurious or useless things that God would have us ask for, but bread, bread for the body and bread for the soul. We should acknowledge God as the giver of every good and perfect gift, and daily look to Him for them, but, like the little birds, make use of the ordinary means which God has appointed whereby we may obtain them: "Give us this day our daily bread."

Sin is here spoken of as debts. God has made it a condition that man must forgive to be forgiven. If any man who has an unforgiving spirit makes use of this prayer with hatred in his heart he condemns himself, for he asks God to do with him as he does with his fellow men: "And forgive us our debts, as we forgive our debtors."

God is sometimes said to do a thing when He only allows it. If we try to go forward in our own strength He may allow us to fall into some temptation whereby we may be overcome. But if we confidently place our hand in His hand He will deliver us from the snares of the devil. This I believe is the true meaning of the words, "And lead us not into temptation, but deliver us from evil."

The gospel plan of redemption by Christ: the power by which it became effective and by which it must be maintained, and the honor and praises for this glorious system of mercy and truth, with the wonderful effects which it produces, belong to God, both in time and eternity, now and forever: "For thine is the kingdom, and the power, and the glory forever."

We should sanction our prayers by an established purpose and an unwavering faith, which may be expressed by saying, "Amen."

Landis ([1912]): 57-60

Prayer from a Right Heart
Peter Riedemann, Germany, 1540

*P*rayer must and ought to be from a right heart—that is, in spirit and in truth—if it is to be pleasing to God. Therefore he who would so pray must prepare his heart, firstly, through the laying aside of all that is wrong, since God heareth not sinners; and must strive, as far as at all possible, to be at peace with all men, above all with the believers; as Christ saith, "If thou comest before the altar to lay thy sacrifice thereon, and rememberest at the same moment that thy brother hath something against thee, then go and first be reconciled to him, and then come and sacrifice thy gift." Therefore each one who would offer the fruit of his lips to God—that is, praise and prayer—must first be reconciled to all, so that none of the believers have aught against him.

Further, he also must have forgiven if he have aught in his heart against any, as Christ teacheth, saying, "When ye stand and pray, forgive, if ye have aught against any: that your Father also which is in heaven may forgive you your trespasses." And when the heart is thus purified it must then be adorned with true faith and real confidence. Yea, the man must have such trust in God that he surely, firmly and certainly believeth that God, as a father who seeketh always the best for his children, will hear him and grant his prayer; as the words of Christ show and indicate, "If ye, who are evil, can yet give your children good gifts, how much more will your Father in heaven give the Holy Spirit to them that ask him?"

Thus, they who pray in faith will receive. And he who prayeth thus in faith ceaseth not to make his request to God, and alloweth no other concern to hinder or delay him; and if there should be delay and it seem as though God will not grant it, he waiteth with all patience in the firm confidence that God will certainly give without delay.

*

If, however, we who are children of Christ's Spirit, know not by reason of our weakness how to come before God so that our desire and request may stand before him, then, saith Paul, "The Spirit upholdeth our weakness; for we know not what we should pray for as we ought: but the Spirit itself intercedeth for us mightily, with unspeakable groaning; and he that searcheth the hearts knoweth what is the mind of the Spirit, because he maketh intercession for the sins of the saints according to the will of God."

Now, it is in this one Spirit that God desireth to be honored and worshipped, and therefore one ought to await his instigation and learn of him. Then what he teacheth and inspireth in us will be heard by God and will be pleasing unto him, and since he heareth us we shall have the petition that we have asked of him.

Rideman (1970): 121, 122

September 17

Words Beyond Sound
Yorifumi Yaguchi, Japan, 1989

The Mute's Testimony

>I can't pray aloud
>My tongue flaps
>but no sound takes shape
>
>Can a voiceless prayer
>fly out
>across space?
>
>When I pray
>an enormous ear strains to hear me
>
>swallows in
>my tiniest thought

*

The Deaf Man's Testimony

>I am
>surrounded
>by a stone wall
>I live
>in a silent universe
>But when I see
>Christ
>I can hear
>the divine words.

Yaguchi (1989): 21, 22

The Modern Idol

John M. Brenneman, United States, 1876

*E*xamine yourselves truly and sincerely, for there are too many idols in our day. True, we have perhaps no graven images or idols (yet we dare scarcely say this of most of us) which we worship with the mouth and serve, as the heathen have; but there are numerous idols besides; and well would it be for us, if in no respect it could be said of us in truth, as it is spoken of by the prophet, "These men have set up their idols in their heart" (Ezekiel 14:3).

That is not idolatry alone, wherein man worships and honors inanimate images made by men's hands, for Paul writes also of such, "Whose God is their belly" (Philippians 1:19). And again, "Such serve not our Lord Jesus Christ but their own belly" (Romans 16:18). There are thousands of such worshipers who offer to their bellies nearly all they can produce, seeking to satisfy them with all kinds of elegant and costly victuals, and intoxicating drinks, and who are "lovers of pleasures more than lovers of God" (2 Timothy 3:4).

*

Mammon is also an idol which many persons very earnestly serve and worship. It denotes wealth, or earthly treasures. Many persons so yield to this idol, with such confidence that they sacrifice their precious time and labor almost entirely to its service in order to obtain it. This mammon worship, through which the true worship of God is neglected, is that which the apostle, in my opinion, had in view when he said, "Covetousness, which is idolatry." Covetousness denotes an earnest and insatiable desire to obtain wealth or earthly possessions.

*

At the present day there are too many of those covetous mammon worshipers, who instead of alleviating the necessities of the poor and widows, would much rather take from them what they have. Luke says (12:13-15): "One of the company said unto him [Jesus], Master, speak to my brother, that he divide the inheritance with me." It appears as if this man troubled himself more about his earthly inheritance than his everlasting salvation, which Jesus proclaimed. But Jesus said unto him, "Man, who made me a judge or a divider over you?" And he said unto them, "Take heed and beware of covetousness: for a man's life consisteth not in the abundance of the things which he possesseth."

*

Not alone are those persons covetous who take for themselves all they possibly can, whether from just or unjust motives, but also those who keep all they can and do not bestow anything. Of this class there are too many, for too frequently is it the case that when something is to be collected for the poor or for the church, frequently the most wealthy give the least, if anything. Where then is the true brotherly love to be seen? Is this then not clear evidence of covetousness, which is idolatry? O brethren! let this not be said of you.

Brenneman (1876): 173-177

September 19

"Thou Shalt Not Kill"
Uria R. Byler, United States, 1963

*T*he evening of September 19, 1757, was a happy one for the Jacob Hochstetler family. The young people of the neighborhood were gathered there for one of those old-fashioned "apple schnitzings" which provided the Hochstetler household with apples to dry for the winter and also gave the young folks a chance to get together for the evening. It was a closely knit little group, boys and girls who had grown up together in the same neighborhood. First they peeled and sliced apples for a few hours, probably laughing and enjoying themselves, as was usual on such occasions. Later, games were played until late, then the "good-nights" were said and the guests went home through the peaceful autumn night. When the last ones had left, the Hochstetlers bolted their doors and went to bed.

The French and Indian War was raging then, and during the last year quite a few white settlers in the neighborhood had been murdered and carried off in captivity. So far none of the Amish had been bothered and the Indians seemed friendly enough. Many times they had come to the house asking for food and clothing.

Tired of the evening's activities, the entire family was now in slumberland, unaware of the danger that was stalking in the forest nearby. There, waiting patiently, were a dozen Indians. Since soon after dark, they had awaited their chance to strike, and now they made ready. They came toward the house. As they were passing the bake oven, the Hochstetlers' dog began to bark. This awakened Jacob Jr., who opened the door to see what the trouble was. A shot rang out and Jacob felt a sharp pang in his leg. He shut and bolted the door and now the entire family were on their feet. In the dimness of night they could see about ten figures gathered near the bake oven.

The two boys picked up their muskets to defend the family. There was plenty of ammunition in the house, and no doubt the Indians could have been detained until daylight and help came. Being nonresistant and not believing in killing, Jacob absolutely forbade such violence as even defending his loved ones. The stalwart sons implored their father to let them use their rifles, but the father believed with all his soul that when the Lord said to Moses, "Thou shalt not kill," he meant just that.

The Indians next set the house on fire. When the Hochstetlers saw this, they all went to the basement. Soon the burning embers began falling through the floor. For a while these were kept extinguished by pouring cider on them. Finally it was apparent that they must leave the house or perish with it.

There was a small window on one side of the basement and through this the family began to leave one by one. Because it was getting daylight the Indians had all left except one, who had lingered to eat a few peaches. He happened to see the Hochstetlers as they were coming out of the window and shouted to his companions, who returned, and soon the entire family was taken.

Jacob Jr. and a daughter were tomahawked and scalped. Another Indian raised his deadly tomahawk over the head of Christian but changed his mind and took him prisoner along with the father. The mother was stabbed to death with a knife and also scalped.

We may well imagine what Jacob Hochstetler's thoughts were when he and his sons Christian and Joseph, hands bound behind their backs, were marched westward toward the Blue Mountains. Behind him lay his dead wife and two children, amid the smoldering embers of his buildings. When they emerged from the basement that morning into the hands of the Indians, he had urged his family to submit to any fate that awaited them.

Jacob was told that they were to be separated and taken to other villages. Sadly they bade each other good-by, not knowing if, and hardly expecting that, they would ever see each other again. The father's parting advice to his sons was: "If you are taken so far away and kept so long that you forget the German language, do not forget the Lord's Prayer."

Byler (1963): 191-203

September 20

The Jewish Bedrock
Sara Wenger Shenk, United States, 1987

Jewish festive traditions are especially well adapted for telling and retelling the faith story. The primary action on a Jewish holiday is usually within the home rather than in the synagogue. Jewish people have a long tradition of sustaining a family-centered worship life from which Christians can learn a lot.

Jewish liturgy and festivals are the source of much of our Christian worship life. Many Jewish celebrations honor a history which we share. The source of their story is also the source of our story. Participation in their festive reenactments of that story brings us closer to our own cultural and historical roots.

The Jews gave us Christ. The prayers, readings, blessings and symbols that Christ used grew out of a thoroughly Jewish context. Christian interpretation of these symbols doesn't so much change the Jewish symbols as it adds a new layer of meaning to them. The meaning of Jewish symbols such as fire, water, paschal lamb and unleavened bread is focused in Christian practice, not negated or obliterated. Understanding the original Jewish meaning of the symbols can restore an historical foundation to our Christian interpretations.

*

It is especially the home-centered quality of Jewish festivals that makes them well suited to enrich our family rituals. Because celebrations happen at home, they have been adapted to include children. The ceremonies for Sabbath and the Passover, for example, are filled with poetic symbols which embrace the mental, the spiritual and the physical. Jewish art and history are woven into the fabric of each festival. For those who can't read, there are bitter herbs to taste and candles to light as a way of entering into the experience.

The festivals often occur around the dinner table where eating and enjoyment of special foods become an important part of the larger commemorative worship drama. Simply by being present at the festive dinner table, a child is introduced to the noblest treasures of the faith. As the drama of lights, readings and symbols unfolds, the child is drawn into profound reenactment of faith tradition. Whether or not the child is aware, he or she is being given a place of belonging, a steady foundation on which to stand. And what more valuable gift can we give our children?

Shenk (1987): 11, 12

September 21

A Mysterious Ethereal Charm
Rebecca Showalter, United States, 1987

When I was a young child, before I had scarcely any concept of values, or comprehension of being prejudiced, the autumn seasons touched me with a mysterious ethereal charm, and with a deep longing for something beyond the scope of our horizons. These longings I now realize will never be satisfied in mortal life.

Autumn conveys an urgent message that life is brief. There is such a short period between seedtime and harvest. It suggests the need of diligent fruit-bearing as we travel through our course of time into eternity.

The tranquility of autumn is a symbol of maturity, fruition, rest and immortality.

Some of us experience the greatest soul stirrings at autumntide, while others are more attuned to spring. Perhaps none of us care so much for the extremes of summer's heat (it is 100° here today) or winter's cold, but let us remember that the power of resurrection which thrills us in springtime was nurtured in the silent frosty hours of winter, and the resplendent glories of autumn were cradled in the heart of summer.

It is well to consider the seasons and speak of their splendors and benefits as they revolve year after year through the centuries.

"Oh Lord, how manifold are Thy works! In wisdom hast Thou made them all: the earth is full of Thy riches" (Psalm 104:24).

Showalter (1987): 8

September 22

The Gospel of All Creatures

Hans Hut, Germany, ca. 1526

Due to an ambiguity in the German translation of Mark 16:15, "preach the gospel to all creatures" could be read to mean "preach the gospel of all creatures"—the gospel which all creatures proclaim. Many southern German Anabaptists exploited this interpretation, which is, however, not legitimate. Nevertheless, the notion that all creation declares God's work has biblical support elsewhere. This belief that God was already partly revealed in all the world through the creatures encouraged mission work. The missionary was not sent into total darkness, but was going forth to fan into flame the sparks of light still present in corrupted Christendom as well as among the Jews, the Turks and the pagans.

*F*irst then, Christ says, "Go ye into all the world and preach the gospel of all creatures." Here the Lord shows how man shall come to the knowledge of God and himself, namely through the "gospel of all creatures." But we must first of all learn and know what is this "gospel of all creatures." For, God have mercy, the whole world is utterly ignorant of it and it is also never preached in our age.

*

In the "gospel of all creatures" is nothing else signified and preached than simply Christ crucified, but not Christ alone as Head, but the whole Christ with all members; this is the Christ which all creatures preach and teach. The whole Christ has to suffer in all members, and not as our Scribes preach Christ (who nevertheless want to be the best, as we hear daily from them), that Christ as the Head has borne and accomplished everything. But then what happens to the members and the whole body in which the suffering of Christ must be fulfilled? Of this Paul bears witness when he says, "I rejoice in my suffering, for I fulfill what is lacking in the suffering of Christ in my body."

And therefore, in a short time, which has already begun, they must with their wisdom be turned into fools, for it is God's good pleasure through foolish, silly and fanatical preaching, as the clever ones call it, to save those who believe it, though these rage against it never so much [as now]. So they must in a short time, for all their wisdom and pride, give way to the poor in spirit who, as Paul says, are simply fanatics to them.

Now this you are to understand with diligence, my dearly beloved brethren, and mark the word which Christ calls "the gospel of all creatures." For it is not here to be understood as though the gospel is to be preached *to* the creatures, cats and dogs, cows and calves, leaves and grass, but as Paul says, the "gospel which is preached to you, in all creatures." This he also shows when he says that the eternal power and divinity will be perceived when a man truly recognizes it in the creatures or works from the creation of the world.

Klaassen (1981b): 48, 49

September 23

The Word of God in Nature
Tennessee John Stoltzfus, United States, mid-1800s

*L*et us look at what is done through the word of God by nature, for us all. See the word of God through the Sun given for us all. She gives light and life to all upon earth. In a warm summer day, we may stand in the sunshine; the earth is warm from the sun about our feet and perhaps a thousand mile around us just nearly as warm at the same moment, as where we stand. What a great wonder through the word of God and a living faith. And by the sun the light of the day cometh and goeth.

Now some may say, "Why is not the moon all the time the same?" The moon gives us the monthly time. That is the word of God seen by the moon. How could we know the time of the month if we had no moon? What a great wonder is seen by the moon, through faith by the word of God.

Now when the sun has made the round for the day, and the moon for the month, and we look up in a clear night to the wonder of the stars to give light to us by the word of God, and living faith, what a glorious sight it is to look at them, like if they were all smiling to us, to give honor and praise to the word of God. And the least one we may point out, seems to stand just as independent as the greater one. People who travel by night and know the stars can go north, south, east and west by the stars. It appears that all have their places to stand and go by. What a great wonder.

Let us look at the word of God in the sea. The great depths and the mountains of rocks through it. The great shores where the waves have to fall silent. At the tides and the immense water running in it and still getting no fuller. What a great wonder to look across the sea where there is nothing but water to be seen below.

Let us look at the beauties of the mountains, valleys, rivers, streams of running water, trees of all kinds, grass of a different kind, fruit trees of many kinds, brutes of different kinds, fishes of different kinds, snakes, worms, insects of most kinds. All this comes by faith through the word of God and, look which way we may, we see the fruits of the word of God.

Paton Yoder (1987): 172, 173

The Spirituality of Visible Things
Leonhard Schiemer, Austria, 1527

*I*n the marvelous creation of heaven and earth and the other creatures God may be known. Paul says that God's invisible essence and his everlasting power and deity can be known, if one comprehends it, ever since the creation of the world. He also says that God has created the visible things in order that through them the invisible may be known. Further he says that the gospel that I have preached to you is being preached to all creatures. In five days God created all creatures. However, because on the sixth day, the day on which man was created, they become beneficial to man, the creation comes to its rest. Man too is not created in order that on the sixth day he remain a man, but in order that he comes into the seventh day, indeed that he becomes deified and comes to God. That is man's true rest and the true holy day.

The means by which the creatures benefit man is suffering. Man kills, cuts and prepares them, and the creatures quietly endure it and suffer for the sake of faith. And even as an animal cannot benefit man as food unless the lamb die, no man will be saved unless he die for the sake of Christ.

Klaassen (1981b): 55, 56

The Parables of Common Life
Hans Hut, Germany, ca. 1526

*A*s the peasant does with his field before he sows seed in it, so does God also with us, before he plants his Word in us, that it may grow and bear fruit. He teaches the gardener the gospel from his trees, the fisherman from his catch, the builder from his house, the goldsmith by the testing of his gold, the housewives from their dough, the vinedresser by his vineyard, vine and shoots, the tailor by the patching on an old garment, the merchant by the pearls, the reaper by the harvest, the woodcutter by the axe laid to the tree, the shepherd by the sheep, the potter by his pottery, the steward and the bailiff by their accounts, the pregnant woman by her childbearing, the thresher by his winnowing fan, the butcher by his slaughtering.

Paul illustrates the body of Christ in and through a human body, and so Christ always preached the gospel of the kingdom of God by the creatures and in parables and without a parable he did not preach to them. And so David says, "I will open my mouth and speak in parables."

From such parables men are diligently to mark how all the creatures have to suffer the work of men, and come through the suffering to their end, for which they were created, and also how no man can come to salvation, save through suffering and tribulation which God works in him, as also the whole Scripture and all the creatures show nothing else but the suffering Christ in all his members.

That is why the whole of the Scriptures is described simply through creatures.

*

That is why Christ always spoke through parables, and these consist not in the speaking, but in the power and the meaning. All animals are subject unto man; if a man needs one he must first prepare, cook and roast it, and the animal must suffer. So it is with God and man: if God is to make use of us or enjoy us, we must first be justified by him and cleansed within and without: inwardly from desire and lust, outwardly from all improper behavior and misuse of creatures.

The peasant sows no corn amongst thistle, thorns, sticks and stones, but he first weeds them out and then sows afterwards. So does God with us: he sows his Word not in a man who is full of thistles or thorns or has desire and affection only towards creatures; that anxiety about bodily welfare which God forbids, must first be rooted out. The builder does not make a house out of whole trees, but first cuts them down and then fashions them as he wills, and afterwards makes a house out of them. In this way we are to learn God's Work and will towards us, which is as a man behaves with a house before he lives in it, which house (Paul says) we are.

*

Therefore all the works which we accomplish with the creatures should be our Scriptures which we closely mark. For the whole world with all creatures is a book, in which is to be seen in act all those things which are read in the written book. For all elect men from the beginning of the world until Moses have studied in the book of all creatures, and have taken knowledge of it by reason, as it is written from nature by the Spirit of God in the heart, because the whole law is expressed in creaturely works. And all men are in this wise concerned with the creatures, as the law shows, even the heathen who have not the scriptural law. The law of Scripture prescribes how a man must kill a beast before it is offered to God, and only after this was it eaten; even so do the heathen who have the law of nature, and who eat no animal alive. So we must first die to the world and live in God.

Klaassen (1981b): 50-52

The Outer and Inner Word

Ulrich Stadler, Moravia, late 1530s

*A*ll things have been ordered and made by God and are good creatures of God in which his eternal power and deity are known if one can perceive it. This includes the Scriptures and the spoken word. Therefore whoever wishes to use the Scripture with true reverence and not to attribute to it more than it deserves or belongs to it, the same must radically separate the Scriptures and the spoken word from the inner word of the heart.

The outer word is that which Christ commanded his apostles to preach when he said: "Preach the gospel of all the creatures. Whoever believes and is baptized will be saved." Here preaching, faith and baptism are all understood and handled externally and are only signs of the living Word, faith and baptism all of which God works through his righteousness. Thus also Paul says that faith comes through hearing the preaching, but hearing through the word of God.

A genuine preacher must receive the true Word of God in the abyss of his soul through much tribulation. That is the Word of God in the abyss of the soul. But the preached word is only the witness or the sign of the true Word. This eternal Word is not written on paper or tablet. Nor is it spoken or preached. God himself assures man of it in the abyss of the soul. It is written into the fleshly heart through the finger of God. This difference is also made by St. John when he says: "I do not write you a new commandment but the old commandment which you have had from the beginning. The old commandment is the Word that you have heard." There he shows that whatever one reads in books, that one hears, that one sees men do or that is in the creatures is not the living Word of God but only a letter or likeness or witness of the inner or eternal or living Word. This living Word is internally witnessed to by the outer word if one pays close attention to it. It is like a sign on an inn which witnesses to the wine in the cellar. But the sign is not the wine.

This is the order of God that something physical always precedes the spiritual. The faith that comes from hearing always precedes justification after which the enduring faith emerges and works powerfully before God and all the creatures. This takes time and does not happen quickly as our scribes say when they persuade the poor people so that they say: "Believe, believe, yes, yes."

Since the word that one hears, believes and accepts is not justified or tried it remains a witness to or the letter of the living Word. It is the opposite of the true Word like a drawn image for the sake of man. With this word the preachers deceive the poor people and point only to the witness that is preached and heard, and that one reads in books. They convince the people that it is the Word of God but the people remain for ever unsatisfied. It is evident that no improvement of life follows. O the boundless deception! With great irreparable injury the world will experience it.

The true inner Word is the eternal almighty power of God, of the same form in man as in God, which is capable of all things. It is given after perseverance in many tribulations in the discipline of the Lord. John calls this the new commandment that is true in him and in you. Only Christ under the holy cross teaches this. According to the true order of God this Word is preceded by the outer word. The preacher is to admonish by means of the external word that one should surrender and listen to the internal teacher and not to allow the people to depend upon the outer word. Otherwise preachers, Scriptures and words become idols. For they are only pictures, signs and instruments. They must disappear so that we are left without the image of the creatures as God also said to Moses.

*

Now man must confess that Christ has become flesh in him and that his flesh is ruled by the Word through the Holy Spirit. All worldly pleasure is renounced as Paul says: "I live, yet not I but Christ lives in me." The world is crucified to me and I to the world. Whoever knows Christ thus may rightly boast that he has the inner Word and can truly testify to the truth. Such preachers we need and will await from God. All the others who come without this confession and who do not get beyond the shouting of the external sound come without Christ.

Klaassen (1981b): 143-146

September 27

The Process of Birth
David Beiler, United States, 1857

Whatever comes from God also leads to God. Whatever of good there is in humanity—that through the Spirit of God is kindled or worked out—is spiritually good or godly, always making allowance for human weakness and imperfection. We must always be like Paul says, "Not that I have already attained it, or that I am already perfect, but I chase after it, so that I may capture the victor's crown; now that I am captured by Jesus Christ. My brethren, I do not make any boast that I have already laid hold of the crown. But one thing I do say: I forget the things that are behind and stretch myself toward the things that are ahead and go after the goal, the precious gem."

When by the grace of God we are this far along, it is like Paul states it, "So then, my dear brothers, we are debtors, not to live according to the flesh. For if you live according to the flesh you will have to die the death; but if by the power of the Spirit you mortify the works of the flesh you will live. For those who are living by the power of the Spirit are the children of God" (Romans 8).

If we by the working of the Spirit are renewed, turned around, changed from

Adam to Christ, from the carnal to the spiritual, and from the earthly to the heavenly—so that we can overcome the carnal lusts and desires that come up in us and seek to attract us to sin—we are experiencing the new birth. The old Adamic self of sin must by the Holy Spirit and its work in us be brought into subjection to Christ.

This would quite evidently be the denial of which Christ spoke, "If any person wants to follow after me, let him deny himself, take up his cross and follow after me. If a person cherishes his life, he will lose it; but that person who loses his life for my sake and the sake of the gospel will find it."

"Marvel not that I say to you, 'You must be born again.'" From the words of Jesus it is simple to understand that there is no assurance of salvation except by way of the new birth; because he said, "You must be born again."

Beiler (1857): 231-233, trans. by Noah G. Good

September 28

Three Questions About Our Call
Ilunga Maurice, Zaire, 1962

We are called to fulfill various tasks by Him who is our Father in Jesus Christ. When God called to Moses, He said: "I am the God of thy father, the God of Abraham, the God of Isaac and the God of Jacob." Then Moses was afraid to look upon God and he hid his face. Are we sometimes afraid to look at God as was Moses?

Why are we afraid? As human creatures, we need the Spirit's power in our hearts. We sometimes try to approach God in our natural state. As Moses had to put off his shoes, we have to put off our own ambitions. Jesus said to His disciples, "If anyone will come after me, let him deny himself, take up his cross and follow me."

Why does our God call us? This is our second question. He said to Moses, "I have surely seen the affliction of my people and have heard them. I know their sorrow; and I am come down to deliver them out of the hand of the Egyptians." One question of course is: how can He deliver His people? By means of Moses as an intermediary. God wants to deliver His people out of the Egyptians' hands. Even today, there are people in the shadow of death for whom you and I are needed as God's intermediaries. The people who have not heard the gospel, those who cannot read the Bible themselves, those who can read but can't understand the Bible's meaning.

In Acts 8:30, 31 we find these questions: "Understandest thou what thou readest?" One answer is this, "How can I, except some man should guide me?" All these people need your presence, your speaking and your abilities as God's intermediaries. God said to Moses, "Come now therefore and I will send you to

Pharaoh." He says to you and to me, "Come and I will send you to those who are in the shadow of death." *We are workers with God.*

Now, our third question is this, "What will be your answer to this call?" Moses, to this call said, first, "Who am I that I should go to Pharaoh and that I should bring forth the children of Israel out of Egypt?" Second, he said, "When the children of Israel will ask me, 'Who sent you to us,' what shall I say to them?" Third, Moses said to God, "O my Lord, I am not eloquent, I am slow of speech and of a slow tongue. But finally he said, "O Lord, send, I pray thee, by the hand of him whom thou wilt send."

*

Dear brethren, let us give ourselves now into His hands. In His hands—in Him—we lose our doubts and fears. He leads us in the path of His righteousness. We are workers with God and His eye is with us.

Dyck ([1962]): 265, 266

September 29

He Would Agree to Be Killed
Million Belete, Ethiopia, 1978

*T*he call of Jesus Christ to his kingdom is for those who are determined to follow through. He is very open about his call. He is not inviting His followers to an easy life. He admits that those following Him must take up the cross and follow Him. Many have done it and many more are doing it today.

This reminds me of a recent story which occurred in an African country. The local government rounded up a group of Christians and put them in prison saying that religion has no place in a revolution. They were of course acting on the words of Karl Marx who said, "Religion is the opiate of the people."

After a few days in prison, all were released except the evangelist. They kept him for a few more days, then said to him, "If you are prepared to sign this document, you will be released." In the document was a statement which said that he would not preach anymore; and that if he did preach, he would agree to be killed. He signed the paper and was released. When the people heard that he had been released, they asked what the conditions were. He told them he had decided to die for Jesus Christ and that he had signed to that effect. He then started to preach boldly, knowing that he would soon be killed. The story spread so rapidly in the town that the authorities found it difficult to arrest and imprison him. I understand that he is still preaching.

Kraybill ([1978]): 38, 39

The Parting Is the Hardest
Maeyken Wens, The Netherlands, 1573

A letter of this beloved martyr to her children, and the account of her death at the stake, can be found on pages 164-165.

Grace and peace from God the Father, through Jesus Christ His only begotten Son, who grant you wisdom and understanding, that you may wisely govern yourself and your children, and bring them up in the fear of God, to which end may the good Father strengthen you, and the Holy Ghost comfort you in your tribulation. This is the greeting and wish of my heart to you my dear and much beloved husband in the Lord.

After all salutation, I inform you that I am still tolerably well according to the flesh, and also according to the spirit I trust I am doing the best; but my best is nothing special, and I regret that I am not more thankful for all that comes upon me, for it is the work of the Lord. We ought to thank the Lord in adversity as well as in that which is agreeable to the flesh; for if the Lord takes all from us, He takes from us no more than what He has lent us, for it belongs to us no longer than it pleases the Lord. Oh, that I could always thank the Lord as well when the flesh suffers adversity, as when it prospers—then we can thank the Lord indeed.

O my dear friend, I should never have thought that parting should come so hard to me as it does. True the imprisonment seemed hard to me; but that was because they were so tyrannical; but now the parting is the hardest of all.

O my very dear and beloved husband, pray the Lord heartily in my behalf, to remove the conflict from me; for it is in His power, if it is His pleasure. Truly the Lord has said: "He that does not forsake everything is not worthy of me." For the Lord well knew that it would come hard to the flesh. But I hope that the Lord will also help me through even as he has helped many, and for which I can simply trust Him. Oh, how easy it is to be a Christian so long as the flesh is not put to the trial, or nothing has to be relinquished; then it is an easy thing to be a Christian.

Herewith I will conclude my letter, and commend you and your children to the Lord, that you may walk in wisdom, to the edification of your neighbor, and the salvation of your soul. I commend you to the Lord and to the rich Word of His grace: this is the good greeting and wish of my heart.

As regards further the visiting, you may do in the manner according to your pleasure; for I should indeed often desire your visit, were it not for the expense. But if you want to make your heart glad, you may come. I dare say nothing else, except that it costs so much, else I should desire to have you come soon. If you come, go to no expense in the way of bringing anything with you, as it costs far too much.

No more for this time, except that you may prosper in soul and body; this is my desire. Greet the acquaintances in the Lord much in my name, and also the friends according to the flesh. My companions also greet you much.

van Braght (1979): 981

October

"They Pushed By Not Pushing!"
James R. Klassen, United States, 1986

*H*oa, the only Vietnamese nurse working with the Montagnard staff at the clinic, told me her concerns. We also discussed our views of following Christ.

"I like your perspective about inviting people to follow Jesus instead of pushing them, but I'm terribly sad about two Vietnamese evangelists who visited my parents," she lamented. "My parents are still Buddhists, and when these two men came to the door and asked to come in, my parents naturally invited them in. These evangelists looked around the room, saw the family altar and made fun of it. They told my parents, 'You're stupid for believing in Buddha.'"

"That sure wasn't very tactful," I said.

"My parents put up with it for a while, but the two men just went on and on about how crazy it was to follow Buddha. My parents are very gentle people, but finally they got so angry that they asked the two men to leave. Is that what evangelism is all about?"

"No," I replied, "not in my thinking. Evangelism is supposed to be good news. But those two men probably figured they had done their duty in presenting the gospel to two hard-hearted unbelievers. I think God holds people more responsible after they have heard the good news, but I don't think your parents really heard the good news at all."

I thought of Phuong-Hang, the Mennonite Central Committee secretary. Just a month earlier, she had told me she had decided to follow Jesus. That exciting news and her additional comments confirmed my philosophy. She had admitted, "My friends ask me, 'Did those Mennonites force you to become a Christian?'" Chuckling, she had added, "I tell them, 'They pushed me by not pushing!'"

Klassen (1986): 108, 109

October 2

We Compel No One

Kilian Aurbacher, Moravia, 1534

*I*t is never right to compel one in matters of faith, whatever he may believe, be he Jew or Turk. Even if one does not believe uprightly or want to believe so—i.e., if he does not have or want to have the right understanding of salvation, and does not trust God or submit to him, but trusts in the creature and loves it, he shall bear his own guilt, no one will stand for him in the judgment.

And thus we conduct ourselves according to the example of Christ and the apostles and proclaim the gospel according to the grace that he has entrusted to us; we compel no one. But whoever is willing and ready, let him follow him, as Luke shows in Acts. That this then also is an open truth, that Christ's people are a free, unforced and uncompelled people, who receive Christ with desire and a willing heart, of this the Scriptures testify.

Klaassen (1981b): 293

October 3

Noah's Story, Part 1

Jan Philipsz. Schabaelje, The Netherlands, 1635

The following four readings are an account of an imaginary conversation in which Noah recounts the details of the Great Flood to a Wandering Soul who has been traveling to points in history.

Noah: I preached, prayed, entreated, exhorted them and pointed them to the ark; telling them, "Behold the time cometh that God will destroy the world by a flood, therefore am I building the ark. Repent, reform and you shall be saved. If not, you must perish and lament your impenitence when too late." But all was in vain—they increased in wickedness daily.

Wandering Soul: But how did it go with them in the end?

Noah: They saw me going on regularly with building the ark. The world increased in wickedness, drunkenness, lewdness, incontinence and all manner of fraud in weight and measure.

*

Wandering Soul: Did the people at that time not begin to reflect?

Noah: Much less than before. In no year was there so much building, so much attention paid to agriculture, so many marriages—mercantile business was never more attended to than during the year before the flood: so that it appeared foolishness to them to preach or to think that the world would be destroyed by a flood.

Wandering Soul: How wonderful, as if God was trying your faith!

Noah: As I knew that the ways of God were wondrous, I was very little startled.

Wandering Soul: Nevertheless, it was something remarkable!

Noah: Your remarks are correct; but what I have further to relate is worthy of your attention. There was in my neighborhood a wealthy and respectable man, the ruins of whose house are yet to be seen: he had four sons and three daughters married this year. At each marriage a sumptuous and splendid feast was prepared—singing and dancing, as usual. The man came to me and told what a splendid house he was about building for his eldest son, for the second son another, and so on. Each was to have a convenient house, and in addition to this, each was to have a portion of land adapted to agriculture, horticulture, etc.; and after his death each was to inherit his portion of the undivided lands. He said, "We are in duty bound to provide for our offspring."

I said to him, "My beloved friend, are you yet so ignorant? Do you not know that the world must be destroyed, and perhaps in this very year? What will then all your providing for be—would it not be much better to learn to know God, and not to be so much concerned about the things of this world?" But all that I could say availed nothing.

He began to reason with himself, saying, "Why would God do all this? He is too gracious, too merciful: he made the world and the things therein, that we should enjoy them," and so on.

I said, "Friend, you are ignorant of the mercy of God, for his mercy is to wean our affections from this world and to prepare us to enjoy another, a better world; and he will not suffer us to remain in the bondage and service of vanity and sin—all has to perish at last."

But all this was useless, he went on in his mad career; sent for the carpenters and stonecutters, laid the foundations for his houses, made ready all the materials. Some of his buildings were already in progress, some knee high, others the height of a man, when the flood came. Some of the remains are yet to be seen.

*

Wandering Soul: I am anxious to know more of this history.

Noah: Where I was residing there was a great festival. They collected from every part of the world; the market places were crowded with all manner of traffic, the taverns were crowded, wine was drunk like water. They were all exulting and triumphing; quarrelling and fighting, carousing, playing and revelling till midnight. Instead of thinking on God, they mocked, inveighed and threatened, saying, "Where is the ark-builder? It appears that the world was to have been destroyed, but we see it is all false—the ark-builder is a liar—everything will continue as it has ever been." And the like derision did they utter. I heard a great tumult at my door and a cry: "Come, carpenter, we will put an end to your world, you impostor, you are only trying to disturb us, to mar our enjoyments; you are a notorious liar." In the meantime I was prostrated before God, and prayed for them with tears, that he would not lay this sin to their charge—my whole family was praying for them during the whole night.

The next day, which was the tenth of the second month, and in the sixth hundredth year of my age, the Lord said to me: "The end of all flesh is come before me; for the earth is filled with violence through them; and, behold, I will destroy them with the earth—come thou and all thy house into the ark. For thee have I seen righteous before me in this generation, take with thee all such animals as I commanded thee, for yet seven days, and I will cause it to rain, and every living substance that I have made will I destroy from off the face of the earth." I did according unto all that the Lord commanded me.

Schabalie ([1834]): 63-67

October 4

Noah's Story, Part 2

Jan Philipsz. Schabaelje, The Netherlands, 1635

Noah: I immediately sent my sons to prepare the ark. They pitched it wherever the sun had caused a rent, after that they prepared the rooms, and the places for the animals, so that every kind might be put in its appropriate place, the larger ones together, and the lesser ones together, and such as were of the same species. To the birds was assigned the upper story, and the creeping things were also to occupy the upper story; and we occupied one of the middle chambers. Then they finished all the necessaries for us and the animals.

Wandering Soul: Father, you had much to arrange and set in order, before you had brought each in its proper place, had you not?

Noah: You are right, my son; besides that I was very much troubled on account of the impending destruction of the children of men, and I warned them again, especially my friends and acquaintances; but they did not regard my admonitions.

Wandering Soul: O their obduracy! But, tell me, how could you get the animals to come to you?

Noah: O son, with them we had no trouble. The divine Power sent them, and in such perfect order, that we were astonished at them; for scarcely were the preliminaries attended to, than came the lion and lioness as lambs. We showed them their place and they went in and laid down quietly. In like manner did the elephant come with his mate, and so did the rhinoceros, the camel, the panther, the leopard, the wolf, the bear, the dromedary, the lynx, the horse, the ass, the groundhog, the swine, the camel-leopard, the phoenix, the hyena, the gryphen, etc., etc.

Likewise did the lesser animals enter, such as the fox, the dog, the cat, the monkey, the rabbit, the squirrel, the weasel, rats, mice, etc., etc. And so did the grasshopper, the flies, silkworms and all manner of creeping things, of each one pair; but of the clean there were seven pair, such as the cow, the sheep, geese, deer, etc., etc.; all went to their places assigned them, in the most perfect order.

Wandering Soul: Father, I hear wonders; I am astonished how these animals would all lie down together, as some of them are very fierce and blood-thirsty!

Noah: God made them all tame. There was not the least difficulty on that account; even the most venomous animals were harmless; for we had dragons, different species of serpents, and other venomous animals; the chameleon, the crocodile, the hippopotamus, the otter, the beaver and the like animals.

The spider was busily engaged in weaving itself a web in the ark to catch the small insects and flies, but she, as well as the serpent, did not give any sign of her malicious nature. The wolf did not gnash his teeth at the sheep; the rhinoceros and the ichneumon did not attempt to harm the crocodile; but they were all as prisoners, endeavoring to save each others' lives.

Wandering Soul: Wonderful interference of God! How glorious a sight to see the animals enter into the ark so orderly, and especially the birds, of which you have told me nothing as yet.

Noah: This is certainly so, my son, for these came flying in on the last day; except those whose bodies are too heavy for the powers of their wings, such as the ostrich, condor, the cock and hen, the duck, partridge and all such, came in at the door. The others generally came into the ark at the window; yet in such a perfect order, that they could easily be distinguished.

Wandering Soul: O what a beautiful sight, but withal a sorrowful scene, as it was to escape such a dreadful calamity!

Noah: There came the noble and only phoenix, the beautiful bird of paradise, the halcyon and his mate, the splendid peacock and peahen, the snow-white swan, the soaring eagle, the green parrot, the crooked billed owl, the keen hawk, the lively sparrow-hawk, the camel-bird, the purple bird, the long-necked crane, the lovely and sprightly canary bird, the goldfinch, yellow and red-breasted robin, the stork, the turtle dove; and all manner of birds, such as the blood-thirsty harpy, the wouwe, the folk, the cuckoo, owls and ravens. At last came the sea gull with doleful cry, plainly foretelling, by its looks, the dreadful tempest which was hastening with acceleration to the general destruction of everything upon earth that had in it the breath of life.

Schabalie ([1834]): 67-70

Noah's Story, Part 3

Jan Philipsz. Schabaelje, The Netherlands, 1635

Noah: The same day when we went into the ark, the weather was remarkably fine; the rye was standing ripe in the fields; everything in full verdure and blossoming. Carpenters and masons were actively engaged and the resounding hammer of the smith was heard. Several houses were building; at others scaffolds were erected. Farmers were engaged in the fields at their hay. Weddings were being held. One said to another, "What fine weather we have, and what a plenteous harvest; everything appears as though the destruction of the world by the flood, was not near at hand."

And while all were merry and joyful, busily engaged in planting, farming, building, marrying and getting married, dancing and singing, without the least thought that God would deluge the world, and that we had all gone into the ark after being mocked by all who saw us build it; and when the Lord had closed the door thereof, then the heavens were spread over with thick, black, lowering clouds, and a tremendous thunderstorm, rain and hail, began—such a tempest as was never seen or heard of. Each ran to his house for shelter, thinking that all would soon be over. The sable night succeeded; nothing but tremendous thunder and the rattling hail and rain was heard. The following day some of the meadows were covered over with water, so that some concluded to drive home their cattle.

*

Noah: Their festivities were dispersed; all their merriments were ended; everyone began to think of his wife and children—but it was with much difficulty that they could get to their houses. They saw the water running into their houses; they looked with the greatest anxiety to the east and to the west, to the north and to the south, to see whether there was not some appearance of change, but there was no hope; for the rain increased every hour—it continued day and night.

On the third day they were attempting to escape to the mountains, that thus they might effect their escape, had the rain continued but for a few days; but it was otherwise. Some got upon their housetops; others climbed upon trees; others fled to the mountains, where they all were for a short time safe.

Wandering Soul: Father, please tell me, did they not then see that this tempest was caused by their sins?

Noah: O son, had you heard the pitiful and lamentable cries as the waters increased, and the roofs were swept from the houses, and the tops of the trees being covered over; mothers catching their children round their necks, men their women, friends and neighbors folding each other in their arms, seeing the dead before them; some were wringing their hands, crying and sighing, beholding the ark at a distance, which was now floating on the surface of the water, but it was too late; the day of grace was gone!

*

Noah: In a few days some of the mountaintops were not to be seen any more—here and there were to be seen roofs of houses, household furniture, trees upon which were dead carcasses, rocking cradles with children, mothers with children at their breasts, some folded in each others' arms, some on the dead carcasses of animals, birds which could fly no longer, and many other animals. There were a few of some of the highest mountains that were not wholly inundated; these were crowded with men and animals, all making a most doleful cry.

*

Wandering Soul: O how dear was their mocking and laughing to them. How painful the reflection that they did not regard the counsel of God!

Noah: They now saw that their false prophets had deceived them in explaining everything as natural occurrences, as if God had not intended to warn them through those portentous signs. What did all their temporal pleasures avail them? Their houses, their lands and their cattle were all destroyed by the flood; the mighty of the earth were no more than the poor and lowly, the tyrants were no more than those whom they sorely oppressed. In short, everyone was now convinced of his vain pursuits.

Wandering Soul: Father, you speak the truth; but be pleased to let me hear more of this history.

Noah: After a few days more, all the mountains were overflowed, so that every thing which had fled to them—all were destroyed, men and beasts, birds and insects, nothing remained alive, except what was in the ark, for it rained forty days and forty nights, so that the water was fifteen cubits high above the tops of the highest mountain before it ceased raining, so that all things perished.

Schabalie ([1834]): 71-75

October 6

Noah's Story, Part 4

Jan Philipsz. Schabaelje, The Netherlands, 1635

Noah: When the forty days' rain was over, the sky became clear, the weather calm, pleasant and agreeable; the sun began to shine, and the stars also appeared. But upon the face of the earth nothing but water was to be seen, and the ark floating upon it; for everything that had life was destroyed.

Noah: After the sun had gone down one hundred and fifty times below the blue horizon, and again arose in the purple east without his rays being obstructed from the face of the waters by trees or houses, and as he advanced in his course and entered Libra, when day and night are equal, it was then the ark struck, and stood still, which did not occasion us little joy, for we hence concluded that the waters were abating. From that time on, the mountain upon which the ark rested became more and more visible, and the waters abated daily; for which we praised God, who was mindful of us, for we were very anxious to get on dry land. When the first day of the tenth month was at hand, and the sun entered Aquarius, we saw the mountains' tops appear, and we concluded that the ark rested in the highest mountain in Armenia, whereof the remains of that mountain bear testimony to this day.

Wandering Soul: Did not the beasts and the birds give some evidence of joy?

Noah: As long as the sun retrograded towards the south they appeared to be dejected; but as soon as the sun approached the zenith and entered Aquarius, some of the animals were heard. Especially the fowls of the air—the lark began carolling most sweetly. The raven seemed to have smelled the dead carcasses; he began to croak and sought the window. When I saw all these signs I began to suspect that the waters had measurably abated. I opened the window on the tenth day of the month, Shebath, as the sun was entering the Pisces, and let out the raven, and he flew to and fro, from one hill to another, which was a sure sign that the waters were not all dried up, although the raven did not return into the ark.

*

Noah: I waited seven days longer, and then let out the dove, who on her return brought welcome intelligence, for she brought an olive branch in her mouth. This was a sure evidence that the waters had abated so much that the trees were everywhere visible. This took place on the twenty-fifth day of Shebath. Seven days afterwards I let out another dove; but this returned not again.

*

Noah: To the delight of the animals and myself, I uncovered the ark; and thus giving free vent to the pure and vivifying air, although none desired to go out of the ark until God gave the command, on the 27th day of the second month, that I, my wife, my sons, their wives, with the animals and all creeping things, should go out of the ark.

Wandering Soul: Was there not great joy among the animals when their emancipation was announced?

Noah: Their joy is not to be described. And how orderly they were in going out when we had prepared the way before them.

Wandering Soul: Be pleased to tell me concerning your coming out of the ark.

Noah: This I will very briefly tell you. After we came out of the ark on Mount Ararat's lofty summit, all the animals followed us by pairs as they entered into the ark, evincing a great degree of sprightliness—leaping and skipping, feeding upon the grass of the earth, which they had not seen during a confinement of one year and ten days. And after I had selected a few to sacrifice, as well as from among the clean birds, as from among the other animals, they all dispersed, each to his respective place.

The herbaceous went into places where was grass; the carnivorous prowled about and lived on dead carcasses; the aquatics retired to fens, marshes and waters; the fowls of the air made for the forests, carolling and praising their Creator—especially the sweet-singing nightingale. Everything that had a tuneful voice was heard to proclaim the great Creator's praise; neither the cuckoo nor the owl could refrain bringing their tribute of praise.

*

Wandering Soul: Father, two questions present themselves which you can answer at once.

Noah: What questions are they?

Wandering Soul: The first is, in what condition did you find the world when you came out of the ark? The other, what was your occupation?

Noah: To answer your last question, I have to tell you as soon as I came out of the ark, and before we descended from the mountain, I built an altar unto the Lord, and offered a burnt-offering for the preservation of our lives. For as every creature is influenced by its *sui generis* (its like), so we, the head of creation, are influenced by our kindred in heaven. And being thus drawn by love, I offered the Lord a sweet-smelling sacrifice—incense of clean animals; and prayed God most devoutly, that he would be pleased to become reconciled, and destroy the human family no more. And the Lord accepted of the sweet smell of the burnt sacrifice; and the Lord said in his own heart, "I will not again curse the ground anymore for man's sake; for the imaginations of man's heart is evil from his youth. Neither will I again smite any more everything living, as I have done. While the earth remaineth, seedtime and harvest, and cold and heat, and summer and winter, and day and night, shall not cease" (Genesis 8:12, 22).

Schabalie ([1834]):76-82

October 7

Why Wash Feet?

Dirk Philips, Poland(?), ca. 1560

The third ordinance is the foot washing of the saints, which Jesus Christ commanded his disciples, and that for two reasons. The first is to give us the knowledge that he himself must cleanse us in the internal person, and we must let the sin which clings so closely, the soiling of the flesh and spirit, be washed away by him, that we may become cleaner day by day, just as it is written. So whoever is clean becomes even cleaner; who is holy becomes even holier; and who is just becomes even more just. And that is necessary, yes, must happen, so that we will be saved.

Therefore Christ said to Peter, "Unless I wash you, you shall have no part in me." Then Peter answered, "Lord, not only the feet, but also the hands and head. Thereupon Christ answered, "Whoever is thus washed needs nothing more than that one wash his feet and he is entirely clean." Thereby he certainly made known that the foot washing (where Christ joins us in washing) is very necessary, and what that signifies, since those whom he does not wash shall have no part with him. And that those who are washed by him do not need more than that their feet shall be washed, and they are entirely clean.

For it is Christ who must wash us from our sins with his blood. And thus those who are sprinkled and washed need nothing more than that the earthly body, the evil lusts and desires of the flesh, will be dead through the Spirit and conquered by him. Thus he is entirely clean out of grace and no sin will be reckoned to him.

The second reason why Christ has instituted foot washing is that we should humble ourselves one to another, and hold the companions of our faith in great esteem; for this reason, that they are the saints of God and members of Jesus Christ; and that the Holy Spirit lives in them. This Christ teaches us with these words: "You call me Lord and Master, and you speak truly about that, for so I am. Thus if I then your Lord and Master have washed your feet, so should you also wash one another's feet. I have given you the example that you should do the same as I have done to you. Truly, truly, I say to you, the servant is not greater than his Lord, and the apostle is not more than the one who has sent him. If you know this, blessed are you if you do that. Be now the blessed who know such and do it" (John 13:14-17).

Dirk (1992): 367, 368

October 8

It Outlived Any Sermon
Robert J. Baker, United States, 1969

*T*he most impressive act I ever witnessed in the fellowship of the believers occurred at the Prairie Street Mennonite Church when I was a teenage boy. That is over thirty-five years ago. And yet the experience is as fresh in my mind as if it were happening this moment in this very room.

It involved two people, one now deceased, the other living today far away from this city of Elkhart, Indiana, where the original memorable event took place. In another sense, however, it involved us all in that church that day. It was hidden from none; it was open to all. What I saw has outlived any sermon I ever heard.

I was sitting near the rear of the church when the tall man came down the aisle. He stopped several benches ahead of me, signaled to a particular man, leaned over and whispered a few words. I was close, but I could not hear the words. Yet I knew what he said. The expression on his face was one of great tenderness and love. I thought he was about to cry. Later he did cry. Knowing what was taking place in that church during that particular service, I did not have to hear the actual words he spoke. I could read his slightly moving lips; I knew why he was there. And my boyish heart was strangely stirred.

*

When I was a boy, kind brethren in the church who knew of the poverty of our family arranged for me to work on Saturdays and after school at a local store that employed only Mennonites at that time. I had not been at that place of employment very long before I realized that two of the brethren did not get along. They had periodic misunderstandings. Voices would be raised and anger was present. As a new Christian I could not understand these differences, the harsh words. I was puzzled, disturbed, hurt.

That Sunday at the Prairie Street Mennonite Church some four pews ahead of me the two men faced one another. The words the tall man said to the older brother on the church bench, the words I could lip-read, were the whispered words, "May I wash your feet?"

*

I watched those two brethren walk to the front of the church. The tall one took a towel from the bench and gently motioned the other to be seated. Both of them were barefoot.

The tall one knelt down, girded himself with the towel and tenderly washed his brother's feet. Then they exchanged places and the act was repeated. They both arose, the towel was laid aside and they stood facing one another in front of that church. The clock stood still; time was frozen for a microsecond; it was like a beautiful painting.

Their faces glistened with tears. Then action once more, gentle, gentle action. They pressed their lips to one another's cheeks. Then it was over, yet it was never over. By that brief act of washing one another's feet they dissolved all the puzzlement, disturbance, hurt that swirled within a young boy's heart.

Hertzler (1983): 145

October 9

Jesus' Way of Love

Pyarelal Malagar, India, 1948

*T*he pattern of life which Jesus left behind in the world is the way of love. This is made plain to us through His teachings and life as recorded in the Gospels. His words in the Sermon on the Mount are still remarkable in this respect.

*

Jesus' way of love implies, therefore, courage to suffer persecution without resentment and retaliation, renunciation of our legitimate rights in the face of opposition, a tolerant and charitable attitude toward our enemies, and nonresistance to evil. To be able to suffer and to sacrifice is the quintessence of Jesus' way of love. Physical force and armament is contrary to the spirit and teaching of Christ. "They that take the sword shall perish with the sword."

Confucius of China was once asked how he would sum up his religion in one word and he exclaimed—"reciprocity." If we were to put the same question to Christianity, what would the answer be? It would undoubtedly be "love"—not of a sentimental type that has no strength and soon withers away, but rugged like the love of the cross. The cross is the emblem of ignominy and shame, but it is also the emblem of self-giving love. Bearing our cross, therefore, would mean living Jesus' way of love.

It is very significant how Mahatma Gandhi, the great political leader of India, adapted a form of this way of love in his political struggle for the freedom of his country and was a great success at it. Three things in which he believed were nonviolence, truth and tolerance. It was a great experiment in the political field on a national basis. Is it not a shame that the great leaders of the so-called Christian countries believe in armament and conscription and go on preparing for war to end war!

The Mennonite Church has believed in this way of life—of nonresistance to evil—since its inception, and has advocated the validity and reasonableness of this Scriptural truth both during war and peace, and we may do well to live up to it. The denial of our own profession will be a great handicap to our Christian lives; mere lip service will be sheer hypocrisy. I believe Jesus' way of love is the natural way, and we must live this way of love if we would save this sin-sick, war-weary world from being plunged into further ruin and disaster.

Hiebert (1950): 121, 122

A Marriage Supper
Melchior Hoffman, Germany, 1530

When now the bride of the Lord Jesus Christ has given herself over to the Bridegroom in baptism, which is the sign of the covenant, and has betrothed herself and yielded herself to him of her own free will and has thus in very truth accepted him and taken him unto herself, thereupon the Bridegroom and exalted Lord Jesus Christ comes and by his hand—the apostolic emissaries are the hand—takes bread (just as a bridegroom takes a ring or a piece of gold) and gives himself to his bride with the bread (just as the bridegroom gives himself to his bride with the ring) and takes also the chalice with the wine and gives to his bride with the same his true bodily blood, so that just as the bride eats a physical bread in her mouth and drinks the wine, so also through belief in the Lord Jesus Christ she has physically received and eaten the noble Bridegroom with his blood in such a way that the Bridegroom and the outpouring of his blood is one with hers—and the broken and crucified Christ Jesus. She is in him and, again, he is in her, and they together are thus one body, one flesh, one spirit and one passion, as bridegroom and bride.

Yea, more. The bride is in truth assured the moment she takes the bread that she has accepted the true Christ for her Lord and Head and eternal Bridegroom in order that ever thereafter his will, spirit, mind and good pleasure may be in her and that she on her part gives herself over unto his will with all her heart, spirit, feeling and will.

*

In such a manner as has been above recounted, a perky little bride, when she receives her engagement ring from her bridegroom, could speak to her childhood playmates and friends, showing it to them: "Look here, I have my bridegroom Jack, Nick or Peter." Now those who hear such words and see the ring understand very well how the bride intends this kind of language, namely, that she does not mean that the ring is physically the bridegroom himself or that the bridegroom is physically contained in the ring but that she has with all her heart, spirit and emotion received a bridegroom by virtue of his will, word, spirit and intention.

It was surely in this sense that the apostles of the Lord Jesus Christ likewise understood the words when the Lord took the bread and gave therewith his body and with the wine his own quickening blood.

*

They understood that through the bread and belief in the Word they should receive that body which sat by them there, that that same body should be their own which would be burned at the cross. And they believed that theirs also was the physical blood which would be poured out from the cross. Such a simple explanation stolid fisherfolk could well understand even when they were still in the first birth, but one over which the wise and greatest scholars of Scripture for their part have become fools and madmen, and still are. They clash and break themselves over such simple words which were said and enacted in a quite straightforward way as by any other human being.

Williams and Mergal (1957): 193-195

October 11

Oh, Delightful Assembly!
Menno Simons, The Netherlands, 1539

*O*h, delightful assembly and Christian marriage feast, commanded and ordained by the Lord Himself! Here no carnal pleasures, the flesh and appetites, but the glorious and holy mysteries, by means of the visible signs of bread and wine, are represented to and sought by true believers.

Oh, delightful assembly and Christian marriage feast, where take place no improper and shameful mockery, and no senseless songs; but the pious Christian life, peace and unity among all the brethren. The joyous word of divine grace moreover, His glorious benefits, favor, love, service, tears, prayers, His cross and death, are set forth and urged with delightful thanksgiving and joy.

Oh, delightful assembly and Christian marriage feast to which the impenitent and proud despisers are, according to Scripture, not invited: the harlots, rogues, adulterers, seducers, robbers, liars, defrauders, tyrants, shedders of blood, idolaters, slanderers, etc.; for such are not the people of the Lord. But they are invited who are born of God, true Christians who have buried their sins and who walk with Christ in a new and godly life. They are invited who crucify the flesh and are driven by the Holy Spirit; who sincerely believe in God, seek, fear and love Him, and in their weakness willingly serve and obey Him, for they are members of His body, flesh of His flesh, bone of His bone.

Oh, delightful assembly and Christian marriage feast, where no gluttonous eating and drinking are practiced, nor the wicked vanity of pipes and drums is heard; but where the hungry consciences are fed with the heavenly bread of the divine Word, with the wine of the Holy Ghost, and where the peaceful, joyous souls sing and play before the Lord.

Menno (1956): 148

A Colony of Strangers

Lawrence Hart, United States, 1992

*I*n the 1830s a Frenchman travelled throughout the United States, taking copious notes along the way. When Alexis de Tocqueville returned to France, he wrote a book that has become a classic, a piercing analysis of life on this continent.

De Tocqueville wrote of the indigenous Americans as a "colony of strangers in the midst of numerous people." I give him credit and respect for not referring to us as "Savages," the word then in vogue. "A colony of strangers in the midst of numerous people."

In the 1830s, the Supreme Court decided that state governments have no jurisdiction on Indian reservations. Attorneys today still use this landmark case as they seek to defend the sovereignty of the various Indian nations in the United States.

Those 1830s events began to alter the relationships between those who came to this country and those who were here. When the French first encountered my own tribe, the Cheyenne, they thought that we were without religion, without political systems and without law.

But yes, we did have a political system. Yes, we did have a religion. Yes, we did have a code of law. One of our culture's aspects that I seek to retain is our council of 44 chiefs. They are called peace chiefs, for they make a commitment when selected to live a life of peace, no matter what the cost. They seek to be peacemakers within their own tribe and with other tribes and peoples.

When I think of the legacy of our peace chiefs, I think of Lean Bear and of White Antelope.

Lean Bear was privileged to meet with President Abraham Lincoln. Lincoln gave him a peace medal and a document verifying that he was at peace and friendly. Yet as he rode unarmed toward a column of troops to show them the document, he was shot and killed. He died violently as a peacemaker.

White Antelope, too, died violently as a peacemaker at Sand Creek, Colorado, in 1864. White Antelope was a peace chief who had been at a meeting just a month before with the territorial governor and a colonel. When he saw troops approach his village, he thought it was a mistake and he cried out for them to stop. When he saw it was a deliberate attack, he did not seek to defend himself. He stood there and began to sing.

He sang a chant of the peace chiefs. "Nothing lives long except the earth and the mountains. Nothing lives long except the earth and the mountains." Many times I think of those words and they remind me of the psalmist, "O Lord, thou hast been our dwelling place in all generations. Before the mountains were brought forth, or ever thou hadst formed the earth and the world, from everlasting to everlasting thou art God."

The psalmist refers to generations. To the earth. To the mountains. And so does White Antelope, even though he didn't know Psalm 90. But the commanding officer of the militia that attacked Sand Creek did know it. He was an ordained minister. Only a few people escaped that massacre; one was the little girl who would become my great-great grandmother.

After the 1830s, times gradually began to change. Soon after the Civil War, the Quakers urged President Grant to initiate a peace policy in dealing with the various tribal groups. More than that, the Quakers made themselves available as government agents in the frontiers so that peaceful relations could be developed. And this did occur.

I have been grateful to those who are a part of the historic peace church tradition since then. We have come to know the good news, the good news of the gospel that respects who we are. The good news that Jesus gives life to us, too.

Hart (1992)

October 13

Plead the Cause of Harmony
Uli Ammann, France, ca. 1720

We are obligated and duty-bound to aid and support faithful ministers and church leaders in the church of the Lord; they are a gift of God. Nor should we leave everything to them and unjustly tread on their toes, nor should we receive any accusation against them, except before two or three witnesses. We should love and respect them and give them the honor and service that is their due.

*

We also consider it necessary and good that a minister be zealous in keeping order by maintaining the old customary practices of the church, and not do much that is new and out of the ordinary, or to break with the old. It is better to hold to the teachings of the divine Word and break down the old sinful life of men and implant a new godly life.

If, however, something that is unhelpful and contrary to the Word of the Lord would be the practice in the church, it must of necessity be dropped and in its place a better practice should be begun in harmony with the Lord's Word. This we believe should indeed be done; but no one should take upon himself the authority to do it without the knowledge and counsel of other ministers and elders. Tobit says, "Always ask counsel of the wise" (Tobit 4). Also "Never do anything without counsel, and afterwards you will have no regrets" (Sirach 32:18).

It is, of course, possible that a congregation may have a practice not found in another, of only unimportant and minor nature not in conflict with the Word of the Lord; against such things there should be no complaining, but one should rather plead the cause of love and peace.

Bender (1977): 3

October 14

Community Across Borders
María Janeth Albarracín, Colombia, 1990

Once the Mennonite brothers and sisters had taught me to live in Christ, and the peace I felt in my heart was absolutely real, I decided to leave the Mennonite community to serve as a missionary for the Lord. Because of the Mennonite foundation that Christians should help one another, I began my voluntary work in health and nutrition in Burkina Faso (Africa), allowing me to put into practice what Jesus teaches us in the New Testament and deepening my faith, peace and hope. "You shall be my witnesses," Jesus said to his disciples before he ascended into heaven, and now I feel like one of his witnesses in the community where I work.

One of my main preoccupations is the lack of personal evangelism. In other words, today more emphasis is put on sharing the message to the masses and not enough attention is given to the individual. For that reason, it would be good for the Mennonites to reflect on this situation and develop a program of personal evangelism. On the other hand, the lack of Mennonite churches in countries where there is much poverty has meant that those less favored do not have the opportunity to share the peace, hope and love of God. I invite the Mennonite brothers and sisters to reflect on this poverty and to go to those places.

It would be good for all Mennonites in the world to communicate with each other and to know what activities they are involved in. I would like the Mennonites to support each other spiritually and to see them carefully study the Mennonite Christian beliefs in their churches. In these times in which we live, I like the work the Mennonites are doing toward peace, understanding and comprehension of other religious philosophies, trying to become one in Christ.

One of my personal experiences while I was serving in Burkina Faso was how those of other churches totally accepted me as a Mennonite. I understood then that all the Christian churches, although they have different names, have the same focus, that is, forgiveness and salvation in Jesus Christ. I also saw that the African Christians are more united because they do not take the denomination so much into account, but instead the strongest view and concern is being one in Christ. If I can make a bit of a comparison with Christians in general, the African Christians are growing stronger in faith.

I am completely convinced that it is not our religion that saves us but our faith and our intimate relationship with God. We can have this relationship wherever we are, without needing to go someplace else to find it. The Lord manifests himself through our lives for the good of humanity and, in one way or another, the Mennonite brothers and sisters provide support for beginning to live in Christ. Being a Mennonite has taught me to live faithfully. It has shown me the correct road while at the same time has provided many satisfactions and opportunities for new experiences. It is in this way that I feel whole and secure in all the facets of my life.

Lichdi (1990): 35, 36

October 15

I Hope To Meet a Merciful Judge
Christian Stoltzfus, United States, 1869

I often have to think of it, especially at night when I often lie sleepless on my bed. After all, how are we poor mortals to do everything which the Great Prophet teaches us in His Gospel? I believe that I have fallen far short of doing everything that I am responsible to do. And I dare not say that I, unprofitable bond-servant, have as yet even once done all that I am responsible for. And even if I should say that I have done all that I am responsible to do, I am fearful that my daily commissions and omissions, and my imperfections would not wholly show it. Then I find comfort in the Word of God, because I believe that good intent is acceptable as genuine, that our Creator knows what poor, weak creatures we are, and that we even yet must strive against an evil enemy.

Yes, says a writer: "On this journey I have three enemies who are constantly against me: the devil, the world and, in addition to them, my own flesh and blood. O God, keep me in your care. Is it not a fact that there are three enemies with which we have to strive? And I believe that my flesh and blood are for me not the smallest of the three.

*

Yes, beloved brother, if we read and meditate on the Holy writ, then we can learn from it that the old patriarchs, prophets and apostles also at times sensed their weakness, but also at times were strong and invincible. Paul says that he knows that neither life nor death, neither angels nor principalities, nor any other creature can separate him from the love of Jesus (Romans 8:38-39) and so on. And the king and prophet David, how much at times he grieved over himself, yet he was nevertheless a man after God's heart. And again at times he was so strong that he says: "With my God I can jump over walls and put soldiers to rout" (Psalm 18:29) and so on.

*

I need to confess that if I regard my poverty and imperfection, I dare not and cannot say truthfully that I have done what I am responsible to do, so I do not dare to, nor can say truthfully that I have received such witness. But yet I hope and believe that the loving heavenly Father is moved to pity me, poor sinner, and that He wants to forgive my past sins if I am to appear before Him on that great judgment day. But through unending grace and mercy, and the price of the shed blood of Jesus Christ, I hope to meet a merciful judge.

Paton Yoder (1987): 147, 148

October 16

Grace to the Humble

John M. Brenneman, United States, 1866

A man, thus truly penitent and humble in heart, truly turning to God, sincerely seeking him day and night in prayer and supplication, wholly offering himself in sacrifice to him, humbly submitting to his powerful hand, and desirous henceforth to live and continue faithful in his service to the end—such a man is, in the Scriptures, called a humble man. And such are they to whom God gives *grace*. As, for example, the woman who was a sinner, and humbled herself at the feet of Jesus, washing them with tears and wiping them with the hairs of her head, unto whom he said, "Thy sins are forgiven. Thy faith hath saved thee: go in peace." All such penitent and humble sinners, seeking grace, shall obtain it of God through Jesus Christ. For "where sin abounded, *grace* did much more abound."

*

Grace is, therefore, the opposite of merit; for when a man gives me that which he owes me, and which I have earned by labor, he gives it to me, not out of grace, but out of indebtedness. But if any one bestows on me good gifts, which I have not merited and which he does not owe me, he bestows them on me purely out of grace.

*

In like manner God has made us partakers of his grace, for he does not owe us any thing; but on the other hand we owe him ten thousand pounds, and have not one farthing with which to pay this great debt. But God will remit it out of pure *grace*, if we but with true penitence of heart humble ourselves before him and confess our sins before him, feel sorry on account of them, and from our heart pray to him in the name of Jesus for pardon; then "he *giveth grace*" to us.

*

Through grace we are regenerated and born anew, and accepted through Jesus Christ as children, and made heirs of his eternal and heavenly kingdom; that is *"he giveth grace to the humble."* He gives grace to them even in this life, insomuch as he pardons their sins and blesses them in body and soul with all manner of good gifts; and in the life to come he bestows on them eternal and heavenly gifts and possessions, and eternal joy, rest and happiness. Oh how unspeakably great is this promise, "He giveth grace to the humble!" For the grace of God is of ten-thousand times greater value than the whole world with all its pleasure, pomp, honor and glory can ever be.

*

I believe sincerely that whoever cannot content himself with the sufficiency of God's grace can never have any real enjoyment; for the grace of God is sufficient for us in time and in eternity. If we are partakers of his grace and confide in it, we have all that we need in order to become happy, glorified and blessed in this world and in the world to come; and what more can we wish? But bear in mind, this grace is given only to the *humble*.

Brenneman (1866): 30-32

October 17

Dreaming of Nature and Life
Anna Baerg, Soviet Union, 1918

October 17: Such beautifully warm days like today come seldom in life and then only in the fall. A mood pervades the world like a beautiful memory—and yet, I cannot understand why, is it the present that is so beautiful—or do all of these presentiments of happiness belong to the future? And if after many years I should look at my diary, then this day is sure to be recorded and I will find myself lying on the river bank dreaming of nature and life. What will it be like then? Will I feel the same impressions I do now? If it were always as quiet and spellbinding as now, and there were no struggles and victories, would one really be able to appreciate days such as this one? I think not, for only in struggle does one learn to treasure happiness and peace.

October 20: It's a glorious Sunday evening. I lie at the open window of our little room and write in the moonlight. What a holy spectacle, such a moonlit night, and yet the more one looks at the bright heavenly light, the darker it seems down below—yes, it is as if the earth were entirely lost in the shadows.

Baerg (1985): 30

October 18

The Flying Saucer
J. Ward Shank, United States, 1961

*I*t was on October 18, 1961, about 3:30 p.m. The day was clear and bright. I was standing in the shadow of a building on our farm when I heard the sound of a jet plane passing overhead. As I often do, I looked up to see if there might be a contrail or glint of sun on the plane high in the air.

Then I saw it. It was moving rapidly to the westward. In fact, it seemed to be moving unusually fast, even for a jet plane. Next I noticed that it was of somewhat unusual shape, more square than the sweptback or delta wings of a jet. It appeared to be very high in the sky, with the sun reflecting from it as it moved. Soon it seemed to change direction and turn in a huge arc back toward the east, even while the sound diminished. My heart jumped. Was I seeing a space ship, a visitor from another planet? I wished that I might have my binoculars, my camera. Then it flew faster and faster, until—

It was then that I realized what I had seen—a fluff of thistledown floating in the sunshine scarcely fifty feet away. Looking up to try to see a jet plane that I had really heard, I became the victim of an amusing optical illusion.

When I told my wife, we laughed heartily over my little fantasy. But how often, under certain circumstances, might our minds come under a strong impression of something unreal? We then tell it as a fact, as reality. People are prone to believe what we tell with sincerity, and so a tale gets started. Some may even be unwilling to believe us in our illusion, but are still unable to deny our fantastic tale because we tell it with an air of assurance and finality.

Much that we hear has little better relation to fact than that floating thistledown had to the reality of a flying saucer. Hundreds of stories float around our communities and through church circles which have little basis in reality. They are not harmless and amusing, like floating thistledown, but often tarnish or destroy reputation.

Sometimes our perspective may be extremely faulty. Nearby things may appear distant and distant things appear to be near. Mountains may seem to be molehills and molehills may seem to be mountains. Serious problems may be regarded as insignificant by some of us, while the side issues loom all out of proportion. It is often helpful to sense how God looks at things, or how they will appear to us in the light of eternity.

Now, someone is bound to tell us that they've really seen a flying saucer. I wouldn't deny it, and neither would I deny their possible existence. I am simply awaiting better evidence. What I like is the stability of fact, the reality of my faith in God, and the actuality of the spiritual and eternal world.

Shank (1988): 167

October 19

The Seed of Happiness
Eberhard Arnold, Germany, ca. 1920

*J*esus' concern was to show His friends and all those who listened to Him the character of the world order to come and of its people. At that time—as today—everyone waited for the new order in man's innermost being and at the same time in the political and economic conditions of nations. People longed for a new kingdom of that justice of which the prophets had spoken. They knew from the prophets and felt with the certainty of the religious conscience that this justice of the prophetic state of the future had to be a social justice. They knew that this social justice must be set up so close to love and grace that it is identical with love. In God's heart, justice and grace dwell so close to one another that the movement of heart they signify is one and the same.

Then Jesus came, and He disclosed this justice to men, both in the depths of its nature and in its practical consequences. He showed them that the justice of the future state must be of an order completely different from that moralistic justice of the pious and holy who until then had felt they were the ones who represented justice. Through His own nature and by the clear words He spoke, He revealed that the justice God does is a living, growing power that develops organically within us, a life process that takes place in accordance with sacred laws of life.

Because of this, Jesus could not stand before men to give them commands about the right way to conduct themselves. He came to them in a very different way. In spirit and in truth He discerned the nature of those who had God's righteousness. He presented their character to men's eyes in this way: "Full of bliss, happy are they who have this character, for they see God; to them belongs the kingdom of the future; they shall inherit the earth; they shall be comforted and satisfied; as sons of God they shall obtain mercy."

Because Jesus himself radiated in His nature the organic unity of all the characteristic traits of this spirit of the future, it was impossible for anyone to try to tear any one sentence of His out of its context and set it up by itself as a law. If anyone places pacifistic action or purity of heart or any other moral or political demand by itself and uses this to claim and set up the new, he is on the wrong track. Certainly it is not possible to take part in God's kingdom without purity of heart, without vigorous work for peace; but unless the good tree is planted, the good fruit cannot be harvested. Unless the change extends to all areas, it is a lost cause to try to emulate Christ in one sphere only.

The Beatitudes cannot be dismembered. They portray the heart of the comrade of the Kingdom, and his veins cannot be cut apart. Because of this they begin and end with the same promise of possessing the kingdom of heaven. Because of this each one begins with the same attribute of inner happiness.

Arnold (1967): 23-25

Questions About Colonialism
Pieter Jansz., Indonesia, 1861

The first modern Mennonite foreign missionary complains of the colonial policies and practices of his native land.

So many things can be listed in which our people dishonor the name of Christ as well as that of the Dutch for these heathen in the Indies: general conduct and behavior; seduction of native girls by Dutch men (by Christians!), the Dutch, of high or low rank publicly whoring and dancing with Javanese prostitutes; exclusion of the Bible in Dutch schools, family devotions sadly neglected everywhere; public religion a dead form; the name of God misused by nearly everyone; the gospel openly and generally called a fable; atheism and free-thinking even taught to the Javanese; requiring the swearing of oaths upon their false gods and errors contrary to God's Word; the all-too-evident worldly goal with which the Dutch come here!; the methods of governing according to the right of the strongest and the rules of self-interest; the pressure of military service and compulsory labor; the crying injustice suffered by the humble Javanese at the hands of their own leaders under Dutch rule! All these things are sufficient to explain why the indigenous peoples show by word and behavior, and sometimes by a frank declaration, that they "do not want Christianity *because it is presented to them by the Dutch!*"

Is it not horrible: Did we receive the blessing of the gospel in our beloved homeland to make the heathen revile it and to despise it ourselves? Did the Almighty *therefore* redeem us from the tyranny of the papacy and superstition through streams of blood of our forefathers, and did the Eternal give his beloved Son—given for us and for the whole world including the Javanese—in order to have us now, rather than bringing them the saving Word of God, sell them opium that brings death and destruction, poverty and misery? Can true blessing rest upon the Dutch treasury, as long as one penny from such a trade flows into it, as long as that trade is carried on by or for the government, or only with its approval in order to derive the profits from it?

Netherlanders, does not a curse cling to the favorable balance of trade from the Indies? Has God given us so many physical and moral privileges, beyond all these peoples, in order that we may deprive them of their beloved and sacred freedom, by the law of the strongest, to force them to work for us, to support us, to make us rich and powerful with the output of their country, leaving them no more than what is absolutely necessary for a very modest living, and to make them a footstool on which we try to elevate ourselves, and which we strengthen only to the extent necessary to carry our weight?

Shenk (1980): 92, 93

A God-Freed Culture

Gerhard G. Giesbrecht, Paraguay, 1984

*T*he Indians in the Chaco who have already lived for decades among the Mennonites and who enjoy their food, clothes and other advantages are basically still rooted in their own culture. They want to be Christians; they want to be free from their fear of evil spirits. However, when their father, mother or one of their relatives dies, their belief in evil spirits surfaces. They want to seek the person who caused the death and revenge themselves on him. The medicine man was their mediator between themselves and the demon world, as well as between them and their neighbors. The medicine man had the power to preserve life or destroy it. He took the initiative when his people expressed interest in a common life as a clan. They ate, they celebrated, they abhorred death together.

*

After ten years of hearing God's word, it found entrance into many Indian hearts. Without the missionaries giving them the rules to follow about what they were allowed to do or not do, they voluntarily quit smoking. They considered exchanging of marriage partners unlawful. They avoided the celebration of the puberty rites because unfaithfulness to their marriage partners occurred at these celebrations. They had experienced Christ in their culture and they abstained from many negative practices which were sin.

*

I wonder several things about the Indians. Are they, in their group, happy as Christians? Is their group organized so that sin is controlled and not allowed to run rampant? Do they allow themselves to be taught by God's word?

My questions are answered when I see a Lengua Indian sitting by the bedside of his sick wife, quietly talking to her, gently stroking her arm. When I see the church collect money for a church project. When a mother gets her child ready for school and sends a snack along. When a man goes to work daily and brings back enough food for his family. When I see the sick person gently being carried to the wagon in order to be interned in the hospital, and, in the case of his death, being buried after a message was brought at the graveside.

*

We must admit that our German-Mennonite culture differs greatly from that of the Indian. However, what does this matter as long as our service and our faith is shared according to God's word? Emperor Friederich Wilhelm the Great coined the maxim, "Each shall be happy in his own way." One could say it this way: Both the Indians in their co-existence with other Indians, and the Mennonites with their belief in God and doing His service, may find happiness through a "God-freed" culture. In this way an Indian in the Chaco becomes an Indian for the second time. And a German becomes a German for the second time.

Giesbrecht (1984): 15

October 22

Keep These Customs!
J.D. Moyo, Zimbabwe, 1967

*A*frica is a large continent with many tribes in it. These tribes have many different customs, and customs are borrowed or copied from one tribe to another. You will find today a mixture of customs among African people. I want to mention some customs which I feel that Africans should keep.

To give and receive with both hands shows that one is respectful and humble. It is an insult to receive something from an elderly person with only one hand. It is also an insult to give with one hand—especially the left hand.

It is a sign of respect and humility to kneel when giving food to grown-ups. I think it is very bad for African women to stand when giving food to people. If food is to be served from the table, it is a good thing for a woman to kneel after everything is prepared and say, "Food is ready." Education and civilization should not destroy Africans' respect and humility.

Sit down to speak to an elderly person. With Africans it is considered very rude to stand when one is speaking to an elderly person. Sitting down to talk shows respect.

Hair left standing at the top of the head showed that a woman was married. This was an important sign. Why do African people despise this good custom? They can keep this custom and still use their headdresses which make them look dignified and Christian. I believe that Africans had good reason to leave this hair up and keep it clean. It was a big marriage crown.

Long dresses for married women. Long before Africans knew anything about civilization, Christianity and education, they made a big difference in their way of dressing. Women wore long dresses while girls wore short dresses—and not too short, either! In many cases today girls and women dress alike. Sometimes you can hardly tell if someone is married or not.

Children not to come in when elders are speaking. In the past it was a bad thing for a child to come in when elders were speaking, unless the child was given permission to do so. In general, this custom is still good.

Obedience and generosity. I asked an old man what good customs he felt should be kept. Do you know what he said? "Obedience and generosity," was his reply. He said Africans used to be very obedient and generous. They gave food without asking money for it. The first thing they thought of when a person came into their home was to see that he had something to eat, and this was free. The old man also said that love is something that is getting finished with Africans. There was a time when it was a big pleasure to keep cousins, nephews and orphans, but today this is a bother and a burden. Each person seems to live for himself and this should not be so.

To answer well when being called. Good mothers, fathers and children should always answer, "Baba" or "Ma," not "We," when being called by other members of the family.

It is very unAfrican to divorce one's wife. Africans kept their wives before they knew the Lord. How much more should they keep them after they have been married to each other as the Church is married to Jesus Christ?

Africans should keep their hair as it is and not try to change it and make it look like the white man's hair. Neither should they try to make their faces look like the face of a white person.

We Africans have many good things in our culture. We should not be quick to throw it all away, but should choose between good and bad customs.

Moyo (1967): 6

October 23

A General Campaign Against Evil
Eberhard Arnold, Germany, 1923

In its early years, the society organized by Eberhard Arnold attracted members from the Free German Youth Movement. The Youth Movement sought a fresh start for civilization after the First World War. Arnold shared this idealism.

*I*t is certain that in the here and now, as we are, there is no sinless state. But the way people everywhere speak nowadays about the necessity of evil and about men's common bondage in guilt unquestionably leads to something like consent to involvement in guilt. People ironically dismiss the world peace to which the prophets witness, the elimination of government proclaimed in John's Revelation, the overcoming of the present social order which comes with brotherhood in church community; they dismiss the communal life which should be—and has been again and again—the self-evident expression of true love. The irony with which people try to dismiss all these things shows quite clearly that in all these critical areas they no longer want to take a stand against evil. They avoid the great either/or that Jesus has shown us: God or Mammon.

By doing this, people turn away from the clarity with which Jesus challenged us to say clearly yes or no, never something between the two, never no when it should be yes or yes when it should be no. Today people turn away from the way of Jesus in the vanity of weak acceptance of man's paradoxical situation in relation to God; all they can say is yes and no or no and yes at the same time to everything all the time and everywhere. Against this we must take up the fight.

One of the present leaders in the dying Movement, who dissolves into speculative paradoxes the decisiveness with which the formerly flaming Youth Movement was charged by God, once called to one of us in a youth meeting, "Surely you don't want to wage a general campaign against all evil?" Yes, this is exactly what it is all about. It was for this that Jesus came to the world; He called us and sent us out so that we might take up and carry on this campaign against all evil in all fields and in all things. He came to destroy the works of the devil. God is light and in Him there is no darkness.

Arnold (1967): 58, 59

October 24

What Is Diplomacy?
Josiah M. Muganda, Tanzania, 1980

Mennonites have often been reluctant to hold government positions due to the coercive nature of the state. A Mennonite diplomat here explains his role in light of Jesus' teachings.

True diplomacy is patient, persevering, nonviolent and persistent. It is considerate and unselfish as well as understanding.

Diplomacy is not thwarting or threatening. Proper diplomacy is not objective, but it is ready to examine and weigh facts, then make suggestions, offer opinions and propose alternatives.

However, since diplomats are not of their own final authorities, they have to adhere to their instructions and should never depart considerably from formal instructions of their home government, "for the one who is sent is not greater than the one who sent him."

In my judgment, diplomatic qualities and approaches seem to march with Christian virtues and aspirations in many ways. At least they don't conflict with each other. Diplomacy requires one to listen to the other person, try to understand his views, reasons, complaints or grievances; then have faith in him and in what he says, and accept him as he is.

Diplomacy is peace-making at conference tables and dinners. Through it misunderstandings, human woes and miseries have been reduced. Diplomacy has diverted wars, has reached agreements and has produced mutual respect and cooperation. The world would have been in chaos if there were no diplomatic consultations.

I think Jesus was diplomatic when he said, "Behold, I send you forth as sheep in the midst of wolves: be ye therefore wise as serpents and harmless like doves" (Matthew 10:16). The world is full of situations like wolves: hunger, greed, selfishness, ignorance, illiteracy, poverty, arrogance and disease. A true and responsible diplomat, like a true Christian, can be as wise as a serpent and help his country acquire or increase modern technology, social change, economic improvement, trade, educational facilities or opportunities, modernization of agriculture and food production.

*

A diplomat, like a Christian, is called to be harmless as a dove. He does what he is instructed to do in the name of his government and for the benefit of the nation. Therefore, he should avoid being self-congratulatory, self-aggrandizing and self-conceited.

*

Diplomacy in its truest sense is patience and nonviolence. It is not arrogance unless it is used by arrogant people.

Let the peace-loving people, the nonviolent and the nonresistant Christians, light their candle and put it on a hill, so that it can shine beyond their borders: To bring peace where there is trouble, love where there is hatred, abundance where there is hunger, educability where there is ignorance and illiteracy, confidence where there is doubt or uncertainty, and light where there is darkness. This is the role of true diplomacy. It is also the role of true Christian love.

Muganda (1980): 14

October 25

Let Us Return Again to Mercifulness
Peter Cornelisz. Plockhoy, England, 1659

Jesus said to them, "The kings of the Gentiles lord it over them; and those who exercise authority over them call themselves benefactors. But you are not to be like that." —Luke 22:25-26 (NIV)

I have seen the great inequality and disorder among men in the world. Not only have evil governors or rulers, covetous merchants and tradesmen, lazy, idle and negligent teachers and others brought all under slavery and thraldom; but also a great number of the common handicraftsmen or laborers (by endeavoring to decline, escape or cast off the heavy burden) fill all things with lies and deceit, to the oppressing of the honest and good people, whose consciences cannot bear such practices. Therefore I have (together with others born for the common welfare) designed to endeavor to bring four sorts of people, whereof the world chiefly consists, out of several sects, into one family or household-government.

Let husbandmen, handicrafts people, mariners and masters of arts and sciences come together, to the end that we may the better eschew the yoke of temporal and spiritual *pharaohs* who have long enough domineered over our bodies and souls. Then let us set up again (as in former times) righteousness, love and brotherly sociableness, which are scarcely anywhere to be found, for the convincing of those that place all greatness only in domineering and not in well-doing. Remember the pattern and doctrine of the Lord Jesus, who came not to be served, but to serve, and gave his life a ransom for many, appointing his kingdom unto his apostles, as it was appointed to him from his Father, answering them when they murmured who after his departure should be the greatest amongst them, said, "If any among you would be greatest, let him be the servant of all."

*

Let us return again to mercifulness which is as well touched with the miseries of the body, as with the miseries of the soul, settling such order or society of mutual love whereby the oppressed (scarcely able to breathe) may be brought to rest and enlargement.

Harder and Harder (1952): 134, 135, revised

October 26

Perpetual Questions
Charles Christano, Indonesia, 1984

I went to Kalimantan (Borneo) with a small number of colleagues to help "start" our mission outreach there. But some of my friends were not ready for the surprises that lay in store for us. I was asked to baptize many new believers, Kantu Dayaks.

The hut where we had our fellowship was a public meeting house in that kampong (village). At the gate we saw ornate decorations made of young coconut leaves, wild flowers and colored papers. Inside there were a few pews and ratan mats. On the wall behind the pulpit hung song sheets written in giant letters so that everybody could read and sing. The translations were their own, using their own images. Those of us from Java felt rather strange. I even overheard one friend who did not want to join the rest, hard-heartedly singing our version of the songs. When I later asked why, he chided me that I was compromising! I was not faithful!

Nor could some of my friends believe me when I baptized our Dayak friends differently. I did not have on my black clerical gown which I always wear for such an occasion in the city churches in Java. Instead I wore a plain batik shirt and no shoes! When we gave our reports and showed some slides to our colleagues in Java, there were a lot of protests, mainly from church leaders! I was called unfaithful to our common practices. They charged me with harsh words. They suspected that I was trying to start a different denomination. These new ethnic groups were not considered genuine Mennonites simply because they do not wear the same kind of dress we do. They do not sing the same songs we sing. They do not use the same liturgy we use.

When some of us heard that our Dayak friends still drink tuak (a domestic strong drink made of fermented rice), we were shocked! They were to be disciplined! They should not be baptized in the first place. But many of us do not know their culture! It is the Dayak custom to have tuak for any important occasion such as a wedding, celebrating baptism, or during harvest time. These people want to share their great joy with the others. Now, how do we give new direction to the new believers about their social life? Shall they completely refrain from drinking or can they drink moderately, without getting drunk?

I have found out that even among my brethren in Indonesia, we have multicultured fellow believers. It is not always easy to accommodate others because we tend to think that we are the genuine Mennonites. We think that everybody has to follow our ways of dressing or our sense of what color is "biblical." When I was confronted with many different ways of doing things, I became aware that what I thought was the right way of doing things happened to be imported from the West. I was blinded by how foreign I had become until I met options my other Indonesian brethren have. And I want to thank God for those different things. I learned that they are not neccesarily wrong. Many of those strange things are just skin deep: not wrong but different! There should be room for differences. We are enriched because of the varied expressions that we have.

Yes, we have much tension. But I call it dynamic tension that stretches us for growth. And love has the capacity for much growth. I believe God is open to many expressions of faith. And He never visits an empty space. He did not come to a vacuum when he came to Bethlehem. He was willing to be wrapped in the Jewish culture. He is willing to condescend, to stoop to become like one of the lowest of the low. So why do not we make ourselves also open to differences?

Christano (1984): 10

October 27

We Ought Not to Dread Death So
Menno Simons, Germany, 1558

Menno wrote these words to Anabaptists living in Amsterdam during a plague.

Elect brethren and sisters in the Lord, I hear that the fire of pestilence is beginning to rage in your vicinity. Therefore I am constrained by the love which

I bear to you and to all the pious who visit you, who are overshadowed by the heavenly light and called into the communion of Christ, to write to you a short letter of consolation, so that you may now and at all times diligently watch for the coming of the Lord and prepare your whole life, heart, mind and conduct for death.

*

If we, with a new, regenerate and penitent soul, firmly adhere to Christ, truly believe His Word, faithfully follow His footsteps, allow ourselves to be governed by His Holy Spirit, and if we mortify the old, sinful life, yes, in every manner die unto the world, the flesh and the devil, if we sincerely seek God's kingdom, righteousness, Word, will, truth, praise and honor, and walk inoffensively in His ways, then we shall live with Him, in Him, and through Him forever, and we shall not be hurt by the second death.

*

Dear faithful brethren, be strong in the Lord, be of good cheer, be comforted. For your whole life and death is lodged in the hands of the Lord. All your hairs are numbered, and without Him not one shall drop from your head. The number of your days, nay, your life, is measured as by handbreadths by Him. Therefore do not fear but willingly serve each other in time of need. Oh, do not let the visiting of the sick vex you, for by this you shall be established in love. And it is also the nature of true love to lay down our lives for the brethren. Reflect on what I advise.

*

Therefore we ought not to dread death so. It is but to cease from sin and to enter into a better life. Nor should we sorrow so about the friends who have fallen asleep in God, as do they who do not look for a reward of the saints. We should rather joyfully lift our head, gird our loins with the girdle of truth and be taken up to the heavenly Canaan. And so with our only and eternal Joshua, Jesus Christ, take the awarded inheritance and so be delivered from the laborious way of our hard pilgrimage, so full of trouble, which we must lead through the trackless, cruel waste, so long as we are in this life. And after that we shall rest in peace.

O elect brethren and sisters, how greatly and gloriously are they gifted of God who, in grace, delivered from the body of sin, and from the emptiness of all transitory things, are taken up into the holy tabernacles of peace, summoned to the eternal, holy Sabbath.

The old, crooked serpent shall no longer bite them in their heels. No ache nor ill shall touch them more. Death, the last enemy, is overcome. Their tears are washed away, and their souls are in lasting rest and peace in the Paradise of grace, Abraham's bosom, under the altar of God. They are come from their great tribulation to Mount Zion, in robes of purest white, worshiping before the throne of God and the Lamb, waiting henceforth until the number of their brethren be complete, then to be glorified together with the glory of Christ, to shine forth as the sun and joyfully to enter into the eternal marriage feast, prepared in heaven for all the chosen ones by the blood and death of Christ.

*

May the God of peace, our merciful Father, by His blessed Son, Christ Jesus, bless you now and at all times, unto greater righteousness, in fuller love.

Your fellow who loves your souls in truth, at present enjoying reasonably good health.

Menno (1956): 1057-1059

October 28

You Will Find Nothing in Me But Patience
Endres Keller, Germany, 1536

In spite of his protest, Endres Keller eventually recanted his Anabaptist beliefs after severe torture.

I hope, dear Lords, that you will not act rashly against me. I say this not from deceitful motives but because I do not want you to incriminate yourselves by doing me violence. What good is it to you to reduce me to this miserable condition? I am distressed beyond misery, I am poverty-stricken and robbed of my ability to work, all of which I cannot overcome in my lifetime. I have been starved so that I cannot now eat or drink, and my body is broken.

How would you like to live for five weeks with only boiled water and unflavored bread soup? I have been lying in the darkness on straw. All this would not be possible if God had not given me an equal measure of his love. I marvel that I have not become confused or even mad. I would have frozen if God had not strengthened me, for you can well imagine how little a bit of hot water will warm one. In addition to this I suffered great torture twice from the executioner, who has ruined my hands, unless the Lord heals them. I have had enough of it to the end of my days.

However, I know that God never forsakes me if I suffer for the sake of his word. I know full well that I have never experienced with great pain the Enemy's temptations against you. May God forgive you and all the dear people who have falsely accused me before you. Many things done long ago I have now been charged with.

However, I know that God works with me for good and that my tribulation is a sign of his love for me. David says: "Blessed is the man whom you, Lord, chastise. You teach him your law so that he may have patience" (Psalm 94:12). The wise man says: "The Lord quickly punishes and chastises him whom he loves, for he gives him his favor, even as a father his child." Therefore, dear Lords, you will find in me nothing but patience in word or deed. I will obey you

347

till I die and I will obey God till I die. But I will not build on this commandment of men, which is against God, as long as there is breath in me. I will not be a hypocrite, either to curry favor or to avoid suffering, but will seek the truth with all my heart.

Klaassen (1981b): 93, 94

October 29

We Remember You
Jakob Hutter, Moravia, 1534

*D*early beloved brothers and sisters! To our great sorrow we have understood that you are in prison, though it is for the sake of divine truth, But we have no idea how you are. Although we have sent brothers out to inquire, we have not heard anything about you.

We are very sad that we cannot speak to you or see you face to face; our hearts are truly suffering with you. We pray fervently and constantly to God; in fact all the believers, the entire Church of God here at Auspitz, does not cease to intercede for you. We remember you before God and reach out to you constantly in holy, brotherly love to comfort you with the comfort we ourselves have received from God.

We ask you to remain steadfast in divine truth to the end through the love and mercy of God. Do not let the threats of the godless frighten you, for they cannot pluck one hair from your head unless it is God's will. Reverence God the Lord in your hearts, as the Apostle Peter says, which means, give honor to God and not to the godless; praise God, glorify Him, trust Him from the very depth of your hearts, and do not doubt His help. At times it may seem that He has abandoned you, but this will never happen. Though God sends you tribulation, He will also lead you out again. Do not forget the comfort of the Holy Spirit, which God has given all His children from the beginning through His prophets and servants.

*

My beloved fellow members in the Body of Christ, see how wonderfully the Holy Spirit comforts us, whatever happens. When a lover of God ponders this and takes it into his heart, it makes his spirit leap and laugh for joy. If a man were sorrowful unto death, these words of comfort should fill him with new life, for all this and much more has been written down for our joy and consolation.

Be comforted then, for God leads into Hell and out again; He makes us sad and joyful again; He gives death and also life, and after great storms He makes the sun shine again. Therefore wait patiently for the redemption of your bodies, and do not grow faint or weary in the race. Do not look back either, but see to it that the love in your hearts does not grow cold and die. Do not be ashamed of the bonds and sufferings of Christ; rejoice in them with your whole heart.

You know that on this earth you are not promised anything but suffering and death, fear and need, and that the godless will persecute, torment and dishonor you. This is the true sign of all God's faithful children; it is the sign of Christ, of the Son of Man and all His members. This sign will appear at the endtime too, according to the Word of the Lord; cross and tribulation are very fitting for all God's children. They are an honor in the sight of God the Most High and of all the believers, a glory and a garland of joy before Him. Christ the Lord had to suffer, and so did all the patriarchs and prophets and disciples, indeed, all chosen from the beginning of the world.

If such things befall us for the sake of truth, we should remember what this means; we are not enemies of God but rather His friends and children. For the Lord himself says, "I will discipline those whom I love."

Hutter (1979): 50, 51, 55-57

October 30

It Seems That There Must Be Tears
Hans Symons, Belgium, 1567

Shortly after writing this letter, Hans Symons was executed with three others in the marketplace at Antwerp. The martyrs were tied to stakes in a temporary hut and strangled. The hut was then set on fire.

O my dear wife, lay to heart the virtues which the Lord has caused to be proclaimed to you, as the prophet says: "He hath shewed thee O man, what is good; and what does the Lord require of thee, but to do justly, and to love mercy, and to walk humbly with thy God" (Micah 6:8).

*

I am much troubled and afflicted in my heart, when I think of you and of my four poor little lambs, whom I must all leave.

I pray you, Tanneken, remember them in your heart as long as you live.

Do not forget my request of you, namely, that you walk in the law of your Lord all the days of your life, and that you be to my and your children, whom the Lord has given us during the time of our wedlock, a pattern in all humility and obedience, in instruction in righteousness; and take for remembrance the Maccabean mother, how she strengthened her children, that they should not forsake the law of God.

*

I do not know what the Lord has seen in me, when I consider that I am so miserable and unworthy to suffer for His name. I can praise and thank the Lord for the great benefits which He has shown to me in my bonds. Well do I now find that the Lord has helped us unworthy ones, especially me.

According to the Spirit, my heart rejoices in the hope of future glory. I hope that I shall soon put off this mortal garment and put on the immortal; may the Lord direct our hearts thereto, for we need help from the Lord of hosts in our tribulation.

See, my dear and much beloved wife and sister in the Lord, take this, with your little children, as a testament and as a remembrance from him who has lived with you in the bonds of wedlock for about five years. We must now part, because of the covenant which we made with God, never to depart therefrom; hence I must now depart from the marriage covenant, for the sake of the covenant which we made with God; I now go (though unworthily), the way which the prophets, Christ and His apostles went, through much tribulation and pain, with many tears, and must drink the cup of bitterness which they all drank.

*

Therefore, my beloved in the Lord, comfort yourself with His Word, and remember that John writes, that the Lord said to His disciples and His friends: "In the world ye shall have tribulation; but be of good cheer, your tribulation shall be turned into joy." Hence, dear Tanneken, rejoice in the hope of future happiness; be patient in tribulation, continue constant in prayer, that the Lord would comfort you and not suffer you to fall into temptation, but with it also make a way of escape.

Commend your matters to the Lord; I hope and trust in God that, if you continue in His laws and constantly keep the Lord before your eyes, He will raise up someone who will help, comfort and assist you. Never separate from the God-fearing. How pleasant it is to be among the Lord's people! I say with Moses: "I would rather suffer affliction with the people of God than enjoy temporal pleasure."

*

O dear Tanneken, it seems that there must be tears; for where no tears are, none can be wiped away. The Lord grant (as I trust in Him that He will) that after this tribulation, which has come upon us for His name's sake, and which is a sore affliction to my heart, we may rejoice together in the kingdom of God and of Christ. For, my dear and much beloved wife and sister in the Lord, whom I love from the bottom of my heart, together with my four little children, it is very hard for me when I think of your heavy burden, the spoiling of our property, and that the Lord has deprived you of the provider of your daily bread. I fain would, had it been the Lord's pleasure, that He had spared us this affliction; however as it cannot be otherwise, we will commend our affliction to the Lord.

*

This is my testament, my dear and much beloved Tanneken. In parting, let me tell you that my mind is still unchanged in the Lord, namely, I, unworthy one, am determined to bear testimony to the Lord, and to seal the same with my blood, in token that it is the truth; nor do I know any other way to be saved through grace, for a witness to the world, to the honor of God and to the salvation of our souls. Amen.

van Braght (1979): 709-711

A Family-Based Revolution of Hope
Sara Wenger Shenk, United States, 1987

What values do I hold most dear? How do I tell my children who they are and where they fit into the vast array of cultures and religions? Either I pass these values on in a haphazard fashion, or I hand them to my children like priceless heirlooms, with care and forethought. Either I take my direction from the loudest, most current voices of the mass media, or I am nurtured by centuries of traditional stories and symbols which have guided countless families in prosperity and in adversity.

Essentially we are all creatures in search of meaning, trying to make sense of the host of options that cry out to us. We can either choose to follow the trends that the dominant culture dictates, or we can select a value system informed from a treasure trove of family memories passed down through generations.

Without a history, without a tradition on which to stand, we are shallow folk indeed.

Handing on the Christian faith to one's children is one of the greatest privileges and most awesome responsibilities of a parent. I do it with joy and trembling. When my sons ask, "Mama, is it a risk to love God?" and "Mama, why doesn't God protect everyone who loves him?", I couldn't *begin* to formulate an answer without the stories of God's people to inform me. I need a history to get my bearings, and, even more so, to orient my sons toward the simple and profound truths of faith. I need tried and true traditions to slow what appears to be a stampede toward high-tech titillation.

I don't want my children to become passive consumers. With a conscious effort to create or recreate family rituals, perhaps our family can join a revolt against the onslaught of depersonalizing dials and digits.

Children form their concepts of God long before they come into direct contact with church teaching. The role of the family in spiritual formation is normally greater than the part played by church or school. What parents hand on is not so much a received doctrine, as a *lived experience*.

Shenk (1987): 7, 8

November

Praying at the Lord's Supper
Klaas Reimer, Russian Empire, 1829

Now we want to prepare ourselves for parting, but let us not depart as an ungrateful people. First and foremost let us praise, honor and thank our mighty and loving God for the great goodness which he continues to evidence to us. For he still allows us to proclaim his service undisturbed. He also allows us to maintain his commandments among each other in good health. Therefore let us praise and thank him in spirit and in truth without ceasing. Yes, to earnestly pray to him that he would maintain us in the right truth, for we do not know if the Lord will again call all of us together here before his table.

Let us also pray to God, that in this last hour he might teach us his truth and that we might evidence his teaching with our daily walk. Let us also pray for the weak and the sick, that they might carry their cross with patience and that they might accept their circumstance as being for the best of their soul. Let us also pray for our youth, that they might truly seize the teachings of Jesus, the apostles and the prophets into their hearts and also be governed by these teachings. We also pray for those who have gone astray, that they would become conscious of what they have fallen from, and that they might find the righteousness-working fruits of atonement for their sins.

Let us also pray for our Czar, his Regents and Princes, for their well-being and that their reign might be just. Yes, that they might find peace and that matters would go well with them and that under their protection we might be able to live out our faith in peace and tranquility.

We are also obligated to pray for all mankind. At this time prior to the end God is sending out his gospel to all people in order that there will be some of these who will thereby obtain the right truth, in order that they would also be able to come to Jesus.

And also for whatever other reason one has to pray to God. May this not only occur here, but also when we are at home in solitude, in the manner which our Savior Jesus has taught us. That we should pray to him with few words and primarily in the spirit, and without ceasing as he says in John 4. "But the hour cometh, and now is, when the true worshippers shall worship the father in spirit and in truth: for the father seeketh such to worship him."

In closing let us now cast ourselves down upon his footstool before his Holy Throne and all together direct ourselves to God.

*

We do not have anything further to present to you at this meal of commemoration and service of love except that I wish you from the heart what God said to Moses, "Speak unto Aaron and unto his sons, when ye shall bless the children of Israel. The Lord bless thee, and keep thee. May the Lord make his countenance to shine upon thee, and be gracious unto thee. May the Lord lift up his countenance upon thee, and give thee peace" (Numbers 6).

I also bless you with the words of David. "May the Lord bless us from Zion, he who has created the heaven and the earth, so that we upon earth might recognize his ways, and all the heathen his goodness" (Psalm 67). Yes, and I also say with Peter, but do grow and increase in grace and in the knowledge of Jesus Christ, for to him alone be glory, honor and praise for his great love and goodness, both now and forever. Amen.

Plett (1985): 208

November 2

A Precious Table
Dirk Philips, Germany(?), ca. 1557

*H*umans do not live by other human words brought forth out of human will, but alone by the words of God proclaimed to us through Christ Jesus and his apostles. Here is the bread of heaven. Here is the water of life. Does anyone hunger after righteousness? Here he finds the bread of life and whoever eats of it will become strong and well in Christ; he will be satisfied in his soul so that he shall not hunger after the leaven of the Pharisees and Sadducees.

Therefore, does anyone thirst after salvation? Here he shall find the most pure fountain and whoever drinks out of this fountain, in him shall come to be a fountain of living water which springs up to eternal life, so that he shall nevermore thirst after the impure water of human teaching. Is anyone desirous after heavenly wisdom let them come to Christ and learn of him, for he is gentle and lowly in heart, and in him his soul will find rest. Then he shall be taught of God and then he shall receive true wisdom.

Christ Jesus is such a master and his Word is of such nature and power that whoever receives and keeps it with a believing heart shall find in the simplicity of the teaching of Christ the unspeakable counsel of heavenly wisdom. They shall, in the words of the cross that in the first glimpse appears simplistic and despised, see and observe much that far surpasses all human cleverness, no matter how high and wonderful it may appear.

Therefore, Paul says to the Corinthians, "I did not act among you as though I knew anything else than alone Jesus Christ, and him crucified" (1 Corinthians 2:2). Every Christian must do the same and have all his desire in the gospel, concern himself therewith day and night, and express himself therein. Then he shall taste the sweetness therein so that he with David shall say, "O Lord, how sweet is your word to my taste, sweeter than honey to my mouth!" (Psalm 119:103).

*

But this sweetness and power of the true heavenly bread no one can taste except he who hungers and thirsts after righteousness and says with David, "As the hart longs for fresh water, so longs my soul for you, Oh God. My soul thirsts for the living God" (Psalm 42:1-2). And again, "Oh God, you are my God, I will seek for you early, my soul thirsts for you, my flesh longs for you in a dry and weary land where there is no water in it" (Psalm 63:1).

*

Oh, what a precious table is this that God has prepared for us in the dry and barren wilderness of this world!

Dirk (1992): 167-169

November 3

What Is Twenty-Five Dollars?
E.J. Swalm, Canada, 1949

*T*he luxurious satisfaction of having a free conscience is worth any price we have to pay for it.

We are reminded of a farmer who was unusually conscientious about his business life. When he retired he sold his entire farm stock and equipment by auction. When a certain cow came into the ring, the farmer stepped forward and told of a defect that the cow had which was not discernable to the public. The cow was sold at a reduced price. The next day when the farmer was asked if he was aware that his little speech in the sale ring cost him twenty-five dollars, he replied, "I told my wife last evening when we retired that I had informed the crowd of the cow's failing and it cost me a quarter of her regular price, but what is twenty-five dollars to a good night's sleep and a free conscience?"

Swalm (1949): 272

Know God Through Himself

Hans Denck, Germany, 1526

Whoever honors Scripture but lacks divine love must look to it, lest he turn Scripture into an idol—as do all scribes who are not "learned" for the Kingdom of God.

You say: "Is it wrong for one who does not as yet know God to value Scripture highly as he may thus be led to knowledge?"

Answer: If one were to give you a letter which promised you great possessions, yet you do not know the writer, how good and rich he is, whether he is as you had hoped, it would be utter folly to rely on the letter. Even if he is what the letter indicates, you can, nonetheless, not rely on the letter until you have discovered for yourself whether this really is the case. If you find that he is indeed good and rich, you will say, "Dear Sir, let me be your servant, I don't care for your letter for I desire no other wages than to be your servant and for you to be my master."

To the one who is not in God's house, the letter is of no use. The one who is in God's house knows without the letter how good the Lord is. Whoever is in God's house, yet is not prepared to do without the letter, implies thereby that he does not trust the Lord without the letter; in other words, he cherishes the letter more than the Lord even though this is expressly prohibited in the letter at risk of losing what is promised therein. For this reason you should never reject the letter, however faithfully you may serve the Lord, for it is also set up as a testimony against you if you should someday commit a wrong. If you do not keep the letter, you cannot draw comfort from it either. If God were not to do more—every moment and hour—than what can be known through his letter alone, how mighty, good and just he is, he would remain unknown for a long time.

Whoever does not learn to know God through God himself has never known him. Whoever diligently seeks God, and is not made aware by God how God has been with him before he ever sought him, has not yet found him and is far from him. Oh, who will give me a voice that I may cry loud enough for the whole world to hear me that God the Lord, the Most High, is in the uttermost depth of the earth waiting for those to be converted who ought to be converted. O Lord God, what goes on in this miserable perverse world that no one can find you, though you are so great; that no one can hear you, though you speak so clearly; that no one can see you, though you are so close to everyone; and that no one knows your name, though you make yourself known to everyone?

Denck (1989): 234-236

Choose a Man of Peace
Mukanza Ilunga, Zaire, 1980

*O*ne day we had gathered to choose a new chief to replace the one who had just died. The men, the women and the young people who had come together to make this choice wondered, "What qualities should we consider?" An old and wise man from this village replied, "Choose a good man, one who loves people, who is hospitable and patient, a man of peace." He continued, "Choose someone who will bring peace into the midst of your families and your clans, into your village, not only during war but also in everyday life."

Furthermore, our tribe has a proverb which says, "Wherever there is a good chief (an old man), there will flow water (the symbol of peace) and not blood (the symbol of war and violence)." Thus, according to our tribal culture, nonviolence means to be spiritually, socially and politically good and also fit to lead others.

This concept is reinforced by the gospel of Christ. On numerous occasions, pastors and evangelists have preached about Christ, about his Sermon on the Mount, and about his pacifist attitude during his arrest, his trial and his crucifixion. We need these sermons so that we can learn to follow faithfully Christ's example. Thus, being a nonviolent Christian in my country means being a person who has learned the lessons of Christ and is ready to follow and obey Him.

On the other hand, nonviolence can also be interpreted, in our country, as a sign of timidity and a lack of patriotism. It would not bother me personally to be called timid and unpatriotic because of my obedience to the teaching of Christ, for it is written that the wisdom of this world is folly in the sight of God (1 Corinthians 3:19).

Ilunga (1981): 20

The Two Kingdoms
Hans Schnell, Germany, ca. 1575

*T*here are two different kingdoms on earth—namely, the kingdom of this world and the peaceful kingdom of Christ. These two kingdoms cannot share or have communion with each other.

The people in the kingdom of this world are born of the flesh, are earthly and carnally minded. The people in the kingdom of Christ are reborn of the Holy Spirit, live according to the Spirit, and are spiritually minded. The people in the kingdom of the world are equipped for fighting with carnal weapons—spear, sword, armor, guns and powder. The people in Christ's kingdom are equipped with spiritual weapons—the armor of God, the shield of faith and the sword of the Spirit to fight against the devil, the world and their own flesh, together with all that arises against God and his Word. The people in the kingdom of this world fight for a perishable crown and an earthly kingdom. The people in Christ's kingdom fight for an imperishable crown and an eternal kingdom.

*

A Christian in the peaceful kingdom of Christ has a loving, peaceable, merciful spirit in the manner of Christ's. He forgives the penitent sinner all sin and transgression. He does not resist evil. He kills nobody physically. He does not preserve his possessions with force but rather presents also the other cheek rather than to oppose the one who strikes him with force. He does not war. He does not injure and kill people but prays for those who persecute and rob him. He who is born again through the Spirit has his Father's nature and qualities in him and is minded as Jesus Christ was minded. Christ not only forbade revenge in his kingdom but also, by his death on the cross, left us an example for us to follow in his footsteps and prayed for his foes on the cross, which believers also do.

*

Christ has redeemed us from the vengeance of the law and established a peaceable kingdom in which the vengeful sword is put away and broken, and warlike weapons have been recast. As Isaiah says: "They shall beat their swords into plowshares, and their spears into pruning hooks."

The believing and peaceable in the kingdom of Christ here on earth dwell safely among one another; none injures or kills another with weapons of war. With this Zechariah also agrees, saying: "And I will cut off the chariot from Ephraim, and the horse from Jerusalem, and the battle bow shall be cut off; and he shall speak peace to the heathen." Of this peaceable people the Holy Ghost speaks (Psalm 46): "Come, behold the works of the Lord, what desolations he hath made in the earth. He maketh wars to cease unto the end of the earth; he breaketh the bow and cutteth the spear in sunder; he burneth the chariot in the fire." Also the 76th Psalm witnesses to this and says; "In Salem also is his tabernacle, and his dwelling place in Zion. There he brake the arrows of the bow, the shield, and the sword and the battle. Selah."

Schnell (1985): 31, 32

November 7

Vote for the Friends of Peace

Amish (?) Minister, United States, 1812

The author of the following piece signed it only "A preacher, Chester County." This may well have been Christian Zook, Jr., an Amish minister in Chester County, Pennsylvania, at the time of the War of 1812. Or the letter might instead be an appeal from a Quaker to members of other pacifist groups. If the author was Amish, then this is a most exceptional document. Amish disciplines do not prohibit members from voting, but neither is this form of participation in government encouraged.

I am an old man, and under Divine Providence I have lived many blessed days. I have endeavored to raise my children in the ways of the Lord, through which they may keep the faith in peaceful piety and eternal truth. For all good things come from the Lord, and those who keep his commandments shall enter into his kingdom and be the sheep of his pasture. As for me personally, I could let the vain things of the world transpire. However, I am concerned for our children and grandchildren and "the land which the Lord gave to them."

It is already more than thirty years since any evil has struck our country, at least no evil to compare with the one we currently must strive against. We have to endure material losses—however, we have peace. I am no "party man," but am opposed to war since it brings sadness, want and death—making the land desolate—takes father from son and son from father—causing widows' and orphans' tears, and is an abomination before God, who alone gives life and alone has the right to take it away. . . .

I fear our rulers have departed from the path of righteousness. We cannot be in the war with them, for our conscience does not allow it: our religious principles forbid it. However, we should be obedient to the laws and "give unto Caesar what is Caesar's." Accordingly, let us obey the statutes, thus having to pay our taxes and having a right to vote for men to make the laws. When we discover that they are not making good laws, we owe ourselves and our families to vote for other men to protect our rights and possessions. . . .

At this time it is our duty to go to the polls and to vote for the friends of peace. When we vote for the friends of peace, we are voting against the war. . . . Oh, my beloved brethren, is it not the duty of every God-fearing man, at such a special occasion, to exercise his political right, while he has the freedom to vote, and while his single vote perhaps can tip the scales? Oh, what a sweet comfort it would be to think back and know that one has contributed to the aversion of this horrible evil.

*

Can any of you, my beloved brethren, consider staying home on election day when by casting your vote in these present times so much evil can be prevented? If anyone who favors the present war party reads this address—if he is a religious man—if he declares himself a Mennonite, Dunkard or Amish, or is in any manner conscientiously opposed to bearing arms, so let him weigh in his own conscience whether he can in present time vote for the war party. At both elections there will be a war-ticket and a peace-ticket. Vote for none but the friends of peace.

Remember that this is no political question—it is not merely a question between Federalists and Republicans—it is a question whether we shall have peace or war.

Luthy (1984): 1-4

Christ and Capital Punishment
Menno Simons, Germany, 1556

*I*t would hardly become a true Christian ruler to shed blood. For this reason, if the transgressor should truly repent before his God and be reborn of Him, he would then also be a chosen saint and child of God, a fellow partaker of grace, a spiritual member of the Lord's body, sprinkled with His precious blood and anointed with His Holy Ghost, a living grain of the Bread of Christ and an heir to eternal life; and for such a one to be hanged on the gallows, put on the wheel, placed on the stake or in any manner be hurt in body or goods by another Christian who is of one heart, spirit and soul with him, would look somewhat strange and unbecoming in the light of the compassionate, merciful, example He has commanded all His chosen children to follow.

Again, if he remain impenitent and his life be taken, one would unmercifully rob him of the time of repentance of which, in case his life were spared, he might yet avail himself. It would be unmerciful to tyrannically offer his poor soul which was purchased with such precious treasure to the devil of hell, under the unbearable judgment, punishment and wrath of God, so that he would forever have to suffer and bear the tortures of the unquenchable burning, the consuming fire, eternal pain, woe and death. Never observing that the Son of man says: "Learn of me, I have given you an example, Follow me, I am not come to destroy souls, but to save them."

Menno (1956): 920-922

Salvation and the Sword
Thieleman Jansz. van Braght, The Netherlands, 1660

*I*t is the duty of every Christian to promote the salvation of his neighbor as much as is possible. But how is this to be done? By external compulsion with fire and sword? Impossible; this touches and affects the body but not the conscience, which must not be compelled, but led and instructed.

The Word of God is the sword with which all error and heresy must be cut down. If the supposed error cannot be conquered with the power of truth, swords will be dull before it. And though a man, through dread of suffering, renounce his belief with the mouth, yet will he not do it with the heart; and thus, instead of converted Christians, dissembling hypocrites are made.

But if a man remain steadfast, and is put to death, how can this tend to his conversion, since every means of conversion is taken away? For, one of two things is certain: if he is a damnable heretic, he is cast down into hell; but if he is not, a saved Christian is put to death—choose whichever you please and an abominable crime is committed.

What is it then, that urges them thus to promote anyone's conversion? What binds them to this? Who enjoins it upon them? Who advises them to it? Yea, who gives them permission to do it? And which of the apostles has set such an example? Truly, such reasons are but fig leaves and covers with which they seek to hide their shame and wickedness. They pretend that they aim at the conversion of men, but in fact seek to secure their own pleasure, honor and lust, in order thus to exercise undisputed despotism in the kingdom of God.

So far is this from being the case—that anyone's conversion is promoted thereby—that on the contrary, all impartial persons conceive an aversion against them. So that even the good (if any good remains, or can be found, in the persecutors), is rendered suspicious; yea, entirely destroyed, inasmuch as their words, however entreating and flattering they may be, can obtain no entrance or credit, neither do they deserve it. For who would expect to learn anything godly or Christian from those who are pregnant with murder, and whose hands are stained with innocent blood? "Do men gather grapes of thorns?" (Matthew 7:16).

van Braght (1979): 359

November 10

Hand In Hand
Stephen Wang, China, 1988

*O*ur children grew up in a different environment than ours and therefore they have a different world outlook. How to train them to have an outlook in accord with ours is a problem that I often think about. They were educated under the atheistic Communist government. Our children respect our Christian faith, but find it hard to accept the religious faith for themselves. It is rather hard to force my children and grandchildren to believe in Christianity, but they may sense someday that it is better to have Christian faith.

For a long time, I have had the idea of sending one of my children to America in order to become acquainted with the Christian faith. Fortunately, my grandson, Guo Xu, recently went to Nanjing to do practice teaching and obtained a Bible at Nanjing Seminary. After reading some chapters, he told me that he is very interested in Christianity and will continue to study its philosophy.

This marvel of Chinese young people beginning to believe in Christianity illustrates that our society needs something more than science, the social sciences and literature. People want to have a spiritual life. More seminaries like the one in Nanjing are needed. Some universities have begun to offer courses on the philosophies of the three great religions: Christianity, Buddhism and Islam.

I have told my children and grandchildren that a person must have a conviction. There is no contradiction between socialism and religion; in present-day China, religion is legal and rightful. Everyone in China enjoys freedom of religion, which the government guarantees through the Constitution. In Changchun, I still attend church. Before liberation, the city had four Protestant churches; after liberation, they were united. I am a Christian and a state cadre at the same time. The Christian faith demands of me that I be a good state cadre.

The people of both China and the United States have a deep love for peace. Although the social systems of our two countries are different, we have many common interests. At present, the only obstacle in the development of normal diplomatic relations is the problem of Taiwan.

Hand in hand, Chinese and American citizens ought to oppose nuclear war and the arms race. Both of our nations have large populations and large territory. If our nations can live in harmony from generation to generation, we will promote peace in the world.

Kreider (1988): 100, 101

November 11

A Marvelous Thing

Jacob S. Lehman, United States, 1903

*T*o us it seems a marvelous thing that, in our advanced stage of civilization and of extensive Biblical research, there should be an occasion to write and teach against the inconsistency of Christians having part in war, since Christ died to redeem us from that power and principle that begets war. The inconsistency and inhumanity of it among civilized people has no doubt been well established; but our purpose is to consider it only so far as it concerns the church; and to direct attention to the unchristian views and practices of popular Christianity concerning it.

All lovers of "peace and good will" would welcome the day when peace and righteousness shall prevail over strife and war. But we may be assured that so long as it is an accepted tenet of popular Christianity that a man may be a politician, a ruler, a soldier or even a conqueror, and yet be a Christian, and so long as their ministers teach from their pulpits that men ought to fight for their country and their homes, and even administer the sacrament to them before the battle, war will not cease to be an art, nor national quarrels be settled by arbitration.

The prophet Isaiah in speaking of the peaceable kingdom of Christ says, "They shall beat their swords into ploughshares and their spears into pruninghooks."

And James says, "The wisdom that is from above is first pure, then peaceable, gentle and easy to be entreated, full of mercy and good fruits." But witness the fruits of the popular teaching. There can be no war between Christian nations without the members of the same churches being arrayed against each other; nor will this ever be different until professed Christianity gets back upon its true foundation.

The Christian is taught to "put on the Lord Jesus Christ," and to "walk in his commandments." And Paul taught, "Follow peace with all men, and holiness, without which no man shall see the Lord." But nothing is more common, nor more generally commended than for the preachers and priests of both sides in a war to vie with each other in invoking the blessings of heaven on their respective armies; and their pulpits resound with applause for the brave and the true. Who upon reflection can fail to see in this a mere trifling with God and with prayer?

Then again, many seem to be distressed by the thought that spiritual darkness hangs as a pall over so many heathen lands, and that the heathen are perishing without the comfort of gospel light. But how frequently does it occur that missionaries of two countries at war with each other profess to jointly promulgate the peaceable kingdom of Christ among these poor heathen, to offer them the doctrine of universal peace, while at home in their own native lands, their fellow-believers are in deadly conflict?

Some of the so-called Christians who are combative admit that it is wrong to fight in an unjust cause; but who is to decide as to the justice of a cause? Men of the finest intellect, with all the advantages of information upon a subject, and after the most careful consideration, have reached opposite conclusions. Such will ever be the case. But Paul makes no distinction as to the cause being just or unjust. He says, "They that resist shall receive to themselves damnation."

Lehman ([1903]): 121-123

November 12

No Ill Feelings
Roy L. Schlabach, United States, 1984

*A*pproximately in the year 1890 an issue came up in the Amish church here in Holmes County that caused quite a controversy. Like it usually goes, truth and gossip were mixed together. The overall issue caused a deep concern in the church. Nevertheless, the problem was there and had to be dealt with. So with a prayerful attitude and taking into consideration the welfare and the future of the church and also the souls of those involved, some older leaders worked on it.

After some consultation it came to the point that Jacob Schrock was expelled and placed under the "Bann." He was an elderly man who had the reputation of having a strong will and of being easily hurt. Therefore, it was very hard for him to accept this verdict and he allowed himself to get very worked up about it.

Jacob was retired and lived in the "Daudy Haus." His son, Emanuel (often known as Mona) lived at home and did the farming. He was a young man, about twenty-two years old at the time.

This particular Sunday evening while doing the chores Mona was in the feed aisle, feeding the horses, when his father came to him, burst into tears (perhaps more self-pity than repentance) and said, "What has been done to me today is far too much. I cannot bear it. I know there are others that feel the same way. If you stand by us, we can make a big thing out of this."

After a pause, Mona said to his father, "*Ach, Daudy, mir welle net so denke. Mir welle des uf uns nehme. Es kann uns zum Guten dienen. Denk mol an Jesu, was er gelitten hat und huts alles gedultich angenommen, und war doch ganz unschuldig.*" (Oh, Grandpa, don't think like that. We want to take this upon ourselves. It can work out for our good. Think of Jesus, how he suffered, and took it patiently upon himself, even though he was completely innocent.)

Jacob seemed reluctant to accept this advice, and expressed a "let down" mood. However, after some time had elapsed, he changed his views and was taken back into full fellowship with the church again.

Years passed by. Mona moved from home and lived on a farm about eight miles away. Old Jacob's health began to fail and Mona often went to visit and help care for his ailing father. One of the last times he was there before Jacob's death, the old man said, "I do not think my time on earth will be long anymore. I want to thank you for that advice you gave me that Sunday evening in the feed aisle. It has helped me more than anything else I can think of. I have a good feeling toward the ministers and the church, and have no ill feelings toward anyone. I have hopes that God has forgiven me, and that I can die in peace."

Jacob died soon afterwards, and we hope he can be at rest with the Redeemer. How this story would have ended had his son supported him in his rebellion, we do not know, but no doubt it would have been quite different.

Schlabach (1984): 40

November 13

On the Meaning of *Ordnung*
Joseph F. Beiler, United States, 1974

The idea of Ordnung *is as old as Anabaptism itself. When Anabaptists formed their own communities separate from the state churches, they adopted agreements by which to "order" their lives together. One Swiss Brethren* Ordnung *circulated with the Schleitheim Confession of 1527. The* Hutterite Chronicle *contains an* Ordnung *from*

1529. The Old Order Amish today still consider Ordnung *("Ottning" in Pennsylvania German) essential for a healthy community.*

*T*he most common definition of *Ordnung* in today's way of thinking is "discipline." That is a surface description, for the true meaning is more than pen and ink can yield. It cannot be defined by any word in any language because church *Ordnung* cannot be lived by the letter. It must be lived by the spirit.

During the nineteenth and twentieth centuries great changes came into our land. Factory-made dress materials, machinery and many other things came upon the American way of living. Our church fathers had a strong desire to hold on to the old way of life, and although much has changed over the years, they have been successful in "holding the line" to the point that we have been separated from the world. This did not come overnight, nor did it come through rash or harsh commands from our bishops, but by making wise church decisions to hold firm the old faith. The bishops and ministers do not make the *Ordnung*. They only attempt to hold the line.

A respected *Ordnung* generates peace, love, contentment, equality and unity. The latter is the key effect of church *Ordnung*. It will focus the individual to one body, one flesh, one mind and one spirit. It creates a desire for togetherness and fellowship. It binds marriages, it strengthens family ties; to live together, to work together, to worship together and to commune secluded from the world.

But a church of *Ordnung* is not without problems. We will always have members that, when they fall prey to sin, will blame the *Ordnung*. A rebelling member will label it a man-made law with "no scriptural base," causing "discord," and a "church-wrecker." We have those who resist *Ordnung*, and they are of two classes. One is prone to look for "greener grass," and the other is made up of those who are unconcerned. They want to live for today, forgetting the lessons of the past.

Obedience is a close associate of *Ordnung*. It signals whether you love the church or if you do not. You are either in the church or you are outside. There is no happy medium.

Only a person who has learned to love and live a respectful church *Ordnung* can fully appreciate its values. Based on the Word of God and the Spirit of Christ, it gives freedom of heart, peace of mind and a clear conscience. A person within the *Ordnung* actually has more freedom, more liberty and more privilege than those who are bound to the outside.

We do know of examples where church ordinances were over-enforced. When self-opinion rules it will go as with the house built upon the sand. A time-proven *Ordnung* over generations and centuries, directed by the Almighty Powers and led by the Holy Spirit, will stand unto the end.

Beiler (1974)

November 14

Convictions?
Edward A. Kline, United States, ca. 1980

*T*he Scriptures do not say much about "convictions." The word has come to stand for a man's position on a matter that he considers to be the truth. But conviction should be no more or no less than Scripture teaches. Many "convictions" today are not much more than a man's own thinking. As in all matters of discernment, convictions need to be put to the test of the Word and the brotherhood. To be overly dogmatic on a "conviction" is a sign of an unsurrendered soul. The Scriptures, however, stand firm, and we need not compromise clear principles of Scripture. Where the application is not clear, the will must be properly exercised so as not to form a divisive "conviction," but must be submissive to the brotherhood for discernment.

"Convictions" have at times become excuses for men to do as they please. Some say that they have no "conviction" to obey a standard or whatever the principle may be. What they are really saying is that they have no desire or will to obey. If a person submits and obeys, even without having the conviction, he will come to see the truth of the matter as he remains submissive and open.

Kline (n.d.): 24, 25

November 15

The Sectarian Virus
Johannes Harder, Germany, mid-1900s

*A*s true as it is that in the biblical message everything begins with a single person and by *the One*, the New Testament reaches far beyond me and marks the beginning of a salvation history for *all*; for it is a matter of universal restoration of the world. ("For God so loved the world"—John 3.) One person is called by another; there is a chain of invitations carried along as in a relay race. The called are gathered and become the *Gemeinde*, which transforms everything that is.

The Anabaptists did not invent the idea of the *Gemeinde* as the most intensive form of human society. They understood themselves as a continuation of the disciples of Christ, as convinced and convincing students of the early church. *Gemeinde* is neither organization nor institution, but rather an *organism*.

*

God turned to the world and that is why conversion (turning around) is possible for every person. There are many, all too many, amputees attached to the body of Christ who against their own will oppose the unifying Lord, whose arms embrace the whole world and who resists every separation between brothers and sisters.

I am speaking of the divisions and controversies within Mennonitism. The virus of separation must be in our blood; otherwise it would be unthinkable that from the beginning we would have fallen prey to so many dogmatic arguments and even enmities. Whoever thinks that he might have more knowledge and confession to offer should ponder the unlimited patience of God. As one's faith grows, so too should grow the ability to carry the brother and tolerance.

As time goes on I can less and less find my way clearly among the dozens of "directions" (movements) in our faith community, some of them very judgmental in character. Difference within the character of a particular *Gemeinde* may well be a strength, as long as it does not become separation, accompanied by judgment and damnation, which is a kind of spiritual sickness. Why should we not live in different houses, as long as they are not fortresses from which we shoot Bible quotations at one another? Are there not differences and tensions enough in our social and political world? Should we not seek to bring our world peace by our unity and forgiving spirit?

The schism in the Russian Mennonite church of the 1860s, which I have gotten to know in its consequences, leads me to ask whether the pious hubbub which took over both the mother church and those who left, did not have its roots in self-righteousness or pride. Is the Bible a textbook for fighting and bickering?

*

Were not our fathers—not to speak of the Bible—anti-clerical and anti-sacramental? But here dogmatic formulations arose as in papal times. I cannot imagine that these scenes of separation made either the mother church or the new groups happier. Is it any surprise if we have been looked upon as sectarians from the beginning and denounced as such?

Loewen (1988): 118, 119

November 16

One Village
Z. Marwa Kisare, Tanzania, 1984

We on the Shirati station set about straightening up our lives both among ourselves, African and African, and between ourselves and the missionaries. It was a time of great joy and freedom. Bishop Stauffer and I came to love each other. We respected each other and each gave to the other the honor and place which was his due.

What was happening at Shirati was not strange to anyone who understood the traditional Luo faith. In our village life we support each other; we look out for each other; we work to build up the strength of the village. If a village member sins, we still support him.

But it is possible for someone to commit so great a sin that covenant is broken between him and his father's village. Suppose a young man kills his brother, someone from his own village. Suppose a young man sleeps with one of his father's wives. Suppose a man sleeps with his own mother. These are terrible things. It is no longer possible for this man to live in his father's village. He is thrown out, *odhi bue*. Usually when someone is caught in such a sin he will run away himself. His sin chases him away. This man has no people; he has no village; he is outside of the village covenant, lost.

When someone is thrown out of his father's village, he cannot return. He may stay out for forty to fifty years. But the time will come when he will become old and he will not want to die outside without a family. So he will send word to his father's village asking to be accepted again by them.

No matter how good a man he may have been or how much the people of the village may have admired him, it is never possible for him to return unless a sacrifice is made which is powerful enough to undo the evil thing which he did. We know in our society that only the blood of a sheep killed in ritual sacrifice has the power to break the curse which that man brought upon himself when he sinned against his father and his village.

After he has confessed, he is symbolically cleansed. This is done by sprinkling him with the prepared liquid. He drinks some of it. He then stoops down in humility and enters the village through the low entrance that was made for him. After he is on the inside of the village enclosure, more cleansing ceremonies are performed. Then he is taken to a small hut, prepared for the occasion, where he eats with members of his father's village.

We believe that sin, that which brings a curse on a person breaking covenant between him and his village, can be knocked off only with blood after confession. We say in Luo, "*Ja chien idolo giremo*—Satan is neutralized only with blood."

To sin is like a person taking hold of a live electric wire. His arm is in spasm and he cannot let go of the wire which is killing him. Anyone who catches hold of him to help him will also be gripped by the current and made helpless. Only by taking a piece of wood can the live wire be knocked from the man's grasp. This is the work of blood in our society; blood alone can knock off the evil which is grasped by a person or village.

That August evening in 1942 the Holy Spirit gave us the insight that both the missionaries and the Africans were all lost from that one true village, the new village of God our Father. It was sin which kept us concerned only with our own earthly families, our ethnic villages. The Holy Spirit showed us that Jesus' sacrifice made it possible for all of us to be brothers and sisters in the same village.

Shenk (1984): 79-81

Am I A Cow?

Family Life, United States, 1989

*T*he hungry cows quickly ran over to the fallen hay that I had just thrown down from the loft. Many of them bit down on a hearty mouthful and began munching. I leaned back against a post, briefly resting my tired muscles from the exertion of tugging a good-sized forkful loose from the big pile in the loft. As I leaned there, I looked down upon the feeding cattle. Something about their behavior caught my attention immediately.

One of the bossiest, and unfortunately the biggest, was spending well over seventy-five percent of her time on the run, chasing the other cattle away from the hay. She would repeatedly dash from one side of the pile to the other, each time dragging with it a clump of hay and stamping it into the mud.

I could take it no longer. My righteous indignation rose in one great bound. What was wrong with that stupid cow anyway?

Not only was the cow missing out on her own breakfast, she was making an uncomfortable breakfast time for the others as well.

But then, just as quickly, my indignation abated and turned into pity. The poor thing, she's so short-sighted that she can't see how little she's getting accomplished. She's spending all her time running to and fro, chasing other cows. She is really to be pitied.

Then another thought struck me. Maybe this is just a fine example, this herd of feeding cattle. Is this perhaps what people are like? Of course, folks don't eat hay, but there seems to be something there that is a striking similarity to people's conduct.

They may not chase folks away from a meal, the way that cow did. Some are heaping up things for their own "meal," maybe pursuing comforts and pleasures for themselves, and disregarding the comfort of others. All the while, others are standing back and meekly enjoying their portion or maybe even stepping aside so that the selfish ones may have a still more enjoyable position.

Then a still more disturbing thought struck me. Perhaps, I'm like that arrogant cow. Maybe I am so engrossed in myself that I fail to see how miserably mistaken I am. Maybe I'm one of those folks that only looks out for myself and mine, and am inconsiderate of others. I hung my head in shame. Cow, I pity you, but you're not the most to be pitied.

"Of Cows and People" (1989): 10, 11

Instantaneous Sanctification

Evangelical Visitor, United States, 1891

*T*here should be no discussion, no question as to the only condition of the soul's attitude to God, yet among the multiplicity of teachings and teachers it is, we fear, too true that the standard of the important half of the gospel has been lowered or lost sight of altogether.

*

The text: "Whosoever is born of God doth not commit sin; for his seed remaineth in him; and he can not sin, because he is born of God," I hear commented upon, perhaps, more than any other. Sometimes in a way that robs God of all glory of saving the lost to the uttermost and leaves us helpless in the hands of sin. This is no holiness or sanctification text. It is the lowest state of grace any believer can enjoy; a life without sin. Justification saves from sin as an act; sanctification saves from sin as a state. There is no knowledge more personal and positive than the knowledge of a personal salvation and there can be no desertion of the Bible standard of justification and sanctification without soul peril for time and eternity.

*

God proposes to spoil the human arrangement to erect the divine. There can be no such a thing as sin in the flesh and purity in the spirit.

*

God's work of cleansing away man's depravation of nature is necessarily instantaneous since it is by faith. It may take a long time to abandon a trust in our own efforts, and repose entirely in God for all needful things, temporally and spiritually, but the step is instantaneous and by faith when taken. Only then can we grow in grace for the simple reason that we are in grace and not under the law of works.

To fearlessly meet the conditions need occasion no fear of the opinions or frowns of men, since he who is Omnipotent and Father, can care for all his little ones. In our experience we found the Divine plan entirely spoiled when the ego or I undertook any cause, but to passively trust our entire needs and all our interests to his care has never failed to gain the Father's most careful attention.

"Holiness" (1891): 369, 370

Free Rein

Family Life, United States, 1986

I was teaching in a neighboring community and as I boarded some distance from the school, I made the daily trip with a horse and buggy. One day in late fall snow fell and caught me unprepared for winter. I decided to cut around on the way home and buy myself a pair of boots at a little country store.

It was almost dusk when I started out. Clouds overcast the skies and darkness came on early. I hurriedly made my purchase and was on my way. Hoping to save a little time, I took a different way home—one with which I was not too familiar, yet I anticipated no problem. By now snow was falling, further decreasing visibility. Old Dobbin obligingly trotted on, but I was not far until I began to have doubts that this road was leading me home. I peered into the darkness, but the faint outlines were all unfamiliar to me. By now the only thing I was certain of was that I was not going where I wished to go. The curves and the angling road had caused me to lose all sense of direction in the snow and darkness. I stopped and looked all around but could see nothing to tell me where I was.

A sudden inspiration came to me and I urged my horse onward. I turned around and headed back the way I had come. Only this time I left it all to good old Dobbin. I knew I was too confused to decide for myself and I believed that my horse wanted to get home every bit as much as I did. When we reached a corner, he swerved quickly around it, telling me he had no such doubts as I had. It was exactly the opposite of what seemed right to me, but I knew my hope was in trusting my horse and God who had given him the homing instinct. No, it didn't seem right, but I had tried my way and it had proved wrong too.

We had not gone far until the faint outlines began to look familiar. Now I knew we were on our road. My horse had found the way!

Is it not the same in our lives? We think we know, only to find ourselves on the wrong track. Our only way back is to turn around, let loose of the reins, and trust Another to lead the way even when it is not what we might choose for ourselves. We know He guides the way and knows our every need.

"Free Rein" (1986): 12

A Prayer for Deeper Life

Leenaert Clock, The Netherlands, ca. 1625

As we, O heavenly Father, have committed ourselves to calling upon your holy name, look upon us with the eyes of your mercy. Incline your ears, open your generous hand and give us cleansed, obedient hearts, that we might lift them up to you, O God and Father in heaven, for there at your right hand we have our Redeemer and Savior, Jesus Christ, your beloved Son. For our justification he ascended into heaven, where we cannot yet follow him as long as we are clothed in our present bodies. But he has comforted us and given us the firm promise that what we ask of you in his name, O Father, you will grant and give us.

Realizing our nothingness, we come before you, dear Father, and pray that you will give us a constant and firm confidence in our hearts, so that we may be able to hear, examine and comprehend your truth, and that you will keep us firm and immovable as you have promised through your son. O Lord, seal this truth in our hearts.

*

Because we ought to call upon you with confidence, O God and Father, free our hearts of vain and deadly thoughts and desires so that no unrighteousness is found in them, and that we may ask or desire only what is pleasing to you, O God, to your praise, and the salvation of our souls.

To that end, make our hearts lowly and humble, so that our prayers do not come back to us empty, but that they may penetrate through the clouds to you, O God and Father. Grant us a heart that willingly forgives our neighbor without retaining any desire for revenge. Break, strike and crush our hearts, to shed a flood of tears which you, O Father, can regard and which will be pleasing to you.

*

And because you alone are wise, and live not only in the light, but are yourself the eternal light, and we are living here in this dark, blind world, so enlighten us, O God, with your divine wisdom, which is a co-worker of your throne. Send it down from your holy heaven and the throne of your glory that it may be with us and work with us, so that we may know what is pleasing to you. For without this grace, O God, we cannot please you. For this wisdom, Lord, we also ask in the name of your beloved Son, Jesus Christ, in whom all the riches of wisdom and knowledge are concealed.

And now, since we are burdened with all kinds of anxieties, we pray to you with David: O Lord, show us your face, and we shall be made well, that we may look upon it and live. For therein rests our salvation and eternal life, which all the saints and the elect possess and enjoy. Let us also enjoy and share in this, in the name of Jesus Christ, your son, who taught us to pray—grant that we may in spirit and truth say: "Our Father . . ."

Gross (Forthcoming)

November 21

The Thirst for Profit

Menno Simons, The Netherlands, ca. 1541

*T*his I write as a warning to the God-fearing merchants and retailers, lest they be like the ungodly and be overcome by avarice. But may they be circumspect in dealing and on the alert against moral danger.

*

Yes, good reader, the whole world is so affected and involved in this accursed avarice, fraud, false practice and unlawful means of support; in this false traffic and merchandise, with this finance, usury and personal advancement that I do not know how it could get much worse. Yet they continue to be the priests' and preachers' Christians, and then call this earning their bread honestly, and doing justice to all.

Ah, my reader, how very different all this is from the faith, spirit and converted life of Zacchaeus. For if we had the spirit, faith and power of Zacchaeus, which we verily should have if we would be saved, then few lords and princes would continue in their violence and luxurious lives; few knights and soldiers in their wicked service and bloody deeds; few judges, lawyers and advocates in their courthouses and offices; few rich persons in the unclean use of their riches; few merchants and retailers in their usury and morally dangerous trade; and few preachers, priests and monks would continue in their salaries, incomes and cloisters. There would soon be a different and better situation because it cannot fail, the righteous must live his faith. Yea, they would with a new and joyful heart say with Zacchaeus, the poor we willingly serve with our goods, and if we have defrauded any one we will gladly reimburse him.

All who with Zacchaeus receive Jesus Christ in the house of their consciences, with him rightly believe the Word of Christ and are truly born by it, these are also given the Spirit of Christ and are of the same mind with Him. Therefore it is impossible for them to defraud anyone of so much as a farthing; the disposition and usage of all true believers being to injure none on earth, but as much as in them is, to assist all; to cheat none, but deal fairly with all. As Paul says, "Let him that stole steal no more; but rather let him labor, working with his hands the thing which is good, that he may have to give to him that needeth" (Ephesians 4:28).

Menno (1956): 369, 370

The Spirit of Community
Andreas Ehrenpreis, Slovakia, 1650

*T*alk of faith and brotherliness does not go together with wearing expensive clothes, dining well every day or piling up riches. The man who saves and accumulates always does it for himself and his family. Whether he lives or dies, his brothers and sisters in the faith have little or nothing to expect from him. How can he speak of love to God, of love to his neighbor, when the desire for wealth is doing its destructive work in him?

When we are filled with the spirit of community, we become simple and modest. We will be satisfied with what little food and clothing we have. On other points, people who honestly call themselves brothers can easily find a common recognition and reach a common agreement in faith; for example that it is God's will to shun war and weapons once and for all.

But about possessions, in spite of the prophets and apostles, men will fight and struggle against the clear truth. Any profits from our work should not be hoarded. The fruits of our work must be put at the disposal of all our brothers in God. They are for the feeding, housing and clothing of the poor, the hungry and the old. It was through love that Jesus became poor and one of the lowliest on earth.

So He commands us as our Lord to love one another in the same way He loved us.

*

We should not think that we are sacrificing our lives only when we face the sword or some other violent death. No. We have to give up our lives in good times too. When we are achieving something and things are going well, we should give our lives to serve our neighbors. Just at such times we are expected to give up everything and not spare ourselves. Paul could have done many things, but he wanted only what was for the good of all. So it is a question of wanting the good for others instead of for oneself. Therefore I will even give up my own judgment, for our good, if it causes a brother to fall. We forfeit the love of God if we cling to our possessions in the face of our brother's need. For we should love, not with words, but with deeds and in truth. The love that works through us must be the same as that love in which God gave His son.

Hutterian Brethren (1978): 25, 26, 28, 29

The Possessions of the Lord

Pieter Pietersz., The Netherlands, 1638

*T*he true believers who evidence themselves as brethren in the Holy Spirit are partakers of one bread and, accordingly, they are truly one bread and one body. The foregoing is a clear example of true Christianity. For in one bread, the fat and lean kernels are crushed and ground together without distinction, they disperse themselves one among the other, are bonded together with water and baked together in the fire. Similarly, the true Christendom is also baptized into one body, blended and kneaded into one dough which is then baked into one bread in the fire of love.

Of this take note, you greedy acquisitors! You who rake in everything only for ourself, and then want to think that you are still a member of the one body and that you are baked and united into the one bread. You have filled your houses with overabundance, your cellars are full of wine, your crocks full of vinegar, brews and roasted meats to excess, your closets are full of all sorts of liquors, your silver beakers and basins, your chests full of ornamental treasures, your superabundance of napkins and tablecloths and all manner of expensive cosmetics.

Everything which you can imagine has been filled to overflowing and everything which you could desire you obtain. The treasures of your eyes are hanging on the walls round about you, full of expensive useless paintings, your overabundance of clothes made of the finest materials, your necks are adorned with precious trinkets wrought of metals and you wives are garnished with expensive embellishments.

In order to achieve all the foregoing you take of the Lord's property, but your indigent brothers and sisters go about clad in cheap miserable clothes, their tables are uncovered as there is hardly enough linen cloth to cover their own bodies, their beds are hard and their blankets are barely sufficient to keep them warm, their beverage is diluted with water, and their victuals are sparse. Finally, the differences in every respect are so great that no comparison can be made. Where is here the one bread and the one body? Is it not present merely in the name alone? For certainly the usage and the power is not present.

*

Now what must one do in order to emulate more clearly this likeness in order that we are truly to become one bread and one body? Follow the word of God. Put aside the clinging sins which are oppressing you. Inspire your arrogant nature, change your hearts of greed, which are only inclined for your own benefit, and seek also the profit of your neighbor. At all times give over what remains as surplus from your own, and distribute that part of your abundance which you can do without. Live according to what is necessary and not according to your own sensuality. Crucify your lusts and desires.

Frequently think of the words of Christ, when a certain man said unto him, "Lord, I will follow thee whithersoever thou goest." But what did your Lord say? "The Foxes have holes, and the birds of the air have nests; but the son of man hath nowhere to lay his head." Therefore also deny yourself everything, flee away from all voluptuousness, and be prepared to carry the Cross of Jesus.

Plett (1985): 338, 339

November 24

Prepared By Love to Serve
Menno Simons, Germany, 1552

The whole Scripture speaks of mercifulness and love, and it is the only sign whereby a true Christian may be known. As the Lord says, "By this shall all men know that ye are my disciples (that is, that ye are Christians), if ye love one another" (John 13:35).

Beloved reader, it is not customary that an intelligent person clothes and cares for one part of his body and leaves the rest destitute and naked. Oh, no. The intelligent person is solicitous for all his members. Thus it should be with those who are the Lord's church and body. All those who are born of God, who are gifted with the Spirit of the Lord, who are, according to the Scriptures, called into one body and love in Christ Jesus, are prepared by such love to serve their neighbors, not only with money and goods, but also after the example of their Lord and Head, Jesus Christ, in an evangelical manner, with life and blood. They show mercy and love as much as they can. No one among them is allowed to beg. They take to heart the need of the saints. They entertain those in distress. They take the stranger into their houses. They comfort the afflicted, assist the needy, clothe the naked, feed the hungry, do not turn their face from the poor, do not despise their own flesh (Isaiah 58:7, 8).

Behold, such a community we teach. And not that any one should take and possess the land and property of the other, as many falsely charge. Thus Moses says, "If there be among you a poor man, of one of thy brethren, within any of thy gates, in thy land which the Lord thy God giveth thee, thou shalt not harden thine heart nor shut thine hand from thy poor brother." Tobias says, "Give of thy bread to the hungry, and of thy garments to them that are naked." Christ says, "Be ye therefore merciful, as your Father also is merciful." "Blessed are the merciful, for they shall obtain mercy."

*

Again this mercy, love and community we teach and practice, and have taught and practiced these seventeen years. God be thanked forever that although our property has to a great extent been taken away from us and is still daily taken, and many a pious father and mother are put to the sword or fire, and although we are not allowed the free enjoyment of our homes as is manifest, and besides the times are hard, yet none of those who have joined us nor any of their orphaned children have been forced to beg. If this is not Christian practice, then we may well abandon the whole Gospel of our Lord Jesus Christ, His holy sacraments and the Christian name, and say that the precious, merciful life of all saints is fantasy and dream. Oh, no. "God is love; and he that dwelleth in love dwelleth in God and God in him."

Menno (1956): 558, 559

November 25

Separating Faith from Unbelief
Leonhard Schiemer, Austria, 1527

*B*ut there is an even greater unbelief that tortures us, namely godless thoughts such as: God will forget me. He will not remain faithful to me. He is a respecter of persons and will not help me as he has helped others. Unbelief cannot be more stupid than to think: if I surrender to God I surrender security. I will perish. If, however, I remain with the world I will soon be safe and not perish so foolishly. If I become or remain a Christian, God will not feed me but if I remain a heathen I will freely feed myself. If I become a Christian my children will die of hunger; if not they will be safe.

To all this I say: clearly you are not yet a Christian but an evil heathen. It is painful until faith is separated from unbelief. It takes a good smeltinghouse, a strong test, a pungent acid; for an uncrucified Christian is like untested ore and like a house the wood of which is still in the tree. Only the fact that we do not know him prevents the love of God in us. Since he is the greatest good it is impossible not to love him alone and above all things if one knows him.

Whoever truly knows God loves him so much that it would be impossible to love anything besides him even if it were commanded on pain of eternal damnation. Indeed, if I truly knew God my spirit and soul would be so overjoyed that this joy would penetrate into the body and it would become unfeeling, impassable, immortal and glorified. Therefore, if man is cleansed from all love of the creatures and even his own life, God brings about this bodily change through that sleep which all the saints share until the resurrection of the dead. Thus we cannot know God until the cover, which hides the divine light in us, that is the creatures, is removed. And the more the creature is withdrawn from us for the sake of Christ, the more the light and the Word of God shines forth. Whoever therefore submits himself to God under the cross is a child of God.

Klaassen (1981b): 55

Brauda Friesen and the Rich Mennonites

David Waltner-Toews, Canada, ca. 1986

Brauda Friesen rose to preach
opened up his Bible wide
opened up his lips like barndoors
let the mares of heaven ride!

How the people sat in wonder
as he preached Woe to the rich!
How they thought that all those *English*
really should be hearing this.

His voice was like an eagle.
Their hearts were on their sleeves.
They knew they'd had a good one
when they all got up to leave.

People thanked him at the doorway
What a work the Lord had done!
People talked of *Brauda* Friesen
all the way from church to home.

Brauda Friesen loved his people.
Brauda Friesen often cried.
No one's sure where Friesen is now,
in an old folks' home, or died.

Only one thing is for certain:
though they praised him for his tongue,
things run just a little smoother
now that *Brauda* Friesen's gone.

Janzen, Yaguchi, Waltner-Toews (1986): 107

I Should Like to Write a Jewel into Your Heart

Soetgen van den Houte, Belgium, 1560

Before being martyred, Soetgen van den Houte penned these parting words to her children—children soon to be orphans, their father having already been sent to his death for his faith.

Grace, peace and mercy from God the Father and the Lord Jesus Christ, this I wish you, my dear little children, David, Betgen and Tanneken, for an affectionate greeting, written by your mother in bonds, for a memorial to you of the truth, as I hope to testify by word and with my death, by the help of the Most High, for an example unto you. May the wisdom of the Holy Ghost instruct and strengthen you therein that you may be brought up in the ways of the Lord. Amen.

Further my dear children, since it pleases the Lord to take me out of this world, I will leave you a memorial, not of silver or gold; for such jewels are perishable: but I should like to write a jewel into your heart, if it were possible, which is the word of truth, in which I want to instruct you a little for the best with the Word of the Lord, according to the little gift I have received from Him and according to my simplicity.

*

Be diligent in prayer and love the poor; for Christ also was poor for our sakes. Be therefore also merciful, even as your heavenly Father is merciful; for such shall be blessed, and shall obtain mercy. Also learn to be meek and lowly in heart; for such are blessed and shall inherit the earth. And blessed are the pure in heart; for they shall see God.

*

My children, be also just in all your dealings; for in the way of the just there is life, and in the beaten path there is no death. It is joy to the righteous to do that which is right, but fear to evildoers. Further, choose to earn your bread by the labor of your hands, and to eat your bread with peace. Seek not to be a merchant nor be anxious for great gain. Better is little with the fear of God, than great treasure and trouble therewith. Better is a dry morsel and quietness, than a house full of sacrifices with strife (Proverbs 15:16; 17:1).

*

O my dear children, I have written this in tears, admonishing you out of love, praying for you with a fervent heart, that if possible, you might be of this number. For when your father was taken from me, I did not spare myself day or night to bring you up, and my prayer and solicitude were constantly for your salvation, and even while in bonds my greatest care has always been that my prudence did not enable me to make better provision for you. For when it was told to me that you had been taken to Oudenarde, and thence to Bruges, it was a hard blow for me, so that I never had a greater sorrow. But when I thought that my coming or providing could not help the matter, and that for Christ's sake we must separate from all that we love in this world I committed all to the will of the Lord, and I still hope and pray constantly that He in His mercy will preserve you as He preserved Joseph, Moses and Daniel in the midst of wicked men.

*

David, my dear child, I herewith commend you to the Lord. You are the oldest, learn wisdom, that you may set your sisters a good example: and beware of bad company and of playing in the street with bad boys; but diligently learn to read and write so that you may get understanding. Love one another, without contention or quarreling; but be kind to each other.

*

Do not easily believe it when evil is told you of another, but examine the matter; and make no commotion when you are slandered, but bear it for Christ's sake.

Love your enemies, and pray for those who speak evil of you and afflict you. Rather suffer wrong than that you should grieve another; rather suffer affliction than that you should afflict another; rather be reproached than that you should reproach another; rather be slandered than that you should slander another; rather be robbed than that you should rob another; rather be beaten than that you should beat another, and so forth.

*

Further, my dear children, Betgen and Tanneken, my beloved lambs, I admonish you in all these same things, as that you obey the commandments of the Lord and also obey your uncle and aunt and your elders, and all who instruct you in virtue. To those whose bread you eat you must be subject in all that is not contrary to God. Always diligently admonish yourselves to do your work and you will be loved wherever you live. Be not quarrelsome or loquacious, or light-minded or proud, or surly of speech, but kind, honorable and quiet, as behooves young girls. Pray the Lord for wisdom and it shall be given you. Diligently learn to read and write and take delight therein, and you will become wise. Take pleasure and engage in psalms, hymns and spiritual songs. Seek for the *only* joy.

*

Herewith I commend you to the Lord, the God of Abraham, the God of Isaac, and the God of Jacob; may He keep you to the end of your lives. Amen.

My dear children, this I leave you as a memorial or testament. If you put it to good use, you will gather more treasure by it than if I had left you many riches, which are perishable; for the riches of this world may be lost through fire, war or misfortune.

My most beloved, though our adversaries tell you that your father and I are not of the same faith, do not believe them; for he confessed the truth concerning baptism and the incarnation of Christ in all that he was able to comprehend, and he valiantly testified to righteousness, giving his life for it, pointing out to you for an example, the same way which the prophets, the apostles and Christ Himself went. He had to go before through the conflict with much tribulation and suffering, and leave his children behind for Christ's sake; hence do likewise, for there is no other way. Give diligence to read the Testament. Amen.

van Braght (1979): 646-650

November 28

The Abundant Life?

Edward Yoder, United States, 1935

The general notion among many seems to be that the abundant life signifies an endless supply of mechanical gadgets and enough money at everybody's command to buy them and wear them out so they can speedily buy new ones or trade for a newer model gadget. The eminent scientist Millikan is quoted as saying that "the progress of civilization consists merely in the multiplication and refinement of human wants."

It is of course just the same old doctrine that capitalists and industrialists have been preaching all along, that prosperity and civilization must be interpreted in material terms, that profit is the basic motive in civilization, and that, in the last analysis, the human beings on this terrestrial sphere exist for the purpose of consuming material goods and an endless procession of gadgets and concoctions. What is to become of human dignity and self-respect under such a Frankenstein profit-monster? The chief end of man is no longer to love God and glorify Him forever, but to consume material goods and provide profits forever. The old catechism needs to be revised and brought up-to-date!

*

No law can be laid down as to what and how many mechanical gadgets any individual needs. But the point is that most folks never consider whether they need or really want a thing. If they have the money or the faith that they will get it and can convince dealers that they can get it sometime, they must get this and that, radio, car, golf outfit or what not, and why? Well, everybody else is getting such things or wants to get them as soon as they can. An abominable reason, I should say! It seems incredible when one stops to think about the matter, that the common practice about us should be such a pressure upon us and our conduct.

We talk about personal liberty and freedom, but how willingly we wear the shackles of social conformity! At our house we are more than glad to be without a telephone. In emergency instances we can telephone from the college, but that is hardly once or twice a year. And radio—it has always seemed to me that any person who values the privacy of home would have no radio about. Especially is the way radio broadcasting in this country is tied up with commercial advertising a veritable shame, and an insult to the listeners. It is only another phase of the doctrine of the abundant life, that millions of gullible folks must be dragooned into buying and consuming material goods so as to make more profit for stockholders. In one of his letters Sir Walter Raleigh remarked that it was the stupid people who make all the work and then do it. "To believe that machinery enriches life is foolishness."

Yoder (1985): 258, 259

November 29

Having Heard Your Word. . .
Leenaert Clock, The Netherlands, ca. 1625

*O*ur gracious, merciful God, dear heavenly Father, you who show and prove to us, your poor children, your abundant generosity and love and have not only given us this desire, zeal and willing spirit to assemble here before you in your holy name, but you have also permitted us to hear your Word (as has happened often and frequently before this) and through it have had your divine will presented and proclaimed—for this demonstrated benevolence, O God, we thank and praise you from the bottom of our heart and from the depth of our souls. We willingly confess our guilt because we have often been admonished and heard your faithful warning, but have not hastened to obey. O Lord, forgive us for the sake of your beloved Son, Jesus Christ.

We also beseech you, dear merciful Father, to make your Word that we have heard and received, alive, powerful and effective in all our hearts, and cause it to bear fruit that will remain unto life eternal;

That we may not only be reborn, thoroughly converted and changed, and renewed completely in your likeness, but also that we may be brought thereby to the perfect stature of Christ and thus grow, increase and be sustained; Yes, that we may set it as a mirror before the eyes of our heart and use it as living water to wash ourselves; that we may thereby become cleansed and pure, that the fruits of righteousness may spring from it and we may become equipped and prepared for every good work;

That our poor souls may also be made alive and well, and that it thus penetrate our hearts so that it will separate soul and spirit, joint and marrow;

That it will bring us to the point that we are not earthly but heavenly minded;

That it may ignite us and make us ardent and fiery unto all virtues;

That we may become utterly humbled and lowly of heart, wholly renewed with a view to showing compassion, grieving for others, and being moved to mercy; also,

That we may thereby taste the sweetness of your divine grace and of the eternal heavenly kingdom, taking our delight in it alone; and finally,

That we may attain the victory over the sly attacks of the devil and all the weapons of the enemy and be eternally kept and saved.

Thus, we ask you, dear Father, for all of our necessities, etc.—all this through your dearly beloved Son our Lord Jesus Christ, who taught us, for attaining your divine grace, to pray: "Our Father. . ."

Gross (Forthcoming)

November 30

Too Conscientious

Family Life, United States, 1983

"Do not be overrighteous, neither be overwise—why destroy yourself?"—Ecclesiastes 7:16 (NIV)

When I became convicted and felt the need of forgiveness at about eleven or twelve, I started to study the little Gideon New Testament given to each of us pupils at public school. But my praying for God's forgiveness and peace was frustrated because I felt I did not have the ecstatic emotional feeling that should follow being born again, according to some of the "Christian" books and literature I read.

*

I still feel grateful to a minister who unknowingly helped me when he preached repeatedly that feelings do not save us; they are not dependable. But God's Word is dependable. It promises eternal life to those that believe. The grace of God through Jesus saves us, not our feelings. It is for us to hold to His promises and keep our attention on Him—not on ourselves.

Really, though, this process of following that minister's teaching was slow. Because I didn't "feel" right with God, I became obsessed with carefulness to please God in every detail. Since confession and restitution for sins is part of repentance, I forced myself to apologize to people, however trivial the offense. At times I was so embarrassed that I could not do it, so my conscience would hound me for weeks until I would get it done.

One reason I was afraid to apologize was because I knew many of the things bothering me were so insignificant to the other person that he'd long since forgotten it.

At times I envied my schoolmates who seemed so carefree, not haunted by a heavy feeling lest some well-meant joke or prank may really have been a sin.

My reading development suffered because I laboriously stared at every word lest I be found lying if I told someone I'd read a book or article, but in reality had skipped a word or two.

By this time I was ripe for another fear—the fear of insanity. I'd heard people who were intellectually inclined—bookworms—were more likely to have mental problems. So I worried.

But I thank God for a mother who cared. My parents kept us children well supplied with physical labor on our farm so I usually slept well immediately upon going to bed. But often early in the morning I'd wake up and think about my troubles. Many times I'd get up before my older brothers and sisters so I could confide in Mom alone. Sometimes I'd sit on the top stair waiting till the sounds from the kitchen told me the time was right to go down.

She was always patient, and now being a parent myself, I can well imagine how she must have groped for ways to permanently help me.

I cannot say that suddenly one morning Mom brought a great Light to focus on me and all my life was changed. No, but I do know that our "early" talks gradually became less frequent. My fears were being replaced by trust that God loved and forgave me. I began to realize that God knows our motives and whether our basic desire is to please Him. Though I came to Mom less frequently, she encouraged me still to come if I needed unloading.

And I still want to do that. But no longer do I need to do it secretly, because I now know that it is perfectly "normal" and necessary for a person to confide in someone he trusts.

"How God Eased My Conscience" (1983): 2, 3

December

The True Celebration
Peter Riedemann, Germany, 1540

*T*o keep a festival or holy day is likewise not for the sake of the outward appearance, for the outward celebration is no more than a shadow and picture of that which is to come. But the essential reality itself is Christ. Since then the essential is Christ, the shadow must give way to him. That is, the outward to the real and true celebration in which the Lord delighteth, which celebration is; namely, to seek diligently to obey God, to do his will, to please him, to meditate upon his word day and night and do what is good and blessed. And, as one saith, to leave off and stop working or reveling in evil and to work in good; that is to say, to live and walk in the Spirit. That is the true celebration that God demandeth, as it is written, "Blessed is the man that doeth this and the son of man that observeth this; that keepeth the sabbath from polluting it, that is, that keepeth his hand from doing any evil."

That is the festival that God commandeth, which we should now diligently observe and keep. But celebrating as it is practiced in the world is an abomination to God. For the evil and shameful things that men are unable to do during the week because of their work, they do on the holy day, using it thereby for the very opposite, and it were indeed better that they had no holy days.

Yet we also have a day of quiet in which we read the Lord's word and listen to it, and thereby revive our heart to continue in the grace of God. Since, however, it is usual for all men to observe Sunday, we, in order to do offense to none (for which day is kept is a matter of indifference), keep the same day; but not because of the law, which is done away with in Christ, but, as we have said, to exercise ourselves in the word of God.

Rideman (1970): 125, 126

God For All Ages

Z. Marwa Kisare, Tanzania, mid-1900s

*A*braham was pitying himself. He has no son. He has no cattle. Before him all is darkness. Sarah, his wife, is barren. He sees that Eliezer of Damascus will inherit his household when he dies. This would be the time for Abraham to say there is no God. This is because people think God must give them everything. But it is not necessary that God enrich you. Some people die before bearing any children. What lack is this to them? None.

Sometimes I think it would have been better if my mother had never borne me. But she bore me and now I have all this trouble. My wife has no son. I have no cattle. All about me the land is dry.

God answered Abraham, "I am your portion." If God is on my side, and it is my business to see that he is on my side, then I have great wealth. If God is not with me, then I am in great poverty. This is wealth, that God is with you. You put your head to rest at a good place if God is with you.

When Abraham was a youth he was discouraged and complaining. But God told him, "My portion to you is great."

My dear young people, people tell you that you have been deceived by the Europeans who told you to follow God. But God's salvation was not concocted by the Europeans. God called Abraham long ago when the Europeans were still barbarous savages. God called Abraham out of savagedom. God called Abraham when the Europeans were still practicing witchcraft and divination, when they were savages. Even if others are deceived, don't you be deceived.

Here I stand, a cattle herdsman, a son of Kisare. There are only two of us here today, sons of Kisare who are following God. Most of Kisare's descendants do not know God. Many of Kisare's descendants who began in the way have turned back. And here I preach among those who are Kisare's people. But even if I am the only one to follow God, I have decided to die with my faith.

There comes a time in everyone's life when he stands alone with his decision. I have experienced much. I have been battered. I am now at a critical place in the battle where I can only go forward on the course I have chosen, entrusting the meaning of my life to God who called me to come out from the traditional ways of my ancestors.

Going back to Abraham, he died in his faith. First he was pitying himself. God told him how great was his reward. Abraham asked God to open his eyes so he could see. Had his eyes been open, then he would not have complained. God opened his eyes, giving him courage to continue on his chosen path.

Abraham lived to be an old man. All that time the land and the people of the land did not get tired of Abraham. The land gets tired of some people, wishing for them to die. But not Abraham. He became very rich. Why was he so greatly rewarded? Because he chose well in his youth. People who have lived to old age see that he who follows God, his life is good. Why? Because God makes up to him that which he lacks.

Shenk (1984): 186, 187

December 3

Do Not Forget Us
Swiss Brethren of Zurich, Switzerland, 1645

*T*he government agitators and policemen who sought after us brought teachers of the State Church along and pestered us day and night with riots, like they did earlier. So many were taken we cannot name them: husbands, wives, pregnant mothers, nursing infants and the sick. There were but few who were not made miserable. Many became widows and orphans, and many were driven out of the land, some to the wilderness and to the mountains, in their efforts to escape and to hide themselves. The searchers went through fields and through the woods after us. They announced it in the State Churches that no one is to help us or house any of us, not even take care of children, and everyone was permitted to help catch us.

Some of those who helped us were punished. (Someone must give a strict account to God.) We believe that the most prominent agitators who caused us so much sorrow and persecution and preach peace are surely bringing condemnation on themselves. The government is preaching that they are the "protectors."

Their faith and service for God give evidence that (Church) leaders are the guilty ones. We can hardly believe that the government knows how cruel the agitators have been to us. We believe the rioters are more responsible. They even stirred up the State Church people so that they thought they were doing God's service. It seems that these gruesome things that happened were not known by the government. We believe that there are many in the court house who are peaceful and merciful and do not want to put any blame on those who are innocent.

Especially do we wish that God will be merciful to those who have been merciful to us. As for the guilty ones, we wish that they might acknowledge their unmercifulness and discontinue it. It is awful to read and speak about it, how they treated pregnant mothers, women nursing infants, the old, the young, husbands, wives, virgins and children, and how they took their homes and houses, farms and goods. Yes, and much more how they made widows and orphans, and without mercy drove them from their homes and scattered them among strangers.

Our children will not be comforted by strangers, and fathers and mothers without their children. With some the father died in jail for lack of food and drink. Some were driven to strange lands so that fathers, mothers, and brother and sister family fellowship must be lived among strangers who do not love them. Now the children are brought up under cursing and ungodly influences which we cannot describe. We must leave it all to God. Do not understand that we are bitter as we write these facts. We wish especially that our descendants will not forget our suffering.

Kauffman (1977): 40-42

December 4

The Danger of Peace
Jakob Guth, Germany, 1702

Y ou dear fellow believers, know that in every language and nation today there are people zealously proclaiming Christ's kingdom, and presenting a great deal in written form as well as in speech about discipleship and other beautiful truths. They are even praising our own fellowship and the persecutions it has endured, including a number of our confessions of faith, and defending them in books, thus opening a large doorway into Christ's kingdom of love. It is therefore our obligation not to be the last in the procession of the spiritual Israel, leading into the land of promise, but rather much more the foremost, for in our ancestors we have, in the strength of God, suffered so very much for this promised land, that is, for this kingdom of Christ our King.

At the same time we should admonish and encourage one another, and by our example edify one another in speaking and in writing, wherever and however this is possible, in order not to experience what Israel, and the churches in Asia and elsewhere experienced, which had degenerated into wild grapevines.

This is especially the case because human nature is so depraved that it cannot endure good days of ease, for then, generally, the human soul is destroyed by its learning to love this world and the things of the world. For when the flesh grows fat and lascivious, it kicks and loses its hold on the rock of salvation, becoming the carnal nation which God complains about in Deuteronomy (32:15). Yes, then usually the spirit grows dry, weary, lazy and weak. It is just like a scales: when one part of the scales goes up the other comes down.

In view of this, dear brothers and sisters, I fear that in the peaceful days we have been enjoying, undisturbed and untroubled by our persecutors, even some of us may have grown lukewarm, discouraged and physically fat and satisfied, and we may indeed have become carnally attached to the world. For we see that the body which is not kept in constant motion easily becomes motionless and subject to all manner of serious, concealed sickness, whereas, on the contrary, the person who suffers in the flesh ceases to sin (1 Peter 4:1).

Accordingly, the cross and shame of Christ, which we are to bear outside the camp and city gate as he did, is the best medicine for all spiritual decline and decrease in faith, love and hope, as well as peace and joy in the Holy Spirit. For under this cross our ancestors and forebears, through the support of the Prince of Life, achieved this kind of experience and testing and this living hope, and thereby grew strong in the fight, and overcame kings (by their faith and patience), and stopped the jaws of lions, so that now all of us can live in peace, each under his own fig tree and vine.

To be sure, it is true that outward peace causes the number of confessing Christians to grow, but it is also true that at such times of ease Satan instigates all kinds of evil counsel and manages in the most subtle ways, with love of self, of the world and of money, and such kinds of most dangerous devices, to entice the believers of truth.

Gross (Forthcoming)

December 5

A New Faith—?

Swiss Brethren, Switzerland, ca. 1570

We desire to believe, live and walk according to the New Testament. If that must be, and ought to be called, a new faith according to the world, a faith which is thus conducted in accord with the New Testament, let it be so, let it remain so; we are therewith content. For we really want to drink of the cup of this New Testament—that is, we have no other desire, through the help of the Lord, than to rule our life according to the instructions of this Testament. Consequently it does not matter to us whether our faith is called old or new, nor do we want to be hostile or offensive to anyone for any other reason.

But even if our faith were new, and if in it we practiced not less but more righteousness than the world, in its old faith: whether even then, for these reasons, the world ought to persecute, revile, seize, torture and put us to death, this, I freely leave to you, my kind reader, and to each one who has understanding to consider and to judge with impartial judgment without regard of person. At that point, if one can come to no other verdict than that this is the course to be taken with us, then the kind reader will have to judge the Jews innocent who persecuted Christ, his apostles and his church, for having carried out such justice.

But if there were someone who had a thievish, adulterous, murderous faith, which would give him liberty in his faith to steal, murder, commit adultery and similar abominations: him or her I dare, out of the fear of God, neither defend nor condemn, neither judge nor damn, outside the guidelines of my Lord's Word (the New Testament). If such a person can support his faith on the basis of divine speech, I will let him work it out and carry the burden himself, even if my own feelings are contrariwise.

Gross (Forthcoming)

December 6

The Hidden Kingdom

Peter Jansz. Twisck, The Netherlands, early 1600s

Now the lamb that was slain, the Lion of the Tribe of Judah, the Root and Offspring of David had overcome and taken the sealed book out of the hand of Him that sat upon the throne and opened it and broken the seven seals, and with the opening of the first seal he showed forth the glory of the kingdom and restored that which had been lost through Adam's transgression or through the fall; for now all those who would overcome should be permitted to eat of the tree of life in the midst of the Paradise of God (Revelation 2:7, 6:2).

*

In the opening of this first seal the glory of God in its full measure was made manifest to the believers, the regenerated and unto those who had been spiritually resurrected, and this had also before been, and of this the angels knew at the time of the birth of the great King, for which reason they also desired to look into the great mystery of God which He now was about to bestow upon the children of men, over which, in great rejoicing, they broke out in harmonious melody upon the fields of Bethlehem, saying: "Glory to God in the highest, and on earth peace, good will to men. For unto you is born this day in the city of David a Savior, which is Christ the Lord."

*

Thus was the King of heaven born poor and hidden (as it were) from the boasting, noisy world in a lowly condition. But notwithstanding His birth was gloriously celebrated, much more so than the birth of any earthly prince or heir to a worldly throne ever was or ever can be. Not only did the humble shepherds rejoice because of the message brought them by the angels and praised God for it, but also princes from the distant East came and made known the mystery of the birth of the great King of kings, whose kingdom was to be an everlasting kingdom and whose dominion was to extend from sea to sea over all the earth.

In the natural appearance, however, he was the most despised of all; he was hated by both Jews and Gentiles, and His disciples (the citizens of His kingdom) had only bonds and tribulation awaiting them. The prophet indicates the reign of the King of the Jews when he says (Isaiah 9:6), "And the government shall be upon his shoulders."

On the other hand, when we look upon the kingdoms of this world, the greater the authority the more honor and service the potentate or sovereign may command. In this kingdom of our Lord, however, the power and authority of the Ruler becomes great through suffering, patience and by enduring the offenses and evil entreatings of men. For this reason also the early Christians praised God when they were accounted worthy for Christ's sake to suffer reproach.

For thus the great King commanded his followers to rejoice when men should reproach and persecute them, and speak all manner of evil against them falsely for His sake. In this manner also the apostles, as its first counselors, ruled this kingdom in lowliness and did not ask others to serve them, but they themselves, at all times, served and recognized that God had placed them as the very lowest, as it were, appointed unto death.

*

That this is the kingdom which God would establish while yet the temporal kingdoms spoken of (namely Babylon, Persia, Greece and Rome) existed, can here be shown or proved in few words; for he says not, "Before or after these kingdoms," but "In the days of these kings" or kingdoms (Daniel 2:44). And that it is the kingdom in which those who arose in the first resurrection live and reign with Christ is shown by the stone which became a great mountain and filled the whole earth (Daniel 2).

Twisck (1913): 20-23

December 7

The Ark of Salvation History
Henry Funk, United States, mid-1700s

*R*egarding Noah's ark and all that was on and in it, there is much to meditate. Here God's love and his desire for the salvation of man through Christ is shown. In the first place the whole world may be taken to be represented by this ark; the lower story the first era of the world; from Adam to the flood; the middle story of the ark, the second era of the world, from the flood to Christ in the flesh; the third or upper story, in which was the window, from Christ to the end of the world.

*

That the ark could have but one window, up in the third story, through which light entered into the ark and gave light to the upper, middle and lower stories (for no light could come into the ark otherwise), plainly prefigures the light of God that shines through Christ. "God is the light and in him is no darkness at all" (1 John 1:2). Jesus said: "I am the light of the world" (John 8:12). "That was the true light which lighteth every man that cometh into the world" (John 1:9).

And since the window was in the upper part or story of the ark, it is believable that there was more light in the upper story than there was in the middle; and more in the middle than there was in the lower. So also according to that which the holy scripture indicates, the light of the comforting gospel of salvation through Christ shone from the beginning into the first or antediluvian era of the world in the preaching of the name of the Lord through the Spirit of God, and that those who believed on it obtained grace of God, as did Noah and others before him.

*

God desires all mankind to come unto him into the ark and church of his covenant, that all may be preserved from the fearful destruction of this world. As the ark had three stories or floors so that all the creatures in the ark were preserved, so also God had in the three eras of the world his believers in the church of the covenant of his blood, by which he redeemed them, and he will also preserve them in the ark of his church, whose Head he is, from the fearful destruction of the ungodly.

And in the last day of the Lord, by his angels, he will gather all his own from the four winds, from one end of the heavens to the other, or from the beginning to the end, and lead them all, young and old, into his fold, which is the heavenly ark of his eternal kingdom.

Because Jesus has the keys, he locked the door behind Noah, so that neither the ungodly nor any other plague could now reach Noah in the ark any more. So also, when the Lord shall have gathered his own in his kingdom, he will shut the door behind his own, so that when the torment of the ungodly begins, neither the devils nor ungodly men, nor any other tribulation, with which the devils and the ungodly are tormented can ever enter the abode of the saved in the ark of the eternal kingdom; for where the Lord shuts the door, no man can open it; neither the devil, nor hell, nor the false prophets, nor ungodly men can ever unfasten the bars of the Lord. Hence the godly will suffer no further tribulation from contact with evil, but will rejoice forever with the unspeakable joy which Jesus has prepared for and bestowed upon them, for Jesus is in all things Alpha and Omega.

Funk (1915): 38-41

December 8

Expectancy
Andre B. Goll, France, 1962

Wonderful and desirable as it is for every soul, conversion can bring only imperfect satisfaction in this life here below. The believer increasingly feels his need for greater and deeper relationship with his God; for this reason a sometimes languishing expectancy becomes apparent in the hearts of many men and women living in the fear of the Lord. Numerous passages in the Psalms especially underline this expectancy: "My soul thirsteth for the living God; when shall I come and appear before God?" (Psalm 42:2); "O God, thou art my God; early will I seek thee: my soul thirsteth for thee, my flesh longeth for thee in a dry and thirsty land, where no water is" (Psalm 63:1).

Pious persons such as Simeon and Anna were also smitten with this nostalgic expectancy of the revelation of the day of the Lord; so they had the blessed privilege of being the eyewitnesses of a marvelous step forward leading to this great day.

In conversing with His disciples, the Lord often repeated that they should not become bound to the things of this world, of which Satan is the prince, but rather to turn their affections to the kingdom of heaven, toward the Father's house where a place will be prepared for each one.

*

In their prophetic messages about the day of the Lord, the Apostles do not fail to emphasize how this position of expectancy should characterize each child of God. On the one hand, expectancy because salvation is not yet complete, awaiting the redemption of the body: "The whole creation groaneth and travaileth in pain together until now. . .we ourselves groan within ourselves waiting for the adoption, the redemption of our body" (Romans 8:22, 23). "For in this we groan, earnestly desiring to be clothed upon with our house which is heaven" (2 Corinthians 5:2).

On the other hand, expectancy as concerns sanctification without which no one shall see the Lord. Sanctification also in order to be made worthy, as it were, of Him who we are awaiting; the King of kings, the Lord of lords, in the name of whom every knee shall bow, in the heavens, on the earth, and under the earth, and every tongue shall confess that Jesus Christ is Lord to the glory of God the Father.

Dyck ([1962]): 84, 85

December 9

The Three Appearances of Christ
Jakob Denner, Germany, ca. 1707

Denner's subjective and spiritualizing emphasis is evident here. The spiritual presence of Christ in the soul is given the status of the historical appearances of Christ at his birth and at the end of the age—making Christ's second coming really his third!

The Holy Scripture, as a testimony of its veracity, presents to us and speaks to us in a number of places about the three appearances of our Lord Jesus Christ. The first is the appearance in the flesh. . . . The other appearance of Jesus Christ takes place daily, hourly and momentarily in all children of God in their inner souls through the Spirit and faith. . . . The third and last appearance of Christ is still in the future, and we will experience it when he comes in great majesty and power as it is described in Matthew 25 and in Luke 21.

If then the first appearance of Christ in the flesh, or the birth of Jesus, is a comfort to us, we want to rejoice in it heartily. I am not speaking here of carnal joy, which unfortunately is the only joy that most people of the world know and experience during these holy days. But rather we want to experience in our souls a genuine heavenly, spiritual and holy refreshing in our hearts concerning the birth of our Savior, and then also the third and last appearance of the same person of Christ with great desire and joyful longing, and in truth; so that we can say with the patriarch Jacob, "Lord, I am looking with expectation for thy salvation," as in Genesis 49:18. And for this we must daily, hourly and momentarily experience the spiritual presence of Christ in our souls. We must taste and experience him, and become more and more like him in spirit.

*

Without this the two others cannot help us or be useful to us. Christ must needs be born in the soul through faith. We must be constantly united with him in love. We must learn to know Christ spiritually.

Denner (1730): 63, 64, trans. by Noah G. Good

December 10

Radical Conversion
Kurt Lichdi, Germany, 1962

What do we mean by conversion? The term itself is related to our concept of turning about, or forsaking a way we have pursued, of giving up a false objective and of turning to a new objective. Religiously speaking, conversion means to turn from the ways of the world in which Satan controls and to turn to God in complete surrender.

The clearest example of radical conversion is found in the life of Saul who became Paul on his way to Damascus. The word of the Lord struck him as lightning until he could only ask, "Lord, what would you have me to do?" Thus, the persecutor of Jesus and of His church was transformed into a chosen instrument of God, the great apostle to the Gentiles.

A similar sudden conversion was experienced by the hearers of Peter's sermon at Pentecost, for they being struck in the heart by what Peter was saying could only ask, "Men and brethren, what shall we do?"

To this question Peter could answer only "repent." Thus, we are given to understand that to repent is close in meaning to the meaning of conversion, being a change of mind and heart and orientation. In this experience the old way in which the spirit has gone is seen as wrong, as evil and contrary to God, and a new spiritual way in a new direction is begun through a new inner orientation towards God. This way leads to salvation in Jesus Christ.

*

But now a Christian must be asked: is conversion always an experience that comes to us suddenly on a certain date and through a specific experience leading to this awakening? The conversion of Paul as we have heard was radical, sudden and dramatic. The same is recorded, for example, about the experience of the church father, Augustine. But there is also a turning about that extends itself over a longer period, that is experienced gradually or in stages.

In this connection we can refer to the experience of Peter. In spite of his tremendous insights as we find them recorded in Luke 5 and 9, Jesus still said to him, "And when you have turned again, strengthen your brethren." We know that Peter actually did deny his Lord. That according to John 21 the Lord following His resurrection tested him concerning his love and that finally Peter did become the great leader and confessor of Jesus Christ.

We also know of development in Menno Simons. He required much time to grow from his earlier life and orientation into the new life, assuming the new way, and finally breaking radically with the old. His was a long road before he finally realized that the teaching and practice of the Roman Church did not agree with the teaching of the Scriptures. It was a long road until he was overcome by his Lord and found his way to a clear and full confession of faith.

Dyck ([1962]): 79-81

December 11

My Experience Can Help You Nothing
Christian Burkholder, United States, 1792

*T*he work of the new birth is a wonderful work, and is effected by God in the soul through Christ. But I am not to dictate to God how he is to go to work to effect the same in you. If you yield yourself up wholly into the hands of God without resistance, he will commence and also finish the work of the new birth in your soul.

*

The new birth takes place in the heart. Therefore the Savior compares it to the wind, which we hear but cannot see. Wind and water are strong elements which are serviceable to the preservation of human life. The spiritual wind which Jesus breathes upon the soul, and the water which he offers it, are the gifts of God for the preservation of the life of the soul. "If thou knewest the gift of God, and who it is that saith to thee, 'Give me to drink,' thou wouldest have asked him, and he would have given thee living water."

*

My experience can help you nothing; nor can your experience help me anything. Besides, boasting much of ourselves is the work of the "old man."

*

If you talk much of your experience and your life shows the contrary, you will become a laughingstock before the world and a hypocrite before God.

*

Christ has given us in his birth a pattern of true humility. Thither, namely, to his manger, we are to direct our course. Indeed he has given us in his birth, doctrine and life an example of child-like humility. Those who are born of Christ have become partakers of his nature and virtues. He, "according to his abundant mercy, hath begotten us again unto a lively hope."

Conversation (1856): 220-222, 224

December 12

Experiences
Edward A. Kline, United States, ca. 1980

"Modern Christianity" builds too much on experiences. An experience of conversion is emphasized, then afterwards other experiences which are supposed to make a man spiritual and holy, or to prove that he is that way! Some people "live" from experience to experience. Not only is this foreign to the Scriptures, but it also does not work! The result is that discipleship and sanctification in exercising our wills is not emphasized much, if at all. It is assumed that it is not possible to do some of the commands in Scripture, unless you have this or that experience.

*

The problem is that there is no following Christ and obedience on a *daily basis*. Such experiences in themselves do not make a man spiritual, rather they exalt the individual.

Many people who profess Christ start doing their own will again after having surrendered it in conversion to Christ. Their life once more revolves around themselves. A new experience is an easy way to feel spiritual once more. The true spirituality of discipleship cannot be practiced in reality unless the will is surrendered and does not function selfishly.

An experience without obedience and discipleship is like an engine that is not running. The engine may be in running condition, and the tank full of fuel, but if it is not running, where is the reality, and of what value is the engine? Experience-oriented people constantly fill the tank, but seldom start the engine. The starting of the engine is like the "working out" of the work of Christ within. It is the responsibility of man.

Closely associated with this worldly concept of experiences is the idea that much activity in religious matters is spirituality. To be truly spiritual is to have the soul (thinking, will and feelings) broken, and in obedience to Christ and His body, the Church. The measuring stick for service to Christ is not the amount of service being attempted, but the source and motivation. Too much activity today springs from minds and wills which are self-centered.

*

The motive of Christian service is obedient love to our Lord. That love seeks no glory for its own. True spirituality is the mind, will and emotions acting not by themselves, but by the spirit in obedience to the Scriptures and Christ. It is not doing more or less than Scripture supports. It is doing nothing of ourselves, but only that which is confirmed by the Scriptures and the Scriptural Church. It does not seek great things, but seeks only to obey. It is "Gelassenheit" and joy in following Christ through pain, distress, cares and suffering, as well as in joy, peace, honor or good report. For the soul that has "lost itself" there is no difference.

Kline (n.d.): 22, 23

December 13

If Christ Is to Be Born in Us

Jakob Denner, Germany, ca. 1707

*I*f Christ is to be born in us spiritually it is essential that we first have a genuine experience of penitence. We must very sincerely be converted before God. We must forsake all unrighteousness and sin. First we need to appropriate John's baptism of repentance and conversion before we can share at all in Christ's baptism to holiness. For John indeed baptized "with water unto repentance, but Christ baptized with fire" as we see in Matthew 3:11. There is no other way that we can attain to Christ's baptism, there is no other way that we can be made one with him, there is no other way that we can be justified and sanctified except by repentance and water baptism, so that true penitence can be experienced in our souls.

But this, unfortunately, is not popular today and people do not want to hear about it. Of course we do want to enjoy Jesus Christ with his forgiveness of sin; but not John with his teaching of penitence and conversion. We do want to have and accept God's grace; but we do not like to come to God in contrition of heart and repentance. We do want the forgiveness of sin from God; but we are not ready to give up sinning. But we find comfort in our sins and make a profession of having experienced the grace of God through Christ, even though we are continuing on in our lustful, carnal way of life, even though not only John, but indeed also Christ himself, preached nothing but this: "Repent, for the time is at hand that the kingdom of God may come in. Make restitution for sin and believe in the gospel."

The message of repentance was not only the beginning of Christ's message, but also his continuing message till the end—for when he took leave of his disciples he said to them in farewell, "Preach repentance and the forgiveness of sins to all people in the world" (Luke 24:47). First comes repentance, then pardon of sins. That is the way God set up the program; true repentance, genuine and sincere repentance, or in other words a complete change of mind (this is actually the literal meaning of the Greek) must come first in order that we can experience God's grace and forgiveness of sin. Without a true turning around and change of heart it does not come about. There is no way without this that we can take any comfort or assurance of the grace of God or of salvation.

Denner (1730): trans. by Noah G. Good

December 14

Courage from the Future
Eberhard Arnold, Germany, 1921

We believe in this new birth of a life of light from God. We believe in the future of love and in the constructive fellowship of men. We believe in the peace of God's kingdom, that He will come to this earth. This faith is not a playing with a future shape of things which exists only in our imagination now. No. The same God who will bring this future gives His heart and His spirit today. His name is the *I Am Who I Am*. His nature is the same now as it will reveal itself in the future. He revealed His heart in Jesus. He gives us His Spirit in Christ's presence among us. In His church, the embodiment of Christ's life, He lives the life of Jesus once again. This church is the hidden living seed of the future Kingdom. The character of peace and the love-spirit of the future have been entrusted to her. Therefore she practices justice and peace and joy in this world, also in the present age.

We speak up in protest against bloodshed and violence from the reality of this life-witness, no matter from which side these powers of death may come. Our witness and our will for peace, for love at any cost, also at the cost of our own lives, has never been more necessary than it is today. Those are in error who reproach us that at a time when this question is not at all urgent, we are speaking of defenselessness, nonviolence, conscientious objection, of discipleship of Jesus in the power of radiating love which makes all violence impossible and excludes us from inflicting any kind of injury on others.

This question is more urgent today than it ever was, and it will become evident that loyal perseverance in an attitude of absolute love requires ultimate courage, manly courage unto death.

Arnold (1967): 62-64

The Peaceful Kingdom of Christ

Peter Jansz. Twisck, The Netherlands, early 1600s

Concerning this glorious time of peace, the holy men of God have written a great deal and desired to see it. They also testified prophetically concerning it. Now (as this time came) the threatening power of the Mosaic law was set aside, and the words of the prophet could be applied, "Comfort ye, comfort ye my people, saith your God. Speak ye comfortably to Jerusalem, and cry unto her, that her warfare is accomplished. . . . Prepare ye the way of the Lord, make straight in the desert a highway for our God. Every valley shall be exalted, and every mountain and hill shall be made low: and the crooked shall be made straight, and the rough places plain" (Isaiah 40:1-4). "He shall feed his flock like a shepherd: he shall gather the lambs with his arm, and carry them in his bosom, and shall gently lead those that are with young" (Isaiah 40:11). "The wolf also shall dwell with the lamb, and the leopard shall lie down with the kid; and the calf and the young fatling together; and a little child shall lead them. And the cow and the bear shall feed; their young ones shall lie down together; and the lion shall eat straw like the ox. And the sucking child shall play on the hole of the asp, and the weaned child shall put his hand on the cockatrice' den. They shall not hurt nor destroy in all my holy mountain" (Isaiah 11:6-9).

"And they shall beat their swords into plowshares and their spears into pruning hooks: nation shall not lift up the sword against nation; neither shall they learn war any more" (Isaiah 2; Micah 4).

All this is fulfilled in the kingdom of Jesus Christ which is the church, from the days of the apostles on until the time when this time shall be fulfilled, and there is none that more fully fulfilled this Scripture than the Apostle Paul, who, like a ravenous wolf, caught and tore the lambs of Christ and took pleasure in the death of the innocent sheep of Christ. Afterwards, however, he became peaceable and prepared so that like a little child of few days (after his regeneration or spiritual resurrection) he led calves and young lions and fatlings together. In persecution he was comforted in the word of truth, in the power of God, through the weapons of righteousness, to his right and to his left, and he testified that now is the day of salvation, the acceptable time in which God will hear us.

Twisck (1913): 11, 12

A Mighty Host, Clean and Fit

Henry Funk, United States, mid-1700s

God has, according to his word, which is truth, accepted all the human creation as clean through Christ, for his service, and for the joy of heaven; and out of these clean creatures who confess Jesus as their Savior by faith, God has chosen for himself a church whose members are to surrender their bodies as a sacrifice for the sake of Jesus and his gospel's, and of whom many thousands have already been offered up. . . . There were and are the holy creatures fit for the sacrifice and ordained thereto by God. As shown by the symbols the cattle, sheep, goats and doves or pigeons were chosen from among the clean beasts for sacrificial purposes; yet there were many other beasts that were clean, but not used for sacrifice, but only for food, by the people of Israel. It is the same with the human creatures. Besides those who have been offered up for the name of Jesus, there is a great multitude of people who are recognized in the word of the Lord as clean and fit for the everlasting kingdom, and yet are not taken as bodily sacrifice for the name of Jesus and his gospel, so that a mighty host will be found out of all nations.

To this host belong, first, the infant children, who by the sacrifice of Jesus were cleansed from the sin of their father, so that no mortal or condemning sin of the parents rests upon them. We do not find that God gave any command to children in their ignorance that would render them unclean, until they come to the years of speech and understanding. A great number of unknowing infants are taken away by death, into the everlasting kingdom, as Jesus promised: "Suffer the little children to come unto me, for of such is the kingdom of heaven. Verily I say unto you, Whosoever shall not receive the kingdom of heaven as a little child, shall in no wise enter therein."

*

No one can take this kingdom from the children, for it is wrought for them and in them by Jesus, as stated above.

Secondly, there are among the heathen nations of the world many people who have not the law and know nothing of Jesus and his gospel, or at least the instruction they have received is not based upon the wholesome foundation of the Spirit of God, but rather it is hidden from their eyes by the teaching of false prophets. Of this condition Paul writes: "For when the Gentiles, who have not the law, these, having not the law, are a law unto themselves, thereby showing the work of the law written in their hearts, their conscience also bearing witness, and their thoughts meanwhile accusing, or else excusing one another."

*

There are other records of the Gentiles and instances can be seen or heard of to this day of Gentiles or heathen many of whom, although they have no written law of God, yet have a law within their hearts, which shows them that there is a God, and that they shall rise again after this life and that they shall then receive a reward according as their earthly life has been: evil if they have lived wickedly; good if they have lived rightly.

*

Love is the fulfilling of the law, and in this respect many heathen are far superior to many so-called Christians, because these latter have Christ simply upon their tongues, but not in their hearts, neither do they confess and reveal him by their works. Inasmuch as God looketh upon the heart and will judge the secrets of the heart, whether it be good or evil, he will no doubt look upon the heart of the heathen in which is the law of the Spirit with the testimony of good works, and it is believable that the Lord will gather from among the heathen a great multitude of clean creatures, from the east and from the west, from the north and from the south, and that they shall sit down in the kingdom of heaven with Abraham, Isaac and Jacob, to the joy of the angels in the everlasting kingdom.

Funk (1915): 210-212

December 17
True Values
Peter Cornelisz. Plockhoy, England, 1659

Shall we never be able to attain to that equal judgment in putting a true value upon real virtue wheresoever it be found: as well in a beggar as in a Prince? And to leave off more to admire the Ornaments of a Magistrate than the Office he sustains? And esteeming less of poverty than of superfluity? Of the honor than of the state? Of a good conscience less than of a popular or vain applause? Of a piece of bread than of delicious dainties? Of Water than Wine? Of a green bank of Turf than of a Costly Couch?

*

We shall be able to do it if we did well weigh that the World's turn is but a short Comedy, and that we are but Actors who appear no more than once upon the Stage. And if we did seriously consider that all things are described and represented to us in the World far otherwise than they are in themselves, but especially when we have well pondered that honest and godly people after a very little while are to expect a participation and enjoyment of another kind of honor and dignity than any the World promiseth.

Shall we never be able to attain to this, to choose rather to lay up our Estates in the hungry bellies of the poor than in a few bags? To lay the foundation of our praise upon the prayers of the poor? To make the cross of Christ our glory and not to eschew the disfavor of man, as the reward of our well-doing? In a word, to put off all desire of revenge, to the judgment of Christ; we shall be able to do all this if we forget not that our God is the most faithful of all Debtors, and the most sure of all Securities; if also we never forget that his praise which shall be given to us in the presence of men and Angels is the most glorious praise, and that his remunerations and recompenses are the most noble and everlasting.

To how happy an hour are we born if we do enter upon this communion or fellowship! And from how many vexations will it release us!

*

But since Christian religion is come into the world, it is a wonderful thing to consider what a light brake in together with it, *viz.* such a light that all they whose hearts were touched therewith, throwing all from them, betook themselves to it for refuge, as to a true and steadfast liberty after a long and horrible captivity, easily forgetting their riches, state, rule and possession, forsaking parents, wife, children, relations and whatsoever before was most near and dear unto them, not being by any temptations of Tyrants to be drawn from the sweetness of the Christian life.

Harder and Harder (1952): 162, 163

December 18

The Light in Japan
Toshiko Aratani, Japan, 1990

When Jesus came to the world, he was a light to many people. To those who were oppressed in darkness, he must have been shining as a light. He was the light of justice for those who were suffering under injustice. It must have been heartwarming and encouraging for those who had never seen such a bright light in their lives before to see the light of Christ.

*

As some of you may know, Japanese society is a very competitive society. Schools are ranked by their academic hierarchy. Your career and future success are quite well determined by the school you graduate from. Children have to study very hard in order to pass the entrance examinations. Parents try to find any possible way for children to do that. Children often go to another prep school after their regular school day is over. Schools in Japan are generally big and classrooms are crowded.

I work at a small Catholic women's junior college which tries to respond to students who live with this kind of pressure. My school is regarded the lowest rank in the city. We intentionally give two entrance exams; the last one after all the other schools in the city have given theirs, so that any one who has failed in other schools can try our exam. We purposely do a group interview, and we start by asking all the students how many schools they have failed. Once they know that everyone else has failed in other schools they seem to feel so liberated and free.

*

At first they are worn out from such competitive examinations and failure in other schools. But we have devoted nuns and dedicated teachers. They all know the students by name. These students have been hiding behind others in class all their lives. But our teachers give them personal attention and the students are no longer "nobodies." In the beginning, the students seem uneasy because many of them don't have good self-esteem. Gradually they begin to feel worthy of themselves as they learn that teachers care for each one.

We have a required course called "Drama in Literature" which we teach in English. Everyone has to act in the drama. Four years ago when I first started teaching at that school, the students did so well in the drama that I asked the county-wide college drama club if we could participate in their annual English drama contest. It was such a joy when we won the golden prize that year. In other bigger schools, only those who love drama make up their drama club, but since we are a small school the whole class takes a role in one thing or another and contributes to the drama. It is a beautiful example of cooperation.

*

The other day I met an American nun who visited us for two weeks for an intensive English course. She had asked us to send photos with names of each student before she came. Sure enough, when she came to Japan she had already memorized all the names and faces. You know how difficult it is to remember all these foreign names. She loved and cared for each of them so much that when it was time to say good-bye to her, the students were reluctant and cried. This is a small personal experience of changes seen in people when they live in the light of love.

Yes, when we are in the light, we make new discoveries and experience joy. Each person will find a different talent and gift. For some it may mean fighting against injustice or straightening the wrong in society. For some it may mean caring for the weak or sitting beside the dying. For each one it will mean finding their own unique, creative way to please the Lord. Verse 10 in Ephesians chapter 5 says, "Walk as children of the light. . .and try to discern what pleases the Lord." Yes, it is a creative and artistic work to find our worthiness and gift in the light from above and to know what to do. It should not be obligatory, legalistic or painful, but enlightening and joyful.

Let us walk in the light and when we find our darkness exposed in the light, let us be brave to repent and correct our way.

Aratani (1991): 15, 16

Sun of Righteousness
Andreas Kolb, United States, 1786

Thou Sun of righteousness, Lord Jesus Christ my life,
Let thy reflection at all times, give me light and brightness
Illumine me inwardly, thou bright Sun of grace,
Lord Jesus, joy of Grace.

I Jesus am the true light, that illumines all men,
That appears inwardly to him, that gives himself to me.
He who asks for brightness shall have as a gift the light of life.

O shine, then, Lord Jesus Christ, brightly into my heart,
And cast out all that is dark, by the candle of thy brightness.
O dear Jesus, let thy reflection which can shine through all things,
Bring to me thy light and brightness.

I will illumine clearly and brightly those who from their hearts love me.
And will reveal to them that which was long in darkness.
O love me then, and I will according to thy will and thy wish,
Fill thee with light and brightness.

O give to me, Lord Jesus, that I might love thee with all my soul,
And follow after thee willingly compelled by pure love.
Just as you have, Lord Jesus, upon this pilgrim way, left to me an example.

Yes, follow me, and do not turn to the right or to the left.
Order your whole life according to my love as my spirit,
Which I gave you, has shown you I am the way to life.

So let me then, Lord Jesus Christ,
Come to the father through you, where all is light and life,
Where the host of the righteous are assembled before your throne.

Kulp (1987): 178

Jesus, Our True Lord

Jakob Denner, Germany, ca. 1707

*B*efore Jesus was born "there went out a decree from Caesar Augustus that all the world was to be taxed," or registered. By this Caesar was saying, in effect, that he was their lord and master, and they were his subjects. And by registering they said, in effect, that they were agreeing to be his subjects and obediently placed themselves in subjection under him.

Adam and all of us are creatures of God made by and for him. God is our all-supreme Lord. So long then as Adam, prior to the fall of man, obediently placed himself in subjection under God, he enjoyed the true state of salvation. But just as soon as he rejected this and determined to be his own master, and did not follow the will of God but his own, he fell into the most abject misery.

And all of us likewise have gone the same way, so there is no other way or means, except that we must turn around and surrender our wills completely to God. He is our sovereign Lord, the true Augustus Caesar, the one who increases the kingdom. For who has it in his power to increase and bless us more than he? So if now we wish to be benefitted by his grace, and have Jesus Christ become reality in our souls and we become partakers of him, we must put ourselves entirely at his disposal in complete submission, humility and obedience, in genuine denial of self and our own wills. We must seek with all diligence to come to the place where we can truly say:

"O my God, you only are my Creator and Lord! Look, I cast myself down to be entirely subject to your holy will, with all that is within me or pertains to me. Here is my heart, my soul, my body, my spirit. Here is all I have and am; I cast it all down and offer it as a sacrifice to you, O Lord, make it genuinely submissive to you. If before now I have resigned this to the world, or if till now I have walked according to my own will, oh, not any more, for from now on all that I have and am is to be subject to your will. Renew this decision day by day more and more, and make me willing and able to follow you in all things and to be obedient."

If we were minded like this and if we could truly say this, we would taste within us and internally experience that Jesus has been born in our souls; we would increase and grow more and more in the grace of God, and this would become more and more real in our souls. It can be no other way. If we want to experience God's grace in us alive, and be firmly assured in our souls, we must be surrendered from the bottom of our hearts and in our wills to him. For how can it be possible for Christ to be born in the soul of the person who opposes God?

Denner (1730): 67, 68, trans. by Noah G. Good

First Christmas

H. Frances Davidson, United States, 1915

As the first Christmas at Macha Mission drew near, a query arose as to how it should be observed, and whether services should be held, since no one could yet speak very well the language. David and Gomo were eager for services, saying that they would put forth every effort to speak to the people about Christ. We longed to give the people something on that day as an expression of our good will, but could not see the way open to do so. At Matepo Mission salt was always given, but in this part of the country salt was very expensive and there was only a little on hand, and we were not prepared to give them meat, as we had little opportunity of procuring game for ourselves. Services, however, were announced for the day, and early in the morning some natives began to arrive, curious to know what the day was like.

In the morning Sister Engle and I were sitting at the table on the veranda, eating our breakfast, speaking of the plans for the day, and expressing a wish that there was some food to be set before the people. While speaking, we heard a goat bleat, and presently two natives, one of whom was carrying a goat on his shoulders, came toward us. They put the goat down on the ground before us, saying as they did so, "The Chief, Macha, sent you this as a present." Here was the answer to our wish and unuttered prayer. Another native headman a short time previously had also presented a goat, and we had bought one, and these three would be sufficient for the dinner. Our praises ascended simultaneously, and we realized that the promise was again verified, "Before they call, I will answer; and while they are yet speaking I will hear."

*

There were ninety-six grown people assembled, chiefly fathers and mothers, heads of families, and these were all seated along the veranda and in the shade of the tent. David took up the subject of Christmas and its origin by first reading from the Zulu Testament which, of course, they did not understand. Before he had read much the Lord sent a first-class interpreter, in the person of a Mutonga native who had worked for some time in Bulawayo, and there learned to read and speak the Zulu language and to understand the Gospel. He was not, however, a Christian, as we learned, but he proved a most ready and excellent interpreter for the day; and as the message was given in Zulu, he as readily interpreted it into the vernacular of the people.

*

At the close of the discourse some of the rest of us spoke for a short time on the same theme, and also explained the cause of our being there among them. Then after a hymn and prayer they were given their food. A bountiful dinner had also been prepared for ourselves, a portion of which we handed over to the two helpers who had so faithfully labored to make the day a success. It is needless to say that they too thoroughly enjoyed their dinner. In every way this first Christmas was one long to be remembered, with nothing to mar the perfect harmony of the occasion.

Davidson (1915): 274-276

December 22

Incarnation: God Is With Us
Jacob J. Enz, United States, 1957

We fear dishonoring Christ by bringing Him too close to man; we fear deifying man by bringing him too close to Christ. In the Bible we do not find such abnormal fear of mixing the two to the detriment of either.

*

Nothing has been quite as devastating to our sense of deep involvement in the incarnation of Christ as the heresy of testamental Christianity. Our common thought about the Bible sees the Old Testament on a low level though we are ready to grant a gradual rise in that level. With the Gospel of Matthew, however, we commonly shift in our thinking to a very high level. With this erroneous conception of the relation of the two testaments we have pushed Jesus above our level of life and have skimmed off His words from His person, turning them into principles which are much easier to ignore than the life of one who lives on our own plane. Whether in the overemphasis on the deity of Christ or in the deification of principle (both done in such a way that permits us to excuse our sin), we arrive at a point far short of the "fulness of the stature of Christ." We have surely "come short of the glory of God."

The first page of the New Testament is a perfect illustration of how we are to think of Christ. In our ordinary reading we quickly skip over the monotonous genealogy to get to the Christmas story. How we dwell on the uniqueness of Christ! And I am not suggesting that we should forget the virgin birth! For me it has an integral place. But proportionwise look at the earthiness, the human side of Jesus! Seventeen verses of genealogy show His deep roots in humanity. The line is hardly a pure one: Abraham, the father of the faithful was also a liar and polygamist; David, the founder of the kingly line, an adulterer. The deep roots in the Old Testament are indicated by the first sentence, "The book of the genealogy. . . ." which is a takeoff on the literary structure of Genesis so that the whole gospel is to be understood as a second beginning closely connected with that very human beginning.

*

This experience in both testaments may be summed up in this: God totally and aggressively accessible to man through Christ, who is the living historical manifestation of the continuing immediate experience by Israel of his saving presence. Reality withholds nothing from a totally responsive man.

That man has the capacity for this is implicit in our doctrine of creation where man is created in the image of God and carries on where God leaves off in the naming process.

*

In addition to the incarnation of God in His people and in Christ there is yet a sin-neutralized incarnation of God in everyone. This is testified to in both testaments. In the judgment scene of Matthew (25:40, 45), to ignore the needy one, whether a child of God or not, is to leave God out in the cold.

*

In this universal indwelling of God in man, either as actively recognized or as neutralized by sin, we find the basis of loving God and neighbor as himself. When we destroy others we are destroying not only God, but also self since in God our own self cannot be separated from the self we destroy in others. The refusal to take the life of another is not a peripheral biblical concern championed by a few eccentrics. It is the inescapable essence of Christianity's most distinctive and foundational conviction—the incarnation.

Enz (1972): 58-63

December 23

Charity and Dignity
John H. Redekop, Canada, 1971

A bit unevenly but with full harmony the singers' voices penetrated the old frame shack. Indian Joe heard them and his face gradually tensed. A year ago, almost to the day, they had sung for him, and left him a hamper and some Christmas tracts. It had lasted him some days and then he was back to his meager fare. They had spent about five minutes at his place; having done their charity for him they left him with more things but less dignity and had rushed back to their upper middle class homes.

Now he heard them again. He could surely use some more groceries but the thought that he was again being used so that some consciences could be a little less sullied—at least for a short time—made him angry. Who did they think he was? A person without feelings? A person who needed food only two weeks a year? A person who could keep his dignity while being used?

The singing stopped. He waited. Someone knocked. Ready to respond with something besides a fake season greeting Joe opened the door. "Donations for the poor please!" a youthful voice appealed. Swallowing his words Joe relaxed, went into his bedroom and brought out a dollar—that left him with two. He actually managed a faint smile. The well-dressed young fellow thanked him and as the twenty-odd well-dressed folk piled into their nice cars, Joe forgot at least some of his long pent-up resentment. He closed the squeaking door firmly. With less money but more dignity he soon turned in for the night.

Redekop (1984):299

December 24

A Place for Jesus
Jakob Denner, Germany, ca. 1707

*J*oseph and Mary went to Bethlehem, to the city of David. This was the place where she was to bring the Son of Love into the world. In Bethlehem the Son of God was to be born. This the prophet Micah had foretold, chapter 5 verse 1, "And thou, Bethlehem, Ephrata, even though thou art little among the thousands in Judah, out of thee shall come the one who shall be Lord in Israel, whose going out is from the beginning and has been eternally."

This Bethlehem, contrary to other towns in Judea, was just a very small place; and in this small place Jesus was to be born. By this we see that Jesus is not to be born in any other place spiritually than in a small, humble and lowly soul. In no other does he want to make himself evident with grace, pardon, salvation, redemption and with all of his kingdom. A soul (or a person) that in himself is big, high and haughty is never fit for this.

For this reason Christ says in Matthew 5:3, "Blessed are the poor in spirit (which is to say, small, miserable, poor, lowly, humble), for theirs is the kingdom of heaven." In nature we see that a lowly place is much more productive than a high one on the mountain. From the mountain the water always flows away, but in a low-lying place it remains and retains it. Just so, a proud and high-minded soul also cannot retain the spiritual water of divine grace, that is Jesus and his Spirit, nor can it be made fruitful in good things. But a soul that is small and humble of heart can achieve this. It is the place where this grace thrives, where such gifts can be preserved. For this reason a Christian poet says so very beautifully, "O lowliness so lofty in praise, yours is the soil that bears many a bloom." And it is Peter who says in 1 Peter 5:5, "God opposes the haughty, but to the humble he gives grace."

This Bethlehem was situated in Judea, and at a former time its name had been Ephrata, as we see in Genesis 35:19, where we have these words, "Thus Rachel died and was buried along the way that leads to Ephrata, which is now called Bethlehem." Ephrata means fruitful. From this we see that the soul in whom Jesus manifests himself will be fruitful in all aspects of life. It will be fruitful in simplicity, in godliness, in holiness and in praise to God and thanksgiving. Such an Ephrata, such a fruitful place or spot, all of us are to try to become, for in such a place Jesus desires to be born.

Denner (1730): 71, 72. trans. by Noah G. Good

Jesus' Birth

Yorifumi Yaguchi, Japan, 1987

When waves of pain contort Mary's body
her face is cramped and pale
Her eyes scuttle apart like crabs
The waves pull, recede again

and attack more violently
She clings to the wagon wheel,
grits her teeth, and her screams
terrify the beasts in the stable

Joseph, pacing nervously,
stumbles and falls
At last, seated, he strokes her back,
grasps her hand; his strength flows into her

Then a tremendous power moves within Mary
Like the sun emerging from a mountain ravine
the infant's head appears slowly, deliberately
Joseph grips it in both hands

Now the baby's cry flies out, rends the night
Joseph's doubts dissolve
On the straw bed
Mary peacefully shuts her eyes

Yaguchi (1989): 13

And Also In Our Hearts

Jakob Denner, Germany, ca. 1707

*T*his was the most holy child, the child without any sin at all, the eternal Word of God, the child of whom Isaiah said (in chapter 9:5-6), "A child has been born to us, a Son was given to us, with majesty on his shoulders, and his name is Wonderful, Counsellor, Power, Hero, eternal Father, Prince of Peace," etc. Oh what great love that God gave his only begotten Son to us as our Savior! Let us be deeply concerned that his birth may also take place in our hearts, that Christ's kingdom may prevail and rule there.

All of us do want to be Christians. Every one makes a claim to faith; in fact, each one thinks he has the best claim to faith. But what does it help us that we imagine this in our minds if it is not truly the fact? Do we have the real faith, and does Christ dwell in us by faith? If Christ has set up his kingdom in us he must make himself evident in us and he must dominate our lives.

If we say we are Christians, let us also demonstrate it in truth: that we truly are, that Jesus lives in us, that he lives and reigns, that he has destroyed the kingdom of the devil with its sins and unrighteousness. It is for this that Jesus taught us to pray, "Thy kingdom come."

Let us show by our actions that through him we are born again, renewed and cleansed. This because he is the only Father; he is also the Prince of Peace, the one who reconciles us with God. So then, where Jesus is in the soul this must be a living reality in us, and it must be felt within that it (the soul) is come into the presence of God, where it has already sought refuge, that while it formerly lived in sin, when it followed after the things of the world, it now pursues after Jesus Christ in godliness and holy love, and in true self-denial, renouncing all folly and pride of the world and what is earthly. This change, this renewal, this turning around, that is what I say the soul must experience within itself in truth, if Christ is in it.

Denner (1730): 74, 75, trans. by Noah G. Good

December 27

An Undivided Messiah
Pilgram Marpeck, Germany, 1531

*O*ne reads in many pagan histories that many, through their reason, have spoken and experienced such lofty things concerning God that even the true believers marvel. But all this occurred apart from the humanity of Christ and the coming Messiah. This Messiah was promised by the law only to the Jews, and the Jews then stood and hoped for the promised Messiah. But, because the Messiah appeared in such a human and weak form, the fleshly reason would not accept such a Messiah or recognize Him. To man, He was a scandal and a folly.

Through this denial of the humanity and deity of Christ, the Jews were like the heathen. Some desired a glorious Messiah, who came only from heaven, and they would not have a carpenter's son whose person and origin they well knew. Some wanted only a man from the seed of David, and not a Lord such as the Son of God, who was Lord over Moses, David, the prophets and the Law, and who could forgive sins upon earth.

The reason of man, and of those who presume to be Christians, works even today in dividing the Messiah. Today, I find mainly three types of spirits or prophets. The first type begins to speak sublime things concerning the deity of Christ and His glorious majesty. When he expounds on the lowliness of Christ and speaks of it as the beginning of His teaching, baptism (on the basis of, and originating from, faith), the Lord's Supper, the laying on of hands, the ban, reproof and similar gifts of Christ (which are gifts only as these things serve us and not we them), then this first type of prophet hinders others because he stirs in them pangs of conscience. It follows that the humanity of Christ is exalted more than His Deity. Thus, the highest becomes the lowest, and the lowest the highest.

The second group of spirits completely rejects the incarnation of Christ, and preaches a salvation exclusive of His humanity. The third group takes only the outward ceremonies of Christ, but without the spirit, as the papists and others do, thereby directing their efforts merely to external appearance and superficiality.

Oh, it annoys the fleshly to the highest degree that the Son of Man, in a physical way, should act and walk upon earth by means of His members, His body, His flesh and bone. It annoys them that those who are regarded by the world as humble, insignificant, simple and foolish, who preach the crucified Christ and follow Him in the cross should have the keys to the kingdom of heaven, to bind and to loose, to forgive and to retain sin upon the earth, and even to capture and to destroy the high reason of these prophets and fleshly ones.

They are irritated, as they were before with the Head, that the members of Christ's body should permit themselves to be released from sin by such despised people, who embody the physical Christ or the humanity of Christ.

Marpeck (1978): 80, 81

December 28

The Same Disposition
Jakob Denner, Germany, ca. 1707

Christ dwells in the soul through faith. But Christ is not a dead Christ, but a living Christ. Where he is, there he must live and work, there his holy life must follow, there the faith must reveal itself alive and powerful in Christ. Where Christ is present, there is his kingdom also, there he dominates, there he reigns. If he is in the soul it has become his empire, and in it he exercises power, and it is then subject to him, and it submits to him in all humility and obedience—then it lives in his holy will and full approval.

Where Christ dominates in the soul and his kingdom is in God's grace, there the kingdom of Satan with all the power of sin must end. In this we can judge ourselves to see how things stand with us. Oh, let us try and seek after Christ to become our reconciliation with God that he may become known in us so that we may through living faith become one with him; so that he may live in us and we in him: he in us through grace alone, we in him in pure humility.

May we constantly acknowledge our own nothingness, abjectness and poverty, that we can do nothing at all without Christ, but that it is he who has to do all things in and through us. He is our reconciliation. It is he who must reconcile us with God, and does it too through his holy blood.

But he is also our sanctification, purification, new birth, through his Holy Spirit, and he does this too, and wants to do it, only on condition that we do not oppose him. It is his pleasure to enter into our soul and heart with his reconciliation and healing if we do not close the door to his entry. He stands at the door and knocks as we see in Revelation 3:20. O let us put on the Lord Jesus Christ.

In our text here it says, "She wrapped him in swaddling clothes and laid him in a manger." So let us also wrap him and find a place for him in our souls, and embrace him in the arms of faith and of love; hold him fast and say with Jacob, "I will not let you go till you bless me." We see here the great humility of Jesus Christ, that although he was God in truth, he still wanted to be born of a poor maid. He rejected all external lordliness; he was wrapped in poor swaddling clothes and was laid in a manger, took his place among the cattle in the stable, although he could have changed all of that.

Do we not need to be ashamed that we seek only riches, greatness, honor and the esteem of the world when this eternal Child of God so humbled himself that he not only wanted to be born man, but even lie among the animals in the stable, and by this means rejected the greatness of the world? Now if he is to dwell in us we must be of the same disposition.

Denner (1730): 75, trans. by Noah G. Good

December 29

Breaking Cycles
Walter Klaassen, Canada, 1973

The cyclical view of events—that is, the understanding that history regularly repeats itself in the cycle of the seasons—has been much more prominent in the human story than the so-called linear view which emerged in Israel a millennium before Christ. It has much to commend it. It is a view that ties man firmly to the earth and invests all that exists with the sacred, with magic and mystery.

But it also locks him into a form of determinism; man is seen as a part of the cycle of nature from which it is impossible to escape into making important decisions of his own. It means that man's ethical responsibility is strongly muted since he is seen to lack the freedom to act. He is simply swept along in the cycle.

Judaic faith was an upsurge of protest against that view of man with the consequences. Israel's story is the account of a struggle against the cyclical view of history. The prophets and sages of Israel affirmed that man is not just swept along, but that, although part of nature, he is accountable to God and before other persons for what he does. One of the central emphases of Israel's faith was that what one does is of great importance and that man is not a slave with no will of his own, but rather a co-worker with God.

That point of view was characteristic of Jesus, and in turn the early church strongly affirmed it in the midst of movements which proclaimed that man could not be responsible since he was in the grip of powers greater than himself.

But within a century or two after Christ the view of history as a cycle became characteristic of christian worship and ritual again. Notwithstanding Augustine in his view of the city of God—that is, that history is moving toward the final great climax, the kingdom of God—the prevalent myth at the popular level remained the myth of the eternal return. This is the idea that the same events keep repeating themselves over and over again. The church year was fixed according to the recurrent cycle of feasts which were repeated annually. Every day the sacrifice of Christ on the cross was repeated in the Mass and thereby made contemporary. Everything was again enveloped in primal mystery which not even the priests, who were the co-creators of it, really understood.

There were, however, also movements in the Middle Ages which attempted to break out of the cyclical view. These were the so-called millennial movements. At various times people were swept up by the expectation of the nearness of the Kingdom of God on earth as the climax of man's destiny and longing. They too saw the course of human events moving toward a grand climax—with anti-Christs, resurrected emperors, prophets, signs and wonders—to a time when greed and covetousness and violence would be absent and perfect harmony and tranquility would reign.

Anabaptism was another similar movement. The ethical imperatives of Jesus outlined in the Sermon on the Mount were again given status. This included a strong emphasis on christianity as doing—with the necessary condition—the possibility of man's actually being able to carry out God's will. The cyclical view of history with all its expression was simply swept away. There was no denial of the sacred or of mystery.

Anabaptism attempted to combine the importance of doing with the importance of the sacred, but, as is almost always the case with such attempts, it was not wholly successful. It did away with emotionally necessary and religiously satisfying ritual, including aesthetics of sound, color and movement. It settled for religious forms that were meaningful beyond doubt but unquestionably impoverished. In Anabaptism, therefore, a satisfying ritual was missing; in Catholicism there was ethical weakness. Anabaptism listened to Jesus the anti-ritualist, while neglecting to notice that he continued to participate in the rituals of Judaism. Catholicism emphasized the rituals and expanded them, while at the same time neglected to hear that the Sabbath was made for man and not man for the Sabbath.

Klassen (1981a): 63-65

December 30

Hope

William Kettering, United States, 1890

*H*ope is represented as being seated on a rock. Worldly hope has for a foundation something that is transitory; something that is perishable. But Christian hope has for a foundation the rock of truth, God's most holy word. Hope was compared to an anchor by ancient writers. Thus Socrates expresses himself, "To ground hope on a false supposition is like trusting to a weak anchor." We see the propriety of this anchor when we consider that the world is like a tempestuous sea, full of dangers.

*

Hope does not remove trouble, it sustains the soul in the time of trouble. The anchor does not quiet the roaring waves, assist the rolling thunder, or bid the winds be still; but it enables the Christian to outride the gale, it keeps him from being driven on the rocks of death. The most pious Christian does not find himself free from the conflicts of life. He often finds himself tossed upon the raging billows, but under these circumstances the hope of heaven as the anchor to the soul keeps him steady.

This hope preserves him in the day of trial; it inspires fortitude and boldness in the cause of God. Hope maketh not ashamed because the love of God is shed abroad in the heart by the Holy Ghost which is given unto us. Take away hope and you take away the enjoyment of prosperity. Deprive man of hope and you take away the only support and solace in adversity. The most happy and prosperous without hope would become the most wretched. The poor and afflicted without it would sink at once into the gulf of despair.

To deprive man of hope is to rob him of his dearest treasure. Extinguish hope and you extinguish life, for who could live without hope? What indeed would life be without hope? It is the last lingering light of the human heart.

Kettering (1890): 26

December 31

Your Biggest Task

Anna Baerg, Soviet Union, 1919

*O*nce again it's the last day of the old year. How different it was last year at Apanlee. Father is no more and the Dicks are no more and so many other things have also vanished. And yet time flows onward, oblivious to our lives and fates, moving in its own rhythm of birth and death. That is how life is.

Yes, the old year was heavy-laden and dark, and the future appears to be no less so. But in spite of it all, today ended very beautifully. The sun has just gone to rest and all the rooftops and hills are steeped in that soft, velvety afterglow of evening. Dusk sets in. We all sit in the corner room, I playing the zither, the others singing along—everyone thinking of Father. Meanwhile, one star after another climbs into the heavens announcing New Year's Eve.

Then—listen! Who is knocking at the door, softly at first, then louder? You open it with a quaking hand. And lo, before you stands a tall and noble form wrapped in a great cloak, staff in hand. She speaks wonderful, heart-stirring words about home and love, then gives a last deep look with her sad, beautiful eyes, points upward and disappears. It is as if life has suddenly been imbued with a higher meaning. The old year has come and gone and much has come to pass.

And the New Year—what will it bring? What will it require of us? And yet, the God of old still lives—therefore, don't give up. His ways may at times be hard to understand, but they are holy. Remain true to Him and serve only Him, Anna Baerg: that is your biggest task in the New Year and don't forget it. All power lies with Him.

Baerg (1985): 54, 55

Bibliography

Aratani, Toshiko.
1991   "The Light of the World in a Low-Ranking Women's College in Japan." *Festival Quarterly* 17, no. 4 (Winter): 15, 16.

Armour, Rollin Stely.
1966   *Anabaptist Baptism: A Respresentative Study.* Studies in Anabaptist and Mennonite History, no. 11. Scottdale, PA: Herald Press.

Arnold, Eberhard.
1967   *Salt and Light. Talks and Writings on the Sermon on the Mount.* Edited by the Society of Brothers. Rifton, NY: Plough Publishing House.

Assefa, Dagne.
1984   "Dis-Quest." *Festival Quarterly* 10, no. 4 (November, December 1983, January): 14, 15.

Baerg, Anna.
1985   *Diary of Anna Baerg 1916-1924.* Translated and edited by Gerald Peters. Winnipeg: CMBC Publications.

Beachy, Monroe L.
1982   "What Does It Mean to be Amish?" *Family Life* (August/September):18.

Beiler, David.
[1857]. *Das Wahre Christenthum. Eine Christliche Betrachtung nach den Lehren der Heiligen Schrift.* Reprint. Gordonville, PA: Gordonville Bookstore, 1976.

Beiler, Joseph F.
1974   "On the Meaning of Ordnung."

Bender, Elizabeth.
1977   Trans. "Copy of a Letter Written by Uli Ammann to the Preachers and Elders of the Congregation at Markirch." *Mennonite Historical Bulletin* 38, no. 4 (October): 2, 3.

Bowman, Esther.
1987   "Satisfaction through Simplicity." *Family Life.* (April): 24.

Brenneman, John M.
1866   *Pride and Humility: A Discourse, Setting Forth the Characteristics of the Proud and the Humble.* Reprint. Hagerstown, MD: Deutsche Buchhandlung, 1988.
1876   *Plain Teachings, or Simple Illustrations and Exhortations from the Word of God.* Elkhart, IN: Mennonite Publishing Company.

Brown, Hubert L.
1976   *Black and Mennonite: A Search for Identity.* Scottdale: Herald Press.

Brun, Washington.
1988   "A Story from Uruguay." *Festival Quarterly* 15, no. 1 (Spring): 18, 20.

Byler, Uria R.
1963   *Our Better Country.* Gordonville, PA.: Old Order Book Society.

Christano, Charles.
1984   "God Never Visits an Empty Space." *Festival Quarterly* 11, no. 2 (Summer): 9-11.

Coggins, James Robert.
1991   *John Smyth's Congregation: English Separatism,*

Mennonite Influence, and the Elect Nation. Studies in Anabaptist and Mennonite History, no. 32. Scottdale, PA: Herald Press.

Conversation on Saving Faith
1857   Lancaster, PA: John Baer and Sons.

Davidson, H. Frances.
1894   "Easter." *Evangelical Visitor.* (March 15): 84.
1915   *South and South Central Africa. A Record of Fifteen Years' Missionary Labors among Primitive Peoples.* Elgin, IL: privately published.

Denck, Hans.
1989   *Selected Writings of Hans Denck 1500-1527.* Translated and edited by Edward J. Furcha. Texts and Studies in Religion, vol. 44. Lewiston, NY: The Edwin Mellen Press, Ltd.

Denner, Jacob.
1730   *Jacob Denners christliche und erbauliche Betrachtungen über die Sonn—und Festtags-Evangelien des ganzen Jahres...* Reprinted from the 1860 edition. Dundee, OH: Jacob A. Hershberger, 1985.

Dirk Philips.
1992   *The Writings of Dirk Philips 1504-1568.* Translated and edited by Cornelius J. Dyck, William E. Keeney and Alvin J. Beachy. Classics of the Radical Reformation, no. 6. Scottdale, PA: Herald Press.

Dyck, Cornelius J.
[1962] Ed. *The Lordship of Christ: Proceedings of the Seventh Mennonite World Conference; Kitchener, Ontario Canada: August 1-7, 1962.* Elkhart, IN: Mennonite World Conference.
[1967] Ed. *The Witness of the Holy Spirit: Proceedings of the Eighth Mennonite World Conference; Amsterdam, The Netherlands: July 23-30, 1967.* Elkhart, IN: Mennonite World Conference.

Engle, Anna R., J.A. Climenhaga and Leoda A. Buckwalter.
1950   *There Is No Difference: God Works in Africa and India.* Nappanee, IN: E.V. Publishing House.

Enz, Jacob J.
1972   *The Christian and Warfare: The Roots of Pacifism in the Old Testament.* Scottdale, PA: Herald Press.

Erb, Paul.
1965   Ed. *From the Mennonite Pulpit: Twenty-Six Sermons from Mennonite Ministers.* Scottdale, PA: Herald Press.

Fisher, Alma W.
1925   "Looking Forward." *The Christian Exponent* (January 2): 5, 6.

Fisher, Nancy.
1971   "Reflections." *Newsletter.* Philadelphia Mennonite Fellowship.

"Free Rein"
1986   *Family Life* (May): 12.

Friedmann, Robert.
1973　*The Theology of Anabaptism: An Interpretation.*
　　　Studies in Anabaptist and Mennonite
　　　History, no. 15, Scottdale, PA: Herald
　　　Press.
Friesen, Peter M.
1978　*The Mennonite Brotherhood in Russia
　　　(1790-1910).* Translated and edited by J. B.
　　　Toews, Abraham Friesen, Peter J. Klassen
　　　and Harry Loewen. Fresno: Board of
　　　Christian Literature, General Conference
　　　of Mennonite Brethren Churches.
Funk, Henry.
1851　*A Mirror of Baptism, with the Spirit, with Water,
　　　and with Blood.* Translated by Joseph Funk.
　　　Mountain Valley, VA: Joseph Funk and
　　　Sons.
1915　*Restitution or an Explanation of Several Principal
　　　Points of the Law.* Translated by Abram B.
　　　Kolb. Reprint. Harrisonburg, VA:
　　　Campbell Copy Center, Inc., 1981.
Funk, Joseph.
1857　*The Reviewer Reviewed. Or, Thoughts and
　　　Meditations on the Sacrifices, Offerings,
　　　Emblems, Figures and Types of the Old
　　　Testament, compared, in their Fulfillment, with
　　　the Antitypes in the New Testament.*
　　　Mountain Valley, VA: Joseph Funk and Sons.
Giesbrecht, Gerhard G.
1984　"Indian and German a Second Time." *Festival
　　　Quarterly* 11, no. 2 (Summer): 14, 15.
Godshalk, Abraham.
1838　*A Description of the New Creature.* Reprint.
　　　N.p., n.d.
Gorter, D.S.
1856　Ed. *Doopsgezinde Lektuur: Tot Bevordering van
　　　Christelijke Kennis en Godzaligheid.* Tweede
　　　Deel. Te Sneek, The Netherlands: van
　　　Druten & Bleeker.
Gross, Leonard.
n.d.　Ed. *Golden Apples in Silver Bowls.* Translated
　　　by Elizabeth Bender and Leonard Gross.
　　　Mennonite Sources and Documents, no. 5.
　　　Lancaster, PA: Lancaster Mennonite
　　　Historical Society. Forthcoming.
Harder, Leland.
1985　Ed. *The Sources of Swiss Anabaptism: The
　　　Grebel Letters and Related Documents.*
　　　Classics of the Radical Reformation, no. 4.
　　　Scottdale, PA: Herald Press.
Harder, Leland, and Marvin Harder.
1952　*Plockhoy from Zurik-zee: The Study of a Dutch
　　　Reformer in Puritan England and Colonial
　　　America.* Newton, KS: Board of Education
　　　and Publication, General Conference
　　　Mennonite Church.
Hart, Lawrence.
1992　"A Colony of Strangers." Akron, PA:
　　　Mennonite Central Committee News
　　　Service (Spring).
Hein, Marvin.
1980　*The Ties that Bind, Moorings of a Life with God.*
　　　Hillsboro, KS: Kindred Press.
Hershberger, Guy F.
1957　Ed. *The Recovery of the Anabaptist Vision. A
　　　Sixtieth Anniversary Tribute to Harold S.

Bender.* Scottdale, PA: Herald Press.
Hershey, Eusebius.
1891　"From Africa's Soil." *Evangelical Visitor* (June
　　　15): 179, 180.
Hershey, Jacob.
n.d.　*Confession of Faith.* Translated by Simon H.
　　　Musser, William A. Kniesly and John M.
　　　Strickler. N.p.
Hertzler, Daniel.
1983　Ed. *Not By Might:* Gospel Herald *Sampler,
　　　1908-1983. Scottdale, PA: Herald Press.*
Hiebert, P.C.
1950　Ed. *Proceedings of the Fourth Mennonite World
　　　Conference; Goshen, Indiana and North
　　　Newton, Kansas. August 3-10, 1948.* Akron,
　　　PA: The Mennonite Central Committee.
Holdeman, John.
1891　*A Treatise on Magistracy and War, Millennium,
　　　Holiness and the Manifestation of Spirits.*
　　　Reprint. Newton, KS: Herald Publishing
　　　Company, 1928.
"Holiness"
1891　*Evangelical Visitor* (December 15): 369-371.
Horst, Isaac R.
1985　*Close Ups of the Great Awakening.* Mt. Forest,
　　　Ontario: privately published.
Hostetler, John A.
1980　*Amish Society.* Third edition. Baltimore, MD:
　　　The Johns Hopkins University Press.
Hostetler, Paul.
1980　*Preacher on Wheels.* Elgin, IL: The Brethren
　　　Press.
"How God Eased My Conscience"
1983　*Family Life* (October): 2, 3.
Hubmaier, Balthasar.
1989　*Balthasar Hubmaier: Theologian of Anabaptism.*
　　　Translated and edited by H. Wayne Pipkin
　　　and John H. Yoder. Classics of the Radical
　　　Reformation, no. 5. Scottdale, PA: Herald
　　　Press.
Hutter, Jacob.
1979　*Brotherly Faithfulness: Epistles from a Time of
　　　Persecution.* Translated and edited by the
　　　Hutterian Brethren. Rifton, NY: Plough
　　　Publishing House.
Hutterian Brethren.
1978　Trans. and ed. *Brotherly Community: The
　　　Highest Command of Love: Two Anabaptist
　　　Documents of 1650 and 1560.* Rifton, NY:
　　　Plough Publishing House.
1987　Trans. and ed. *The Chronicle of the Hutterian
　　　Brethren.* Vol. 1. Rifton, NY: The Plough
　　　Publishing Corporation.
Ilunga, Mukanza.
1981　"Dis-Quest." *Festival Quarterly* 7, no. 4
　　　(November, December 1980, January): 20.
**Janzen, Jean, Yorifumi Yaguchi and David
Waltner-Toews.**
1986　*Three Mennonite Poets.* Intercourse, PA: Good
　　　Books, 1986.
Kauffman, John E.
1977　Trans. *Anabaptist Letters from 1635 to 1645:
　　　Translated from the Ausbund.* Third Edition.
　　　Atglen, PA: privately published.
Kettering, William.
1890　"Hope." *Evangelical Visitor* (January 15): 26.

Kitondo, Kusangila.
1987   "The Three Things That Concern Me Most."
        Festival Quarterly 14, no. 1 (Spring): 8.
Klaassen, Walter.
1981a   *Anabaptism: Neither Catholic nor Protestant.*
        Revised Edition. Waterloo, Ontario:
        Conrad Press.
1981b   Ed. *Anabaptism in Outline: Selected Primary
        Sources.* Classics of the Radical
        Reformation, no. 3. Scottdale, PA: Herald
        Press.
1988   "Menno Simons: Molder of a Tradition." *The
        Mennonite Quarterly Review* LXII, no. 3
        (July): 368-386.
Klassen, James R.
1986   *Jimshoes in Vietnam: Orienting a Westerner.*
        Scottdale, PA: Herald Press.
Kleinsasser, Jacob.
1988   "Whosoever Will, Let Him Come." *The
        Plough* 19 (May/June): 7-9.
Kline, David.
1990   *Great Possessions: An Amish Farmer's Journal.*
        San Francisco: North Point Press. New
        York: Farrar, Straus & Giroux, Inc.
Kline, Edward A.
n.d.   *The Theology of the Will of Man, and Some
        Practical Applications for the Christian Life.*
        Baltic, OH: Amish Brotherhood
        Publications.
Kniesly, Sallie.
1888   "Cheerfulness." *Evangelical Visitor* (July 1):
        164.
Krabill, James and Jeanette Krabill.
1984   "The Resurrection According to Matthew."
        Festival Quarterly 11, no. 2 (Summer): 43.
Kraybill, Paul N.
[1978] Ed. *The Kingdom of God in a Changing World:
        Proceedings of the Tenth Assembly Mennonite
        World Conference; Wichita, KS; July 25-30,
        1978.* Lombard, IL: Mennonite World
        Conference.
Kreider, Robert.
1988   Ed. *James Liu and Stephen Wang: Christians
        True in China.* Newton, KS: Faith and Life
        Press.
Kulp, Isaac Clarence Jr.
1987   Trans. "Plates: Explanations-Translations of
        Some of Them." In "Andreas Kolb,
        1749-1811" by Mary Jane Lederach
        Hershey. *The Mennonite Quarterly Review*
        LXI, no. 2 (April): 178-186.
Landis, Samuel K.
[1912] *A Call to Obedience.* Scottdale, PA:
        Mennonite Publishing House.
Lehman, Jacob S., et al.
[1903] *Christianity Defined: A Manual of New
        Testament Teaching...* Lancaster, PA:
        Reformed Mennonite Church.
Lesher, Christian.
1850   "The Spiritual Clockwork." Translated by
        Noah Good. Brethren in Christ Archives,
        Messiah College, Grantham, PA.
1971   *The Small Spiritual Magazine.* Translated by
        Laban T. Brechbill. N.p.
"A Lesson in Patience"
1987   *Family Life* (June): 13.

Lichdi, Diether Götz.
1990   Ed. *Mennonite World Handbook 1990:
        Mennonites in Global Witness.* Carol Stream,
        IL: Mennonite World Conference.
"The Little Man's Bad Check"
1990   *Family Life* (April): 15.
Loewen, Harry.
1988   Ed. *Why I Am a Mennonite: Essays on
        Mennonite Identity.* Kitchener, Ontario:
        Herald Press.
Loewen, Howard John.
1985   *One Lord, One Church, One Hope, and One God:
        Mennonite Confessions of Faith in North
        America: An Introduction.* Text-Reader
        Series, no. 2. Elkhart, IN: Institute of
        Mennonite Studies.
Luthy, David.
1984   "An Important Pennsylvania Broadside of
        1812." *Pennsylvania Mennonite Heritage*
        (July):1-4.
M., H.B.
1889   "The Experience." *Evangelical Visitor* (April
        1): 109.
**MacMaster, Richard K., with Samuel L. Horst
and Robert F. Ulle.**
1979   *Conscience in Crisis: Mennonites and Other
        Peace Churches in America, 1739-1789:
        Interpretation and Documents.* Studies in
        Anabaptist and Mennonite History, no. 20.
        Scottdale, PA: Herald Press.
Marpeck, Pilgram.
1978   *The Writings of Pilgram Marpeck.* Translated
        and edited by William Klassen and Walter
        Klaassen. Classics of the Radical
        Reformation, no. 2. Scottdale, PA: Herald
        Press.
Martin, John D.
1971   Comp. *Christopher Dock: Pioneer Christian
        Schoolmaster on the Skippack.* Reprint.
        Harrisonburg, VA: Christian Light
        Publications, 1977.
Masiye, Agrippa V.
1967   "It Was on the Same Road!" *Good Words*
        (June): 8.
Mast, John B.
1950   Trans. and ed. *The Letters of the Amish Division
        of 1693-1711.* Oregon City, OR: Christian J.
        Schlabach.
Menno Simons.
1956   *The Complete Writings of Menno Simons.*
        Translated by Leonard Verduin. Edited by
        J.C. Wenger. Scottdale, PA: Herald Press.
The Mennonite Hymnal.
1969   Scottdale, PA: Herald Press. (No. 40 "I Sing
        with Exultation" translated by Marion
        Wenger, 1966.)
Mennonite World Conference
[1984] *Proceedings: Mennonite World Conference XI
        Assembly: Strasbourg, July 24-29, 1984.
        Theme: God's People Serve in Hope.*
        Lombard, IL: Mennonite World
        Conference.
Miller, Ervin.
1989   "Are Your Words True?" *Family Life* (May): 10.

Miller, Levi P.
n.d.   "Teaching Emphases That Hinder
        Discipleship." Baltic, OH: Amish
        Brotherhood Publications.
Moyo, J.D.
1967   "Keep These Customs!" *Good Words*
        (December): 6.
Muganda, Josiah.
1980   "Should Mennonites Be Involved in World
        Diplomacy?" *Festival Quarterly* 7, no. 2.
        (May, June, July): 14.
Müntzer, Thomas.
1988   *The Collected Works of Thomas Müntzer.* Edited
        and translated by Peter Matheson.
        Edinburgh: T. & T. Clark.
Musser, Daniel.
[1868] "An Awakening Call." Reprint. Lancaster,
        PA: Reformed Mennonite Church, n.d.
N., R.M.
1969   "The Bus Driver's Game." *Family Life*
        (February). Reprinted in *Family Life*
        (January 1989): 14.
Ndlovu, Fetty Mae.
1970   "I Collided with Myself." *Good Words*
        (November): 4.
"No Peaches on Sunday"
1974   *Family Life* (January). Reprinted in *Family Life*
        (January 1989): 15.
Nyce, Dorothy Yoder.
1983   Ed. *Weaving Wisdom: Sermons by Mennonite
        Women.* South Bend: Womensage.
"Of Cows and People"
1989   *Family Life* (May): 10, 11.
Ortíz, José, and David Graybill.
1989   *Reflections of an Hispanic Mennonite.*
        Intercourse, PA: Good Books.
Osborne, Philip.
1989   *Parenting for the '90s.* Intercourse, PA: Good
        Books.
Oyer, John S.
1984   Trans. "An Amish Sermon." *The Mennonite
        Quarterly Review* LVIII, no. 3 (July):
        296-317.
Peachey, Paul.
1971   Ed. "Answer of Some Who Are Called
        Anabaptists Why They Do Not Attend the
        Churches." Translated by Shem Peachey
        and Paul Peachey. *The Mennonite Quarterly
        Review XLV, no. 1* (January): 5-32.
Peters, Victor.
1965   Ed. *Zwei Dokumente: Quellen zum
        Geschichts-Studium der Mennoniten in
        Russland.* Winnipeg: Echo-Verlag.
Plett, Delbert F.
1985   *The Golden Years: The Mennonite Kleine
        Gemeinde in Russia (1812-1849).* Steinbach,
        Manitoba: D.F.P. Publications.
Redekop, John H.
1984   *Two Sides: The Best of Personal Opinion,
        1964-1984.* Winnipeg: Kindred Press.
Rideman, Peter.
1970   *Confession of Faith: Account of Our Religion,
        Doctrine and Faith Given by Peter Rideman of
        the Brothers Whom Men Call Hutterians.*
        Second Edition. Rifton, NY: Plough
        Publishing House.

Risser, Johannes.
1827   Letter to his cousin. Translated by Elizabeth
        Horsch Bender, revised by John D. Roth.
        Mennonite Historical Library, Goshen
        College, Goshen, IN.
Rodriguez, Luis Elier.
1988   "Four Challenges for Latin America." *Festival
        Quarterly* 14, no. 4 (Winter) 20,21.
Ruth, John L.
1978   *Mennonite Identity and Literary Art.* Focal
        Pamphlet No. 29. Scottdale, PA: Herald
        Press.
Sauder, Menno.
1945   Ed. *Companion of a Solution to World Problems
        or the Christian Faith as Portrayed throughout
        the Bloody Theatre or Martyrs Mirror and
        Other Authors.* N.p.
Sauder, Nancy.
1987   "A Fair Chance." *Family Life* (February): 30,
        31.
Schabalie, John Philip.
[1834] *The Wandering Soul, or Conversations of the
        Wandering Soul with Adam, Noah and Simon
        Cleophas...* [Translated by I. Daniel Rupp.]
        Reprint. Millersburg, OH: John D.
        Hershberger, 1975.
Schlabach, Theron F.
1974   Ed. "An Account by Jakob Waldner. Diary of
        the Conscientious Objector in World War
        I." Translated by Ilse Reist and Elizabeth
        Bender. *The Mennonite Quarterly Review*
        XLVIII, no. 1 (January): 73-111.
1988   *Peace, Faith, Nation: Mennonites and Amish in
        Nineteenth-Century America.* The
        Mennonite Experience in America, vol. 2.
        Scottdale, PA: Herald Press.
Schnell, Hans.
1985   "The Two Kingdoms." Translated by
        Leonard Gross and Elizabeth Horsch
        Bender. *Christian History Magazine* IV, no.
        1: 31-33.
Shank, J. Ward.
1988   *The View from Round Hill: Selected Writings of
        J. Ward Shank.* Edited by Paul L. Kratz.
        Harrisonburg, VA: The Sword and
        Trumpet.
Shenk, Joseph C.
1984   *Kisare: A Mennonite of Kiseru.* Salunga, PA:
        Eastern Mennonite Board of Missions and
        Charities.
Shenk, Sara Wenger.
1987   *Why Not Celebrate!* Intercourse, PA: Good
        Books.
Shenk, Wilbert R.
1980   Ed. "Mission and Politics in the Nineteenth
        Century: Pieter Jansz' Tract." Translated
        by Anne-Marie Vischer, Elizabeth Bender,
        Roelf S. Kuitse. *The Mennonite Quarterly
        Review* LIV, no. 2 (April): 83-104.
Showalter, Rebecca.
1987   "Which Is Best?" *Family Life* (November): 8.
Sider, E. Morris.
1989   Ed. *My Story, My Song: Life Stories by Brethren
        in Christ Missionaries.* Mt. Joy, PA:
        Brethren in Christ World Missions.

1989   *Missionary Reminiscences: An Autobiography.*
        Grantham, PA: privately published.

Smith, C. Henry.
1962   *Mennonite Country Boy: The Early Years of C.
        Henry Smith.* Mennonite Historical Series.
        Newton, KS: Faith and Life Press.

Stahl, Martha Denlinger.
1987   *By Birth or by Choice: Who Can Become a
        Mennonite?* Scottdale, PA: Herald Press.

Steiner, M.S.
1903   *John S. Coffman, Mennonite Evangelist: His Life
        and Labors.* Spring Grove, PA: Mennonite
        Book and Tract Society.

Stoltzfus, Eli
1969   *The Serenity and Value of Amish Country Living.*
        Strasburg, PA.: privately published.

Swalm, E.J.
1949   Ed. *Nonresistance Under Test: A Compilation of
        Experiences of Conscientious Objectors as
        Encountered in Two World Wars.* Nappanee,
        IN: E.V. Publishing House.
1969   *"My Beloved Brethren...": Personal Memoirs and
        Recollections of the Canadian Brethren in
        Christ Church.* Nappanee, IN: Evangel
        Press.

Toews, Aron A.
1990   *Mennonite Martyrs: People Who Suffered for
        Their Faith 1920-1940.* Translated by John
        B. Toews. Hillsboro, KS: Kindred Press.

Twisck, Peter Jansz.
1913   *The Peaceful Kingdom of Christ or An Exposition
        of the 20th Chapter of the Book of Revelations.*
        Translated by John F. Funk. Reprint.
        Moundridge, KS: Gospel Publishers, 1974.
1982   *A Father's Gift of 1622.* Translated by Titus B.
        Hoover. Port Trevorton, PA: privately
        published.

Umble, John.
1948   Trans. and ed. "Memoirs of an Amish
        Bishop." *The Mennonite Quarterly Review*
        XXII, no. 2 (April): 94-115.

van Braght, Thieleman J.
1979   *The Bloody Theater or Martyrs Mirror of the
        Defenseless Christians.* Twelfth Edition.
        Translated by Joseph F. Sohm in 1886.
        Scottdale, PA: Herald Press.

"When Children Pray"
1989   *Family Life* (February): 22.

Williams, George Huston, and Angel M. Mergal.
1957   Eds. *Spiritual and Anabaptist Writers.* Volume
        XXV: The Library of Christian Classics.
        (First published 1957 by SCM Press Ltd.,
        London and The Westminster Press,
        Philadelphia.) Louisville, KY:
        Westminster/John Knox Press.

Witmer, Beth.
1988   "Footprints." *Family Life* (January): 9.

Yaguchi, Yorifumi.
1989   *Jesus.* Translated by Ross L. Bender. Edited
        by David Hershey. Goshen, IN:
        Pinchpenny Press.

Yoder, Clarence T.
1987   "The Harmony in Nature." *Family Life* (May):
        5.

Yoder, Edward.
1985   *Edward: Pilgrimage of a Mind: The Journal of
        Edward Yoder 1931-1945.* Edited by Ida
        Yoder. Scottdale, PA: Ida Yoder and Virgil
        E. Yoder.

Yoder, John H.
1973   Trans. and ed. *The Legacy of Michael Sattler.*
        Classics of the Radical Reformation, no. 1.
        Scottdale, PA: Herald Press.

Yoder, Paton.
1987   Ed. *Tennessee John Stoltzfus: Amish
        Church-Related Documents and Family
        Letters.* Translated by Noah G. Good.
        Mennonite Sources and Documents, Irvin
        B. Horst, Series Ed., no. 1. Lancaster, PA:
        Lancaster Mennonite Historical Society.

Zimmerman, Caleb.
1985   "24 Minutes of Devotions." *Family Life*
        (April): 5.

Zimmerman, Eli Z.
1982   *Precious Memories of Terre Hill and Vicinity.*
        Fleetwood, PA: privately published.

Zorilla, Hugo.
1989   "Interpreting the Fourth Gospel through
        Those Who Give Up Their Lives." *The
        Mennonite Quarterly Review* LXIII, no. 2
        (April): 150-170.

Index of Writers

babwe and Zambia). She was the first member of the Brethren in Christ to receive an academic degree (B.A., M.A., Kalamazoo College, Michigan). 118, 405

Denck, Hans
(ca. 1500-1527), German Anabaptist leader, scholar, Bible translator and mystic, he was possibly influenced by Thomas Müntzer, and himself greatly influenced south German Anabaptism. 68, 70, 76, 100, 148, 187, 209, 226, 247, 272, 273, 355

Denner, Jakob
(1659-1746), Pietistic German Mennonite-Dompelaar minister at Altona, whose emotionally warm sermons have been widely read among Mennonites and others. 32, 116, 143, 256, 280, 392, 396, 404, 408, 409, 411

Dirk Philips
(1504-1568), Former monk who joined the Dutch Anabaptists and became their most skilled theologian. He worked alongside Menno and was active from Friesland to Poland. 158, 194, 324, 353

Dirks, Heinrich Sr.
(1842-1915), First foreign missionary sent by Russian Mennonites, went to Sumatra, Indonesia. After ten years in Indonesia he returned to the Ukraine and served as an elder and evangelist, all the while promoting missions. 216

Dock, Christopher
(d. 1771), German-born American colonial schoolmaster, fraktur artist and hymn writer. He wrote the first American treatise on education. 205, 291

Doerksen, Viktor G.
(b. 1934), Canadian Mennonite Brethren historian. 245

Dyck, Abram
Early 19th-century school teacher in the Ukraine. 35

E

Ediger, Alexander
(1893-1938?), Teacher and elder in the Ukraine, exiled to Murmansk, later to eastern Siberia. Nothing was heard from him after 1938. 185

Ehrenpreis, Andreas
(1589-1662), Outstanding Hutterite minister in Moravia and Slovakia, where he was made bishop; a prolific writer of tracts, letters and hymns. 108, 173, 190, 197, 275, 373

Enz, Jacob J.
American seminary professor of Old Testament. 107, 406

F

Felbinger, Klaus
(d. 1560), Hutterite preacher, missionary in Bavaria and martyr. 69, 95, 166, 177, 191

Fisher, Alma W. 27

Fisher, Nancy
Social worker living Chester County, Pennsylvania. 72

Flores, Gilberto
Guatemalan church leader. 130

Friedmann, Robert
(1891-1970), Austrian-born historian of Anabaptism, Jewish emigrant to the United States in 1938. 71

Friesen, Abraham
(d. 1849), Kleine Gemeinde elder in the Ukraine. 89

Friesen, Abraham
(b. 1933), American historian of Anabaptism. 169

Friesen, Dorothy A.
(b. 1949), American service worker to southeast Asia, peace and justice activist. 134

Friesen, Peter M.
(1849-1914), Mennonite Brethren minister, educator and historian in the Ukraine. 295

Funk, Henry [Heinrich Funck]
(d. 1760), American immigrant bishop and writer who helped sponsor and supervise the first American publication (in German) of *Martyrs Mirror*. 154, 188, 198, 390, 399

Funk, John F.
(1835-1930), American bishop and pioneer in Mennonite publishing; he founded the *Herald of Truth* and other periodicals, and published Menno's works and the *Martyrs Mirror* in English; was instrumental in settling Mennonite emigrants from Russia in North America. 87

Funk, Joseph
(1778-1862), Virginia publisher and singing teacher, noted especially for revising and collecting hymns. 110

G

Gerber, Samuel
Swiss elder. 91, 181

Giesbrecht, Gerhard
(1906-1977), Ukraine-born Mennonite Brethren schoolteacher and minister in Paraguay, known especially for his work among the Indians. 339

Godshalk, Abraham
(1791-1838), Minister and farmer in Bucks County, Pa. 92, 263

Goll, Andre B.
French Mennonite leader. 391

Grebel, Conrad
(ca. 1498-1526), Co-founder of the Swiss Brethren, who performed the first baptism of the Anabaptist movement. 179

Greenwalt, Margaret
Dutch Mennonite. 182

Guth, Jakob
German Mennonite leader and possible compiler of *Golden Apples in Silver Bowls*, a doctrinal and devotional book of great influence. 387

H

Harder, Bernhard
(1832-1884), Minister, teacher and poet in the Ukraine. 117

Harder, Johannes
(1903-1987), Russian-born German scholar, teacher, minister, activist and novelist. 151, 365

Harding, Vincent
Former minister and voice for racial justice among Mennonites, currently professor of ethics and theology. He is no longer a Mennonite. 42

Hart, Lawrence
Minister and Cheyenne peace chief in Oklahoma. 330

Hein, Marvin
American Mennonite Brethren minister. 244

Hershey, Benjamin
(1697-1789), German-born bishop in Lancaster

County, PA., who led the community through times of war and schism. 224

Hershey, Eusebius
(1823-1891), American evangelist and first Mennonite foreign missionary from America; died in West Africa five and a half months after arriving there. 159

Hershey, Jacob
(1792-1842), Lancaster County (Pa.) River Brethren. 219

Hildebrand, Kornelius Sr.
(1833-1920), Industrialist in Ukraine. 157, 162, 218

Hoffman, Melchior
(ca. 1495-1543), German furrier who first took Anabaptism to the Netherlands; died in prison for his faith. 328

Holdeman, John H.
(1832-1900), American, the organizer of the Church of God in Christ, Mennonite (also called Holdeman Mennonite) 94

Horst, Christian
(1821-1907), Conservative Mennonite of Franklin County, Pennsylvania. 99

Hostetler, John A.
(b. 1918), American sociologist and author of several books and articles, recognized as a leading expert on the Amish, the community in which he was raised. 284

Hostetler, Paul
(b. 1925), American Brethren in Christ, college information director. 96, 237

Hubmaier, Balthasar
(1480?-1528), German Anabaptist pastor and polemicist whose congregations at Waldshut, Germany and Nicholsburg (Mikulov), Moravia, were organized along the lines of "official" or territorial churches. 66, 126, 153, 240

Hut, Hans
(d. 1527), Veteran of German Peasants' War, then Anabaptist missionary in Austria, Germany and Moravia. He was extremely effective in winning converts, and broad in his influence. 149, 274, 306, 308

Hutter, Jakob
(ca. 1502-1536), Tirolean Anabaptist whose leadership of communal Anabaptists in Moravia and Austria led to their being called "Hutterites." After severe torture, he was martyred at the stake. 160, 348

I

Ilunga, Mukanza
Zairean church leader and member of the International Mennonite Peace Committee. 356

J

Jansz., Anneken
(d. 1539), Dutch Anabaptist associate of David Joris, martyred by drowning at Rotterdam. 50

Jansz., Pieter
(1820-1904), First Dutch Mennonite missionary of modern times, sent to Java, Indonesia in 1851, later published the Bible in Javanese. 38, 338

Janzen, Jean
(b. 1933), Mennonite Brethren poet from California. 257

K

Kabalu, Milolo
(b. 1952), Zairean teacher and church women's leader. 56

Keller, Endres
Bavarian Anabaptist who later recanted after months of prison and torture. 347

Kettering, William
(1847-1901), Pennsylvania Brethren in Christ farmer. 414

Kisare, Zedekia Marwa
(b. 1912), Tanzanian bishop; first African Mennonite bishop. 43, 81, 115, 232, 233, 366, 385

Kitondo, Kusangila
Zairean pastor and influential church leader. 231

Klaassen, Walter
(b. 1926), Canadian historian of Anabaptism and the Middle Ages. 61, 412

Klassen, James R.
(b. 1947), American service worker and missionary to Vietnam during and after the Vietnam War. 316

Kleinsasser, Jacob
(b. 1922), Canadian Hutterite (Schmiedeleut) elder, living at Crystal Spring Colony in Manitoba. 215

Kline, David Jr.
(b. 1945), Ohio Amish farmer and nature writer. 202

Kline, Edward A.
(b. 1951), Ohio New Order Amish, lumber company manager. 365, 395

Klopfenstein, Joseph
Alsatian (France) Amish minister. 298

Kniesly, Sallie
Ohio Brethren in Christ. 140

Kolb, Andreas
(1749-1811), Pennsylvania schoolteacher and fraktur artist. 403

Kossen, Hendrik B. (b. 1923),
Dutch minister. 105

Krabill, James
(b. 1951), American missionary to Côte d'Ivoire (Ivory Coast), worked closely with the indigenous Harrist church. 119

Krabill, Jeanette
(b. 1951), American missionary to Côte d'Ivoire (Ivory Coast), worked closely with the indigenous Harrist church. 119

Kreider, Eleanor Graber (b. 1935),
Born in India, raised in United States, director of the Resource Centre, London Mennonite Centre. 55

Kremnitzer, Helga
German Mennonite youth worker. 131

L

Landis, Samuel K.
Resident of Lancaster, Pennsylvania. 297, 299

Lehman, Jacob S.
(d. 1924), Reformed Mennonite writer in Pennsylvania. 184, 361

Lesher, Christian
(1775-1856), River Brethren/Brethren in Christ bishop and writer active in Pennsylvania. He was influenced by radical pietism. 88, 210

Lichdi, Kurt
German minister and businessman. 393

Lind, Millard
(b. 1918), American minister, editor and professor

of Old Testament. 29
Loosli, Theo
Swiss minister. 276

M
M., H. B.
Lancaster County (Pa.) Brethren in Christ. 230
Malagar, Pyarelal Joel
(b. 1927), Indian bishop and onetime president of
Fellowship of Reconciliation in India. 327
Mantz, Felix
(ca. 1498-1527), Co-founder of the Swiss Brethren
and first Anabaptist martyr at Protestant hands. 31
Marpeck, Pilgram
(d. 1556), Austrian mining and civil engineer,
noted for his many booklets and letters which
show his clear mind and moderate disposition.
45, 46, 109, 129, 150, 152, 167, 193, 249, 255, 410
Martin, Jonas H.
(1839-1925), Conservative bishop of Lancaster
County, Pennsylvania, who organized the Weaverland Conference, known as Old Order Mennonites. 87
Masiye, Agrippa V.
(b. ca. 1930). Zimbabwean Brethren in Christ   pastor-teacher and bookstore owner. 242
Maurice, Ilunga
Zairean minister.   312
Menno Simons
(ca. 1496-1561), Dutch priest who joined the
Anabaptists and became their most influential
leader. The name "Mennonite" is derived from
"Menno." 46, 59, 67, 79, 113, 180, 208, 221, 227,
234, 250, 260, 287, 329, 345, 359, 372, 375
Mesdag, Jaques
(d. 1567), Flemish Anabaptist miller and weaver,
martyred at the stake at Courtrai, Belgium. 294
Miller, Ervin
Indiana Amish. 88
Miller, Levi P.
(b. 1954), Ohio Amish minister, sawmill worker. 160
Moyo, Jacob D.
(d. ca. 1987), Zimbabwean Brethren in Christ
pastor-teacher and editor. 340
Muganda, Josiah
Tanzanian diplomat, served as a counselor in Education and Cultural Affairs at the Tanzanian Em-
bassy in the United States. 342
Müntzer, Thomas
(ca. 1489-1525), German mystic, pastor and apocalyptic revolutionary whose spiritual ideals influenced several early Anabaptists. A leader in the
German Peasants' War, Müntzer was captured
and soon executed. 73
Musser, Daniel
(1810-1877), Reformed Mennonite bishop and physician of Lancaster County, Pennsylvania who
wrote extensively, expounding and defending that
group's positions. His writing on nonresistance
was esteemed by Tolstoy. 74

N
N., R. M.
American; Lancaster County, Pennsylvania. 86
Ndlovu, Fetty Mae
Zimbabwean Brethren in Christ. 31

O
Ortíz, José
(b. 1939), Puerto Rican minister and teacher, living
in Indiana. 290
Osborne, Philip
(b. 1943), Kansas psychologist and educator. 195

P
Pietersz., Pieter
(1574-1651), Dutch Waterlander minister, devotional writer and windmill maker. 156, 223, 374
Plockhoy, Peter Cornelisz.
(ca. 1620-ca. 1700), Dutch-born social reformer in
England and America. The communal settlement
he founded in Delaware in 1663 was destroyed by
the English the next year. 343, 400

R
Redekop, John H.
Canadian Mennonite Brethren columnist, professor of political science, church leader. 407
Redekop, Magdalene
Canadian author and literary scholar. 100, 267
Reesor, Christian
(1833-1915), Canadian Old Order Mennonite
bishop. 96
Reimer, Klaas
(1770-1837), Founder of the Kleine Gemeinde in
the Ukraine. 352
Reublin, Wilhelm
(ca. 1480-ca. 1560), German-born priest who became early supporter of radical reform and peasant unrest. He was active as an Anabaptist in
Switzerland, Germany and Moravia, but after in-
volvements with a wide spectrum of Anabaptists,
he abandoned the movement. 176
Riedemann, Peter
(1506-1556), Silesian Hutterite minister and missionary in Austria, Germany, Moravia and
Slovakia, whose "Confession of Faith" became a
Hutterite standard. 300, 384
Rinck, Melchior
(1494-ca. 1545), German Peasants' War veteran
and later Anabaptist leader and martyr. 154
Ris, Cornelis
(1717-1790), Conservative Dutch Mennonite minister. 254
Risser, Johannes
(1787-1867), German minister, later emigrated to
United States. 44, 229
Rodríguez, Luis Elier
Puerto Rican church leader. 133
Roosen, Gerrit
(1612-1711), Widely influential German minister,
writer and businessman. 97
Ruth, John L.
(b. 1930), American lecturer, historian, author, film-
maker and minister. 41

S
Sakakibara, Gan
(b. 1898), Japanese historian, writer, translator and
professor. 258

Sattler, Michael
(ca. 1490-1527), German ex-monk Anabaptist leader and martyr; probable author of the influential "Brotherly Union" (Schleitheim Confession). 69, 175, 201, 211

Sauder, Nancy
Ontario Old Order Mennonite. 48

Schabaelje, Jan Philipsz.
(1585-1656), Dutch Waterlander deacon and minister in Amsterdam and Alkmaar; writer whose most influential work was *The Wandering Soul*. 33, 101, 102, 112, 121, 189, 269, 270, 277, 278, 317, 319, 321, 322

Schiemer, Leonhard
(d. 1528), Austrian Anabaptist missionary and martyr; pupil of Hans Hut. 275, 308, 376

Schlabach, Roy L.
(1915-1991), Ohio Amish bishop. 362

Schlabach, Theron F.
(b. 1933). American historian. 39

Schlaffer, Hans
(d. 1528), Austrian Anabaptist missionary and martyr, a former priest who was converted to Anabaptism by Hans Hut. 111

Schnell, Hans,
Also known as Hans Beck, was a Swiss Brethren elder active in southern Germany in the latter sixteenth century. 356

Schreiner, Sally
American Mennonite church worker. 127

Schrock, Simon
(b. 1936), American Beachy Amish minister and author. 228

Scott, Stephen
(b. 1948), Old Order River Brethren of Lancaster County, Pennsylvania, author of several books about ways of life among the Amish and other plain groups. 137

Shank, J. Ward
(b. 1904), Minister, author and editor in Virginia. 335

Shenk, Sara Wenger
(b. 1953), American teacher, writer on family concerns and pastor. 57, 304, 351

Shillington, George
Canadian Mennonite Brethren minister and Bible teacher. 178

Showalter, Rebecca 305

Shutt, Joyce M.
(b. 1936), Chaplain in Adams County, Pennsylvania. 123

Sider, Lewis B.
(b. 1911), Brethren in Christ missionary to Zimbabwe, retired in Pennsylvania. 83

Smith, C. Henry
(1875-1948), Historian, educator and banker; of Amish Mennonite background from Illinois, first American known to have received the degree of Ph.D. (University of Chicago, 1907). 192

Smyth, John
(d. 1612), English Puritan minister and refugee in Amsterdam who joined the Mennonites in 1610. Members of his congregation who did not join the Mennonites returned to England and founded the Baptists. 213

Soto, Elizabeth
(b. 1959), Native of Puerto Rico, serving Mennonite Central Committee in the United States. 283

Stadler, Ulrich
(d. 1540), Austrian Hutterite leader in Moravia, noted for a deep spirituality of *Gelassenheit* (yieldedness, detachment, composure). 172, 310

Stoltzfus, Christian
(1803-1883), Amish deacon in central Pennsylvania. 333

Stoltzfus, Eli L.
(b. 1923), Lancaster County Amish, former caretaker of a replica Amish farmstead open to tourists. He later became a Seventh Day Adventist. 253

Stoltzfus, "Tennessee" John
(1805-1887), Progressive Amish deacon with broad contacts; lived in Lancaster County, Pennsylvania until age 67 when he moved to Tennessee and organized an Amish congregation there. 281, 307

Swalm, Ernest John
(1897-1991), Canadian Brethren in Christ bishop and evangelist. 125, 206, 354

Symons, Hans
(d. 1567), Flemish Anabaptist martyr. 349

T

Tanase, Takio
(b. 1929), Japanese minister and teacher in Hokkaido, later pastor in Tokyo. 161

Toews, Johann J.
(1878-1933), Minister and teacher in Ukraine, died in exile in northern Russia. 75, 246

Twisck, Pieter Jansz.
(1565-1636), Dutch elder, writer and merchant. 163, 204, 286, 293, 389, 398

U

Umlauft, Hans
Bavarian Anabaptist evangelist and mystic; a former monk, he became a cobbler. In later years he probably joined the Hutterites. 268

Unger, Abraham
(1820-1880), Elder of Einlage congregation, Chortitza, Ukraine; instrumental in forming the Mennonite Brethren. 139

V

van Braght, Thieleman Jansz.
(1625-1664), Dutch minister and cloth merchant, best known as compiler of the *Martyrs Mirror*. 84, 165

van den Houte, Soetgen
(ca. 1520-1560), Flemish Anabaptist martyr. 378

van der Zijpp, Nanne J.
(1900-1965), Dutch pastor, historian and professor; instrumental in refugee and youth work. 168

van Straten-Bargeman, Christina
(b. 1931), Dutch teacher and church worker. 81

W

Wagner, Jörg
(d. 1527), Bavarian radical (not Anabaptist) and martyr. 115

Waldner, Jakob
(b. 1891), Hutterite conscientious objector from South Dakota during World War I. He later lived in Manitoba. 136

Waltner-Toews, David
(b. 1948), Canadian poet and veterinary epidemiologist. 377

Wang, Stephen
(b. 1905), Chinese youth worker, teacher and professor of chemistry. 360

Wens, Maeyken
(d. 1573), Flemish Anabaptist martyr. 164, 314

Widjaja, Albert
Indonesian. 147

Witmer, Beth
Resident of Elkhart County, Indiana. 139

Y

Yaguchi, Yorifumi
(b. 1932), Japanese pastor, poet and professor. 36, 122, 135, 261, 301, 409

Yoder, Clarence T.
(b. 1956), Amish minister in Wisconsin. 148

Yoder, Edward
(1893-1945), American professor of classics. 237, 239, 242, 292, 380

Z

Zimmerman, Caleb.
Old Order Mennonite of Lancaster County, Pa. 146

Zimmerman, Eli Z.
(1903-1992), Old Order Mennonite of Lancaster County, Pennsylvania. 282

Zorilla, C. Hugo
(b. 1940), Colombian missionary to Spain and professor in the United States. 132

Geographical Index

For locating readings by country of origin.

Chronological Index

For locating readings by year of origin.

Scripture Index

Page numbers refer to the first page of the reading in which the reference is found.

Index of Subjects

Page numbers refer to the first pages of the reading in which the reference is found.

About the Author and Compiler

Raised in Lancaster County, Pennsylvania, Craig Haas has had lifelong contacts with Mennonites. He joined the Mennonite Church in 1982 after reading about Anabaptist history and thought.

Craig graduated from Millersville University in 1980, and received a master's degree in philosophy from the University of Chicago in 1982. He later studied at the Associated Mennonite Biblical Seminaries in Elkhart, Indiana.

He has served as a church planter and a pastor, and is presently employed by the People's Place in Intercourse, Pennsylvania.

Craig and his wife Christine live in Manheim, Pennsylvania and are members of the Blossom Hill Mennonite Church near Lancaster.